CALVIN'S OLD TESTAMENT COMMENTARIES
THE RUTHERFORD HOUSE TRANSLATION

Editor-in-Chief

D. F. WRIGHT

General Editors

D. F. KELLY, N. M. DE S. CAMERON (1984-1994)

Consultant Editors

T. H. L. Parker, J. H. Leith, J. I. Packer, R. S. Wallace

Contributing Editors

R. C. Gamble, D. C. Lachman, A. N. S. Lane, J. G. McConville

CALVIN'S OLD TESTAMENT COMMENTARIES

Calvin's Old Testament Commentaries

Volume 18

EZEKIEL I

(Chapters 1-12)

Translated by

D. Foxgrover and D. Martin

WILLIAM B. EERDMANS PUBLISHING COMPANY, GRAND RAPIDS

THE PATERNOSTER PRESS, CARLISLE

Published 1994 jointly by Wm. B. Eerdmans Publishing Company and
The Paternoster Press, P. O. Box 300, Carlisle, Cumbria, CA3 0QS UK

Printed in the United States of America

00 99 98 97 96 95 94   7 6 5 4 3 2 1

Library of Congress Cataloging-in-Publication Data

Calvin, Jean, 1509-1564.
   Calvin's Old Testament commentaries.
   Includes bibliographical references and indexes.
   Contents: — v. 18. Ezekiel I, chapters 1-12
          — v. 20. Daniel.
   1. Bible. O.T. — Commentaries — Early works to 1800.
I. Wright, David F. II. Kelly, Douglas, 1943-   .
III. Cameron, Nigel M. de S. IV. Title.
BS1150.C35   1993   221.7   93-206
ISBN 0-8028-0751-8 (pb)
ISBN 0-8028-2468-4 (cloth)

British Library Cataloguing in Publication Data

Calvin, Jean
   Ezekiel 1: Chapters 1-12. — Rev. ed. —
   (Calvin's Old Testament Commentaries Series; Vol. 18)
   I. Title II. Foxgrover, David III. Martin, Donald IV. Series
   224.407

   ISBN 0-85364-598-1 (cloth)
   ISBN 0-85364-599-X (paper)

Contents

CONTENTS

General Preface

John Calvin is widely known as a man of one book — the author of the celebrated *Institutio* of the Christian religion. Yet for all the influence of that work, Calvin's most substantial legacy is his expositions of the Bible — the sermons, lectures, and commentaries on which he expended so much energy throughout his ministry at Geneva. Their qualities have often been praised. They remain more accessible and more instructive to the modern student of the Scriptures than any other corpus of biblical exposition from the sixteenth century.

English translations of Calvin's commentaries began to appear soon after they were first published. (As conventionally used, the category of commentaries encompasses both the lectures and the commentaries strictly so called; for the distinction see T. H. L. Parker, *Calvin's Old Testament Commentaries* [Edinburgh, 1986].) A complete version of both Old and New Testament commentaries was produced in the nineteenth century by the energies of the Calvin Translation Society. The New Testament ones were retranslated more recently under the editorship of D. W. Torrance and T. F. Torrance (Edinburgh, 1959-71). Given the distinctive place accorded to the Old Testament in the Reformed tradition of which Calvin was the most significant creator, it is only proper that his Old Testament commentaries be similarly set forth in a new translation.

The aim of the translation is simply stated — to let Calvin speak in his own words, as far as translation into another language allows. Annotation has been kept to a minimum, and the temptation to comment on Calvin's comments has been strictly eschewed. The translation has been done from the original sixteenth-century editions. The only feature of these editions not reproduced in this version is the text of the Hebrew Bible which some of them set alongside

Calvin's own Latin translation of it. In the course of his translation and commentary Calvin often cites Hebrew words. Where he does not provide a transliteration, one is given in square brackets, which are used to identify any such additions. For example, when Calvin includes words or phrases in Greek or French without translating them into Latin, an English translation is provided in square brackets. The sign 'Mg.' in the notes indicates that the following biblical reference is given in the margin of the sixteenth-century edition used.

In such an enterprise editors become debtors to many other labourers in the same field. We wish in particular to pay tribute to the encouragement, counsel, and critical reading of the Consultant Editors, and the participation of the Contributing Editors, of whom A. N. S. Lane painstakingly checked references and J. G. McConville the Hebrew, D. C. Lachman provided the bibliographical introduction, and R. C. Gamble assisted from the resources of the Meeter Center. And not least are thanks due to Dr. Nigel M. de S. Cameron, the first Warden of Rutherford House, for his energetic contribution to setting this translation project on course.

Our prayer is that these new translations will enable a new generation to appreciate the Old Testament expositions of one who was content to be known as the servant of the Word of God.

Rutherford House   The Editors
17 Claremont Park
Edinburgh

Translators' Preface

A major reason for the continuing relevance of Calvin's commentaries is his ability to explain a verse or word in view of its context and the writer's purpose. The "Spirit's plan" or the "sum of the whole," as Calvin liked to put it, determines the meaning of a phrase or verse. Although modern interpreters may disagree with Calvin's expositions of particular passages, and although their knowledge of this period of biblical history may be more sophisticated, all will recognize Calvin's skill in grasping the writer's purpose and keeping that purpose uppermost in mind as he interprets the text.

We wish to make two comments about our translation. The first applies to the text of Ezekiel. Calvin translated the Hebrew quite literally, and we have followed Calvin very closely. Therefore, our translation may appear stilted and halting. But it does give the reader a sense of Calvin's own procedure. After all, he was lecturing from the Hebrew text, without notes. Later, in his comments, Calvin often renders a smoother translation of key phrases or sentences.

Second, in spite of Beza's comment in his preface to Coligny that Calvin "spoke much the same as he wrote," the reader of the *Institutes,* the commentaries (in the proper sense), and the letters will quickly recognize that the style of the lectures is not as nuanced. At times the reader suspects that Calvin is stalling for time as he ponders a point or moves on to a new topic, repeating a word or phrase that would have been omitted in a written commentary. We have avoided the temptation to "improve" the style by deleting connectives and repetitions or by constructing clauses.

We extend our appreciation to David Wright and the other Editors for their support, and to the Meeter Center of Calvin Theological Seminary, Grand Rapids, Michigan, for a research grant and for the gracious hospitality of its staff.

David Foxgrover, Donald Martin

Bibliographical Note

Calvin's lectures on Ezekiel were his last. In his preface to "all truly Christian readers," Charles de Joinviller tells us that Calvin began to interpret Ezekiel on January 20, 1563, though he was so afflicted by severe diseases that in the course of the year he had often to be carried to the lecture hall in a chair. After completing the twentieth chapter on February 2, 1564, he was compelled to remain at home, almost always being confined to his bed. But in spite of his ill health Calvin diligently revised the greater part of these lectures with his own hand, a revision that de Joinviller tells us he has carefully preserved with the rest. Theodore Beza, in his dedication of the work to the Admiral Gaspard de Coligny, laments the premature death that prevented the completion of these lectures on a prophet he regards, particularly toward the end of the book, as the most obscure of all. Perhaps sensing the difficulty many had with the work he had been expounding, Calvin particularly exerted himself to perfect those lectures he had already delivered, even though he had little prospect of completing the work as a whole.

The first edition, from which this translation has been made, was published posthumously:

> *Ioannis Calvini in viginti prima Ezechielis Prophetae capita Praelectiones*, Ioannis Budaei et Caroli Ionvillaei labore et industria exceptae. Genevae, Ex officina Francisci Perrini, M.D. LXV.

The French translation, which Joinviller promised would follow shortly for the benefit of our people who did not understand Latin, was published the same year.

> *Leçons ou Commentaires & Expositions de M. Iean Calvin, sur les vingt*

> *premiers Chapitres des Revelations du Prophete Ezechiel: . . . Le tout*
> *fidelement recueilli premierement en Latin, par Iean Budé & Charles*
> *de Ionviller: & depuis traduit nouvellement en Francois. A Geneve,*
> *De l'Imprimerie de François Perrin, M.D. LXV.*

The standard, and for many the most accessible, Latin edition is in

> *Calvini Opera* 18 (*Corpus Reformatorum* 40: Braunschweig, 1889).

The first and previously the only English translation was that of the Calvin Translation Society by Thomas Myers:

> *Commentaries on the First Twenty Chapters of the Book of the Prophet*
> *Ezekiel,* two volumes; Edinburgh: Calvin Translation Society, 1849-
> 50.

*John Calvin's Lectures
on the First Twelve Chapters of
The Prophet Ezekiel*

*Taken down by the effort and industry of
Jean Budé and Charles Joinviller*

*With a Preface by Theodore Beza
dedicated to the most noble Gaspard de Coligny,
Admiral of France*

*Two Very Full Indices Are Added, the First of Words and Subject-Matter,
the Second of Passages Cited*

*[Enter in through the narrow gate: for wide is the gate and spacious the
way which leads away to destruction. Matthew 7:13]*

Geneva

*The Press of François Perrin
1565*

Ioannis Caluini in

VIGINTI PRIMA

Ezechielis Prophetæ capita
Prælectiones,

*Ioannis Budæi & Caroli Ionuillæi labore
& industria exceptæ.*

Cum Præfatione Theodori Bezæ ad generosiss.
Gasparem à Colignio Galliæ Amiralium.

*Additi sunt Indices duo copiosissimi, prior ver-
borum ac sententiarum, posterior
locorum qui citantur.*

lata est porta & spatiosa via quæ
Introite per arctã portã: quoniam
abducit in exitium, Matth. 7. 13.

GENEVÆ,

Ex officina Francisci Perrini.

M. D. LXV.

Theodore Beza

*Grace and peace from the Lord to Gaspar de Coligny, Grand Admiral
of the French, most noble lord, illustrious in piety and other Christian
virtues, from Theodore Beza, minister of the church of Geneva*

I am confident, most noble lord, that the fruit which you have been accustomed
to gather from the other writings of John Calvin you will also obtain from this
"swan song" of that great and truly excellent servant of God.

Nevertheless, I have no doubt that what has happened to me in writing
this will happen to you in reading it. That is, at the name of such a man, the
intense sorrow that we experienced so recently at his death will arise again
with overwhelming feeling. And certainly this sorrow is too proper and even
too necessary to allow of — let alone require — its quick removal. Thus, I
think it is even lawful to indulge in it.

No one can be ignorant of the storms that the church of God has endured
in the past few years, since they have shaken the whole world. Indeed, we
now can truly proclaim that saying, "What region on earth is not full of our
toil?"[1] But many have not given sufficient credit to the champions who have
defended religion. God raised up you Gideons and Samsons, not only in
Germany but also in England and Scotland, and recently even in our France
(under the auspices of that illustrious leader, the Prince of Condé). Risking
your very lives at every danger, you deflected every sword from the necks of
the pious. But surely the chief enemies of the church are not flesh and blood,
since they can harm only the body. And so, although such defense is a special
service of God, and your praise before the very angels of God is exceedingly
great, because at a most opportune time your courage repulsed so great a power,
nevertheless you had to wage war at the same time with far different enemies

1. Virgil, *Aeneid* 1:460.

3

and also with far different weapons. And even now it is being waged. Although it is not so frightening in appearance, yet it is far more dangerous since it brings with it complete ruin to the house of God. I speak of the spiritual wickedness by which Satan tries both to infect doctrine itself and to corrupt morals. With these lost, it is inevitable that the church will not only be imperiled, but completely destroyed. The leaders in waging this war are undoubtedly those whom God has appointed pastors, teachers, and elders of his church for this very purpose, so that by teaching and refuting and praying (for these are the weapons by which those hostile troops are overthrown) they might administer the kingdom of God.

If you have regard to empty names, that type of person is numerous; if you consider substance, that type is rare indeed. Nevertheless, this age of ours has had a large enough number of this latter type, of whose constancy and labors we ourselves are the fruit and harvest. But the world is unworthy of such, as is shown by our loss within three years, at a most inopportune time, of the best and bravest. Indeed, we see only a few surviving of those great heroes who, as we remember, bravely and successfully cast down the Antichrist from his height, like Heinrich Bullinger, who was recently saved for us from the plague by God's beneficence; Guillaume Farel, an elderly man of invincible strength; and Pierre Viret, who even today struggles successfully in the church of Lyons in the front lines.

The beginning of the recent slaughter was made with Philipp Melanchthon. Peter Martyr did not long survive him, after returning from the Colloquy of Poissy to his post at Zurich. Soon after him followed Wolfgang Musculus, and after him Andreas Hyperius, as if the hand with which God strikes switched between north and south: Philip in Saxony, Hyperius in Hesse, and the remaining two have died in Switzerland. O, what great men! and how precious!

However, while John Calvin survived, that truly great man and πολλῶν ἀντάξιος ἄλλων [pollōn antaxios allōn; "worth a regiment"],[2] he mitigated all these calamities; and although these losses were very great, while he still lived they became much lighter. And, behold, him too have our sins snatched from us in the past year. None can estimate how much the church has lost in him who was not an eyewitness of his labors. What did that man not accomplish? Who could be compared with him in preaching, lecturing, and writing? Who was more succinct than he in teaching and at the same time so solid? Who was more successful in solving problems, more forceful in rebuking, more persuasive in consoling, and more definite in refuting errors?

I know that on the one hand some Epicureans will ridicule what I say (for why not ridicule the servant when they make fun of the Lord himself?), and on the other, it will be despised by those stupid and dull souls for whom the highest wisdom is to know nothing. Nevertheless, I know that there is not one of these

2. Homer, *Iliad* 11:514; literally, "equal to many others."

4

cunning enemies of God who does not agree with me silently to himself. Each faction among the followers of Antichrist has and praises its own patron, not without deprecating the others. Let such foolish and profane partisanship be removed far from us. We do not boast of Cephas, of Paul, or of Apollos. The language of Canaan we know is one. The Lord by whom we swear is one.

But since the limbs of one and the same body have different functions, we prefer the eyes to the hands and feet. And since the eyes of such a body are many, we realize that some are more clear-sighted than others. But we praise and adore God in the individual parts of his body. May this praise therefore belong completely to our Lord and God. One who does not realize that in some special sense Calvin was entirely indebted to God realizes nothing. But why this praise? The pleasure of these heavenly blessings, solely by their remembrance, enormously both benefits and delights. Hence, the power of examples is twofold. The only goal and purpose of sacred history in particular is that while reading it we might be as deeply moved as if we experienced events there and then.

And so in this sorrow, when the death of such a man inevitably upsets all truly pious and good people, and especially those who even daily received remarkable benefits from his presence, his unique teaching and his truly admirable wisdom, we ought to be consoled primarily by two things. First, we are aided in no small way by the fresh and beautiful examples of both his sayings and his deeds, until we ourselves complete the course of our voyage and are escorted into the same port. Second, no one person stands out in our memory who has left so many and such finished monuments of his teaching. If the Lord had granted us the benefits of such a light for another year or two, I indeed do not see what could have been lacking for a thorough understanding of the books of both covenants. There are books left, the ones called "historical," which he did not illumine with his commentaries — except Joshua and also Job and the two books of Solomon. However, his French sermons on Job, Samuel, and 1 Kings will fill this deficiency in part, for they were taken down word for word. For that great man had obtained this too from God, that he spoke much the same as he wrote.

Of the prophets, he illumined Isaiah with appropriate commentaries; his lectures on the others are extant, taken down with great diligence and faithfulness by two men endowed with extraordinary piety and learning. Jean Budé, son of the great Budé, and Charles Joinviller. But his premature death prevented him from completing Ezekiel. This is a great loss to the church, because Ezekiel, especially toward the end, remains the most obscure of all the prophets. And I have no idea when someone will finally arise to complete this picture begun by such an Apelles.[3] We reckon we have no need to explain why we believe this unfinished work should nevertheless be published.

3. A famous Greek painter of the fourth century B.C.

5

But if, perhaps, someone should ask why we have dedicated this to you rather than someone else, I say honestly that I have as the author of this plan that man himself, who was free to decide about his own work as he pleased. But I would have done the very thing he wanted of my own accord and for the strongest and best reasons. And why should I not concur with his judgment? In war and peace for an entire twenty months I was an eyewitness of the great gifts of body and soul that he clearly esteemed and admired in you from a distance.

He asserted in the prefaces of his books that he followed in the footsteps of Paul, whose only reason for saluting some by name in his epistles was to present to the churches specific, chosen individuals for others to contemplate and be enflamed by their examples to true piety and other virtues. How true his judgment of you would be if your modesty permitted you to be praised openly! Of if it were right to seek out witnesses, as is usual in doubtful matters, how numerous and reliable would be those we could cite! But there will be another place, I hope, to speak more fully of these things.

Now I prefer to consider something else, something more pleasant for you. Though a great man, you are the least ambitious of all. However much you have done, I want to urge you, most noble lord, to do the very thing you are doing — to apply yourself completely, as you have so successfully begun, to reading, listening, and meditating on these sacred writings carefully, and also to using them in practice. And not only this, but also to protecting and preserving the churches by all the just means appropriate to your dignity and courage of mind.

Those who think that they cannot stand if religion survives do not hide the fact that, as deadly enemies of you and all the pious, they are attacking primarily you alone. But either I do not know you, or such things sharpen rather than dull your powers. You yourself have experienced and observed God's concern to defend his own. Innocence itself and integrity defend you well enough against all incriminations. You — if any of your rank — have that inward and invincible defense in your heart, which even profane people call a "brass wall." I speak of a good conscience. Supported by this alone, you will easily overcome all adversaries, believe me.

In these struggles a diligent comparison of the prophetic and historical writings will strengthen you like nothing else. There future events are not deceptively foretold from some observation of past things, as people commonly do. False counsels are not taken, and outcomes are not obstructed by that ambiguous coincidence of secondary causes. You will stand among the counsels of God himself and behold the true causes of changes, and beginnings, processes, and outcomes, and all declared plainly and clearly.

Although the prophets have their riddles, everything becomes clear by making careful comparisons, knowing the prophets' idioms, and especially by relating the outcome of things to the predictions themselves. It is like peering down directly from heaven at human affairs — especially when you depend upon that faithful leader who takes you along a sure path, through rough and inaccessible places. There is no reason to despise these things as common or to scorn them as stories of happenings long out-of-date, as they appear to certain prattlers today.

The prophets do not deal with small or common matters, as some think who are unskilled in such things. But in these books we find decrees and judgments about the greatest monarchies, unlike any we have today, about the status of the highest kings and princes, about the safety and destruction of the finest cities in peace and war, about that great God of hosts sitting upon the judgment seat. The kings of those times were profane and impious. But they did not do as some today, who are so ashamed to inquire from the mouth of God speaking through his servants that they heed nothing more and dare to accuse of ambition the faithful servants of God who are fulfilling their duty. Indeed, at that time no nation decided serious matters without consulting its prophets, as all the histories relate.

When I say this, I am not placing ministers of the Word on the thrones of kings or princes or any magistrate, and I do not nurture their ambition. But I speak of what is fact, and what experience itself proves of late, as I remember you yourself, most noble lord, noticed in time and even predicted. And then, to say something about the times, their pattern, I confess, has certainly changed, but the Lord is the same, his providence is the same, his mercy toward us is the same, and his indignation against the wicked is the same. These things are constant and unchanging, and even firmer foundations ἀποδείξεων [apodeixeōn, "of proofs"] than are found in mathematics itself. If there is any stability and constancy in things (whatever these might be), it all depends on the nature and will of God himself. We will find the most illuminating declaration of these things not only in general in the law, but in particular in the prophetic writings, if only we compare the past with our own times and with those things about which we daily inquire.

You ask for an example? It has already been four years since the churches of France promised themselves great peace and tranquility at the celebrated Colloquy of Poissy, and their adversaries had nowhere to turn. But at that very time our man of God dedicated his lectures on Daniel to these churches and gave vent to these words: "If we are to face still more contentions (and I warn you that tougher battles remain than you think) with the full violence of the madness of the godless, that boils so fiercely as to stir up the entire underworld, you will recall that your course is set by the heavenly master of the contest. We must obey his laws all the more promptly because he strengthens his own to the very end." At the time he gave this warning, many promised themselves the contrary. How truly he spoke by the prophetic spirit is shown by the countless catastrophes that followed, the end of which is still not in sight.

7

the contrary. How truly he spoke by the prophetic spirit is shown by the countless catastrophes that followed, the end of which is still not in sight.

Whence came this prediction? you ask. Certainly not from false and profane divination and astrology that he, if anyone did, condemned from God's Word. It came from the very books of the prophets that he was interpreting at the time. When he saw the very same evils ruling among the French, for which the Lord habitually harshly castigated his people and avenged his enemies with just punishments, why not pronounce that the same measures hung over the unrepentant? For similar reasons, Luther foresaw and predicted the recent destructions in Germany due to contempt for God's Word. If only he had known better the specific causes! Thus, at this very time, it is easy to observe among the French those whom you would least expect not only defending the superstitions and manifest idolomania that are well enough known to all, but also, with everyone listening and laughing, tolerating unpunished explicit Epicureanism and horrible blasphemies that no one heard in earlier ages. In the end, there is no place left for justice and equity, and edicts and laws are passed in vain.

Who is so blind that he cannot foresee horrible punishments awaiting the authors and defenders of these sins — and perhaps (may I be a false prophet in such a matter!) the whole kingdom as well? Surely heaven and earth will pass away rather than the Lord allow them (which horrify even the Turks) to remain unavenged. And the longer this punishment is put off, the harsher will it appear when it does come. I know that some will ridicule these warnings, as Noah himself was ridiculed. Others will accuse harshly, as Jeremiah was treated as a man of strife. But God's truth will still stand firm.

I pray him, most noble lord, first, that he clothe his Royal Majesty above all with every holy virtue, which already has been done in part and all hope and wish henceforth to see done. And second, that he grant him many counselors like yourself (which I say without flattery) and a few others — adorned, that is, with the holy prudence of the Spirit and zeal for piety and justice. By their counsels very many faults could be thoroughly corrected, and holy and righteous governance by the sacred Word of God and his Royal Majesty's authority successfully instituted.

And finally, may God happily confirm and preserve you, with your truly Christian wife and children and your noble brothers and their holy families, and all the assembly of the pious who look — after God and his Royal Majesty — to the illustrious Prince of Condé (I hope we will be given another place to speak of him), and to you and the rest of the godly and committed nobility.

Geneva   January 18, 1565

Charles de Joinviller

Greets All Truly Christian Readers

Our most eloquent and faithful pastor, Theodore Beza, with singular skill and productive genius, seems to have omitted nothing from the preface to these lectures which he addresses to the Admiral of France, a most noble man noted for admirable piety. Nevertheless, whoever reads and looks deeply, with some attention and level-headedness, will not judge superfluous what I now offer in passing. I trust it will not be useless, but acceptable and approved by all the pious.

First, whether you consider the consistent integrity of his life or his rare learning joined with extraordinary piety, no words can adequately express the loss to God's church when that most outstanding and utterly godlike man, John Calvin, our excellent parent, was taken from this life to eternal peace. Who surpassed him in sanctity of character, unbelievable friendship, unbroken greatness of spirit, extraordinary tolerance, or any of the highest virtues? His almost limitless writings plainly testify to his marvelous erudition. Some have been published; others will see the light shortly, God willing, for the great benefit of all the pious. A large number of his remaining writings were taken down from his sermons or preserved by his friends; for instance, letters in French and Latin that he sent to people of all classes. These sources will reveal the acute and productive genius with which that man was gifted and the keen and sound judgment in which he excelled.

But I will say no more on this here, lest my recounting these things appear out of place. It is enough that I mention only a few matters that are more relevant to these lectures. On January 20, 1563, he began to interpret Ezekiel in the public school, even though he was afflicted constantly by a variety of serious diseases and often had to be brought to the auditorium by chair or was forced to come on horseback. Though the power of his weakened

9

body was failing, he did not give in to these violent diseases for an entire year, but continued to fulfill his duties of preaching and reading.

Finally, about February 1 the following year, when he was only four verses short of completing chapter 20, he was forced to stay at home and keep to his bed almost continuously. Even while he could scarcely draw breath, he still continued studying, dictating, and often even writing. It is hard to believe how much he accomplished even when ill health kept him at home. Among other things, he diligently emended a good part of these lectures, as is obvious from notations by his own hand in the copy I have carefully preserved with the others.

We must all deeply lament that this man, so well versed in the teaching of the prophets, was taken prematurely by death and could not expound all of Ezekiel. All the godly are aware that the prophet's predictions which follow are most necessary to the church of God. What if this man had clarified them? To make up this loss in some measure, several men of great authority and learning thought it much better to publish these lectures than to hold them back any longer, since they would be of great value to all pious people.

Therefore, Jean Budé, my dearest brother, and I, relying on the judgment of those men, have undertaken the task most willingly. We have spared no expenses, trouble, or labor in publishing them as soon as possible. And shortly, if God wills, we will ensure that our people understand them when we have translated them into French, like our French lectures on Jeremiah that were type-set nine months ago and are now at last in print. If I am not mistaken, these will be of great service to our folk unskilled in Latin. So that this Latin edition should lack nothing, we have made sure that whatever was missing from the manuscript is restored carefully at the end. And since a great treasure is enclosed in this book, a very full index has been drawn up by a learned scholar. His guidance will make it possible to draw easily upon unbelievable riches with no trouble. Another index has been added of the scriptural passages that are cited and explained. Moreover, in bringing out these lectures we have applied the same industry, care, and diligence as in the volumes already published. It is unnecessary to repeat more fully here what has been made perfectly clear elsewhere about the method we employed in taking down Doctor Calvin's extemporaneous expositions.

Therefore, good readers, it remains only for you to enjoy the labors of such a great man and to welcome the profit you will gain from them as coming from the great and good God, and sincerely to give him immortal thanks. How much profit you receive from your reading, you yourselves will judge better and more certainly than I can explain with many words. Farewell, then, and may you always resolve to direct all your energies to the glory of God alone.

Geneva   January 18, 1565

Ezekiel 1–12

**The prayer with which Doctor John Calvin was always
accustomed to begin his lectures:**

*May the Lord grant that we might meditate upon the
heavenly mysteries of wisdom and progress in true piety,
to his glory and to our edification. Amen.*

Lecture 1

At the very beginning of his book, Ezekiel indicates the time at which he filled the office of a prophet; understanding his message depends on this point. Unless we grasp why God raised him up, we will hardly be able to follow his thought, much less receive the proper benefit from his teaching. Therefore it is necessary to begin here, that is, with the time. He says,

CHAPTER 1

1 *And it was in the thirtieth year, in the fourth month, and on the fifth of the month, and I* [that is, "when I was"] *in the middle of the captivity* ["among the captives"] *by the river Chebar, the heavens were opened, and I saw visions of God.*
2 *On the fifth* ["of the month"], *it was the fifth year of the captivity of King Jehoiachin.*

We see that our prophet was called to the teaching office in the fifth year after Jehoiachin had voluntarily surrendered to the king of Babylon and had been dragged into exile along with his mother.[1]

He says, however, *that was the thirtieth year.* Most follow the Chaldaean paraphraser[2] and interpret this phrase as dating from the discovery of the Book of the Law. It is generally agreed that that was the nineteenth year of King

1. Mg., 2 Ki. 24:15.
2. I.e., Targum.

13

Josiah's reign; but in my calculations I do not subscribe to the view that understands this as dating from the discovery of the Book of the Law. To call it the thirtieth year for this reason would be too obscure and forced a way of speaking.

We never read that later writers started their counting from that point. Besides, there is little doubt that among the Jews the usual method was to begin counting years from a Jubilee, which was like the beginning of a new era. Thus I have no doubt that the year was called the *thirtieth* after a Jubilee.

This is not a new invention, for it is mentioned in Jerome.[3] He wrongly rejects the right view, however, because he was deceived by a divergent view. But since the Jews certainly used the method of calculating that begins from the "Jobel," that is, the "Jubilee," then the words *that was the thirtieth year* make very good sense.

Someone might object that nowhere do we read that the eighteenth year of Josiah's reign was that festival year, when everyone returned to his fields, freedom was given to the slaves, and there was a complete restitution of the entire people.[4] The solution is easy: although it has never been discovered in what years the Jubilee occurred, it is enough for us that the Jubilee was a festival year and that the Israelites followed this custom in numbering the years. In the same way, the Greeks had their Olympiads and the Romans their consuls, and from them calculated their annals. Similarly, the Hebrews were accustomed to begin with the Jubilee year when they numbered years, up to the next renewal, as I said.

It is very likely that this was a Jubilee year, for Josiah is said to have celebrated the Passover with such great splendor and display that there had been nothing like it since Samuel's day.[5] The best conjecture that can be offered is not that he celebrated the Passover every year with such magnificence, but that he was persuaded to do so by the nature of the occasion when the people were renewed, all the people returned to their own lands, and even slaves were set free. As it was a Jubilee year, the pious king was led to celebrate the Passover far more splendidly than was his custom. He even surpassed David and Solomon. Although he reigned thirteen years after this, we do not read that a Passover with such unusual display occurred again.[6] No doubt he celebrated the Passover annually but in the customary way. That observance was extraordinary, and we can conclude that it was a Jubilee year. Although this is not explicit in Scripture, let it suffice for us that the prophet numbered the years according to the usual manner of the people.

3. *Commentary on Ezekiel* 1:1.
4. Mg., Lv. 25.
5. Mg., 2 Ch. 35:18.
6. Mg., 2 Ki. 23:23.

He says, *that was the fifth year of the captivity of Jechaniah,* who is also called Jehoiakim.[a]

Jehoiakim succeeded Josiah and reigned for eleven years.[7] The thirteen years left of Josiah's reign and these eleven make twenty-four years. Jehoiachin passed directly into the hands of King Nebuchadnezzar and was his captive from the beginning of his reign. He reigned for only three or four months.[8] Afterward, the last king, Zedekiah, was installed arbitrarily by the Babylonian king. Thus we see that twenty-nine years are completed. Add to that the time in which Jehoiachin reigned, and there is no doubt that it was the *thirtieth year* following the eighteenth year of Josiah's reign. It is true that the Book of the Law of God was discovered that same year,[9] but here the prophet accommodates himself to the received rule and custom.

We must now come to God's purpose in taking Ezekiel as his prophet. For thirty-five years Jeremiah had not ceased to speak out, but with little success. Since the prophet (that is, Jeremiah) had so exhausted himself, God wanted to give him a helper. It was certainly a great relief for Jeremiah, who was in Jerusalem, to learn that the Holy Spirit was speaking in similar tones through another voice, for in this way the truth of Jeremiah's teaching was attested.

In the thirteenth year of Josiah's reign[10] Jeremiah assumed the prophetic office; thus eighteen years remain. Now, let us add the eleven years of Jehoiakim, and there will be twenty-nine. Next, add one year and five more, and we will have thirty-five years. Jeremiah's difficult task was to speak out continually for thirty-five years among the deaf and even the mad. Therefore, in order to relieve his servant, God gave him a companion to teach among the Babylonians the same things that Jeremiah had not ceased proclaiming in Jerusalem.

This benefited not only the captives but also the remnant of the people who were still left in the city and the land. This confirmation was necessary for the captives because they had false prophets, as we see in chapter 29 of Jeremiah:[11] there were Ahab the son of Kolaiah and Zedekiah the son of Maaseiah, who proudly boasted that they were gifted with a spirit of revelation and promised the people miracles. They ridiculed the compliance of those who had left their homeland. They said they preferred to fight to the very last and to risk their lives rather than willingly abdicate their divinely promised inheritance. In this way they taunted the captives. Then there was Shemaiah the

---

a. An error for Jehoiachin. Calvin in this lecture uses several forms of *ch.*
7. Mg., 2 Ki. 23:36.
8. Mg., 2 Ki. 24:8.
9. Mg., 2 Ch. 34:14.
10. Mg., Je. 1:2.
11. Mg., Je. 29:21.

Nehelamite,[12] who wrote to the high priest Zephaniah and rebuked him as lazy and lenient for not severely suppressing Jeremiah as a fanatic and impostor who falsely assumed the office of prophet.

Since the devil had his agitators there, God raised up his prophet in opposition. Thus we see how useful — even necessary — it was that Ezekiel carry out the prophetic office in that place. But the usefulness of his teaching extended more widely since those in Jerusalem were compelled to hear what Ezekiel had prophesied among the Chaldaeans. When they realized that he agreed with the prophecies of Jeremiah, they would inevitably at least inquire what this agreement meant. It was no accident that one in Jerusalem and another in Chaldaea should prophesy with a single voice, like two singers harmonizing with each other. One could not desire a finer or more harmonious melody than appeared between those two servants of God. Now we see the significance of what our prophet said about the years: *in the thirtieth year,* he says; then, *in the fourth month* (the word "month" is understood); and *on the fifth day I was in the middle of the captivity.*

Before proceeding further, I will briefly sketch what Ezekiel deals with. He has almost everything in common with Jeremiah, as we said, but especially this: he threatens the people with final destruction because they incessantly heaped sin upon sin, thereby provoking the vengeance of God more and more. Therefore he threatens them — and not just once — because the people's hardness was so great that conveying God's threatenings three or four times was insufficient; he must repeatedly drive them home.

He also shows, however, that God determined to treat his people severely because they were contaminated with so many superstitions. They were faithless, avaricious, cruel, and full of greed toward one another. They were also given to luxury and inclined to passion. All these things were recited by our prophet to show that the vengeance of God was not excessively severe; the people had reached the limit of impiety and the height of every wickedness.

In the process he gives here and there a little taste of God's mercy, for all threats would be empty unless some promise of grace were available. In fact, as soon as God's vengeance looms large, it drives people to despair, and despair thrusts them into a frenzy. Whoever is aware only of the wrath of God is inevitably agitated, and then like a raging beast wars with God himself. This is why I said that apart from a taste of God's mercy all threats are empty.

The prophets find fault with people for no other purpose than to drive them to repent. But repentance is not possible unless those who are alienated from God are convinced that he can be reconciled to them. This is the reason why our prophet, like Jeremiah, tempers his harshness by interjecting promises while upbraiding the people. He also prophesies against foreign nations, again

12. Mg., Je. 29:24.

like Jeremiah chiefly against the sons of Ammon, the Moabites, the Tyrians, Egyptians, and Assyrians.[13]

But from chapter 40 he treats more fully and copiously the restoration of the temple and the city. He claims explicitly in that section that the condition of the people would be renewed; the royal dignity would flourish, and the priesthood would recover its original excellence. Right to the end of the book he describes the singular benefits of God that were to be hoped for after seventy years. It is appropriate to remember what we saw in Jeremiah:[14] while false prophets promised the people a return after three or five years, the true prophets predicted what would in fact happen so that they would not be broken by the length of years but patiently submit to God and even undergo just correction peaceably.

Now that we grasp our prophet's concerns, the purpose of his teaching and its substance, I will follow the text. He says that *he was in the middle of the captivity.* Some explain the prophet's words too subtly and think that he was not actually among the exiles; they refer this to a vision, as if when he says תוֹך [*tôḵ*] he means that he was in an assembly of the entire people. But the prophet's purpose is far different. He says that *he was in the middle of the captivity,* in order to show that, despite being an exile along with the others, he was given the prophetic spirit in that polluted land. Therefore *in the middle of the captivity* is not taken for "assembly"; the prophet simply relates that although he was far from the holy land, God's hand reached even there, so that he might excel in the gift of prophecy.

This refutes the stupidity of those who foolishly say that our prophet had the spirit of revelation before he went into exile. They lapse, however, not so much through error and ignorance as through incorrigible arrogance, for nothing is more irksome to the Jews than God's reigning outside the holy land. To this day they are hardened because they are dispersed throughout the whole world and scattered through every region. Nevertheless, they still retain something of their former pride. But at that time when there was still some hope of returning, it seemed to them an intolerable profanity that the truth of God would shine elsewhere than in the holy land, especially outside the temple.

Here the prophet shows that he had been called to the teaching office while among the exiles, as one of them. In this matter God's inestimable goodness was highly visible, in raising up a prophet as though from among the very dead. Babylon was like the deepest abyss, from which the Spirit of God emerged with his own instrument; that is, he publicly brought forth this man to be the minister and herald of both God's vengeance and God's grace. Thus we see how wondrously God brought light out of darkness when our prophet was called to his office while in exile.

13. Mg., chaps. 26–29, i.e., Ezk. 25–32.
14. Mg., Je. 28.

17

Although his teaching ought to have been useful to the Jews who still remained in the homeland, God did not want to call them back to himself without some mark of disgrace. Because they condemned every prophecy that arose at home, in the temple itself and the sanctuary on Mount Zion, it was necessary for them that a teacher who was immersed in that deep abyss be brought forth from that cursed land, as I just said. So we see how God humiliatingly castigated that wicked contempt of his teaching. For a long time Isaiah had fulfilled the prophetic office, followed by Jeremiah; but the people never changed. Therefore, when prophecies streamed forth from the fountain itself, they were scorned by the Jews. As a result, God raised up a prophet for them from Chaldaea. Now we see the point of the prophet's plan.

He says *by the river Chebar,* which many understand to be the Euphrates; but they offer no reason, except that they found no other famous river in that land. When the Tigris flows into the Euphrates, its name is dropped; and from this they divine that the Euphrates is there called the Chebar. But we do not know the region in which our prophet was exiled; he could have dwelt in Mesopotamia or beyond Chaldaea. Moreover, since the Euphrates divided into many branches, it is likely that names were given to each separate stream. But because we are not certain about any of this, I prefer to leave the matter undecided.

Because *the prophet received a vision on the bank of the river,* some ingeniously conclude that the waters were somehow consecrated for revelations. When they seek to offer an explanation, they say that water is lighter than earth; and since it is necessary that prophets rise above the earth, water is suited to revelations. Others refer it to the power of cleansing and think that even baptism is represented.

But I disregard these ingenuities, which vanish on their own. I gladly ignore them because arguing this way leaves no solid foundation in Scripture. We know that speculations of this sort are plausible, but in Scripture we ought to seek certain and firm teaching on which to rest. They also ineptly distort this passage, "by the rivers of Babylon, we sat down and wept,"[15] as if the people went to the riverbanks when they wished to pray and devote themselves to worship. It is more likely that the setting of the area is described, since it was well irrigated, as I said earlier.

He says *the heavens were opened, and he saw visions of God.* God opened his heavens — not that they were actually parted. But when all obstacles are dissolved, God enables the eyes of the faithful to penetrate as far as his heavenly glory. If the heavens were parted a thousand times, whose vision is so keen that it could reach the glory of God? The sun appears small to us, even though it far surpasses the earth in magnitude. Then the other planets (except the moon) are like little sparkles, and so are all the stars. Since

---

15. Mg., Ps. 137:1.

light itself grows dark before our sight can penetrate that far, how will our vision reach the incomprehensible glory of God? Consequently when God opens the heavens, he also gives new eyes to his servants, because otherwise they would fall short not only in midcourse but one-tenth or one-hundredth of the way. When Stephen saw the heavens opened,[16] his eyes were undoubtedly illumined by an extraordinary power so that he could see beyond human capacity. Similarly at Christ's baptism, the heavens were opened;[17] God appeared in such a way that John the Baptist seemed to be lifted above the clouds. This is the sense in which the prophet now says *the heavens were opened.*

He adds that *he saw visions of God.* Some think that this expression describes the visions as extraordinary, because in Scripture whatever is excellent is called divine. Very high mountains are called "mountains of God," and likewise "trees of God." But this interpretation is frigid. I have no doubt that he calls prophecies "visions of God" and in this way professes that he was sent by God. That is, God somehow divested the prophet of his humanity when he assigned him the role of teaching.

It is not surprising that he speaks of visions of God, because otherwise it would have been incredible that any prophet could emerge from Chaldaea. Nathanael inquired "whether anything good could come from Nazareth,"[18] even though Nazareth was in the holy land. How then could they be persuaded that the light of heavenly teaching was shining in Chaldaea, that the testimony of God's grace would arise there, and that God would carry out his judgments through the voice of a prophet in that place? No one would ever have believed this unless the call of God had been sealed in a rare and unusual manner.

He adds *that was the fifth year of the captivity of Joachim,* or Jechoniah, or Jechaniah. Undoubtedly he indirectly censures the people's obstinacy with these words. If God afflicts us harshly, we will be agitated at first, but inevitably we gradually become tame. Since the people's stubbornness was not conquered within the five years, we can conclude how fiercely rebellious they were against God.

In the meantime, he does not spare the rest. Those in Jerusalem reckoned that affairs had gone admirably well for them because they had not gone into exile with their brothers. So they despised them, as we often saw in Jeremiah. Since those who still remained in the homeland were pleased with themselves and considered their fortunes the best, the prophet here noted the time, because their harshness had to be overthrown. When they opposed the prophecies of Jeremiah in the same way, God added a second hammer with which to beat them. This is why he speaks *of the fifth year of Joachim's captivity.* Next:

16. Mg., Acts 7:56.
17. Mg., Mt. 3:16.
18. Mg., Jn. 1:46.

19

3   *The word of Yahweh was to Ezekiel the priest, the son of Buzi, in the land of the Chaldaeans, by the river Chebar; and there the hand of Yahweh was upon him.*

He does not repeat the copula found at the beginning. It may seem surprising that he begins the book with a copula, for when he says *and it was,* it seems that something previous is implied. Since there is nothing before this, the copula appears absurd. But an unstated antithesis or comparison is probably implied between the prophecies that had flourished for a long time in Jerusalem, their proper and natural setting, and this prophecy that arose in Chaldaea. It is as if he said, "even among the Chaldaeans," for the particle ו [*w*] is equivalent to גם [*gam*]. The meaning is that after exercising his servants in vain, even to the point of weariness, for many prophets fulfilled their office in Jerusalem, God now also speaks in Chaldaea. Therefore he says: *the word of Yahweh was to him.*

I do not know why some dream that here Jeremiah is called Buzi, unless because the Jews were persuaded, quite ignorantly, that the father of a prophet is never mentioned unless he too was a prophet. Their ignorance is refuted in other passages; but here their curiosity is clearly shameful when they insist that Buzi was a prophet. Because they find no prophet of that name they imagine he is Jeremiah — as if it were probable that the father was left behind in Jerusalem while the son was exiled. There is certainly nothing plausible about that.

It is because he was of a priestly family that it says *he was the son of Buzi.* Our prophet had to have a notable name, because if he had been an obscure commoner, no one would have listened to him. Therefore the dignity of the priesthood had some influence in their accepting him more readily.

Now he states explicitly what I said before, *in the land of the Chasdim;* as if to say that although God had never been accustomed to raise up his prophets in faraway lands — especially defiled lands — now he changed this pattern, because even among the Chaldaeans someone was endowed with the prophetic spirit. Moreover, the particle שם [*šām*] is added for emphasis: *was upon him there,* he says.

Otherwise the Jews would have been horrified by Ezekiel, like some monster, when they heard that the Word of God came out of Chaldaea: "What? Would God pollute or contaminate his teaching that it should arise thence? What kind of people are the Chaldaeans that God could erect his throne there? He has his dwelling on Mount Zion; this is where he is worshiped and invoked. His light must burn here, as the prophets have often testified." The prophet opposes such boasts: "God has already begun to speak in Chaldaea, and his power is evident there."

He says *the word of Yahweh was given to him,* because we know that

God alone ought to be heard, and the prophets are to be heard only if they present what has come from him. Therefore all teachers of the church must first be disciples, so that God alone retains his right and remains the only teacher and leader, and authority dwells with God alone. When the prophets demand to be heard, they add that they do not advance their own inventions but faithfully hand on what they have received from God. So it is with our prophet. I have dealt briefly with these matters, because they have been treated more fully elsewhere.

Finally he adds *the hand of Yahweh was upon him.* To expound "hand" to mean "prophecy," as some do, seems to me weak and superficial. Accordingly, I take "hand" to mean "power," as if Ezekiel said that he was endowed with the power of God, which established that he had been chosen to be a prophet. Therefore "the hand of the Lord" was a testimony of new grace to enable Ezekiel to subject all the captives to himself, as sovereign, because he bore the personal authority of God.

This could also refer to the efficacy of his teaching, for the Lord not only furnishes his servants with words but also works by the hidden inspiration of his Spirit and does not allow their labors to be in vain. The passage could be taken in this sense; but because the prophet assumes for himself only what is necessary and thus claims for himself the position and standing of a prophet, I have no doubt that when he speaks of the hand he is indicating an inward working, as it were.

There is certainly also this inner efficacy of the Holy Spirit when God offers his power to those who hear, so that they embrace his Word by faith. But even if all the listeners were deaf and the Word of God disappeared in smoke, the inner power of God would still be in the prophecies themselves. This is what Ezekiel's words indicate: *was given to him by God.*

I will finish here because otherwise I would be forced to stop suddenly, and we must come to the vision that is the most difficult of all.

Almighty God, you deemed your people worthy of the continued grace of your Spirit when they were cast forth from their inheritance, and you raised up a prophet from among the very dead to recall them to life when they were already without hope. Therefore, grant, I pray, that although the church today is miserably afflicted by your hand, you will not leave it without consolation, but show us that even in the midst of death we are to look for life from your mercy, to the end that we may bear all your chastisements patiently, until, reconciled to us, you are pleased to show us that you are our Father, and so at last we may be gathered into that blessed kingdom where we will enjoy our complete happiness, in Christ Jesus our Lord. Amen.

Lecture 2

Now we must analyze the vision, whose obscurity so frightened the Jews that they forbade anyone to undertake, or even attempt, its explanation. But either God appeared to his prophet in vain or to some benefit. To affirm the former would be very absurd. If the vision is to be useful to us, we must understand it at least in part. If someone objects that it was offered to the prophet and not to others, that quibble is easily dismissed, because the prophet wrote what we read here for the common use of the entire church.

If someone asks whether the vision is clear, I confess that it is very obscure, and I do not profess to comprehend it. Nevertheless, it is not only permissible and useful to inquire into what God has set before us; it is also necessary. Therefore it would be shameful laziness voluntarily to close our eyes and not attend to this vision. Besides, if we taste only a little of what God intended, that will be of some importance; and not only a moderate but even a slight understanding may suffice for us.

I wanted to preface these brief remarks; now I come to the prophet's words themselves.

4 *And I saw, and behold, a whirlwind* [or, "a storm"] *coming from the north; a great cloud, and a fire turned in on itself* [or, "whirling"]; *and brightness all about it. And from its center like the appearance of hasmal, from the center of the fire.*

The purpose of this vision must be considered first. I have no doubt that God wished to furnish his servant with authority and then to strike terror into the people. Therefore the frightening form of God described here for us ought to be referred primarily to reverence for teaching. The prophet was dealing

22

with hard and unyielding people, as has been sufficiently noted and as we will see more clearly as we progress. It was necessary to subdue their arrogance; otherwise the prophet would have been speaking to the deaf.

But God also had another purpose. There is an analogy or likeness to be maintained between this vision and the prophet's teaching. This is one point. As far as the vision itself is concerned, some understand the four creatures to be the four seasons of the year and conclude that God's power in governing the world is being celebrated. But that is completely amiss. Some think that the four virtues are represented, because, as they say, the image of justice shines in the man, prudence is represented by the eagle, fortitude in the lion, and temperance in the ox. Although this is subtly worked out, it has no solidity.

Others take it quite differently, seeing the four passions here designated: fear and hope, sadness and joy. Others conclude that the three faculties of the soul are denoted, for in the soul τὸ λόγικον [to logikon] is the seat of reason; θύμικον [thymikon] is the irascible part, as they say; and ἐπιθυμήτικον [epithymētikon] is what they call concupiscence. Fourth they add συντέρεσιν [synteresin], which is conscience. But these ingenious arguments are childish.

Formerly, the accepted opinion was that the four Evangelists are depicted in this figure. They think that Matthew is compared to a human being, because he begins with the genealogy of Christ; Mark to a lion, because he begins with the preaching of John; they think Luke is like an ox because he begins by talking of the priesthood. John is the eagle because he penetrates as far as the secrets of heaven. But in these figments too there is nothing solid; all of them dissolve if they are analyzed more closely.

Others conclude that the glory of God in the church is depicted, and therefore they think the creatures are to be taken for the "perfect," who have made greater progress in the faith. The wheels are the weak and simple. After that they pile up many ineptitudes that are better buried immediately than rebuffed at great effort. I repudiate all these notions.

We must now see what the prophet himself intended. I have already said that God's plan was to honor the prophet in the act of giving him his commands, so that his teaching would not be scorned. But we must at the same time consider the special reason that I touched on: with this symbol God briefly showed why he was sending his prophet, for the visions resemble the teaching as much as possible. This is why, in my judgment, Ezekiel says that *he saw a north wind*. The people had already experienced God's vengeance, when he used the Assyrians as well as the Babylonians to castigate them. Jechoniah voluntarily went into exile, as we have seen; nevertheless, the Jews imagined that they would have a tranquil nest in their city and homeland. They ridiculed the compliance of those who went into exile so quickly. Therefore the prophet says that *he saw a whirlwind from the north*. The rush of the wind or storm here mentioned must surely refer to the judgment of God, for he planned to strike the Jews with horror to prevent them becoming sluggish in their security.

After speaking of the whirlwind or storm, he added that *he saw four creatures and four wheels interconnected,* to indicate that their movements did not arise by chance but came from God. Therefore these two ought to be joined: the storm was aroused from the north, and God, the author of the storm, was seen on his throne. But meanwhile, so that God's majesty might impress the Jews more strongly, he also says *I saw four creatures and four wheels joined together.* He understands the four creatures to be cherubim. It is not necessary to seek an explanation elsewhere, for Ezekiel himself testifies in chapter 10 that when he saw God in the temple, these four creatures were under God's feet, and he says they were cherubim.[1]

Now we must see why he records four creatures, when two cherubim encircled the ark of the covenant; and then why he ascribes four heads to each one. If he wished to accommodate his language to the pattern of the sanctuary,[2] why did he not specify the two cherubim with which God was content? He seems to depart from God's own prescription. Surely four heads and round feet do not fit the two cherubim that encircled the ark of the covenant.

But the solution is easy: the prophet alludes to the sanctuary, but he bends his language to fit the people's ignorance. Religion had almost died out at that time, and there was such contempt for the law that the Jews did not even know what the sanctuary was to be used for. They worshiped God as if he stood at a distance from them, and they disregarded his providence in human affairs. We see that their stupor was so impenetrable that, although often struck down, they were never aroused.

It was necessary that a new pattern be presented to the Jews, because they were almost completely senseless. The prophet therefore borrows half from the sanctuary itself and adopts a second half besides, as was necessary for such a dense people. But he made up nothing out of his own head; I am now speaking of the Holy Spirit's plan. God did not want to draw the Jews away from the sanctuary (for that was the foundation of all right understanding); but because he saw that the pattern of the law was not sufficient, he added fresh support in giving four heads to each of the cherubim and wanting there to be four cherubim instead of two.

As for the number of cherubim, I have no doubt that God wanted to teach that his power is diffused through all regions of the world. We know that the world is divided into four parts, and therefore in order for the people to know that God's providence rules everywhere in the world, four cherubim are presented. It is also appropriate to remember that angels are designated by

1. Mg., Ezk. 10:20.
2. Mg., Ex. 25:18-20; 37:7-9; Nu. 7:89.

cherubim or seraphim, for what are called cherubim in this passage and in chapter 10 are called seraphim by Isaiah in chapter 6.[3] Moreover, we know that angels were powers and principalities, and we know that they are distinguished by these titles — as if Scripture called them God's own hands.[4] Therefore, because God works through angels and uses them as the ministers of his power, God's providence and power in ruling the entire world are highlighted when angels appear. The reason why not only two but four cherubim are set before the prophet's eyes is that God's providence in earthly affairs had to be made obvious. At that time the people imagined that God was confined to heaven, and therefore the prophet teaches that God not only reigns in heaven but also governs earthly affairs. This is how and why God extends his power throughout the four regions of the world.

But why does he attribute four heads to each creature? The answer is that in this way angelic power in all living creatures is displayed to us. This is by synecdoche,[5] however, because God works through his angels not only in humans and other living beings but in all created things. Because inanimate things have no motion from themselves, and because God, as I said, wished to instruct that ignorant and dense people, he set forth an image of all things in those creatures.

As far as living things are concerned, humans hold the principal place because they are formed in the image of God; the lion rules the wild beasts, while the ox represents all domesticated or tame animals, as they say, because it is the most useful. Since the eagle is a royal bird, all birds are included in this word. I am not fabricating allegories here but merely embracing the literal sense. It seems to me all but certain that God indicates angelic inspiration by the four cherubim and extends that to the four regions of the world.

Now to make it clear at the same time that no creature moves of itself but that all motion is from the hidden impulse of God, he attributes four heads to each creature. It is as if he said that the angels exercised the rule of God in the whole world, not only in a certain part, and then that all creatures are moved as if they were joined with the angels themselves. He says there were four heads for each of the creatures, because if we consider God's government of the world through the eyes of faith, that angelic power will appear in every motion. It is just as if the angels bore the heads of all living creatures; that is, they included in themselves clearly and obviously all elements and all parts of the world. So much for the four heads.

Concerning the four wheels, I have no doubt that they signify all the transformations that are commonly called "changes." We see the world con-

3. Mg., Is. 6:2.
4. Mg., Eph. 3:10; Col. 1:16.
5. A rhetorical figure in which a part is substituted for the whole.

25

tinually changing and putting on, as it were, a new appearance, as if a wheel turned itself or completed its course by some external impulse. Since there is nothing stable in the world but constant change is discerned everywhere, the prophet joins wheels to the angels, as though saying that whatever change is discerned in the world does not arise by chance but is dependent on something outside itself, namely, the angels. The angels do not move anything by their own power but only inasmuch as they are God's hands, as we already said.

Because those transformations are so intricate, the prophet says that *he saw a wheel in a wheel.* The course of things is not continuous; when God begins to do something, he seems to withdraw, as we will see again. Also, many things coincide with each other, and on this ground the Stoics concoct "fate," as they call it, out of the connection of causes.

But here God teaches his own something far different, namely, that the transformations of the world are so interconnected that every movement depends on the angels, whom God governs according to his own will. Accordingly the wheels are said to have eyes. There is no doubt that God opposes this shape of the wheels to foolish opinions, for people fabricate blind fortune and imagine that everything turns by chance according to some kind (I know not what) of turbulent impulse. Although God compares the transformations that occur in the world to wheels, he nevertheless says that *the wheels had eyes,* as if to show that nothing happens by chance or by the blind impulse of fortune.

Certainly that notion comes from our blindness. We are blind in the light, and therefore when God acts, we conclude that he turns everything upside down. Because we dare not spew forth such crass blasphemies against God, we say "fortune" acts indiscriminately. In so doing, we transfer the rule of God to fortune. Seneca refers to a certain jester who belonged to his father-in-law.[6] When he became old, he lost the use of his eyes and complained that he in no way deserved to be cast into darkness. He concluded that the sun no longer shone in the world, but it was he who was blind. The same thing happens to us. We are blind, as I said, and then we want to assign the cause of our blindness to God. But since we dare not incriminate God openly, we impose the name of fortune on him. For this reason the prophet says *the wheels had eyes.*

We now grasp the essence of the vision and must come to the details. After saying that *a wind arose from the north, and a great cloud,* he adds that *there was also a fire folded inward.* In chapter 9 of Exodus Moses uses the same word of the whirlwind that God raised up in Egypt.[7] The *fire was folded inward* or twisted, and *the fire was brilliant.*

---

6. *Letters* 50:2.
7. Mg., Ex. 9:24.

Some expound this part quite cleverly, stating that the fire was brilliant because the judgments of God are not obscure but revealed before the eyes of all. I do not know whether the prophet intended that; I am not convinced. Rather, God's majesty is depicted for us, according to the manner used by Scripture. Therefore he says the *fire was brilliant all around.*

Finally, he says *in the middle of the fire there was like the appearance of hasmal.* Many take hasmal to be an angel or some unknown figure, but unjustifiably in my judgment. I have no doubt that hasmal is a distinctive color. Following the Greeks,[8] Jerome translated it "electrum."[9] I wonder why he would say it is more precious than gold and silver, for electrum is made of gold and one-fifth silver. Therefore it does not surpass either gold or silver, and Jerome was mistaken in this matter.[10] But whether it was electrum or another exceptional color, the majesty of God is so clearly made known to the prophet that he ought to be seized with admiration.

The vision was not offered privately for his own sake, however, but (as I have mentioned) for the benefit of the whole church. Thus the color differed from the fire so that the prophet would understand that the fire was divine. It was a symbol of God's glory and therefore did not appear like an ordinary fire. Now follows:

5 *And in the middle of it the likeness of four creatures, and this their appearance, the likeness of a human being.*

We have already stated why God showed his prophet four angels under the form of four creatures. It was necessary to deviate slightly from the form of the sanctuary because all worship under the law had grown cold to the profane. God therefore descended from heaven in a recognizable form, as if to say that he not only reigned above among his angels but exercised his power here, since his angels are engaged on earth and occupy all the regions of the world. The point is that God's providence encompasses everything.

Then he says *there was the form of a human being in those creatures;* but this does not seem to agree with the context. A little later he will say there were four heads for each of the creatures and that their feet were round, or calflike, as others translate it. But here he says that there was the form of a human being. The solution is that although there were some differences, the form of the human being was primary. The cherubim were undoubtedly seen by the prophet as angels of God. Moreover, wings do not suit human beings; but he means that their stature, as they call it, was human. Although they were

8. Septuagint.
9. Vulgate.
10. Jerome, *Commentary on Ezekiel* 1:4.

not exactly similar to humans, there was a human likeness as far as the entire body was concerned. Now we understand why he says *there was the likeness of a human being.* Next:

6 *And to each one four faces, and to each of them four wings.*

Now he comes to the head and wings. Many take this to mean that there were four heads to each creature, and then four forms to each head. They also multiply considerably the number of wings because they attribute four wings — others even sixteen — to each of the four heads. But this does not seem to agree with the prophet's words. He simply says *there were four heads to each one,* and then *four wings.* The wings and heads correspond to each other, but each creature had only four heads. Therefore it had no more than four wings, and this will be clear again from the context. Next he adds:

7 *And their feet a straight foot, and the sole of their feet like the sole of a calf's foot* [in this passage, I conjecture that the points have been changed, because עָגָל *('āgāl)* means "round," and here it is pointed עֵגֶל *('ēgel),* that is, "calf." I do not know why the prophet says the feet were calves' feet or similar to a calf's foot; this seems out of place. But I do not quarrel over details], *and they sparkled* [others translate it, "and sparks"] *like the appearance of polished metal.*

This seems to be added by way of explanation. Because the prophet spoke of the form of a human being, he added that *the feet were straight,* although he says the feet were round or calflike. As for the straightness, I refer it not only to the feet but to the legs themselves. It is just as if he had said that the creatures stood as humans usually do, for we differ from the brute animals who look down on the ground. As the poet aptly says while commending the unique grace that God conferred on people:

> He gave man a face uplifted,
> And ordered him to behold the heavens
> And hold his face erect toward the stars.[11]

The prophet expresses the same idea when he says the *creatures had straight feet.* Therefore he says that the creatures were not like beasts but bore a human likeness or image.

In any case, he says the *feet were round,* which seems to refer to agility or to a variety of directions, as if he said that the feet were not pointed in only one

---

11. Mg., Ovid, *1 Metamorphoses,* i.e., 1:85-86.

direction. But in whatever direction God moved the creatures, they easily went forward because their feet were round. If someone wished to turn either left or right and at the same time go backward, he would realize he was going against nature. But if the feet were round or shaped like a calf's foot, he could direct his course in all directions. So the creatures' agility seems to be referred to here.

Concerning the phrase *they sparkled like bronze,* or polished metal, we know this likeness appears more than once in Scripture, for when God seeks to make his servants attentive he sets forth new figures to capture their attention. The same thing happens to our prophet, because if only the color of flesh had appeared in the creatures, it would have gone unnoticed, or at least the prophet would not have considered the meaning of that sight so attentively. But when he sees the glowing legs and the sparks glistening in all directions like polished metal, then his mind had to apply itself more intensely to this vision. We now see why he says the appearance of the legs was like *polished metal* and that *sparks glistened.* Next:

8 *And the hands of a human being under the wings* ["from under the wings"] *on four sides* [or "corners"]; *and to the four of them faces and wings.*

The prophet also says there were *hands under the wings.* Since we know that hands are our chief means of acting, all actions are often denoted by this word. Pure or impure hands signify human works that are either clean or unclean. In saying that the *creatures were furnished with hands,* however, the prophet shows that they were equipped to carry out the task assigned them. Whoever lacks hands lies useless and cannot assume any work. Therefore, in order to express the angels' power, the prophet says that the creatures had hands. This also refers to the human figure, but "hands" designates something in particular: the agility of the creatures that enabled them to carry out whatever God commanded.

But he says that the hands *were under the wings.* With these words he indicates that the angels had no motion of their own, did not move wherever they pleased, but were activated from above; in short, all their actions were guided by the will of God himself. There is no doubt that by *wings,* in this passage as well as in similar passages, something more than human is to be understood. Since the wings with which the creatures covered themselves signify nothing other than the hidden power of God, it follows that the phrase *the hands under the wings* merely points out that the angels do not move by their own intrinsic (as they say) power but are impelled by another source, the power of God himself. They are not moved hither and thither by chance, but God governs all their actions, bends and directs them in whatever direction he pleases. This is why the prophet says that he *saw hands among the creatures* and that *those hands were under the wings.*

He repeats for the second time that there *were faces and wings for the four.* It is also noteworthy that he says *on the corners,* as though he said the creatures had the power to move in all directions, not that there were four hands each. At first glance it seems that this is meant when he says *on four corners,* or "on each corner"; but he means only that the hands appeared on the creatures in such a way that they were ready to act in whatever direction God wanted to move the creatures. Now follows:

9 *They were joined each to another of the wings* [that is, the wings were joined each to the next of the wings] *of them* [the creatures]; *in proceeding they did not turn back* [that is, "when they advanced, they did not turn back"]. *The man* [אִישׁ *('îš),* or "each," that is, "each creature"] *advanced directly toward its face* [or literally, "from the region of its face"].

Now he says the *wings were joined,* which he will explain more clearly a little later. He will say that the wings were joined above, and two wings were extended in such a way that they clothed or covered the body. But here he deals briefly with what he will treat more fully later. Thus *their wings were so joined* that one touched the other.

Later he will deal with another point, namely, *the creatures so traveled as not to go backward.* A little later he seems to contradict himself when he says that the creatures ran about like lightning and then returned. These statements agree quite well, however, because later he will explain that the creatures moved in such a way that they went in a continuous course toward their goal or destination. It does not follow that afterward they stayed there. Therefore, when the creatures proceeded, they did not turn aside this way or that, nor turn back, but persisted in their allotted course. Subsequently they had different encounters, like lightning.

The hour does not allow me to explain what he means by this. I will defer until tomorrow.

Almighty God, we are so fixed on the earth by our dullness that even when you stretch forth your hand to us, we are unable to reach you. Grant that, having been aroused from above by your Spirit, we might learn to raise our senses to you and struggle against our laziness until in drawing closer you become so intimately known by us that we at last may arrive at the enjoyment of full and perfect glory, which is kept for us in heaven, through Jesus Christ, our Lord. Amen.

Lecture 3

We must see why the prophet says that *each creature walked toward,* or opposite, *its face.* I interpret it simply to mean that their course was straight, so that they did not go astray or turn away either to left or right. Those who turn their face in this or that direction often stumble and then deviate from the right way. The creatures were so attentive that they always moved toward their goal and did not divert from the set plan.

We see here a definite and, as they say, inflexible rule commended in the divine actions. Human beings suddenly change their plans and fluctuate; and when they have something set before them, if a divergent thought sneaks in, they are carried off in a contrary direction, as if forgetting what they were doing. But God wishes to show that his actions are so arranged that nothing in them is either askew or astray. We said that the creatures represent angels, and then the angels represent an image of the governance of the entire world. One must understand that they are like the hands of God, because he directs them to obey him. Now follows:

10 *And the likeness of the faces the face of a human being, and the face of a lion on the right side of the four; the face of an ox on the left side of the four, and the face of an eagle on the four.*

Now he comes to the faces or the countenances of these creatures. "Face" properly refers to the entire body, but here the prophet understands only the countenance. He says *on the right was like the face of a human being and a lion, but on the left the face of an ox and an eagle.* We explained yesterday that he ascribes four heads and as many faces to the angels of God because the people's stupor was so great that they failed to acknowledge God's providence in every

31

region of the world. We know that they were so inebriated with foolish confidence that they wanted, as it were, to confine God in a prison. To them the temple was like a jail for God. The prophet therefore makes it clear that God's providence shines in all parts of the world. Since there is power in living things, he represents it by synecdoche in these four principal species.

One question remains, however — and a difficult one at that. In chapter 10 he puts "cherub" for "ox."[1] Some think, or at least respond, that at a distance it appeared to be the face of an ox, but closer up it was a cherub. They all realize that this is quibbling, but because they cannot otherwise escape the problem they concoct this groundless figment. Others surmise that the cherub is the same as the ox, which can easily be refuted by numerous passages. Cherubim do not have heads like oxen, as is well known.

I have no doubt that something different was in the second vision when God appeared to his prophet in the temple. It is called the same vision because of the similarities, but it does not follow that it was completely identical. This conjecture should not be rejected out of hand, because, as I already said, when God revealed himself to his servant in Chaldaea, he wanted to censure the people's dullness with this complex figure. But when God appeared the second time in the temple, there was something more divine. That is why there was this variety; instead of the ox, each creature had the face of a cherub. Besides the shape of the entire body, there was also some distinguishing symbol by which the prophet more directly and intimately knew that these creatures were cherubim or angels.

This reasoning seems to accord with God's showing his prophet a form that quite closely resembles the form of the sanctuary and the two cherubim that encircled the ark. Some further suppose that the heads were arranged so that the head of the human being looked east, while the opposite head looked west. But there is little doubt that the four faces were all visible at once and that their eyes looked in the same direction. To the right were the two forms of which we spoke, the human being and the lion; to the left were the ox and the eagle. Next follows:

11 *And their* ["the creatures' "] *faces* [some stop here and take the next phrase in an adversative sense: "But their wings were spread out." Because there is a copula in both places, I think it may be better to read this as a single construction: so "their faces"] *and their wings were spread out* [or, "divided"] *from above, with each one* [now he speaks of the wings] *joined to the next; and with two they covered their bodies.*

He says that the *faces as well as the wings were spread out,* because the four faces emerged from one body. The prophet is not saying that the

1. Mg., Ezk. 10:14.

faces were joined together as if a fourfold form could be seen in one head: the form of a human being and next the form of a lion, as in one mirror various forms that correspond with one another appear at different times. The reader could make the same error, as if different faces stood out from one head. Hence the prophet says they were *spread out from above,* or divided. Therefore he indicates a diversity of heads. He says of the wings that they *were extended,* and he also expresses the way in which they were extended, that *two wings were joined* or bound together so that each creature was joined to the one next to it. The prophet thus means that the four creatures were united by their wings.

He says that the remaining wings covered their bodies, and thus we see that there is some similarity between this spectacle and what was presented to Isaiah, as he relates in chapter 6. Why the *wings were also joined upward* seems sufficiently clear: God has divergent impulses in stirring the earth, yet in such a way that, even though seeming to conflict with each other, they harmonize perfectly.

Therefore, *were joined upward* is said in respect of God himself, because on earth horrible confusion is often evident, and the works of God, as I mentioned, seem to conflict with one another. But if one lifts up one's eyes to heaven, one will see that happenings which appear to conflict with each other here below (that is, as long as we dwell on earth in the present state of things) agree exceedingly well. Next he adds:

12 *And each one walked to* ["against"] *its face; according to whither the spirit was for walking* [that is, "as the spirit moved them to walk"], *they walked; they did not turn back as they walked.*

Here the prophet repeats that the creatures followed a straight course, *with each toward* (or, "against") *its face.* He will say the same thing a third time a little later. This narration is not without purpose, because as we said yesterday and will say again a little later, we can hardly be induced to give glory to the God of wisdom. Because of our dullness we suppose that God mixes all things indiscriminately, as if he were in darkness. Because God's actions seem tortuous to us, it was necessary that this phrase be repeated often: *the angels advanced against their face,* that is, they were intent on obedience. Even the son wishing to obey his father, or the servant his lord, is often upset and perturbed by what must be done. Because some confusion is always evident among God's creatures, the prophet diligently asserts that *the angels walked toward their face;* that is, they were so intent on their goal that they did not turn aside this way or that.

What he states about the angels ought to be referred to God himself, however, for God's purpose was not to extol angelic wisdom. He sets

33

before us God's ministers so that therein we might perceive one of the principles of our faith: God so orders his actions that nothing is contorted or erratic.

He adds: *wherever the spirit was for walking, they walked.* Here "spirit" is taken for mind or intention. We know that it is often taken metaphorically for the wind and also for a person's soul. But here "will" ought to be understood; yet the prophet alludes to that impulse by which the angels are seized when God uses their efforts. The prophet seems to allude to this likeness because there is so much power and swiftness in the angels that they are like the wind.

It says in the Psalms that "God makes the winds his ministers,"[2] and the apostle applies this appropriately to the angels themselves in Hebrews 1.[3] Therefore this analogy will work very well: the *angels walked wherever the will bore them.* By this word "will" the prophet designates the secret motion by which God directs his angels as he sees fit.

He also confirms what we saw earlier, that the angels are not drawn here and there by chance but have an appointed goal, because God, the fount of all wisdom, works through them. He says once more *they so walked that they did not turn back;* that is, they did not change their course. Later, however, he will say that they *turned back.* But this is easily reconciled with the earlier statement, because it indicates only that their course was not disrupted. While they proceeded in one direction until they completed the distance, "they walked," and they then returned like lightning.

God does not so apply his angels to a task only once that they rest after that; rather, each day — each moment — he exercises them in obedience to himself. Since the angels are so conscientious in their work, it is not surprising that the prophet says *they went and returned.* Yet when he says *they did not turn back,* this agrees very well, because they did not return until they had satisfactorily completed their duty.

Finally, the only purpose of this vision is to let the prophet know that God does not abandon his works in midcourse, as it says in the Psalms.[4] Since there is nothing incomplete or deficient in God's works, the angels press on right to the post and complete the distance. Afterward they return like lightning, as he will say a little later. Next:

13 *And the likeness of the creatures, their appearance, like the coals of a glowing fire, like the appearance of torches rushing among the creatures; and brilliance in the fire, and lightning issued from the fire.*

2. Mg., Ps. 104:4.
3. Mg., Heb. 1:7.
4. Mg., Ps. 138:8.

As I said yesterday, something divine must shine forth in this vision. By presenting the face of a human being, an ox, an eagle, and a lion, God accommodated himself to the people's stupidity, as we said, and to the capacity of the prophet himself. Since we are human, we are unable to penetrate beyond the heavens. Therefore God was concerned about his prophet and all the pious but wished at the same time indirectly to reproach the people's stupor. If the human face did not differ from its ordinary form, the vision would not have attracted the prophet's amazed attention. Thus something heavenly had to be mixed with the earthly figures. This is why the creatures were *like burning fire*.

Now we understand the reason for this diversity. If nothing wonderful had happened when God appeared to Moses, he would not have concluded that he was called by God. But he recognized God in the bush because he saw it burn without being consumed.[5] Then he became aroused and thought to himself that the vision was presented to him from heaven. The same point is to be diligently observed in this passage, and from this we also gather how humanely, even indulgently, God deals with us. God sees how limited is our capacity and therefore condescends to us. This is the reason for the creatures' faces, the stature of their bodies, and what we related before.

Because God sees us languishing on earth, lying dead as it were, he raises us up. This is the point of what Ezekiel recounts: *the appearance of the creatures was like fiery coals*. Because coals taken out of a fire sometimes go out, he says *those coals were burning*. Therefore the prophet could not help but be moved when he saw that the creatures were not merely creatures, that is, when he saw something heavenly in the creatures' form, something that exceeded the limits of nature and surpassed human senses. This also benefits others. When we read this vision, we acknowledge that what the prophet recounts was so clearly manifested to him that God shone forth in it and did not allow his prophet to waver. The prophet's teaching, sealed by such definite marks, is thereby better confirmed for us.

It is also appropriate to recall what we said yesterday, that there was something terrifying in this vision, because the people were hardened to all threats, even blows. God had carried out severe judgments not only against the kingdom of Israel but also against the city itself and the whole land of Judah. Nevertheless, the captives were champing at the bit and murmuring at being dragged into exile. Meanwhile, those who remained in the city thought all had gone remarkably well for them. Because they were so secure, it was necessary to terrify them, as we will also see a little later.

It is also said that the *fire burned before God,* where he not only wanted his glory to be seen by us but also to strike fear, as he did in promulgating the

5. Mg., Ex. 3:2-3.

law.[6] In Psalm 18 David narrates that God appeared to him in this way when he saved him.[7] He surely means that God demonstrated his terrifying power against unbelievers. In this passage the prophet likewise says that the *appearance of the creatures was like burning and fiery coals.*

Then he adds another analogy: *they were like lamps,* although some explain this as firebrands or burning wood. But another sense is more widely accepted and more appealing to me: the prophet now expresses more clearly the appearance of the fire, that *those coals were like lamps.* Lamps emit their splendor farther and seem to disperse their rays in all directions, like the sun shining in the still air. In sum, the prophet means that the fire was not dim but sparkling brilliantly, and that its rays spread out, like burning lamps.

Next he says that they *walked among the creatures.* The fire assuredly appeared among the creatures as if lamps were moving back and forth, for he does not pointlessly say that the *fire walked among the creatures.* The prophet saw something like a burning form in the midst of the creatures; but he also saw a fire sparkling in all directions, as if burning lamps were moving back and forth among the creatures.

In this way God wished to show the strength of his Spirit in every action, so that we should not measure him by our standards — a depraved tendency inborn in us. When a word is spoken about God's works, we conceive what our reason can grasp and we want to limit God in some way to our imagination. But God demonstrates that when he works, his power is miraculous, like a fire rushing back and forth. God's strength is beyond our comprehension.

Next he says that *the fire was brilliant* and *lightning issued from the fire.* This could affect the prophet's mind even more when he saw the fire unusually brilliant. We know that fire is often bright, especially when it flares up. But here the prophet designates something extraordinary; the fire was not the kind seen when wood bursts into flame, but truly brilliant. It is easy to gather that here God is making his glory visible.

For the same reason he says that *lightning issued from the fire.* The brilliance just mentioned bears on this — the fire was mixed with lightning. We know that we cannot see lightning without trembling, for the sky seems inflamed in a moment, as if God wanted somehow to consume the world. The appearance of lightning is always terrifying to us. To make the prophet more frightened at the vision, God purposely displayed the appearance of lightning. He had no wish to frighten his prophet beyond the need to humble him.

As I urged at the outset, this vision was not presented to the prophet for his private use but to benefit the entire people. Insofar as the prophet himself was human, he needed this preparation in order to be humbled. We always

6. Mg., Ex. 19, 20.
7. Mg., Ps. 18:8-15.

carry around so much pride, which dulls our senses so that they are not capable of God's glory. Therefore, when God wishes to be known to us personally, he strips us of all pride, all security. In brief, his humbling is the beginning of true understanding. Now we grasp why *lightning issued from the fire.* He confirms this same point later.

14 *And the creatures ran about and returned like lightning* [he uses another word, but it means the same. בזק *(bāzāq)* and ברק *(bārāq)* are the same. They mean "lightning" as well as "shimmering"].

Here the prophet expresses more clearly what would otherwise be obscure. He says that *the creatures ran about and returned like lightning;* he is undoubtedly indicating the creatures' great quickness. Lightning (as Christ uses that comparison when he speaks of his advent)[8] issues from one part of the world and in an instant reaches the opposite. Such is the quickness of lightning that it races through the boundless heavens in a moment, and hence the prophet says the *creatures ran about and returned like lightning,* that is, the creatures were ready to obey God in whatever direction God sought to dispatch them. As we said, the angels were prepared to obey God's commands; but we cannot comprehend the extreme swiftness of their course except by this comparison with lightning.

Now we see how well these two agree: the creatures did not return and they did return. As I said, they did not return until they reached their goal; for even if many impediments arise, God breaks through them so that his actions never fail. The devil by his obstacles certainly tries to force God's withdrawal, but here the prophet shows that when God has decided something, the angels are at hand to govern the world. They are so strong that they follow through to the limit, inasmuch as God inspires them with his power. There follows next:

15 *And I looked at the creatures* [that is, "when I looked at the creatures"], *behold, one wheel upon the earth near the creatures, facing each of the four.*[a]

Now the prophet comes to the wheels that were joined to the creatures. Each creature had a double wheel, as we will see later; that is, one wheel was inside another. That the prophet did not immediately notice the wheels standing near the creatures must be due to the magnitude of the vision. Although he was attentive and had certainly been given a spirit of understanding by God and, in a way, was taken up into heaven, he was convicted of his weakness

8. Mg., Mt. 24:27.
a. Literally, "to the four, to the face of each one."

37

by his inability to comprehend at once such a great vision. He was alerted to this wonderful mystery so that he would attend to the entire spectacle with greater reverence. Therefore he says, *when he had his eyes fixed on the creatures, the wheels immediately appeared.*

He uses the singular, but afterward he declares clearly that there were four wheels. Now he removes all uncertainty: *behold,* he says, *one wheel.* In what sense "one"? Namely, *near the creatures, facing each of the four.* So we see that there was a wheel for each creature. This is easily understood from the prophet's words.

I said yesterday that through these wheels God wished to convey to his servant, and to us as well, the transformations that appear repeatedly in the world. If we consider the condition of the world, it is rightly compared to the sea — a tempestuous sea. As the sea is subject to contrary winds and storms rise up here and there, so nothing in the world is stable or tranquil. The condition of the world is constant change, like a turning wheel.

The wheels stood near the angels, because the world is governed by the secret inspiration of God. When everything seems to revolve randomly by blind impulse, God still has his ministers to control every movement so that there is nothing turbulent or disordered in them. This is why *the wheels moved about and stood near the angels,* as he will repeat immediately. Now follows:

16 *The appearance and work* [that is, the "craftsmanship" or "form"] *of the wheels like the appearance of Tarshish: and a likeness of one to the four* [that is, there was a certain equality of proportion among the four wheels, so that one was completely similar to the others], *and their appearance and form* [or "work," or "their craftsmanship"] *as if a wheel was in the middle of a wheel.*

Now the prophet uses the plural in saying that there were *four wheels.* He says the color was like a precious stone. Jerome translated it "sea," because the sea that faced Cilicia, viewed from Judea, is called Tarshish. For some reason the color of the sea or sky seemed right to him. Be that as it may, the word is not used simply for the color of the sky; Tarshish is a precious stone, as is clear from Exodus 28[9] and many other places. The Greeks[10] translated it "chrysolite," but I do not know if that is right; it does not make much difference. Let us hold that it was a precious stone whose color was so exquisite that it attracted attention.

Under the figure of the wheels God wished to set before his prophet something earthly but at the same time to arouse his mind by that color, whence

9. Mg., Ex. 28:20.
10. Septuagint.

the prophet could ascertain that the wheels were unusual; they were not made of wood or any earthly material but were heavenly wheels. The color should attract the prophet's attention so that he would know that heavenly mysteries were being revealed to him.

Like the appearance of Tarshish, he says; next, the *likeness of each one to the four.* This could refer to the creatures, as some have imagined; but I have no doubt that the prophet teaches that the wheels were so much alike that one did not differ from the other. This proportion and equality shows that in all of God's works there is perfect ordering. This is not obvious (in fact we are more likely to assume that everything revolves by some disorderly impulse); but if we lift up our senses above the world, no doubt we will be enabled to acknowledge what the prophet describes: in all God's works there is a disposition so well ordered that no line could be better drawn. While God visibly changes the world, from his standpoint he maintains an even course so that what are called transformations or revolutions are in no way irregular in his regard. Each wheel was coordinated with all the others.

Finally, he adds: *their appearance and craftsmanship,* or form, *was as if a wheel was in the middle of a wheel;* thus one wheel intersected the other. He does not mean that one wheel was larger and the other smaller, but that one wheel was set within another so that they intersected each other.

Now we must see (I touched briefly on this yesterday) that the wheels were doubled because God does not seem to hold to a straight course: he has various transformations apparently contrary to one another, as if his activity were dispersed when he inspires his creatures with power. Therefore it says *one wheel was in the middle of another wheel.* In short, God presents to us in a lively fashion what experience teaches. First, the world is borne along like running wheels but in no simple fashion. Such variation occurs that God seems to drive to the right and then the opposite to the left. It is just as if two wheels were set within each other.

I can go no further now; I defer the rest until tomorrow.

Almighty God, since you have proposed to subject us to so many changes that we cannot dwell on earth with peaceful minds, grant, I pray, that being exposed to such varying fortunes, we may seek our rest in heaven and always aspire to behold your glory, so that what our eyes cannot discern may shine upon us. And may we acknowledge that the entire world is governed by your hand and power so that we might rest in your fatherly care, until we arrive at the enjoyment of that blessed rest which has been won for us by the blood of your only-begotten Son. Amen.

Lecture 4

17 *In walking they went to their four sides; they did not turn back when they walked.*

What he had already explained sufficiently he repeats for confirmation: *they walked in the four sides,* that is, each creature maintained its own straight course. What he says about *not turning back* relates to their perseverance; they did not proceed further than their completed course but without interruption proceeded directly to their goal. I am merely touching briefly on these things that have already been adequately explained.

18 *And rims to them* [literally, "backs"; but he means "rims," or "tires," which are iron bands], *and height to them, and terror to them; and their backs* [that is, "their rims" or "tires"; therefore, "their rims"] *were full of eyes around all four of them.*

His statement that there were *rims on the wheels* may seem superfluous, but it refers to the second part of the verse where he says that the rims were full of eyes. We must now deal only with their *height and terror.* He indicates that the wheels were large, but since they were round, their height could not be greater than the breadth. Thus when he says they *were tall,* he undoubtedly means that they were so large that merely looking at them caused terror (which he adds again, later on). To sum up: those wheels were uncommon in so exceeding the usual size that their height or magnitude was frightening.

The purpose of all this was to make the prophet more attentive to the vision, for if the Lord does not violently grasp us to himself, we become torpid in our laziness. The prophet had to be affected in various ways so that when he realized that something uncommon was set before his eyes, he would reverently apply all his senses to considering it.

By saying that the *rims of the wheels were full of eyes,* he indicates that the wheels were not turned by chance but moved with deliberation. If the eyes were in other parts of the wheel, they would have been of no use; but since the wheels turned on their rims, that is, on their iron bands, the prophet saw that the eyes were fixed there. We now see that although God appears to turn the world this way and that, nothing is done without reason or plan. By *eyes* the prophet indicates providence that never errs.

He does not say that each wheel had two eyes but that *the rims were full of eyes;* this is a more forceful expression than merely "the wheels had eyes," like saying that even the slightest movement of the wheels was ordered with or was guided by the highest reason.

This refutes the error of those who think that years are denoted by the wheels within wheels. I believe this idea was borrowed from the Egyptians, for in hieroglyphics a year is represented by the image of a serpent that is twisted so that it bites its own tail. It is certainly true that the continual succession of time is so intertwined that one year draws another after it, as Virgil also says: "the year turns upon itself by its own footsteps."[1]

But that idea is quite foreign to this passage, where the prophet speaks of movements that seem confused to us but nevertheless are orderly, because God never acts by chance or recklessly. Now, then, we understand the meaning of this section. He adds:

19 *And when the creatures advanced, the wheels near them advanced; and when the creatures were lifted up from the earth, the wheels were raised up at the same time.*

In this verse the prophet teaches that all the transformations of the world depend on some other source, namely, heavenly motion. We said that the creatures represent for us the angels whom God inspires with hidden power in order to work through their hands. When he says that the wheels progressed by virtue of that higher motion, it follows that there is nothing fortuitous in the world. God directs all things in accord with his incomprehensible wisdom, so that nothing happens except by his inspiration, hidden and imperceptible to our eyes.

The prophet's teaching is like a mirror in which we ought to contemplate what is hidden to human minds. We observe many happenings and therein suppose that numerous and complex motions are confused. But the prophet opposes this perverse notion and teaches that the wheels, which in themselves

1. Mg., *2 Georgics,* i.e., 2:402.

are motionless, are driven in accord with a higher motion. As the creatures —
the cherubim — are moved by that impulse, so too are their wheels.

Now that we have grasped the Holy Spirit's purpose, we should also
note the usefulness of his teaching. When we see people devising many
schemes to disturb the whole world, when we see numerous conspiracies and
everything prepared to carry them out, let us know that all these matters are
governed by God but in a secret way that surpasses all our senses. When we
see a great deal often happening inopportunely, to our judgment, let us understand that the angels are discharging their duty, and those things that have no
motion of their own are impelled by the angels' inspiration and motion.

The same point must be said of other matters. If winter is mild or
excessively severe, let us consider in that extreme what the prophet teaches
here, that God so governs the disposition of the times in accord with his will
that nothing happens except by this inspiration. Thus he says *when the creatures advanced, the wheels near them advanced at the same time;* as if to say
that the course of the creatures was like a pattern by which the wheels directed
their own course. *When the creatures were lifted up,* he says, *the wheels were
lifted up at the same time.* Next:

20 *Whither the spirit was for going they walked, thither the spirit was for
going* [this is how I construe it. To join it, as others do, with the second part
of the verse is too forced. The prophet repeats what he said; he is quite verbose;
next he adds:] *the wheels were also lifted up* [here "to lift up" is understood
in a general sense as "to raise," not as before and in the next verse; "they
were lifted up"] *with them, because the spirit of the creature was in the wheels.*
[Let us also add the next verse.]
21 *In walking they walked* [that is, when the creatures walked, the wheels
walked], *and when* [the creatures] *stood still,* [the wheels also] *stood still; and
when they were raised up* [here a verb of lifting, נשא (nāśā'), is used strictly;
but earlier he spoke without a modifier], *the wheels were lifted up with them
at the same time, because the spirit of the creature in the wheels.*

He continues the same thought, that the wheels were as if fixed, not lying
down but standing without moving. We know this is unnatural, for a wheel cannot
stand on any part of its rim without falling to the right or to the left, or rolling on.
But the prophet says the wheels were as if immobile; from this it follows that
their motion was "extrinsic," as they say. Later he confirms the same point with
more words; *the wheels stood with the creatures, as they walked,* and then *were
raised up.* The prophet recounts what he mentioned briefly earlier.

Although the matter is obscure, he arouses our attention by this abundance of words to let us know that the motion of the wheels is not pointlessly
attributed to the creatures but because its cause resides with them. If he had

said this briefly, it could have been conveyed carelessly. But when the prophet says so many times that the wheels moved as they were drawn by the creatures, it follows, as I said, that all the transformations that we see in the world arise from another source. The reason is repeated: *the spirit of the creature* (that is, "of the creatures") *was in the wheels.*

He changes the number, as he did earlier. The prophet means that the spirit of the creatures was in the wheels not because the wheels had any understanding but because they received their power from the creatures, just as the moon derives its brilliance from the sun. So let us be aware that the wheels were driven, but not because the creatures' intelligence was poured into them. God does not give mind and counsel to winter or summer, or to peace and war, or to the calm and the storm, or to pestilence and other things. What then? Neither air nor sea nor land has any power of itself but only insofar as God through his angels directs the earth for this or that use, or when he channels human plans this way or that, to war or peace.

Now we see plainly what is meant by *the spirit of the creatures was in the wheels,* namely, that God pours out his power through the angels so that not even a sparrow falls to the ground apart from his providence, as Christ says.[2] Therefore, whenever confusion makes us anxious and desperate, let us remember this sentence: *the spirit of the creatures was in the wheels.* Surely when we tremble repeatedly in uncertainty, what would happen unless we rest in the teaching that the outcome of all things will be whatever God has decreed, because nothing occurs except by his will. There is no motion or action under heaven except what he himself inspires through his angels. Now follows:

22 *And a likeness of the firmament* ["expanse"; רקיע *(rāqîaʿ)* is the noun used by Moses in his history of creation][3] *above the heads of the creature* [that is, "creatures"], *like the appearance of terrifying crystal* [others translate it "ice"], *stretched* [the firmament, or the expanse extended; נטוי *(nāṭûy)* is used for רקיע *(rāqîaʿ)*] *over their* [the creatures'] *heads from above.*

The prophet now tells what is most important in this vision: God seated on his throne. If he had spoken only of the creatures and the wheels, the vision would have been of little use, or at least incomplete. But when he places God on his throne, we conclude that the angels who inspire movement in other things do not move by themselves and have no power of their own.

In brief, the prophet here teaches that the angels so cause whatever happens under heaven that nothing should be ascribed to them of their own doing. Why? Because God presides over them and governs their actions.

2. Mg., Mt. 10:29; Lk. 12:6.
3. Mg., Gn. 1:6.

This is the point of the last part of the vision, which must be expounded now.

The prophet says that there was the *likeness of a firmament over the creatures' heads.* With these words he wished to lead us gradually to God himself, and God has also dealt with his prophet by setting various steps by which the prophet might himself ascend, little by little, according to the capacity of the human mind, to limitless heights. The prophet therefore does not speak of God's throne but only of the firmament.

When we lift up our eyes, God's glory appears nearer to us above than on the earth. It certainly shines everywhere, above and below; but heaven is in itself more excellent than the entire earth. And since heaven approaches more closely to God, his image is brighter there. God exercises his power and wisdom there much more brilliantly than on earth. How many miracles does the sun contain? If we examine each planet and then consider the stars, we will be bound to be seized with wonder a hundred times. So when the prophet speaks of the firmament, in effect he raises us up so that little by little our minds reach God.

He saw a likeness of the firmament. If he had simply seen the firmament that is exposed to the eye, it would not have been a vision. I do not know why the Greeks[4] translated it στερέωμα [*stereōma*] and the Latins followed them, for רקיע [*rāqîaʿ*] is neither similar nor related to that word. Nevertheless, I use the accepted word. Because the sky is visible to all, it could not attract the prophet's attention as required. But *he saw a likeness of the firmament,* whence he knew it was not the sky but a new form that was set before his eyes, as if God were leading him to heaven with an outstretched hand.

Over the heads of the creatures רקיע [*rāqîaʿ*], an expanse, was expanded. There is another participle, נטוי [*nāṭûy*], which means "extended"; נטה [*nāṭâ*] means "extend" or "expand." He says *as the likeness of terrifying crystal.* Thus this sky that the prophet saw had the color of crystal; but God added the terror, because, as already said, we are so sluggish that God must employ something shocking when he wants to bind us wholly to himself.

Over the heads of the creatures themselves, he says, *from above,* so that we might understand that these creatures have been subjected to the rule of the Most High God, as we will see later. Next:

23 *And under the expanse* [or, "firmament"] *their wings straight, each one toward its companion; to each creature two wings with which it covered itself, and to each one two wings with which they covered themselves, their bodies* [or, "in their bodies"].

4. Septuagint.

There is some obscurity in these words, but this can be easily removed if we note that there are two modes of covering. The wings that extended above covered the creatures themselves, that is, their faces; but the other wings connected to their bodies covered the body itself.

Some think this is repetitive: "the two wings with which they covered themselves and their bodies," as they put it. But this seems to me absurd, and so I have no doubt that what we saw before is repeated: two of the four wings covered the creatures when they were raised above. The wings were joined together so that each creature was connected with another. That was one form of covering; but there was another as well, when the other wings were lowered to cover the whole body. In sum, the prophet offers nothing new but emphasizes what he said before. Next:

24 *And when they walked, I heard the voice of their wings, like the voice of great* [or, "many"] *waters, like the voice of God* [or, "the voice of a strong man"; or, "a strong voice," which is more acceptable to others], *the voice of speech like the voice of a camp* [that is, "an army"]; *when they stood still, they lowered their wings.*

By saying that he *heard the voice of wings,* the prophet is explaining his earlier teaching, when he said that the wheels followed the course of the creatures and stood still unless they were drawn by the creatures. Now he explains this idea more clearly by *voice.* We know that commands are expressed by voice, and this is the way people communicate with each other, so that the one in command orders by voice what he wants done. Since what we said above was obscure, that the wheels were moved by the creatures, the prophet says there was *a voice in the motion of the wings.*

He has already stated, and he repeats it, that the creatures occasionally rested and lowered their wings. When the wings were lowered, there was no motion in the wheels. Since the wheels conformed to the motion of the creatures, he says that the *wings were vocal* — not because the wheels were furnished with ears or could hear commands. But the prophet could not otherwise express what I have already said, that heaven and earth are animated by angelic motion, than by saying there was something like a voice in that motion, which is like saying that whatever happens obeys God's command. But obedience cannot be engendered unless there is a prior voice. Therefore we now see the prophet constructing his statement to express and confirm more effectively by a new form of speaking what we saw before: the wheels were moved by the creatures, because a voice was heard in the wings.

He adds that it *was like the voice of many waters,* or great waters. We know that when a rushing river overflows it creates a great noise. Nothing is more terrifying than that sound, for it is like a crash that threatens to shatter the whole earth. It is this vehemence that the prophet now expresses.

He adds, *the voice of God.* It will be hard to speak this way about God. Even if speech is often attributed to him, we know it is done metaphorically. There had to be some external likeness, however, to show the prophet what in itself was not visible. But that does not suit the "voice of God" unless we take the phrase to mean "thunder," as in Psalm 29: "The voice of God shakes the cedars and the mountains so that the animals in the forests miscarry."[5] Here David calls thunder the voice of God. But I am not sure whether this metaphor fits the present passage. Yet if the translation "God" is acceptable, we cannot take the words to mean other than thunder.

Some translate שדי [*šadday*] as "strong man" or "violent man," which is not inappropriate, except that a general expression cannot be adequate for this passage. The images set forth here must raise the prophet's mind on high. If it simply said, "the voice of a strong or a violent man," what would that amount to? So I dare not reject the view that thunder is meant. If this exposition displeases anyone, it will have the same force as "loud-sounding" or "terrifying," for Scripture calls cedars and mountains "of God" because of their outstanding eminence.[6]

He says *when they walked,* because otherwise there was no motion. He said that the wings of the creatures were lowered when they stood still. There was no necessity for earthly things to move, unless there was a prior inspiration in the creatures, that is, in the angels.

He adds *the voice of speech.* Here Ezekiel goes a step further and says that the voice was understandable. It is true that inanimate things cannot hear a voice; but as I said, the prophet wished to assert that the wheels were so obedient that it seemed they were instructed and God had eloquently and distinctly commanded whatever he wanted done. It was as if the wings had spoken in an intelligible manner so that the wheels turned not by chance but in response to a command they received.

He says *like the voice of a camp.* This likeness ought to be noted carefully, because in an army the numbers hardly allow troops to have that regard for one another that produces good order, which military discipline requires. There is great clamor and confusion in the camp, but when each accommodates himself to the others, order is preserved. Therefore the prophet means that although an infinite number of matters occur simultaneously, nothing is out of line since God governs all earthly motion with more reason than a commander rules his army, even one who excels in unusual wisdom. Thus we see what the Spirit means in this part of the vision: he compares what

5. Mg., Ps. 29:5-6, 9.
6. Mg., Pss. 80:11, i.e., 80:10; 36:6.

occurs in the world to a vast army; but he says that in this multitude there is order and reason, so that although there is a clamorous tumult, all things come together properly.

Again he says *when they stood, the wings were lowered.* A question could be raised here: how could the creatures rest, since God always works? As Christ says, "The Father and I work until this day."[7] Since the power of God is never idle, what could the resting of the creatures mean? God works through the angels, as we have already seen. If they rest, then God has an occasional respite; but that is absurd. When the prophet says *rested,* he only wishes to note the variation in human affairs. Sometimes things are so tranquil we conclude that God has taken leave or a holiday in heaven. This is not because he has ceased to act but because we do not perceive the actions that would plainly demonstrate his power in movement and action. Therefore the prophet merely wanted to note variation, not that we ought to imagine that sometimes God does nothing or that his angels cease to act. Rather, they do not always work in the same or a similar manner.

> *Almighty God, although we wander far from you, grant that, having been taught by your Word, we may hold to the right path by which to approach you, and by faith contemplate those things that are hidden from us so that we may depend on you alone. And grant that we may so lean on your providence that we do not doubt our security, since our life and salvation are in your care. So when we are upset by various storms, may we remain at peace until at last we enjoy that blessed and eternal rest which has been prepared for us in heaven through Christ our Lord. Amen.*

7. Mg., Jn. 5:17.

47

Lecture 5

25   *And there was a voice from above the expanse that was over their head;*
when they stood still, they lowered their wings.
26   *And above the firmament* [or rather, "expanse," as we said] *that was*
above their head as a vision [or, "appearance"] *of sapphire stone, the likeness*
of a throne; and above the likeness of the throne as the appearance of a human
being, above it from above.

We said in the last lecture that because the prophet intended to speak
about God's glory, he spoke of the firmament, for human minds cannot reach
to such heights except by degrees. Therefore the prophet describes for us
the expanse of heaven. Now he adds that *there was the likeness of a throne*
above the firmament, and seated on the throne the likeness of a human
being. He is careful to mention the degrees when he says *above the expanse*
was a throne, and on the throne was a human being. He repeats what he
said earlier about the expanse of heaven. Just as God regarded the prophet's
weakness, so now he accommodates his word to the meager measure of our
understanding.

It is worth observing that he says *he saw the likeness of an appearance;*
we gather from this that he did not actually see the heavens, that the throne
was not formed of any material, and that it was not really a natural human
body. The prophet expresses these things clearly to prevent anyone imagining
there is anything visible in God. Some fanatics conceived God to be corporeal,
and from this passage someone might ignorantly conclude that God can be
seen and confined to a place — seated like a human being. Lest any of these
fabrications steal into people's minds, the prophet testifies that he saw neither
a human body nor a material throne; what was offered to him were these forms

48

or appearances. No one should think that the prophet is needlessly wordy in matters sufficiently clear.

He says *above the expanse that was over the creatures' head.* We have already explained that he deals again with the creatures' heads because all of the earlier vision should be referred to God himself. He adds *the expanse* because we could not ascend to God from the creatures without some aid. The firmament is brought before us so that we might reach the heights of God as if by a ladder.

He now specifies *the likeness of sapphire stone,* to inform us that only figures were situated before the prophet's eyes. This also applies to the likeness of a throne. We know that in earlier times the Anthropomorphites[1] disturbed the church with their madness in thinking that God was like us and had a throne on which he sat. In order to prevent such inventions the Holy Spirit says that the prophet saw not an actual throne but *the likeness of a throne.*

This was especially necessary concerning the human figure. This passage and similar ones, incorrectly interpreted by the Anthropomorphites, provided an occasion for their error in supposing that God is corporeal and confined to a limited space. These people progressed to such fury that they rushed in like an army to stone all those who opposed their wickedness. Therefore the prophet says that *he saw as the likeness of an appearance of a human being.* He could surely have used one word, but because we are so prone to vague and erratic ideas, he adds *appearance* to *likeness.* We see that whatever those ancient heretics fabricated earlier about a visible form of God is explicitly excluded.

One might ask why God assumes human form, both in this passage (that is, in this vision) and in others similar to it. I gladly embrace the opinion of the Fathers who say that this was a prelude to that mystery which was finally made known and which Paul extols magnificently when he exclaims, "this is a great mystery, that God at last was manifest in the flesh."[2] Jerome's view that these words are said of the Father himself is harsh.[3] We know that the Father never was clothed in human flesh. If he said simply that God was represented here, there would be nothing absurd. Remove all mention of persons, and it will be entirely true that the human being who sat on the throne was God.

At the end of the chapter the prophet also testifies to this when he says this was the likeness of God's glory.[4] There he uses the name "Yahweh," which expresses God's eternity and fundamental essence. It would be acceptable that God is represented in this figure. But what John says in chapter 12

1. Those who attributed a human body to God.
2. Mg., 1 Tim. 3:16.
3. *Commentary on Ezekiel* 1:22-26.
4. Mg., v. 28.

must be added, that when Isaiah saw God seated on his throne, he saw the glory of Christ and was speaking of him.[5] What I have already cited from the Fathers fully agrees with this, that whenever God appeared in human form, an obscure glimpse was given of that mystery which was at last made manifest in the person of Christ.

In the meantime, the ravings of Servetus[6] should be rejected, for he is easily refuted by the prophet's words. Servetus contends that this likeness was human in essence, and that Christ was a son in a figurative sense, because he was God in visible form, composed of three uncreated elements, as he says. These are the most detestable blasphemies and not worth refuting; but because that wicked dabbler has fascinated many gullible people who deserved to be punished for their foolish curiosity, it is useful to touch on those errors in passing.

Servetus imagines that from the creation of the world Christ was God in visible form, and he infers that in this way Christ was the image of God. He acknowledges no person in the Father but says that the Father was the invisible God and that Christ — insofar as he was the image of the Father — was also a person. He claims that Christ was composed of those three uncreated elements. If he merely said "out of three elements," Christ would not be God; but he invents for himself "uncreated elements" that take their origin from the essence of God. But he says that these elements were so ordered that they had human form. Thus he does not say that Christ merely appeared in human form but that Christ was fashioned as a human being in the divine essence.

Finally, he says that Christ was made human from the seed of Abraham, because a fourth element, which he acknowledges to be created, was added to the three. Thus he says that Christ was human because he imagines a mass brought together in a confused way out of that visible deity and the seed of Abraham. According to him, Christ was a human being only for a time, because that visible God was mingled with flesh. He says, however, that the flesh of Christ was absorbed by the deity. Just as God was made human not by union but by confusion, so now he says that his humanity was deified and that Christ's flesh is of one essence with God and in that sense has nothing human about it.

This is how he ridicules us who teach that we cannot participate in Christ unless we ascend to heaven by faith, for he imagines that Christ's body is everywhere and without limit. How so? It has been deified, he says, and does not retain any vestige of human nature. Now we see the kind of monstrosities that impostor has fabricated; but our prophet smashes such trifles when he says *there appeared the likeness of an appearance of a human being.*

5. Mg., Jn. 12:41.
6. Antitrinitarian burned to death at Geneva in 1553.

God's throne is described more distinctly for us in Daniel: "a human being, who bore at least a human form, was led to the Ancient of Days."[7] There God is placed on the highest level, and then Christ is joined to him as mediator. Daniel says that Christ was brought to the Ancient of Days, because just as Christ descended from the Father, so he has been received into his glory and now has been given the highest rule and power — as taught there at length.

But what is pertinent to the present passage ought to suffice for us; that is, the prophet saw God only in the person of Christ, for what is said about the human likeness cannot be transferred to the person of the Father or of the Spirit. Neither God the Father nor the Spirit was ever manifest in the flesh; but God was manifest in the flesh when Christ appeared to us, and the fullness of divinity dwells in him.

Paul says in Philippians 2 that Christ was made in human likeness, and in form and condition appeared human[8] — but in a different sense. He does not make Christ human in a figurative sense, and he does not deal expressly with the essence of Christ's body; rather, he emphasizes the condition of Christ's body when he descended to us. Therefore he says that he was humbled, so that he in no way differed from ordinary human beings in appearance. Moreover, Paul uses a word that distinguishes essence from appearance, namely, μορφή [*morphē*]. We now understand Paul's intention when he says that Christ was found to be like a human being in condition; in our flesh he was an outcast and contemptible. But in this passage in Ezekiel the Holy Spirit teaches something else, that Christ appeared in human form, although he was not yet human.

If someone asks where this body was taken from, the response is easy: it was not a created body, in substance, but this form was created only for a time. As is sufficiently well known, God at times gives his angels bodies, which afterward vanish. But there was another reason for this vision: Christ did not appear in human form in order to eat, as some angels did,[9] but only to accommodate himself to the prophet's capacity.

In brief, it was the likeness of a body in appearance only, as the prophet says, but not in essence. From this we gather that when God alone is mentioned, the entire essence, which is common to the Son and the Holy Spirit with the Father, is understood. It would be absurd to understand Christ alone under the name Yahweh. It therefore follows that the entire essence of God is to be understood here.

When the persons are compared to one another, however, then to say "he was in human form" applies to Christ alone. Therefore God in his entirety

7. Mg., Dn. 7:9-10, 13, 22.
8. Mg., Phil. 2:7.
9. Mg., Gn. 19:2-3.

51

appeared to his prophet, and in human form. But neither the Father nor the Holy Spirit appeared, because when that which is proper or unique to Christ is mentioned, then the persons begin to be taken into account.

This must also be noted because fanatics are now spreading a new error, as if Christ were a God distinct from the Father, and the Holy Spirit was still another God. One of them was that impostor, George Blandrata of Piedmont,[10] who resided among us under the guise of a physician and hid his impiety as long as he could. But when he realized he was detected, he fled into Poland and infected that entire area with his poison. He is not worth mentioning, but because he wanted to become famous through his blasphemies, he has just that fame which he desired. Because this error has spread so widely and all Poland has been infected (as I already said) with this diabolical madness, those who are not well trained in Scripture ought to protect themselves, to avoid falling into those snares.

As I was saying, they imagine that Christ was God, but not that God whom Moses and the prophets honor. Accordingly, whenever God is mentioned in the Law and the Prophets, they restrict this to the Father alone — even though they confess that Christ was God. But when they are pressed more closely, they say that he was made God in his essence,[a] because the Father communicated his own essence to him, as if by transfusion. Thus according to them Christ is a fabricated[b] God, because he is not one and the same God with the Father.

They think their wicked notion is confirmed whenever the Father is called simply "God." But the solution is easy, for in such a case a comparison is made of the Father with the Son: "God so loved the world that he gave his only-begotten Son."[11] The Father is certainly called God, but the Son is added. Therefore it is not surprising if the foundation of deity is given the highest rank. At other times, when there is no comparison of persons, the entire deity, which is common to the Father, Son, and Holy Spirit, and which is one and simple, is denoted.

In sum, when the persons are not under consideration, there is no relating one to another; but when the persons are an issue, then indications of relationship arise. The Father is placed separately, and then the Son in his rank, and then the Holy Spirit. I will not gather up all the testimonies of Scripture; it is enough that I point out such foul errors, so that those who are less skilled are not caught in these traps.

When Paul says that God was manifested in the flesh,[12] he is certainly

---

10. George Blandrata, 1515–88(?), a Piedmontese physician, known for promulgating Unitarian views in Poland and Hungary after encountering Calvin in 1558.

a. *Deum essentiatum.*

b. *factitius.*

11. Mg., Jn. 3:16.

12. Mg., 1 Tim. 3:16.

not speaking of a secondary or foreign essence. The essence of God is one. Therefore the entire deity was manifested in the flesh, and for that reason he says God was manifested in the flesh, just as Christ said: "I am in the Father, and the Father is in me."[13] Elsewhere when he teaches that the entire fullness of deity dwelt in Christ, we ought not to conclude from this that the essence of God was torn, as if one part was with Christ and another with his Father.

Thus, when John says in his canonical epistle that Christ was truly God ("This is the true God and life eternal"),[14] it would surely be intolerable blasphemy to claim that the true God was other than the Father. Of whom could this be said except the one God? If this affirmation were denied to the Father, he would cease to be God. Thus, if Christ is truly God, it follows that his essence does not differ from the Father's.

When Paul says that the church has been redeemed by the blood of God,[15] it is clear that the name of God is used simply and without qualification. As long as that impostor restricts the name of God to the Father, how can that agree with Paul's view? God, he says, redeemed the church by his own blood; if God redeemed it by his own blood, then the God of glory who has been from eternity and whom Moses and the prophets adore must be understood.

Now we understand how Christ, in respect of his "person," appeared in human form, and yet the fullness of God appeared. That Christ appeared can be proved and is clearly stated in John 12,[16] which I have cited. Both Isaiah and Ezekiel plainly testify that God appeared in his fullness: "I saw Yahweh seated on a throne."[17] Who is Yahweh, if not the God of Israel, of whom Moses earlier proclaimed, "Your God, Israel, is one God"?[18]

But how does John apply this to Christ? In respect of his person. We see how well these things agree, that the fullness of God appeared in the perfection of his glory and unlimited essence — and yet appeared in the person of Christ alone, for neither the Father nor the Spirit was ever clothed in human flesh.

I have dwelt on this teaching a little longer because many not well versed in reading the Fathers cannot easily make their way through them. These questions are quite thorny, but I have tried to deal as briefly as possible with this obscure and perplexing matter, and to explain it so that anyone equipped with even a modest understanding and judgment can easily comprehend what I have said. I will not pursue further the sentiments I could bring forward on this matter, for nothing is more useful in this than to be modest and sober in wisdom.

13. Mg., Jn. 14:10, 11.
14. Mg., 1 Jn. 5:20.
15. Mg., Acts 20:28.
16. Mg., Jn. 12:41.
17. Mg., Is. 6:1.
18. Mg., Dt. 6:4.

God appeared in visible form to his servant. Could Ezekiel ingeniously philosophize about God's essence, as the scholastic theologians have done who put no end or limit to their disputations? Hardly. Ezekiel kept within definite limits. Paul was caught up to the third heaven, but he says that he heard ἀπόρρητα [aporrēta], things that it were sacrilege to reveal.[19]

Let us be content with solid teaching that adequately fortifies us against all the snares of the devil. So he says *on the throne the likeness as of the appearance of a human being above it.* Next:

27 *And I saw as the form of hasmal, as it were appearance of fire within and around; from the appearance of his loins and above, and from the appearance of his loins and below, I saw as the appearance of fire; and brightness to him all around.*

With these words the prophet indicates that God appeared visibly in the form of a human being, and in such a way that his brightness still dazzled his eyes. The appearance of Christ was such that the prophet was able to consider each part, as when I observe a man I not only direct my eyes to his form from head to foot but consider the quality of his eyes and then his sides and his stature, whether tall or short.

When we consider human beings and trees, our sight is sufficient for examining the individual parts. But if we wish to direct our eyes to the sun, immediately they weaken, for the brilliance of the sun is so great that it dazzles us. If our eyes are unable to bear the splendor of the sun, how can the power of our minds reach to God and examine fully his glory?

This is the prophet's purpose when he says, *he saw as the appearance of hasmal.* We said that some understand this to be an angel, but in my judgment that opinion cannot stand, and therefore I reject it. I have no doubt that some sort of color is indicated. Jerome[20] translates it "electrum," but I leave that undecided. His statement that it is more precious than gold or silver is groundless,[21] because it is composed of both metals. Nevertheless, its color was extraordinary because it not only captivated the prophet's eyes but dazzled them with its splendor so that he recognized it as something heavenly and divine. Therefore he adds that it was *like the appearance of fire within,* which we explained before, *and all around.*

Moreover, the fire appeared this way so that the prophet would understand that these were marks of God's glory, and, as we will see in the end, that he might know that the vision would be useful only if he modestly contained

---

19. Mg., 2 Cor. 12:4.
20. Vulgate.
21. *Commentary on Ezekiel* 1:4.

himself within limits. When the majesty of God appears, it can overwhelm the angels themselves. What then will happen to us? But God accommodates himself to our capacity in such a way that visions are useful to us only if we are not prideful and do not get carried away with foolish and daring curiosity.

He also says that *the fire appeared above and below,* that is, above and below the loins; and the *fire was bright all around.* Later he adds:

28 *As the likeness of a rainbow* [the verb "I saw" from the previous verse must be repeated], *as the appearance of a rainbow that is in a cloud on a day of rain* [that is, "when it rains"], *so was the appearance of brightness all around. This vision of the likeness of the glory of Yahweh; and I gazed, and I fell on my face, and I heard the voice of someone speaking* [others translate it, "a voice speaking"].

Now the prophet adds that *the likeness of a heavenly rainbow was presented to him.* The profane call this Iris and suppose that she carries out the commands of the gods, especially Juno. But Scripture calls it the "rainbow of God," not because it was created after the flood, as many falsely conclude, but because God wished to increase our hope by that symbol whenever heavy skies obscure the heavens. We seem to be submerged under those heavenly waters, and therefore God wished to confront our lack of faith by having that heavenly rainbow as a pledge and witness of his grace.

When Moses says "I will place my rainbow in the heavens,"[22] some twist him to mean that a rainbow appeared for the first time. But there is little doubt that God wished to imprint a witness of his grace on something barely appropriate, just as he freely uses all creatures to do his will. The heavenly rainbow is often a sign of lengthy rains, and it somehow seems to attract rain. Therefore, since its appearance can strike terror, God says to the contrary that whenever the rainbow appears, it is clearly established that the earth is protected from a flood.

But when some attribute a witness of grace to this present passage, I am not convinced; that notion is repudiated by the vision. It is certainly plausible that the rainbow appeared because God wanted to show himself propitious to his servant, just as they interpret the passage from Revelation 4,[23] where John saw the throne of God encircled by a rainbow because God had been reconciled to the world through Christ. I do not dispute that interpretation of the passage in Revelation; but to say the same thing about Ezekiel would be completely out of place, because this entire vision was terrifying, as I said from the beginning. To mix contrary things this way would pervert the whole thrust of the vision.

22. Mg., Gn. 9:13.
23. Mg., Rev. 4:3.

Why then is the heavenly rainbow mentioned here? We have said that the heavens appeared to the prophet so that he might ascend little by little to reflect on God's glory, because in the heavens the marks of deity are more remarkable than on earth. If we consider the things unfolded before us, God certainly is never ἀμάρτυρος [*amartyros,* "without a witness"], as Paul says in Acts 14,[24] but his majesty shines more clearly in the heavens.

When the rainbow appears, however, a new reason is added to glorify God, for in the rainbow we have a more explicit expression of God, as we meditate on how magnificent is the handiwork of heaven and turn our eyes upon all the stars and planets. There, I confess, God surely compels us to admire his glory; but the rainbow has something extra that must not be despised, as if God added something more to the unadorned appearance of the heavens.

Now we understand that the prophet saw the heavenly rainbow that he might be increasingly moved when God revealed such remarkable signs to lead him to consider his glory. Therefore what some interpreters adduce about a symbol of reconciliation is completely inappropriate.

He says *I saw the appearance of a rainbow, which happens,* or which is *in a cloud on a day of rain.* If someone asks whether those colors have any substance, it is certain that they arise from the sun's rays in a vacuous cloud, as the philosophers teach. When the prophet says *a rainbow happens on a day of rain,* he simply means that it stood out or became visible, not that those colors have any substance, as I just said. While the rays of the sun are reflected among themselves in a vacuous cloud, they produce a multiplicity of various colors.

Afterward he adds again, *as the appearance of brightness all around.* Again the prophet confesses that his eyes were dazzled, because he could not bear such splendor. God reveals himself closely to his servants, but not to nourish that curiosity to which humans are too prone. Therefore God wished to disclose himself as far as was useful, but not as far as the demands of human desire, which always runs to excess.

Because people become so agitated that they easily weaken, we must stress what the prophet asserts once again, that *there was seen an appearance of brightness all around.* But what was that splendor like? It so dazzled the prophet's eyes that he became aware of his weakness and no longer desired to know more than was proper, but in modesty subjected himself to God.

Finally, he says that *this was a vision of the likeness of the glory of Yahweh.* These words confirm what I mentioned before, that he saw God's glory in such a way that God did not appear as he is but as he can be seen by mortals. If angels tremble at the appearance of God and even cover themselves with their wings, what will happen to us who crawl on the earth?

24. Mg., Acts 14:17.

Therefore we must remember that whenever the prophets and holy fathers beheld God, they saw *as the likeness or appearance of the glory of God;* they did not see the glory itself. They were not capable of that. This would be like measuring with our hands a hundred and a thousand heavens, earths, and worlds. God is without limit. Thus, since the heaven of heavens cannot contain him, how could our mind comprehend him?

Although God has never been seen in his limitless glory and has never revealed himself as he is, nevertheless it must be maintained that he has appeared in such a way as to leave his servants with no doubts. They knew they had seen God. Expressions that otherwise might seem harsh apply to this same point, for example, "I have seen God to face."[25] Was Jacob so foolish to think he saw God as one sees a mortal human? Hardly. That appearance must refer to certainty, as if he said that it was not some specter that was offered to him, or something he might have imagined, as the devil deludes us if we are not attentive and cautious. Jacob distinguishes the vision that mastered him from all the deceptions in which profane peoples took pleasure.

An "appearance face to face" means "personal knowledge." As I just said, God never allowed himself to be seen by the fathers except in accord with their meager measure, for he always considered the nature of their abilities. This is what the prophet has in mind when he says *this vision was of the brightness of the glory of Yahweh.* Moreover, since it is certain that he saw Christ, then Christ is Yahweh, that is, the eternal God. Although Christ is distinct from the person of the Father, nevertheless he is entirely God — God who in himself is the Father. Even though there is a distinction between the persons, the essence cannot be torn apart except in wickedness.

I defer the rest until tomorrow.

Almighty God, in your limitless goodness you have deemed us worthy of such honor that you descended to earth in the person of your only begotten Son, and each day you appear to us intimately in your gospel where we contemplate your living image. Therefore grant that we may not abuse such a benefit through senseless curiosity but be truly transformed into your glory, and thus more and more advance in the renewal of our mind and entire life, so that at last we may be gathered into that blessed and eternal glory which has been obtained for us through your only-begotten Son, our Lord. Amen.

25. Mg., Gn. 32:30.

57

Lecture 6

After the prophet recited the vision whose purpose was to confirm his call, he adds that *he fell on his face.* These words teach us that he was thoroughly convinced about the manifestation of God's glory, for only the knowledge of God truly humbles us. The prophet teaches at the same time, however, that people cannot be brought to order until they have been brought low.

He does not say only that he was prepared to accept the commands of God, and he does not commend his docility. Instead, he indicates that he was violently cast down. He did not immediately put off the affections of the flesh; we know that confidence is inborn in us. Hence because the prophet was not by nature sufficiently disposed to obey God, it was necessary that he be *cast down by fear, so that at last* he would voluntarily humble himself. Now he adds:

CHAPTER 2

1 *And he said to me, "Son of man, stand on your feet, and I will speak with you."*
2 *And when he spoke to me, the Spirit came into me and stood me on my feet, and I heard him speaking to me.*

Here the prophet tells that he was raised up by the command of God. God does not cast down his own to leave them lying on the earth but immediately raises them up. As far as the reprobate are concerned, they are so terrified by the sight of God that they promptly fall down and do not rise again.

But it is not so with the faithful, because the pride of the flesh is corrected in them, and then God extends his hand to them and restores them from death to life.

We must note this distinction carefully, because we see that the wicked are often terrified when God speaks. Even if they shamelessly reject him when he speaks, they are frightened by his hand when signs of his anger and vengeance appear. Yet they remain lifeless. It is common for the faithful to be frightened when God speaks, but the result is far different, as we see here. After God humbles them, he commands them to have courage and shows them that his purpose is none other than to establish them by his power.

The prophet also teaches that nothing was accomplished by this voice until the Spirit was added. Certainly God works effectively through his Word, but we must affirm that its efficacy is not contained in the sound itself but comes from the hidden power of the Spirit. Therefore the prophet sets forth both ideas; on the one hand, he relates that *he heard the voice of God that he should stand on his feet.* God wished to inspire him with confidence. But he also adds that he was not raised up by that voice until *the Spirit stood him on his feet.* In this way the work of the Spirit is joined with the Word of God.

This distinction is made, however, so that we might know that the external Word is of no importance by itself, unless it is animated by the power of the Spirit. If someone objects that the Word is superfluous because it is not effective by itself, the solution is easy. Because it pleases God to act this way, there is no reason we should object. But a clearer response is offered to us: although God always works in human hearts through the Spirit, the Word is not without benefit. God gives us light through the sun; nevertheless, he alone is the "Father of lights,"[1] and the splendor of the sun is of no use except insofar as God uses it as his instrument. The same ought to be maintained about the Word, because the Holy Spirit penetrates our hearts and illumines our minds. All power of acting resides with the Spirit, and therefore absolutely all praise ought to be offered to God.

Who can prohibit the Spirit of God from using instruments? Therefore we maintain that when God speaks, the efficacy of his Spirit is added at the same time, for otherwise the Word would be fruitless. Nevertheless, the Word does not lack effectiveness, because the instrument must be joined with the author of the action.

A brief explanation of this teaching is sufficient to refute those foolish objections that flutter about from all who flaunt human free choice. They say that we are able to heed the Word that is presented to us or reject it. But we see what the prophet is saying. If anyone is fit to render obedience to God, surely the prophet excels in this regard. But the Word of God had no effect on

1. Mg., Jas. 1:17.

59

LECTURE 6

him until the Spirit gave him the strength *to get up on his feet*. We conclude from this that we do not have the power to obey whatever God commands us unless it comes from him. Now follows:

3 *And he said to me, "Son of man, I send you* [literally, 'sending I you'] *to the sons of Israel, to rebellious* [or, 'apostate'] *nations who have rebelled* [this is the same word] *against me; they and their fathers have behaved faithlessly toward me to this very day."*

Now the prophet explains more clearly that the vision, which he mentioned before, was presented to him so that he would be furnished with authority and then could more freely fulfill the prophetic office among the Israelites. We know that God claims for himself alone the honor of being heard in his church, and that is proper. It is not in vain that he is called our lawgiver,[2] and our only wisdom is to depend on his Word.

Therefore, since God alone ought to be heard, any mortal who thrusts himself forward can be rejected unless he comes in the name of God, creates confidence in his calling, and really wins conviction that he speaks only God's command. So that Ezekiel might not play his role in vain, he had to have some sign of divine sanction; and that was done by means of the vision.

Now he explains the purpose of the vision more clearly. It is to be noted that apart from the Word, signs are illusory. If the prophet only saw a vision, and no Word of God had followed, what would have been the result? But when God confirmed the vision by his Word, then the prophet could tell effectively that he saw the glory of God. This can also be applied to the sacraments, because if only the signs are presented to us, they will be like dead specters. Therefore God's Word in effect brings the sacraments to life, just as we said about visions.

Whenever Ezekiel uses this expression, saying *he was called "son of man,"* I have no doubt that God wished to act in advance so that the people would not reject the prophet as one of the crowd, for he had been dragged into exile in disgrace. Since he appeared no different from the common people, his teaching could be condemned and repudiated. But God seized him, and in a kind of concession called him "son of man." Nonetheless, he indicates that his teaching should not be judged by its external condition but on the basis of his calling.

It is true that his speech was rather prolix, and we see how much our prophet differed from the others. His speech breathed an exotic quality, for he inevitably picked up many imperfections of speech, since they were in exile. The prophet was not careful about elegance and brilliance. Since he was

2. Mg., Is. 33:22; Jas. 4:12.

60

accustomed to the common speech, he spoke that way. But I have no doubt that God deliberately wished to present him as one of the crowd, contemptible in outward appearance. He truly lifted him above every mortal, however, because he honored him with the gift of prophecy.

Now we must see how God prepared him to carry out his office. *"I send you,"* he says, *"to the sons of Israel, a rebellious nation, recalcitrant,"* or a faithless nation. The prophet could merely have fled when he saw that an odious task had been enjoined on him; its difficulty alone could have terrified him. But a double testing was added in that he saw that he was entering a struggle with countless enemies. For however many Israelites there were, he provoked them all to conflict. This was the most serious test.

The other was that he saw that he was not only "beating the air,"[a] as the common proverb puts it, but he could also regard it as a profaning of heavenly teaching if he spoke among wicked people and, in the end, only exasperated them more and more. Therefore we see that the prophet had no reason, according to the flesh, to urge himself to fulfill his role. If God wished to use him, he ought to give him some hope of success, or at least keep him in suspense so that by remaining uncertain of the outcome he would attempt and try everything.

To start with, he is faced with the difficulty of dealing with a perverse and unyielding people, then he is drawn into such a hateful struggle, and third he is ordered to "throw what is holy to the dogs" and "cast pearls before swine,"[3] and thus to prostitute God's Word. He certainly could have despaired a hundred times when he pondered these things. Nevertheless, it was God's plan to arm him with indomitable perseverance so that he would press on in the course of his calling.

The main point that we must grasp is that when God wishes to move us to obey him, he does not always promise a happy outcome to our labor; but sometimes he wants to test our obedience to the point that he will have us be content with his command, even if people ridicule our efforts. Indeed, at times he indulges our weakness, and when he orders us to undertake some task he testifies at the same time that he will not allow our labor to perish and our efforts to be completely useless. Accordingly, God spares us. But sometimes, as I said, he tests his own, so that whatever the outcome, it should be enough for them to obey his command. We easily gather from this passage that our prophet was tested in this way.

---

a. *aquam verberare,* literally, "beat water," i.e., in a mortar (Erasmus, *Adages* II.i.59). Calvin equates the two proverbs in *Sermon 28* on 2 Timothy (*Calvini Opera* 54:339; trans. Laurence Tomson [London, 1579], p. 988), citing 1 Cor. 9:26 (cf. Erasmus, *Adages* I.ix.84).

3. Mt. 7:6.

We read the same thing about Isaiah, for when he was sent by God he not only heard that he would speak among the deaf, but God presented him with something far more difficult: "Go," he says, "make blind the heart of this people, make their ears heavy and their heart obstinate."[4] Therefore Isaiah saw not only that he would be exposed to mockery because his efforts would have no success, but that his speaking had no other purpose than to blind the Jews and finally to destroy them two and three times over — even though once would suffice.

But as I have already said, sometimes God wants his servants to rest in his authority so as to labor even with no hope of success. We must note this carefully, for whenever we are called by God, before we prepare ourselves, these thoughts enter our minds: "What will be the result?" and "What will I accomplish by my labor?" When the outcome does not accord with the longings of our heart, we become despondent. But to do this annuls the role of God's will.

Although our labor may be useless, it is enough that it pleases God. When we are ordered to do something, let us learn to leave the outcome in God's hand. Although the whole world may deride us, and although despair makes us cowardly, let us pull ourselves together and struggle on whatever may happen, because it ought to be sufficient for us that our obedience pleases God.

This is why Paul says that although the gospel is the "odor of death to death,"[5] it is a pleasing odor before God. When he says that the gospel brings death, our natural reaction may be that nothing would be better than to abandon it. Paul objects and says that the gospel should not be judged on the basis of its success. Although people not only remain deaf but also fall into a worse state, even though in a rage they rush headlong against God, nevertheless the gospel always retains its pleasing fragrance before God. The prophet's teaching has the same purpose.

Now if someone objects that God acts cruelly in deliberately blinding people so that those who are already truly lost perish three and four times, a response is easy. God offers his Word in common to the good and evil but works through his Spirit in the elect, as has been said. As far as the reprobate are concerned, teaching is useful in rendering them inexcusable and then breaking their stubbornness. Because they deliberately refuse to yield to God, they are condemned and inevitably succumb.

Therefore, when God sees that the reprobate are unyielding, he smashes them with the hammer of his Word. At last he takes away all excuse of ignorance because, like it or not, they are convicted by their own consciences; they are their own judges, and their mouths are stopped. Although they do not

4. Mg., Is. 6:9-10.
5. Mg., 2 Cor. 2:15-16.

stop clamoring against God, they are oppressed by his judgment. Although it may seem absurd that God sends his prophets to blind the people, his plan should be considered with reverence, even if its purpose is hidden to us for the time being. As I have just said, we know in part why God struggles with the unyielding and intractable.

Now, since Ezekiel is warned about the outcome from the start, there is little doubt that God wanted him prepared when he began to carry out his office, so that he would not give in to any obstacles. For some, who otherwise seem quite willing to obey, resist in midcourse when obstacles and difficulties appear. Many even retreat. So we see that some renounced their calling because they conceived great hopes and brilliant plans. But when the outcome does not correspond to their notions, they think they have been discharged from their call. They even murmur against God and throw off their burden, or rather shake off what was imposed on them.

Many shrink back from a course embarked on when they fail to experience the success that they imagined for themselves or presumed in their minds. So before Ezekiel began to speak, God anticipated temptations of this sort and warned him that he would be dealing with an incorrigible people.

He says that *"the sons of Israel are apostate nations."* מרד [*mārad̲*] means to fall away and also to rebel or resist; the word "rebel" is sufficiently appropriate. Thus *"I send you to rebellious nations,"* because immediately afterward the word מרדו [*mārᵉd̲û*] follows; that is, *"who rebelled against me."* We know that among the Jews this was a word of reproach. Whenever they call us גוים [*gôyim*], it is as if they called us profane, rejected and completely foreign to God. To them this word גוים [*gôyim*] means pollution and stench. Therefore to the Jews we are like a dung heap and the excrement of the world, because we are גוים [*gôyim*].

There is no doubt that this pride occupied the peoples' minds during the prophet's time. But God called them *"rebellious nations."* I admit that "nations"[b] is sometimes taken in a good sense, but because Scripture often calls גוים [*gôyim*] foreigners who do not share in God's covenant, it is a mark of shame and disgrace among Jews. There is little doubt that God wished to abolish the title of honor with which he had distinguished them — "a holy nation and a priestly kingdom."[6] Therefore, when God called them גוים [*gôyim*], it was like saying they had been stripped of all that dignity in which they earlier excelled, and that they in no way differed from the profane and rejected nations.

A similar picture is found in Hosea.[7] The prophet was commanded to

b. *gentes.*
6. Ex. 19:6.
7. Mg., Hos. 1.

take a prostitute for a wife. He says that he fathered a son and a daughter. The son he named עַמִּי לֹא [lō' 'ammî], because they were "not the people of God." Then the daughter was called "not beloved." The prophet shows by that vision that the Jews were rejected, so that God no longer considers them his children but rejects them as foreigners. In this passage, too, rejection is noted, when the prophet says that God called them גוֹיִם [gôyim].

Moreover, he uses the plural number to express better that defection had spread throughout the whole people. If there were only a few faithless people, the prophet might be encouraged. But God pronounces the most serious judgment, that the entire people, in whole and in part, were rebellious. This is the reason for the plural number.

But one might ask if there was not one person remaining among that people who embraced the prophet's teaching. The answer is easy: the pronouncement does not concern individuals but the people as a whole. Whenever the prophets spoke this way,[8] when they called the Israelites degenerate and illegitimate, children of Sodom and Gomorrah, and the offspring of Canaan, they inveighed against the multitude indiscriminately. They certainly had a few disciples who could not be classed in that category. We must recall what is said in Isaiah 8: "Bind my testimony among my disciples."[9] It is as if the prophet were commanded to speak separately to the faithful, of whom a small number remained, and to speak as if the writings were closed and sealed. But he openly proclaimed this speech to the entire people. In the same way, when God proclaims that the children of Israel *are rebellious nations,"* he looks to the people as a whole.

Meanwhile, there is no doubt that God always preserves some seed, although it is hidden seed. Daniel was in exile at that time with his compatriots, and he was certainly not a rebel against God. But as I have just said, it is enough that the wickedness had spread throughout the entire people. Moreover, God says that he was already sufficiently familiar with the kind of people they were: *"they rebelled,"* he says, *"against me."* These words indicate that he was not making a test, as if he did not know what these people were like. He says that their obstinacy was known to him by many trials; nevertheless, he says, *"I send you,"* because (as I already said) he wished to cut off all excuse of ignorance. He also wanted to break their stubbornness, which was otherwise indomitable.

He says *"Both they and their fathers behaved faithlessly against me, even to this day."* He does not diminish their crime when he says that they imitated their fathers' example; rather, he amplifies the people's wickedness in saying that it was not beginning only now. They were begotten by wicked

---

8. Mg., Is. 57:3; 1:10; Ezk. 16:3.
9. Mg., Is. 8:16.

parents — "like father, like son,"c as the common proverb puts it. Furthermore, nothing here serves as a valid pretext for error when we mention the fathers as an example, as today papists hold up this shield against God. When they talk constantly of the fathers, they surmise that this serves to defend themselves against every wickedness. We see, however, that it is not only meaningless to God but also increases the crime when the children's obstinacy is based on their fathers' evil examples.

The prophet does not wish merely to teach that it was a frivolous pretext for the Jews to object that they patterned their lives on imitation of their fathers; but, as we see, he shows that they were doubly damned because right from the start they did not stop provoking God. Thus wickedness and contempt of heavenly teaching prevailed among them continuously in every age.

Moreover, this passage admonishes us not to abuse God's great tolerance. We see the purpose for which God sent his prophet. The people were already doomed to final destruction, but God wished to plunge them deeper, even into the deepest abyss. Let us beware that nothing similar happens to us if we remain obstinate. When God sends prophets to this area and that, we must be called to repent. We must see to it that this Word, which is properly appointed for human salvation, be not the "odor of death to death" for us as it was to that ancient people. Next:

4 *"And the sons stern of face and hard of heart: I send you to them, and you will say to them, 'Thus says Sovereign*d *Yahweh.'*
5 *And they, whether they hear or desist, for they are a house of rebellion, and they will know* [the copula is redundant and ought to be changed to an adverb of time or an adversative particle: 'nevertheless, they will know'] *that a prophet has been among them."*

God continues the same speech but uses other words to express how rebellious the people were, that they were not only obstinate and hard of heart but also had a stern countenance. He ascribes this hardness to both the heart and the face. Certainly קְשֵׁי [qᵉšê] and חִזְקֵי [ḥizqê] are different words. "Stern faces": we could translate this as "wicked" or "stubborn" (for stubbornness appears in the face); or it would not be inappropriate to translate it as "impudent." But we ought to keep the literal meaning of the word. For "hard of heart," however, it would be acceptable to say "unyielding"; or if this allusion is more agreeable, we could render it: "an unyielding look" (as the wicked are said to have a "shameless look") and then "unyielding in heart."

c. *mala ova malorum corvorum*, "bad eggs from bad crows." Cf. Erasmus, *Adages* I.ix.25.
d. *Dominator* (not *Dominus*, "Lord"), and so throughout.

65

The point is that the Jews were not only obstinate toward God and filled with haughty contempt, but they were so desperately wicked that they opposed God without dissimulation, liked horned oxen or raging bulls. We know that hypocrisy often lies hidden in the soul, and although people swell up with malice, they do not disclose what they are nourishing within. But the prophet shows that the Israelites had abandoned themselves to such wickedness that their open enmity toward God showed in their faces.

In sum, while he prepares himself to carry out God's mandates, the prophet must tell himself that when he approaches the people, his teaching would not only be useless to them since it will not be received with the reverence it deserves, but beyond that it would also be exposed to much ridicule. The Israelites were not only filled with hidden contempt of God but openly displayed their hostility; they were, as I said, so shameless that they did not hesitate to reject the prophet openly.

Thus, *"the sons are stern,"* and so forth; *"nevertheless, I send you to them."* God once again brings forward his command so that the prophet would rest simply in this word alone, that he was sent by God. What if he upsets people? Let him be content to have his work approved by God. This is the point of the expression *"I send you to them,"* which is repeated a second time.

The prophet could take exception: "What will I do? If they have hearts of brass and faces of iron, I will labor in vain." God responds in turn, "A prophet should not be anxious, because it is enough that he has a mandate." God deals with his servant like a prince who does not explain his entire plan to his ambassador but still orders him to serve. This is how God deals with his servant.

We see here that God magnifies his own authority. This should be noted diligently so that we do not always try to bargain with God, as we are accustomed to do. If God does not immediately show us the results of our labor, we languish; and thus we try to exempt ourselves from his command by making excuses. God opposes us with this phrase: *"Behold, I send you."* The rest tomorrow.

Almighty God, since today you deem us worthy of the honor of your Word resounding daily in our ears, grant that it may not encounter hearts of stone and minds of iron; but may we subject ourselves to you with all due docility so that we truly sense that you are our Father. And may we be established in the confidence of our adoption for as long as you persist in speaking with us, until at last we enjoy not only your voice but also the sight of your glory in your heavenly kingdom, which has been won for us by your only-begotten Son through his blood. Amen.

Lecture 7

After God warned his servant that he was going to undertake a very difficult task, he now confirms him and exhorts him to act with invincible freedom. *"You,"* he says, *"will say, 'Thus says God' "* — as if he said that the mere fact that he is carrying out God's business is enough to overcome all obstacles. Here God does not give specific commands; he will do that later in its place. *" 'Thus says Yahweh' "* is a general expression that means, "I offer nothing of my own but faithfully speak what God commanded." We see that God's purpose was to set his name against the people's obstinacy; now that the prophet has been endowed with this authority, God commands him to be strong and bold in spirit, even though he has oppressive and harsh enemies.

Next he adds, *"whether they have heard or desisted, nevertheless, they will be aware that a prophet has been among them."* Here God again exhorts his servant to persevere, whatever the outcome of his labor. If things do not turn out according to our ideas, we are inclined to despair. But God wants us to persevere in the course of our duty, even if everything turns out unhappily.

Furthermore, he shows that his labor will have some results even though the people reject whatever he says because of their depravity. When God's servants discern no benefit from their labors, it breaks their spirits. We always desire to do something worthwhile. God therefore indicates that his teaching has a result other than bringing salvation to humankind. That is, it removes all pretext of error and uncovers the wickedness of those who grasp for cover-ups. Even if hypocrites willingly and knowingly perish, they still assume that they are excusable unless God opposes them with the light of his teaching.

The point of all this is that although the prophet's teaching did not benefit the Israelites, nevertheless it would be useful in another way: *"they will realize at last that a prophet has been with them."* Some think that the prophet's

67

speech is too abrupt, but there is no corruption here, although a key word seems to be missing when he says *"if they have heard* and *if they have desisted, because they are a house of rebellion, and they will recognize that there was. . . ."* We said that the copula ought to be taken as an adversative: *"nevertheless, then they will recognize."* They will not accomplish anything by their stubbornness except that God holds them convicted.

Let us learn from this passage that although the wicked furiously try to reject the teaching of God, they accomplish nothing except to bring forth their evil more and more. Let us also learn from this that God's teaching is precious to him and that he cannot tolerate our despising it. The wicked never condemn heavenly teaching with impunity, because it is just as if they trampled on an invaluable treasure. Those who forsake the Law and the Prophets still do not escape the hand of God, because conscience is enough to deprive them of any excuse.[1]

When God invites people to himself, draws nearer to them, and offers himself to them in a special manner as Father and Teacher, then if they reject such a wonderful benefit, their ingratitude certainly deserves the greatest severity. Whenever God raises up for us prophets and faithful ministers of his teaching, let us remember what is said here: unless we embrace such a great benefit, we will in the end know that a prophet was with us because God will bring about horrible judgment against the contempt of such great kindness. Now follows:

6 *"And you, son of man, do not fear them and do not fear their utterances, because they are rebels* [this is not the word מוֹרְדִים *(môredîm),* but they translate it 'rebel.' Perhaps it means something else, for it is not commonly used by the Hebrews], *and thorns with you* ['over against you'], *and you dwell with scorpions. Do not fear their utterances and do not be broken by their face, for they* [are] *a rebellious house."*

God again instructs his servant to press on bravely, even if the people close off all approaches by their malice and wickedness. Because we often fall away through fear and terror, God arms his prophet with invincible confidence against the people's threats and against all words whatsoever. He offers no reason except that *"they are a house of rebellion,"* or they are a rebellious and obstinate nation. We said that at first glance this explanation seems to be frigid, but it suffices to encourage God's servants when they consider that God orders nothing by chance.

When they recognize that it pleases God that they squander their words on the deaf, thereby they do not fail to carry out their role, even though they

1. Mg., Rom. 2:12.

may wear themselves out in vain as far as the world is concerned. Moreover, when the thought arises that God will be on their side, their confidence and courage are increased. Thus it happens that they despise every threat and terror and boldly carry out their duty.

For this reason he now says, *"You, son of man, do not fear them, and do not fear their utterances."* I take "utterances" to mean not simply threats but also the scorn with which we know the servants of God were weighed down. Hypocrites rise up with great confidence and complain that they have been wronged, and then they brashly hold up the name of God. So today the papists not only spew forth threats to disturb us but arrogantly boast that they are the church. They confirm this by "perpetual succession," and then that the church will never be without the Holy Spirit, and therefore it is not possible that God would ever desert them.

We see that the domestic enemies of God not only speak threateningly against God's servants but also advance many false pretexts to burden true and faithful prophets with their envy and hatred. However plausible such malicious charges appear, as the enemies of truth unjustly oppress us, God commands us to go forward with invincible courage.

"Do not fear them," he says, *"or their utterances."* Because this same expression is repeated a little later, we conclude that God is presenting something extraordinary. It is worth noting that God proclaims once and then twice that the prophet should not fear the utterances of those who boast that they are the church of God and do not hesitate shamelessly to flaunt his sacred name as if they were in a game. Since we have God's authority to despise such words, there is no reason why today the papists should leave us dejected, when they puff themselves up and thunder forth the name "church" and "apostolic authority." Proper honor is not offered to God unless all the pomp of the world is brought into line so that only teaching from the mouth of God is exalted.

He adds, *"because,"* or "nevertheless," for this causal particle can be taken as an adversative: *"even though they are rebels, and thorns, even though you dwell among scorpions, nevertheless, do not fear their utterances and do not be broken by their face."* חתת [*ḥātat*] means to be broken and worn down, but it is also applied to the soul; and here it is taken in a metaphorical sense for "broken in spirit." It is as if he said, "Be bold in taking on every threat and false charge, *because they are a house of rebellion.*"

This passage teaches that no one is fit to carry out the prophetic office who is not armed with the courage to persevere whatever may happen, so that one does not fear any threat or stumble and vacillate when oppressed by unjust slanders. That is why Paul says that he advanced through ill report and good report, because he was unfairly misrepresented by the wicked.[2] Therefore,

2. Mg., 2 Cor. 6:8.

69

whoever wishes to prepare faithfully to take up the office of teaching must be equipped with the constancy to oppose with an iron will all slander, every curse, and any threat or terror.

There is certainly no doubt that the Israelites were thoroughly exacerbated when they heard themselves called *"thorns and scorpions."* But it was necessary to sting them, because if they were merely threatening a mortal, they could exalt themselves far more impudently. But since God pronounces that *"they are thorns and scorpions,"* and since they see the prophet boldly and unhesitatingly carrying out these mandates, it is inevitable that they are driven into outrage or that they fall silent. But although they struggled as far as their obstinacy and hardness could take them, in the end God succeeded in making them retreat in shame. The prophet, furnished with such great courage, served the truth — and the truth prevailed.

We also see from this passage that the prophets often spoke harshly when the wickedness of the people with whom they were dealing demanded it. Nevertheless, they were not carried away with excess, nor did they rail intemperately against their adversaries. There was no other way they could assert their teaching against the wicked who were driven by diabolical fury to struggle against God himself.

Hence we must understand that although their speech was cruel and harsh, nothing but human concern inspired their hearts. Our prophet was not a barbarian who was moved by indignation to spew forth harsh reproaches against his own people; but, as we see, the Spirit of God dictated what might seem excessively harsh to tender and delicate ears. Next:

7 *"And you will offer my words* ['you will proclaim my words'] *to them, if they have heard or if they have desisted* [that is, 'whether they have heard or refused to hear'] *because* [or, 'surely'] *they are rebels* [or 'people of rebellion']."*

He repeats again what he had said but with slightly different words. The point is the same, however: that the prophet should not stop in midcourse if he sees that he is not attaining what he desires and hopes for. When we undertake what God orders, we certainly ought to be optimistic and also to want our labor to have some results. We can entertain hopes and desires, but if it turns out differently than what we expected, we ought to leave the outcome in God's hands and carry out our calling to the limit. This is the purpose of this sentence: *"You will offer my words,"* or proclaim my words, *"whether they have heard or desisted";* that is, "Even if it means 'singing your song to the deaf,' as they say, you will not stop proclaiming my word."

Then he adds an explanation: *"because they are a rebellious nation."* God warns his servant in advance that there is no reason why he should change his course, even though he sees that his labor is without result. The prophet ought, once and for all, to fortify his soul with the thought that although the people have no ears, he still must speak in the name of God.

It is certain, as we mentioned yesterday, that there were a few for whom the teaching was useful; but here it is the people as a whole that is at issue. So let us learn that when God calls us to the office of teaching, we must not consider the kind of people to whom God calls us. If God chooses to exercise us while we struggle with rebellious and stubborn people, we must still offer his Word, because that is what he orders. Next:

8 *"And you, son of man, listen to what I say to you, lest you become rebellious as this house* [or, 'as the house of Israel is rebellious' — this is to be understood]. *Open your mouth and eat whatever I put before you."*

God continues to confirm his servant, but he removes a stumbling block that could break the prophet's eagerness. When he sees that the house of Israel is so stubborn, he could a hundred times abandon the desire to teach. So God adds a stimulus and urges him to persevere, even though he is aware that the house of Israel is so ruined by its stubbornness: *"You,"* he says, *"listen to whatever I say to you."* Here we see that no one can fulfill the teaching office without having so far advanced in the school of God. All who wish to be considered true teachers must be disciples of God, and it is paramount that they listen to God when he speaks.

Then he removes the stumbling block that we mentioned: *"lest you become rebellious like the house of Israel."* We know that a crowd often has the power to disturb us, for the consensus of the entire people is like a violent storm. When all conspire together, even those who are not evil are carried along with the rush. Because it is not unusual for the crowd to carry along even God's servants, God prevents this and throws a bridle on his prophet: *"lest you become rebellious like the house of Israel."*

He is not speaking indifferently of any people whatsoever but of that nation which boasted that they were chosen by God and bore in their flesh the symbol of adoption. God wanted his prophet to ignore the popular consensus, because we know that the Israelites arrogantly boasted that they were the holy and special people of God. As today the papists boast, so the Israelites at that time dealt violently with all the prophets.

We ought to note this passage diligently, because today many completely vanish when those magnificent titles are brought forward. But we know that this is nothing but smoke, by which Satan tries to dazzle us while falsely brandishing the names "God" and "church." We certainly ought to receive with modesty and veneration whatever comes from God, so that as soon as God's name appears, it moves us within. But at the same time, we must be prudent and discerning so that we do not become numb when Satan bears the name of God to delude us. Discretion must be brought to bear, and here God shows us its rule. If we are thoroughly persuaded that the teaching which we profess and follow is from God, then we can safely look down on — as if from heaven — every mortal and even the angels themselves. Nothing is so excellent that it can outshine the truth of God.

Since the Israelites frequently pretended to be the people of God and adorned themselves with the signs of the church, we must affirm that the name "church" is frivolous when hypocrites rule it, or rather exercise a wicked tyranny and oppose themselves to God and his teaching. Today we can turn this passage against the papists, or rather aim it at them directly, whenever they reproach us with that smokescreen of "Catholic Church" and "bride of Christ." God himself has said once for all that we must not rebel although the entire house of Israel is rebellious. That is, those who hold up God's name may conspire among themselves with diabolical stubbornness, but we must not consider what they do so as to subscribe to their wicked conspiracy.

We read the same thing in Isaiah 8: "Do not call 'conspiracy' what this people calls 'conspiracy'; do not be afraid or tremble for fear of them, but bless the Lord of hosts."[3] Peter also quotes this passage because at that time the Jews who stubbornly opposed the gospel caused the weak to stumble because of their boldness in claiming to be the church. Nevertheless, they rejected and abhorred the new teaching that was then being professed. Peter quotes this same passage from the prophet, that although the house of Israel wickedly conspired against God, such stubbornness must be rejected.[4]

Later the prophet adds, "Behold, I and the children whom God has given me are a sign and a portent."[5] He states that these little ones, who were worshiping God purely and who withdrew from the widespread wickedness, were like portents and lived as if they were abnormal. The author of the Epistle to the Hebrews effectively applies this passage to the kingdom of Christ.[6]

Today we are certainly a portent to our enemies who boldly and in desperate shame exalt themselves against the pure teaching of the gospel. To them we are heretics, schismatics, dogs — the refuse of the world. But although we are a sign and a portent to them, it is enough for us that we are acknowledged by God. We must separate ourselves from that wicked conspiracy unless we want to be separated from God himself.

What is consensus with the papists or union with such refuse except dissension from God himself? Since today we cannot extend a hand to the

---

3. Mg., Is. 8:12-13.
4. Mg., 1 Pet. 3:14-15.
5. Mg., Is. 8:18.
6. Mg., Heb. 2:13.

papists or cultivate brotherly concord except at the cost of denying God, let all that cursed consensus be gone, and let us learn to separate from them courageously, as we are clearly ordered to do in the person of the prophet.

He said a little earlier that a "prophet dwells among them," and this was expressed clearly so that he would watch out for himself more carefully. It is difficult to walk among thorns and scorpions without being pricked and without the scorpions striking us with their poisonous tails. God commands us to be so attentive that we can walk among thorns and not be scratched and that the venom of scorpions not touch us. This will happen if we ask heaven for the wisdom that we do not possess, for if the Spirit of God governs us, it will keep us untouched by the sting of any serpent and from every wound and injury.

Next: *"Open your mouth and eat whatever I put before you."* With this crude symbol, God confirms Ezekiel in his calling. He orders him *"to eat a book,"* and this was carried out in a vision. Jeremiah uses the same metaphor in chapter 15 but with a slight variation in that our prophet seemed to have actually eaten that scroll. But Jeremiah indicates only that he digested the words of God like food; not that he tasted them with his tongue but that they were fixed inwardly in his soul as if he actually consumed or digested them.[7]

God wished to confirm our prophet in a different way, however, when he presented that scroll to him and ordered him to eat it. There is little doubt that the scroll included whatever the Spirit of God dictated to the prophet later on. It was as if God made a mortal into an instrument of his Spirit; as if he said, "You will offer nothing human or earthly, because you shall offer what my Spirit has already written in this book."

Here we see a distinction between the true servants of God who seriously fulfill their office and those talkative people for whom it is enough to excel in eloquence — or empty wit. There are many clever people who disgorge what they have never digested in their minds. Their teaching immediately vanishes. This is what Paul means when he says that "the kingdom of God does not consist in words but in power."[8] Those who are truly consecrated to God not only learn what to say but digest it like food so that they take God's Word within and hide it away in the innermost recesses of their hearts, and then bring forth the food that they have thoroughly digested.

Now we understand why God wanted the prophet to eat the book, which comes next:

9 *And I looked, and, behold, a hand extended to me; and behold, in it the scroll of a book.*

7. Mg., Je. 15:16.
8. Mg., 1 Cor. 4:20.

10 *And he unrolled it before my face, and behold, the scroll was written on the front and backward* [that is, "on the front and the back"], *and the writing* [what was written in it] *lamentations and dirges and woes.*

Now the prophet teaches more fully about the meaning of these matters we mentioned before. He relates that *the scroll of a book was offered* to him; that is, a book was offered in the form of a scroll. The word מגלת [*megillat*] that he uses is derived from "to roll," גלגל [*gilgēl*], as is *volumen* (scroll) among the Latins. They were formerly accustomed to write on scrolls; that is, books did not have the compact and concise form that we use now. They had scrolls, which the uncultured call "rolls." Ancient documents were written in this way; everything ancient in the archives of princes was written on scrolls. Thus the phrase "In the scroll of the book it is written, etc."[9]

Now the prophet says that *such a scroll was offered to him to eat;* but he says that *it was offered by a hand that was extended.* By this symbol, God shows more clearly that the scroll was not compiled in the air and that it could only have come from heaven. If the prophet had seen only a scroll before him, he could have disputed with himself whether it was sent from God. But when a hand offering the scroll appears, a hand extended by God, then everything needed for complete and enduring certainty is present.

He says, *after the scroll was unrolled, he saw that it was written on both sides;* these words make him realize that nothing brief was being ordered, but a long period of time was being imposed on him. If he had spoken only about the scroll, the Jews could have rejected him with contempt after three or four days, as if it had come to the end: "Yes, a scroll was presented to you; but you have already spoken three or four times. Isn't that enough?" Hence to prevent such scorn, he says that *the scroll was written on the front and backward.*

Now he describes the nature of its contents: *the writings were only lamentations,* he says. הגה [*hegeh*] sometimes means "meditation" or simply "speech"; but because it is used here with lamentations, there is no doubt that it is taken for songs of mourning. Finally, הי, *"hei,"* a particle of lament, is added.

The prophet's point is that the teaching contained in the book was not sweet or humorous but full of sorrow, because God presents in it signs of his anger, and only matter for sorrow and lamentation can be seen in it. Now we understand that the Israelites were more and more exasperated when the prophet said that he came only as a herald announcing war in God's name and had no mandate of peace.

As far as the rest of the people are concerned, we will see later on in

---

9. Mg., Ps. 40:8, i.e., 40:7-8; Heb. 10:7.

many passages that the prophet was a preacher of God's mercy. But it was necessary to arouse the Jews in this way so that they would understand that God was opposed to them. The prophet was sent for this purpose alone, that he might appear among them like a soldier and thunder forth in the name of God himself.

I cannot go any further at this time, even though what follows is part of this context.

Almighty God, since today you have deigned to summon us to yourself through the testimony of your fatherly favor, grant that we may not be like wild beasts but peacefully subject ourselves to you and thus follow where you call us, so that we may truly sense that you are our Father. May we thus abide under the protection of your hand for as long as we are sojourners in this world, so that at last, gathered in your heavenly kingdom, we may be completely joined to you and to your only-begotten Son, who is our happiness and glory. Amen.

Lecture 8

CHAPTER 3

1 *And he said to me, "Son of man, eat what you find to eat, this scroll; and go, speak to the house of Israel."*
2 *And I opened my mouth, and he fed me the scroll.*

When he ordered him to eat whatever he got, this ought not to be extended to whatsoever he might come upon. The prophet is forbidden to refuse the book, no matter what it tastes like. A harsh or bitter taste could make him reject God's threats. Finally, he notes the quality of the book, that it contained nothing but sadness.

He continues, *I opened my mouth* out of obedience. This indicates that he was not being curious or fussy in trying to taste it. Instead, he set aside all disputations and took what was offered to him from heaven. Now he adds:

3 *And he said to me, "Son of man, feed your belly, and fill* ['you will fill'] *your stomach with this scroll that I give you." And I ate, and it was in my mouth like honey in sweetness.*

Ezekiel follows up what we saw before: a scroll was given to him to eat, because the servants of God ought to speak from the inner affection of the heart. We know that many have a fluent tongue but do nothing except show off; in the meantime, God makes a laughingstock of their vanity because their labor bears no fruit. Thus we should note what I quoted from Paul: "The kingdom of God consists in power."[1] But the efficacy of the Holy Spirit does

1. Mg., 1 Cor. 4:20.

76

not manifest itself except when those called to the office of teaching seriously devote themselves to carrying out their office. This is the reason why Ezekiel was commanded to *eat the scroll.*

Now he says that *it was sweet to him like honey.* A little earlier, however, he related that it was filled with curses. Therefore he is either devoid of all humanity, or he ought to be touched by grief, when he saw that he was appointed as the herald of God's vengeance. But elsewhere we have seen that God's servants are furnished with two types of feelings. They were rigid and harsh whenever necessary, but they still sympathized with the miserable people. But their anguish did not prevent them in any way from bravely persevering in the course of their calling.

The reason Ezekiel now says that *the scroll was sweet to him* is that he rested in the command of God, and although he pitied his people, he knew that it had to be that way, and he accepted God's just judgment. Thus by the word *sweetness* he indicates nothing other than approval, because he embraced the office enjoined on him, and he was so obedient to God that he forgot all the sadness contained in the book. The justice of God prevailed and to an extent extinguished the extreme kindness that otherwise could have inhibited him.

Jeremiah speaks the same way in chapter 15.[2] He says that he found the words of God and they became to him a joy and delight in his heart. We saw that he was not only anxious but extremely sad when he realized that complete destruction threatened the people. But as I just said, these two fit together nicely, that is, the prophets wanted the people to be saved, and they devoted themselves as much as possible to saving them.

At the same time, they were strong and steadfast and did not hesitate when necessary to condemn the people and to bring forth the threats of God that were enjoined on them. A little later Jeremiah says that he was filled with anger. "Your words were found," he says, "and I ate them; and this brought joy and delight to my heart, because," he says, "your name was invoked upon me, Yahweh God of hosts"; that is, "because I was filled with the power of your Spirit, and just as I was called to this office, you also reached out your hand to me so that I could faithfully and steadfastly carry out what you ordered. Therefore, your words were a delight to me."

Next he adds: "I did not sit in the council of the scorners, nor did I exult in shaking off the yoke. Since I clearly perceived that I must obey you, and since I was contrite, I did not sit with scorners; but I sat alone," he says, "because you filled me with indignation."[3] Now then we see in one man two emotions, very diverse and contrary in kind. He was filled with indignation, and yet he found delight in God's words. Now Ezekiel adds,

2. Mg., Je. 15:16.
3. Mg., Je. 15:17.

77

4 *And he said to me, "Son of man, go to* ['enter'] *the house of Israel and speak to them in my words.*

5 *Because you have been sent not to a people obscure^a in speech* [this is a collective term; therefore, the number is changed to 'a people obscure in speech,' literally] *and difficult in language, [but] to the house* [that is, 'of Israel'].

6 *Not to many peoples obscure in speech and difficult in language whom you do not understand* [that is, 'whose speech you do not understand']. *If not, I would have sent you to them,^b and they would have listened to you.*

7 *But* [here the copula is taken as an adversative] *the house of Israel will not be willing for listening to you* [that is, 'will refuse to listen to you'] *because if they are not willing to hear me, for the entire house of Israel stern of brow* [or, 'stubborn'] *and hard of heart."*

Now God uses more words to explain that he wanted his servant to eat the scroll in his outstretched hand so that he would be prepared to approach the children of Israel. He could not come empty-handed. We know that people contribute nothing solid of themselves. Hence it was necessary that Ezekiel accept from God what he was going to hand over to the Israelites. Let us, then, hold to this order: the scroll was given to the prophet, and then he was sent to the people.

But *God* commands him *to offer,* or speak, *his words;* this is worth noting and refers to the same idea. If Ezekiel ought to make known only what he received from God, this rule ought to be valid for all God's servants, so that they do not spout their own inventions but proclaim what they have learned from God, just as if it came from his mouth. Finally, Peter's words are always valid: "Let one who speaks in the church speak the words of God."[4]

Now he adds, *"I do not send you to a people obscure in speech and difficult in language but to the house of Israel."* Some surmise that the prophet is being encouraged to do his duty because God requires nothing too difficult of him. If he had been sent to remote nations with whom there was no common language, he could excuse himself by saying that the burden was more than he could bear. The difficulty would be like an obstacle. Therefore they reason that remote and foreign nations are being contrasted with his own people so that he would quickly fulfill his duty; as if he said, "I do not send you to foreigners, for they would not understand and would be like barbarians to you.

a. Calvin's following comment about the "collective term" is based on the plural *profundos labiis,* "obscure in speech." Since "people" is the singular *populum,* Calvin changes the first phrase to the singular *profundum labio.*

b. This translation is the one given by Calvin below. As it stands the Latin would mean: "If I had not sent. . ."

4. Mg., 1 Pet. 4:11.

But because you are familiar with your own people, you will have no excuses when I send you to them."

But that view does not convince me, because I read these three verses in the same context, as if they fit together. There is no doubt that God is stressing the people's wickedness with this comparison. This idea is primary: the Israelites would be deaf even though the prophet used the common and vernacular speech, as they say. This is the first point. The cause is also made obvious, that is, because *"the people are bitter."* God means that nothing stands in the way of the Israelites progressing in the prophet's teaching except their own malice and wickedness. This is the reason he says, *"I do not send you to a people obscure in speech."*

I do not know what gets into the minds of those who think that wise and educated people are denoted by this epithet, for "people of obscure speech" and "people of difficult language" mean the same thing. What is a difficult language if not a barbaric tongue? Now we understand the genuine meaning, namely, the prophet was not sent to a people whose language was unknown, because he would be a barbarian to them and not understand them. So *"I do not send you to them but to the house of Israel."*

Now he adds: *"not to many peoples."* Those who translate this "great" do not follow the prophet's meaning, for God spoke of all the people in the singular, and now he uses the plural, as if to say: "I do not send you to the Egyptians or the Chaldaeans, or to other nations far away — as indeed the land is bound on all sides by people whose tongue is unknown to you. I do not send you to them."

Next: *"if not."* Jerome translates it, "If I had sent you to them," as if there were no negative particle לֹא [*lō'*]. It is literally, however, "if not." But because this is a difficult expression, some surmise that this is the phrase אִם־לֹא ['*im-lō'*] used in oaths, which they explain affirmatively as בֶּאֱמֶת [*be'emet*], "truly" or "certainly." But this would be a defective use of the language if we take it this way, for later on they take אִם ['*im*] to mean "again." These two words אִם־לֹא ['*im-lō'*] mean the same as if an oath were inserted. What meaning, then, can be properly drawn from these words? "I will certainly send you to them; they will listen to you." But that meaning we see is very forced.

Some explain it thus: "If I had not sent you to them, they would have listened to you" — as if God would censor the people's nature to desire empty and false prophecies rather than submit to the truth. It is as if he had said, "If some humbug would pour out darkness on them, they would immediately embrace his fables and lies, because they are so inclined to vanity. Because I send you, however, they do not listen." But this exposition does not fit either, because we will see it a little later in its own place.

So this is how I favor construing it: *"if not, I would have sent you to them, and they would have listened to you.* " As if he said, "If a difference in speech did not stand in the way, I would rather have used you among foreign nations." In this way, however, God expresses his scorn, when he says that he would rather have sent the prophet here or there than to the Israelites, except for the lack of a common language.

Since their languages were different, this obstacle kept the prophet within his own boundaries, so that he was sent to his own people. There is nothing forced in this interpretation. *"I do not send you to many peoples obscure in speech and difficult in language, because you would not understand their speech. If this were not an obstacle, I would have sent you; they would listen to you."* We see what I mentioned a little earlier, that the Israelites are compared to foreign and uncircumcised nations, not because of ignorance of language but because in the hardness of their hearts they repudiated the teaching offered to them.

Isaiah says[5] that God's Word will be difficult and obscure even to the Jews, but in another sense, as if he compares his prophecies to a sealed book because God blinded them as they deserved. Since they were reduced to a reprobate mind and deprived of sound reason, he says that his teaching would be like a closed or sealed book and he like a barbarian using an unknown tongue.[6]

But in this passage God clearly shows that the only impediment to the house of Israel advancing in his Word is that they did not want to listen. He says that the gentiles would be compliant if they could participate in such benefits. Therefore, if the prophet's language had not been unknown to the profane and uncircumcised gentiles, he would have found attentive and obedient disciples among them, just as God testifies.

Why is it that the house of Israel would not listen? There follows, *"But the house of Israel does not want to listen"*; that is, "the house of Israel does not want to listen to you because it does not want to listen to me," he says. But we see clearly that the cause of this negligence is ascribed to the people, because they deliberately repudiated the Word of God and hardened themselves to the point of stubbornness. But he ascends higher: they were unyielding not only to the prophet but to God himself, just as when Christ urged his disciples to persevere in teaching, saying, "Therefore, they will not listen to you because they do not listen to me; and why do they hate me and my teaching, except that they do not receive my Father?"[7]

This offense usually breaks the spirits of the pious when they see their teaching rejected with such arrogance. This reproach usually diverts the servants of God from their course. But this warning is set before them openly: "God himself is condemned." Why then do they take it so hard to stand in

5. Mg., Is. 28:11, 13.
6. Mg., Is. 8:16; 29:11.
7. Mg., Jn. 15, i.e., 15:18-23.

the same position in which God himself is cast? It seems to them unworthy that their labor is rejected with such contempt and disgust. But does not God deserve to be heard more than all the angels? Since unbelievers in their pride and haughtiness are opposed to God himself, is it any wonder that they do not accept with reverence what is proposed by a mortal?

Now we see the point of God's plan when he says, *"the house of Israel will not listen to you, because they do not hear me."* The prophet should not be upset when he sees his work come to nothing or even when the children of Israel rise up against him. If he experiences from them the same reproach with which they dare to battle against God himself, he ought to bear it patiently.

Next: *"because the entire house of Israel are hard of brow* (or, stubborn of brow), *and stern of heart."* He repeats what we saw before but with different words, namely, that the people's hardness of heart was invincible. They were not only stubborn of heart but also violent in appearance, so that they put off all sense of shame. Finally, he indicates a desperate obstinacy when he joins a "thick head" to a "hard heart." Next:

8 *"Behold, I have set your faces* [that is, 'your face'] *hard against their face, and your brow hard against their brows.*
9 *I have set your brow like iron, harder than stone* [or, 'rock']. *Do not fear them, and do not be broken by their face* [or, 'by their presence'], *because they are a house of rebellion* [מרי המה *(mᵉrî hēmmâ),* about which we spoke before]."

Ezekiel was forewarned about the people's stubbornness — yes, their desperate wickedness. Now God confirms him so that he does not lose heart when he sees the struggle he will have with such lost and deplorable people. What else was this but to battle against stone? If Ezekiel had been ordered to strike a mountain, it would have been no worse than being ordered to speak among such a people. He needed this confirmation: *his brow would be ironlike against the people's hardness.*

If he had hoped for more success from his labors, perhaps that confidence would have made him lazy. Confidence makes us more remiss when the work at hand is neither demanding nor difficult. Therefore the prophet might have been more unresponsive if he were definitely persuaded that the people would be docile and he approached them confidently. God aroused him when he spoke of their obstinacy.

But just as it was useful for the prophet to realize that the duty to which he had been called in obedience was very arduous, so too it was necessary to be armed with the power of God. Otherwise it would have been easy to succumb to the difficulties. This is the reason why God now adds that *he had given him a hard brow and a hard face against the people's face and brow.*

81

Furthermore, in this way he was admonished to hope for strength from another source, so that he would not consider his own power; but it would be obvious that he was governed by the Spirit of God. When we consider the nature and extent of our faculties, it is easy for us to melt and flow away, or at least become limp, so that we do not carry out our office with as much determination. Therefore God recalls his prophet in another way when *he says that he has given him a face* — as if he said that he was not a soldier in his own strength but was armed with heavenly power.

Although this was said at that time for Ezekiel's personal benefit, it pertains to us all. Let us realize that when God calls us to the office of teaching, we should never measure the outcome of our efforts by the yardstick of our own capacity or consider what we can do; we are to rest in that power outside ourselves, which God extols here with fullest praise. Whoever acknowledges that God is capable of overcoming all obstacles will bravely prepare for the task, but those who delay in order to estimate their powers will not only become weak but completely fall apart.

We see also that we are instructed in modesty and humility so that we claim nothing for our own strength. Thus it happens that when many are filled — even bursting — with confidence, they merely blow like the wind. Let us learn to seek the bravery we lack from God alone. We are no more distinguished than Ezekiel. If he had to be strengthened by the Spirit of God, how much more necessary is it for us today!

Finally, we gather from this that although the whole world would rise up against God's servants, his power will be superior, just as we saw in Jeremiah: "They will fight against you, but they will not prevail. Hence there is no reason why the violent assaults of all our enemies should terrify us. Although the world is shaken, there is no reason why we should tremble, for the strength of God in us will always be more powerful."[8] Therefore there is added: *"I have made you,"* he says, *"like iron, harder than stone. Therefore do not be afraid."*

God says, *"I have made the prophet's brow like iron,"* not because the prophet struggled with the people's wickedness or audacity, but because God set the confidence with which he provided Ezekiel against the people's raging impudence. This is the sense in which the *"prophet's brow"* is said to be *"like iron."*

Now he adds, *"do not fear them, and do not be broken by their face,"* or "presence." These seem to be at odds with each other, that the *"prophet should not be broken and not be afraid,"* and that since he nevertheless excels in invincible courage. God so tempers his grace that the faithful always need incentives, even though he encourages them and supplies them with abundant strength.

God works in his servants so that they accomplish nothing except as they

8. Mg., Je. 1:19; 15:20.

are ruled by his Spirit; but at the same time they need his teaching, so that exhortations are never useless. Profane persons think that there would be no need for teaching and that all exhortations would be frivolous, if, when God leads us by his Spirit, he not only begins but also continues and completes his work. But Scripture shows that these two fit together perfectly: God confirms us by his Spirit and renders us invincible, but in the meantime he fills us with power through his exhortations and causes them to flourish among us and to be effective.

In this way God strengthened his prophet on the one hand by giving him a head like iron and harder than stone, giving him an invincible spirit; on the other hand he urged him not to fear. So we see that God governs his own from within, and yet adds his teaching as the instrument of his Spirit.

Finally, he adds, *"because* (or, 'although') *they are a house of rebellion."* The particle **כִּי** [*kî*] is often used in an adversative sense, as we have said elsewhere. If we agree to take it in its proper sense, however, it works out well, *"because they are a house of rebellion,"* as if to say: "There is no reason for the prophet to be afraid, because he has been forewarned in time, and nothing new will happen." We tend to be frightened by novelty more than anything else. But when we have considered what happens, we are not disturbed, and we certainly do not stop or hesitate. Because the prophet had already learned that *"the house of Israel was rebellious,"* he persevered, for he experienced nothing new or unusual. Next:

10 *And he said to me, "Son of man, receive in your heart and hear with your ears all my words that I speak to you.*
11 *And go ['proceed'] to the exile [that is, 'to the captives'], to the sons of your people, and speak to them and say: 'Thus says Sovereign Yahweh,' whether they will listen or will stop."*

He repeats the same teaching. We said that our prophet is more verbose than Isaiah or even Jeremiah himself, because he was accustomed to the form of speaking found among the exiles at that time. He is neither concise nor polished. But we must affirm that he accommodated his speech to his disciples, because he was dealing with a people who were not only crude and dense but also obstinate. Their language had degenerated as well as the purity of their faith.

The prophet deliberately set aside elegant language. Whatever the case, nothing was pointless among people so slow and stupid. Hence he says what we saw before: *"he was ordered to speak all the words."* But earlier he says that *"he was ordered to take them to heart and understand them with his ears."* The order is inverted, because "understand with your ears" comes before "take them to heart." They philosophize more cleverly than truthfully who say that hearing inwardly takes precedence, because ears are struck with sound in vain if the heart is not already teachable. Although God prepares his elect to hear and "gives them ears to hear," the teaching does not penetrate their souls before it has been taken in by the ears. There is no doubt that this is an example of ὕστερον πρότερον [*hysteron proteron*], as they call it.[9]

The point is that the prophet hears God speaking and is thereby certain of his calling. This was not said for that reason, however, but so that he could confidently boast that he was God's disciple and would present nothing but what he heard from the mouth of God himself. He was ordered *"to listen to God's words"* so that he might confidently battle against the people's wickedness.

What we saw before about the heart is also repeated, namely, that the prophet might freely boast that he did not offer merely windy eloquence, like profane people who have no other purpose than to capture people's applause. The prophet therefore says that he was *"ordered to take God's words to heart."*

Now he adds that *"he should go and proceed to the captivity, to the sons of his people."* We see that God does not consider the prophet as much as the Israelites, because they never yielded willingly to the prophet when he brought such an unpleasant commission. Nothing could be more sad or hateful to them than to hear threats and curses. Hence because they had never willingly turned to obedience, he is sent with this testimony: first, to offer whatever he learned in the school of God; then, he learned from God to add nothing of his own; and finally, to speak without being broken by the people's stubbornness. *"Whether they will listen or will stop, nonetheless you must proceed."* Why? *"You will say, 'Thus says God.'"*

We have explained that this phrase means that we ought to be persuaded that our efforts are pleasing to God even if they are without results among the people. It ought to suffice that we have been sent by God. Then he wants to test our constancy, so that when we see that we labor in vain we do not quit, but instead are prepared to obey, whatever may happen.

Almighty God, since you wish to set before us today the teaching of your prophet so many centuries after his death, grant that we be neither rebellious nor hardened. May we submit ourselves to you with proper reverence and obedience, so that the labor which issued in condemnation for the people of old because of their stubbornness may be saving for us today. May we follow what you teach us through them so that we may make for the goal to which you call us and persevere until the course is completed, so that at last we may be gathered in your heavenly kingdom, through Jesus Christ our Lord. Amen.

9. "The last first," the rhetorical device of putting the last item in a series first for emphasis.

Lecture 9

12 *And the Spirit lifted me up, and I heard behind me the voice of a great noise, "Blessed the glory of Yahweh from his place."*

The prophet confirms again, as we saw before, that God had worked in his soul by the secret inspiration of his Spirit. Although God had exhorted him to be brave, the Lord himself provided what he required of him. In sum, the prophet was strong in God because God exercised his own power in him. He says that *he was lifted up by the Spirit,* which means simply that there was no movement in him except by heavenly inspiration. It was necessary for him to be lifted up outside himself for a time so that nothing human appeared in him. More will be said about this a little later.

He adds that *he heard the voice of a great noise,* that is, a very loud sound that differed from normal human speech. By the crash or tumult of the sound the prophet was able to distinguish it from a human voice. *"Blessed,"* he says, *"the glory of Yahweh from his place."* There is no doubt that this utterance ought to be adapted to the present case that is at issue. When that voice sounded forth, God wished to nullify the clamorous voices of the people, since they believed that they had been wronged. We know that the people complained and continually murmured since they felt that they were treated more harshly than was fair. Thus the glory of God is set against all the Israelites' wicked and sacrilegious blasphemies that they constantly spewed forth against God, as if he had treated them cruelly.

In sum, that voice restrained all the false charges with which the wicked had tried to bury completely the glory of God. He says *"that glory is blessed,"* because even if the people do not dare to spew forth crass and open abuse against God, they nonetheless curse his glory whenever they detract from his

85

justice and reproach him for being too rigorous. Therefore *a voice is heard* in opposition, *"Blessed is the glory of God."*

I understand the phrase *the place of God* to mean the temple. I admit that in many passages of Scripture heaven is described in this way, not that the limitless essence of God can be enclosed in a space. As heaven is called his throne, or seat, so earth is called his footstool[1] because he fills all things with his immensity. But here and elsewhere, the temple is often called the dwelling place of God, because in a sense God dwelt there with respect to people.

Furthermore, this is said with respect to the exiles as well as the rest of the people who remained at Jerusalem. The exiles did not take sufficiently to heart that they had been expelled from their homeland and dragged off to a faraway place by God's righteous vengeance. Since the captivity was not enough to subdue them, it was necessary for God's name to be set before them so that they would know that they had not been deprived of their homeland by the power and fury of their enemies, but they had been expelled by the judgment of God.

The prophet was concerned, no doubt, with the Jews who remained at home. They boasted that God was seated in the temple and imagined that they would always be safe under his protection. As we will see a little later, however, the prophet proclaimed that a penalty similar to what happened to the others was awaiting them. It is as if he said that God abides in his temple so that his glory might shine there for all to see.

Just as he wanted to humble the Judeans as well as the ten tribes, so he wanted to lessen the sorrow of all with some consolation so that they would not cease to hope for the promised restitution. The calamity itself could hurl them into despair so that they might think that their salvation was imperiled, or even that God was somehow dead and his power gone. What was the purpose of worshiping God? What was the reason for the splendor and dignity of the temple except that God would protect his own? But they had been abandoned by him.

This would be reason to despair, if it were not counteracted. Now this is what the prophet does, since on the one hand he warns that God was a just avenger of wickedness when he allowed the ten tribes to be dragged into exile. On the other hand he will still be their liberator because he does not stop ruling in his temple, even though profane people imagine that God has been overcome and that they triumphed over him with unlimited insolence.

Now we understand the prophet's meaning, for this sentence would have no impact if it were taken in a general sense. But when it is applied to the present issue, we see that God's glory is not extolled in such a statement in vain, nor is the temple mentioned without reason. Next:

1. Mg., Pss. 11:4; 103:19; Is. 66:1.

13 *And the voice* [Jerome[2] correctly suggests that "I heard" is repeated ἀπὸ τοῦ κοινοῦ *(apo tou koinou);*[a] therefore "I heard the voice"] *of the wings of the creatures, embracing each its neighbor; and the voice of the wheels near them, the voice* [I say] *of a great noise.*

Now the prophet seems to express the source of the voice to which he referred. I do not think that the voice came from some other place, and the creatures then harmonized with the wheels. But it seems to me that he is explaining what otherwise would have been ambiguous, that God's glory was celebrated by the creatures and the wheels.

It is not surprising that a voice is attributed to the creatures, because we saw that they were cherubim or angels. By the wheels God wanted to designate all actions and motions — motions, I say, that seem to be fortuitous but that are ruled by the creatures whom God inspires with his power when he wants to carry out his plan. Thus he exercises his rule in all creatures. Everything that happens is governed by his will.

Therefore the sound came from both the creatures and the wheels to extol God's glory and to show that he still ruled in his temple during that sad and miserable destruction of the people. In fact, he ruled supremely at that time, because he was the judge in punishing their wickedness, and because he would be the redeemer of his people in that he promised redemption after seventy years.

He says that *he heard the voice of the wings when they embraced one another.* For פֿשׁנ [*nāšaq*] means to embrace. Others translate it, "When they beat their wings" or "contended with one another." But he indicates this touching in the metaphor of embracing. Hence when *each wing embraced its neighbors,* the voice emerged. He adds the same thing about the wheels. Finally, he repeats what he said, *there was the voice of a great noise.* Next:

14 *And the Spirit lifted me up, and took me away; and I went bitter in the indignation of my spirit, and the hand of Yahweh was strong on me.*

He confirms, as we saw a little earlier, that he was led by the Spirit of God so that in a sense he was outside himself. But not as profane people conceive of ἐνθουσιασμους [*enthousiasmous*].[b] Their diviners were carried away, and the devil so twisted them that they lost their minds. The prophet did not mean that he was carried away, because the prophets of God always had

2. *Commentary on Ezekiel* 3:13.
a. Literally, "from the common," used of two clauses (see v. 12) sharing a word in common.
b. "Fanatics."

87

a calm and composed mind; he means that he was governed by God's Spirit so that he was not himself, and that he breathed nothing earthly. Finally, he means that visible marks had been inscribed on him to secure authority for his teaching among the entire people.

It was more than necessary that the prophet be adorned with these signs, because of the people's foolishness. Furthermore, his commission was detestable, and he had never fulfilled the teaching office before this time. Therefore it was necessary for him to be renewed so that the people would acknowledge that he was somehow divine. He had been personally involved with his own people, and his appearance and manners were well known.

As I said, however, God separated him from everyday life so that he might represent something heavenly. The purpose of this was to create faith in and reverence for his teaching, as we said. He himself was certainly aware of the movement of the Spirit, but there is little doubt that the people also understood. Otherwise there would have been little confidence among them when he spoke of himself. This direction by the Spirit was therefore made obvious so that the Israelites would understand — if only they had eyes and attended to the miracle — that the prophet somehow had been renewed.

But what follows seems to conflict with an earlier sentence.[3] He said that the scroll was sweet like honey, but now he relates that he *went away bitter in his spirit*. But as I explained briefly yesterday, these can be easily reconciled. The prophet was not completely devoid of understanding. Although he was totally consecrated to God and was completely diligent and prompt in everything, he still retained some humanity. From this comes the bitterness of spirit about which he speaks, and therefore he mentions *his spirit*.

There seems to be a tacit antithesis between that motion which seized him and that affection, by no means depraved, which is somewhat distinct from the grace of the Spirit. The prophet burned with such zeal that when he undertook the commands of God, he almost forgot himself. Nevertheless, he sensed within himself something human, so that the power of the Spirit did not extinguish all sorrow. Thus we understand that the prophet was somehow carried away by the Spirit, and yet *his own spirit was bitter*.

He adds, *and the hand of Yahweh was strong on me.* Some understand "hand" to be prophecy, but ignorantly in my judgment. I have no doubt that it means the same as "power" or "rule." He says *the hand of God was strong,* because it was necessary that he obey God, even though the bitterness of which he spoke might draw him in a different direction. As Paul says that he was constrained by zeal for God,[4] the prophet means that he was constrained by the secret inspiration of the Spirit so that he did nothing in a human manner

3. Mg., v. 3.
4. Mg., 2 Cor. 5:14; Phil. 1:23.

and did not govern himself according to the wishes of his mind. Moreover, he did not follow his own counsel but was completely intent on promptly obeying God.

This is the sense in which he says *the hand of God was strong on me.* Otherwise one could object: "Why did he not give up when he was so oppressed with grief and anxiety weighed on his spirit?" He responds, *the hand of God was strong,* and that is how he prevailed. It would have been easy to give up a hundred times, if he had not been supported by the power of God.

We see a conflict in the prophet, because as a human being he was consumed with sadness; but he was so ruled by the power of the Holy Spirit that he denied himself and all human affections. Next:

15 *And I came to the exile* [that is, "to the captives"] *in Tel-abib. They were sitting* [or literally, "the exile of those sitting"] *near the river Chebar. There they sat, and I also sat there bewildered* [or, "desolate"] *in their midst for seven days.*

Now he says that he had returned to his own people, not because he had moved to another place but because through a vision he had been drawn away from the companionship of other people. God revealed himself to him on the bank of the river Chebar, but he was alone. Since this happened in a vision, there is no doubt that he was always among his own.

In what sense does he say that *he had returned?* Because that vision vanished, and he was situated once again with the other captives. Some in their subtlety take this to mean he was a monk, but that is frivolous. They say he was horrified by the people's wickedness, and he sought solitude so that he would not contract any blemish. But this is unlikely. I have no doubt that the prophet means that after he heard God speak and the vision was offered him, he returned to his earlier way of life.

He says that *he sat for seven days,* somehow absorbed in wonder or sadness. שׁמם [šāmam] signifies both solitude and astonishment, as well as wonder. But because the prophet says that *he sat in quiet and silence for seven days,* there is no doubt that God prepared him in this way so that later when he began to speak he would attract greater wonderment from all the people.

It should not seem absurd that he was silent even though he had been sent by God. This was not done out of laziness or some hesitation that could be ascribed to a failing. But although the teaching office had been conferred on him, he still had not been given definite commands. It was as if one might be chosen as an emissary by a king or senate but only later on is given direction concerning one's orders.

In the same way, the prophet was called to the prophetic office, but he still did not know what he would be saying. Yes, he ate the scroll, but God

89

had not yet told him where he wanted him to begin and then how he ought to direct his teaching. Ezekiel had not yet been led to that point; for that reason *he says that he sat* either in great amazement, or in great despair, as they say.

This spectacle itself could arouse people's minds to find out what this unusual sadness meant. Whatever the case, we see that this silence was to prepare him to carry out his office more effectively and with better results. His word ought to have met with greater reverence afterward, *since he remained silent for seven days.*

He says that *he came to the exiles who sat in Tel-abib.* I gladly subscribe to the judgment of those who think that this is the proper name of a place; and the ancient interpreters have also left these two words. The Septuagint translates it μετεώρον [*meteōron*], as if it were "raised up." תלל [*tālal*] means "to raise up." But it ought to be תלול [*tālûl*] if the prophet is saying that he was raised up. But that does not fit here. Rather, he recounts that he was like one of the common people after the vision had been withdrawn. Others translate it "eminent," but I do not know where they get that. As I said, the judgment of those who teach that this was the proper name of a place is most probable.

Jerome[5] translates it "heap of fruit," which is not bad. There is little doubt that the name was given to the place from its situation, just as cities, regions, and mountains are often called after their setting and other qualities. In this same way that place was called Tel-abib, for תל [*tēl*] means "heap," and אביב [*ābîb*] means "ear" or "stalk of grain." Thus it could be that the place was called Tel-abib because of its fertility, since many crops were gathered there. But this is not of great importance. The principal point to be maintained is what we said, namely, the prophet was seen with that sad and despondent expression: *he was silent for seven days.* Now follows:

16 *And it happened at the end of seven days* [that is, "after seven days"], *done* ["it happened" or "was done"; the same word is variously repeated] *that the word of Yahweh to me, saying,*
17 *"Son of man, I have placed you* [or, 'I have appointed you'] *a watchman to the house of Israel. Therefore you will listen to the words from my mouth, and you will warn them from me."*

Now the prophet shows more clearly why he remained silent for seven days; although he had been made a teacher, the right time to carry out God's commands had still not come. He therefore waited until he received a definite word. Thus he says that *at the end of seven days, a word from the Lord was given to him.* We gather from this that first he was chosen, and the burden of a commission was placed on him; then for a time he remained in suspense,

5. Vulgate.

because he still did not grasp with certainty what he was to say, or where he ought to begin. It appears from this that God leads his servants by degrees, so that he claims them for himself and then he shows them generally why he requires their work and labor. Finally, he sends them out to the task itself, or to carry out their duty.

We see that this was done with our prophet. First, he learned that he was chosen by God; then he was warned in general terms to carry on bravely and not to succumb to any threats or terrors. Finally, God presented those commands that he wanted him to take to the people. It does seem that God is still speaking in general terms, but it amounts to his proclaiming that the time had come for the prophet to gird himself for the task. Thus *"Son of man, I have appointed you a watchman,"* he says, *"to the house of Israel."* What Ezekiel heard pertains to all teachers of the church: they are appointed to and placed in a watchtower by God, to keep watch over the common welfare of all. All who from the beginning have been made ministers of heavenly teaching must be watchmen.

If only in the papacy — where this name has been given to blind, deaf, and dumb idols, and where those with great bombast call themselves bishops — if only they had been admonished about their calling! We know that the word "bishop" means the same as "watchman." But although they boast that they are bishops, they have been immersed in the darkness of impenetrable ignorance and overwhelmed with their pleasures and foolishness. There is no more intelligence in those creatures than in an ox or ass. At least oxen and asses spend their energies in helping people! But these creatures are not only destitute of all judgment and reason but completely useless!

We must uphold what I said, that when God elected prophets they were placed in a watchtower to act as watchmen for the welfare of the entire church. This also must mean that pastors acknowledge that they have been stationed in a place where they keep watch. This is one point. Now this could not be so, unless they are furnished with many extraordinary gifts, or at least prevail through the Spirit over the common people. It is not enough that pastors live like private citizens; they must be far more attentive, as if they were lifted up into a high tower. This requires acuteness and skill. This is the second point.

Now he adds, *"You will listen to the words from my mouth, and you will announce them to them from me."* Here a general rule is prescribed for all prophets and pastors of the church: they must listen when God speaks. With this statement God wanted to exclude whatever people fabricate or concoct on their own. There is no doubt that God wished to claim for himself alone the right to speak; therefore he commands all people to be silent and not to offer anything of their own. Moreover, when he commands *"them to listen from his mouth,"* he bridles them so that they mix in nothing or lust after their own concoctions, or dare to conceive this or that.

91

Finally, we see that when God alone wishes to be heard, everything that people contribute of themselves is abolished. God does not mingle with others in an uproar, as if he wished to be heard only in part. Therefore he assumes for himself what we properly ought to attribute to his supreme rule, namely, that we attend only to what comes from his mouth.

If this was said to Ezekiel, how do people of no account dare to bring in their own concoctions, as we see the papacy has done? What kind of religion is that, except a confused hodgepodge of countless human concoctions? They produce an immense chaos of errors from many brains. But they want us to adore whatever foolish people have dreamed up as if they were oracles of God. But who among them will boast that he surpasses Ezekiel? Even if all come forward at the same time, will they dare to compare themselves with him alone? If they dared to do that, who would tolerate such arrogance? We see that Ezekiel was bridled along with all the prophets so that he spoke only what he heard from the mouth of God.

It follows: *"you will warn them from me."* The word that the prophet uses means "to admonish" as well as "to beware." There is little doubt that he means the admonitions that make people cautious so that they do not perish because of error and thoughtlessness. After God subjected the prophet to himself and ordered him to be a disciple, he now appoints him to be a teacher; it was not enough to listen, unless one called to rule the church hands on what he received from God. Therefore God orders his prophet to speak after he ordered him to listen.

He adds, however, *"from me,"* so that the people understand that God alone is the author of the teaching. False teachers in their pride plead the name of God, as we see it sounded forth in that papist axiom: "The church of God is ruled directly by the Holy Spirit and therefore cannot err." But these two things must be brought together: the person appointed a teacher must listen to God speaking; then he must warn in God's own name. That is, he must profess that he is a minister and witness of God, so that the teaching is not thought to be from himself. Those who praise genius, erudition, and eloquence often obscure the name of God. Although to start with they profess that what they teach they received from God, afterward they speak as if it came from themselves; that is, they ingratiate themselves with an empty display. In this way neither the majesty of God nor the efficacy of the Spirit appears in their profane manner of teaching.

So after God imposed a law on the prophet to offer only what he had heard, he adds the other phrase: *"that he must warn the people."* He should not warn them only on his own, however, but always speak God's holy name and thereby show that he had been sent by him. This is why Moses said, "What am I and my brother Aaron?"[6] We see that Moses had spoken for God; that

6. Mg., Nu. 16:11.

is, he professed to be God's minister, since he testified that he was nothing, that he assumed nothing for himself, and that he did nothing according to his own plan or initiative.

> *Almighty God, today you condescend to take care of our salvation and raise up your servants to be like eyes for us, so that we know that you keep watch lest we perish. Therefore, grant, I pray, that we be so moved by the sacred warnings that come from you through their ministry and effort, that if we have turned aside from the right way, we may quickly return and thereafter persevere in our course and struggle with such persistence that at last we attain the enjoyment of that blessed rest which has been won for us by the blood of your Son. Amen.*

Lecture 10

18 *"When I say to the wicked, 'You will surely die,' and you do not warn him and do not speak to him to warn the wicked of his wicked way, to give him life, the wicked himself will die in his iniquity, but his blood I will require from your hand."*

Now the prophet is taught that he is assuming a very difficult and even dangerous task. First, God laid down a law that he should advance nothing on his own. Now it is added that he is set as a watchman over the people such that he must render an account if he is not diligent in maintaining his watch. It is as if it had been said that souls were committed to his care and trust, so that if they perished through his negligence, he would be subject to punishment before God.

It is right to weigh up these words: *"If I say to the wicked, 'You will surely die,' and you do not warn him, he will indeed perish, but I will require his blood from you."* In the first place God confirms what we saw yesterday, that it is not granted to mortals to condemn or absolve according to their own judgment. When God sends out his servants, he does not give up his power but retains supreme rule for himself. "There is one lawmaker," as James says, "who can save and destroy."[1]

Elsewhere, Ezekiel reproaches the false prophets for bringing life to souls that were dying and killing souls not given to death.[2] We know that the proud have always tyrannized over consciences when they presume to the name of prophet. But they put themselves in the place of God, as the papacy has done.

1. Mg., Jas. 4:12.
2. Mg., Ezk. 13:18-19.

94

The pope pretends that he does nothing in his own name but at the same time arrogates to himself what is proper to God and is seated like an idol in a temple.

Nothing more properly belongs to God than to rule our souls through heavenly teaching; but the papists pile up their own inventions and consequently torture consciences in misery and plunge them into final destruction. They bring in laws to suit their own desires and always add the condition that these laws must be observed under penalty of eternal damnation, or mortal sin, as they put it.

Therefore we must carefully note this passage where God claims for himself alone the power or right of condemnation: *"if when I say,"* he states, *"to the wicked."* We conclude from this that all are sacrilegious who bind consciences with their laws, decrees, and maxims, or command this and forbid that. They seize from God what he wishes to be ascribed to himself. In short, pronouncing judgment belongs to God alone; the prophets are merely heralds.

At the same time, we must repudiate those fanatics who, on the pretext of this passage, want to be given a license to sin and make no distinction between good and evil because it is not ours to condemn. Properly speaking, we do not claim anything for ourselves when we tell what has proceeded from the mouth of God. God condemns adulterers, thieves, drunkards, murderers, slanderers, and the envious and greedy. If someone reproves an adulterer, if another upbraids a thief, and if a third inveighs against a drunkard, will we say that they have rashly claimed for themselves more than they should? Hardly! They do not make these pronouncements on their own, as we said; God has spoken, and they are witnesses or heralds of his judgment.

We must therefore maintain moderation to avoid condemning anything out of peevishness, as many immediately curse whatever displeases them and cannot be brought to inquire more diligently. Let inquiry come first; but when God has spoken, let us follow the rule given to the prophet: *"if you do not warn him,"* he says, *"and speak to warn him."*

This is said with respect to the role imposed on Ezekiel. The same does not apply to private persons not bearing the title "prophet." Let us note that this is not a general statement referring indiscriminately to all and sundry. It applies to the prophet called to be a watchman. If those who undertake such a burden do not warn people, no excuse remains for them except to render an account to God about those who are lost. The repetition demonstrates that this is not to be done in a perfunctory manner, but prophets are to be urgent and persistent in recalling sinners.

This sentence was clear enough: *"if you do not warn the wicked after I have spoken";* but the phrase is added: *"and if you do not speak to warn him."* It seems this sentence is repeated for no purpose. But God means that if the prophet does not continually warn those who sin, he is not absolved, since he spoke once in passing and was done after only one word. Let us note that rebukes are to be pressed repeatedly so that sinners return to the way.

This is the import of Paul's teaching to Timothy, "Be urgent, in season and out of season."[3] If it were sufficient to warn those who err in a soothing way and afterward to spare them, Paul would have been content with such kindness. But he said "be urgent out of season," so that a minister of the church should not stop repeating those same warnings. He says the same thing elsewhere, to the Philippians: "It does not pain me to repeat often these same things to you."[4] We know what he professed in Acts 20, "I did not cease," he says, "to warn each of you, night and day, in public and in private."[5] That persistence which Paul shows he had used is prescribed here for all the prophets and servants of God.

He says, *"to warn him of his wicked way,"* that is, "let him beware." As we said yesterday, זהר [*zāhar*] means to beware. But here it is taken in the active voice, *"unless you speak to teach him to beware of,"* or to return from, *"his wicked way."* One could ask why God touches on only one part of the teaching and buries the chief part. Why was the law given and why were prophets called out, except to gather the people to God? But this is the obedience of faith. We know that God cares about nothing more than binding miserable souls together in the hope of eternal life.

This is the chief end of the law and the gospel: that people be reconciled to God and worship him as Father. Castigations, threats, and terrors follow next, but let them now only be mentioned. But the condition of the people must be considered, as we have already seen. Wickedness and contempt of God and every kind of sin had grown so strong at the time that the prophet could not address them in a friendly and pleasant manner.

We must certainly consider that passage from Paul: "What do you want? How should I come to you? With a rod or in a gentle spirit?"[6] He gave the Corinthians a choice, whether they would have him come in a spirit of gentleness or armed with a whip to castigate them. Why? Since they were content in their vices, Paul could not treat them as children, as he usually did, and could not deal generously with them. He was forced to assume an alien role and present nothing but austerity or strictness.

The Israelites were the same. Thus it is not surprising if God overlooks his mercy, promises of grace, and whatever is sweet and pleasing to people. They were not fit to hear God's fatherly voice, unless they were first subdued. This could be done only by force, so great was their obstinacy. We must also note that the more odious the commission, the more the prophets have to be prodded. If only God's grace is offered and if only the hope of eternal life is

3. Mg., 2 Tim. 4:2.
4. Mg., Phil. 3:18, i.e., 3:1.
5. Mg., Acts 20:31.
6. Mg., 1 Cor. 4:21.

set forth, it is easy to present freely whatever is commanded, because there is nothing in teaching of that kind which would greatly offend or irritate souls.

But when people must be called — or rather dragged — before God's tribunal where they are to be terrified with the fear of eternal death, and where the minister appears "armed with the vengeance of God," as Paul says,[7] then the resulting offense sometimes drives people to fury, because only with difficulty can they withstand the onset of God's Word. Therefore even the prophets must be aroused because they would fail or at least tremble. Now we understand that God speaks only of his threats and terrors and mixes no taste of mercy, because the Israelites were not fit for sweetness. Moreover, the prophet would never have dared to carry out so eagerly the office imposed on him if this threat had not been added.

We will see in other passages that the prophet was commissioned by God to reconcile those miserable exiles to God. He will present many testimonies about the kingdom of Christ and the restoration of the church, and he will prophesy about the mercy and pardon of God; but before he brings any pronouncement of grace, it was necessary that he grapple with the people's desperate obstinacy. So it is that God says only that *"the wicked must be warned to turn from their wickedness."*

It might seem absurd to add *"to give him life,"* because earlier all hope of repentance had been taken away: "They are a rebellious and bitter house; you will accomplish nothing among them."[8] But now it seems that results from his labors are promised, since the issue here is the life of those who will repent when warned. In the first place, we must realize that there are always some who can be healed, even if the people as a whole seem hopeless. When God said earlier that the Israelites were all rebellious and incorrigible, he was considering the entire body. But as he usually preserves for himself a few seeds, there were a few left among that people who could still be converted by the prophet's efforts. This is one point.

It is also appropriate to note that even if our labor yields no results, we ought to be as satisfied as if a better outcome had occurred according to our own desires. For example, if we deal with the wicked multitude, wherever we turn our eyes contempt of God and such depravity appear that our effort seems wasted. But while we find cause for despair in people's wickedness, we ought nonetheless to pursue our course as if the seed already bore some fruit. Although Ezekiel had heard from the mouth of God that the people were rebellious, he should have devoted his work to God as zealously as if he could discern or hope for some success. Let us also remember what I mentioned: God always has a few seeds left, even though the people as a whole have fallen into wickedness.

7. Mg., 2 Cor. 10:5-7; cf. Rom. 13:4.
8. Mg., 2:5, 6, 8.

97

Now he adds, *"the wicked will die in his wickedness; but his blood I will require from your hand."* Here God says that he called his servant with the stipulation that he render an account if someone perishes through his fault. As I mentioned earlier, this passage shows that those called to the teaching office take up a very dangerous task. Nothing is more precious to God than the souls that he created in his image, and of whom he is Redeemer and Father.

Therefore, since our souls and their salvation are so dear to God, we gather how urgently all prophets and pastors ought to be engaged in their office. It is just as if God committed souls to their trust, stipulating that they render an account for each one. It is not enough that they warn this one or that, but unless they have tried to recall everyone from destruction to life and salvation, we hear what God will pronounce. That passage from Paul also applies here: "Woe to me if I do not preach, for necessity is laid on me."[9]

In sum, to arouse the prophet to carry out his office, God announces that a penalty would hang over his head if he does not try diligently to recall all the wayward to the path of salvation. But because people think that ignorance will be an adequate defense, this quibble is removed, for God adds that they will perish even though they have not been warned. This exception was added deliberately, so that people will not flatter themselves by casting the blame on their pastors when they perish in error.

Even though someone has not been warned, he will die; and although the pastor will render an account of his negligence and continue to spare himself, he will have no excuse before God. Thus we see that negligence in prophets and pastors borders on faithlessness, when they knowingly and willingly allow souls to perish through their silence. It is not surprising if God sentences to death those who have not been warned. It is enough that their consciences convict them; however much today they plead error and ignorance, it is certain that they perish willingly. There follows next:

19 *"And if* ['But if'] *you warn the wicked and he does not turn from his wickedness, from his wicked way, he will die in his iniquity; but you have acquitted your soul."*

Here the prophet is taught how beneficially he will establish his work, even if it appears that he has accomplished nothing. This alone ought to be sufficient, that he demonstrated his zeal to God. Even if one being led back to the way by holy exhortations remains obstinate, the servants of God ought not disdainfully to abandon this responsibility as useless. They acquit their own souls.

Earlier it was said that necessity was laid on them, because if they were

9. Mg., 1 Cor. 9:16.

dumb dogs, the destruction of souls would be imputed to them. But when they have fulfilled and adequately carried out their duty before God, should it not be sufficient for them to be absolved in his judgment? Hence we see that the prophet is encouraged by this consolation, lest it vex him to warn lost and stubborn people. If the teaching is not useful to them in any way, he will still benefit.

Christ's words are well known: "Whatever house you enter, bless it. If the house is unworthy, the blessing will return to you."[10] So it is when the prophets zealously strive to recall the wandering sheep and gather them into the sheepfold. If they experience such brazenness that their work is useless, its benefit will nevertheless return to them. Now we understand God's purpose in these words, *"you have acquitted your soul."*

He puts not only *"wickedness,"* however, but *"wicked way,"* for the sake of explanation. One may wish to make a distinction, so that "wickedness" would be inner malice of heart, but "wicked way" would be the outward life, including all actions. This is perhaps more likely, but it is acceptable to take "wicked way," after he has spoken of wickedness, as epexegetical. Now follows:

20 *"And if a righteous person turns away from his righteousness and commits iniquity, and I place a stumbling block before his face* [or, 'then I will place a stumbling block before his face'], *he will die because you did not warn him; he will die in his offenses. And his righteous deeds because* ['which'] *he did will not be remembered, but his blood I will require of your hand."*

Here God adds another part of the task that he imposes on all prophets. They are sent first to bring back to the way those who are alienated from God but also to retain those who are already in the flock, to lead to the finishing post those who have already entered the race. We see that the prophets ought to be intent on both concerns: not only to recall to obedience to God those whose desires have led them astray but to confirm those willing to be taught and exhort them to persevere and not allow them to perish.

After God has spoken of correcting sinners who have strayed, he now adds another part: *"if a righteous person,"* he says, *"turns away from his righteousness, and you do not warn him, he will die; and I will require his blood of your hand."* In sum, God indicates that the prophets would be guilty not only if they failed to exhort to repentance those who have led themselves away from the right path but also if they failed to retain in their duty those who have already entered the right course. We must do both: recall those who have fallen into various errors and keep those in the flock from wandering off and strengthen them in perseverance.

10. Mg., Mt. 10:12-13; Lk. 10:5-6.

Thus it is now added: *"if a righteous person turns aside, he indeed will die, but his blood I will require. . . ."* It is asked, however, how the righteous could "turn aside," since there is no righteousness without the Spirit of regeneration, and the Spirit is an incorruptible seed;[11] its grace could never be completely extinguished. The Spirit is the pledge and seal of our adoption, and God's adoption is irrevocable, as Paul says:[12]

Thus what is said here, *"the righteous person departs and turns aside from his righteous path,"* seems absurd. That saying of John is also noteworthy: "If they had been of us, they would have remained with us; but since they have been estranged, that defection itself is sufficient testimony that they were never of us."[13] But we must note that here the word "righteousness" is used of what has only the outward form but no root. Once the Spirit of regeneration begins to flourish, as I said, he abides forever.

We will occasionally see people carried away with a wonderful ardor and zeal to worship God and motivated to advance God's glory more than even the best. We will see this happen, but "the Lord knows who are his own," Paul says.[14] For this reason it is not surprising if in this passage God commends under the name of righteousness those virtues that merit praise from others, even if they do not come from a pure source. Thus we often see it happen that the righteous are estranged and *"they depart from their righteous path."*

This passage ought to arouse us urgently to seek from God the Spirit of perseverance. Because we are so prone to sin, we immediately flow away like water unless the Lord establishes us. Therefore when we see the righteous themselves depart from the way, let us be afraid; in addition let us be certain of the constancy of our faith, provided that our confidence is founded on the aid of the Holy Spirit and not on ourselves. Meanwhile, we see that Christ's pronouncement is not in vain: "Blessed are those who persevere to the end,"[15] because many fall in the middle of their course or going backward turn away from God.

Now we must note carefully what follows: *"his righteous deeds will not be remembered."* Many wish to bargain with God, that if for a time they display some desire for piety, that might be taken into account and serve to acquit them. But we hear what God pronounces: *"if someone falls away, none of his righteous deeds will be remembered."* We have no reason to flatter ourselves into security and sloth when God shows that unless we persevere to the end, to our race's goal, whatever we accomplish will be useless.

11. Mg., 1 Pet. 1:23.
12. Mg., Rom. 11:29.
13. Mg., 1 Jn. 2:19.
14. Mg., 2 Tim. 2:19.
15. Mg., Mt. 24:13.

As for the text, he says, *"if he falls away from his righteousness,"* or "goes back," or literally, "turns away, *and does wickedness."* We must note this carefully, because we know that even the best often slip; but here is denoted that falling away when someone casts himself into iniquity. Therefore "to do wickedness" means to dedicate oneself completely to wickedness. When John says that those who have been born again of God's Spirit do not sin,[16] he means that they are not addicted to sin, even though they still carry around many weaknesses and vices. As Paul also says, "sin dwells in us, but it does not rule."[17] Therefore to sin is to prostitute oneself to sinning.

He says, *"I will place,"* or "to place," or "if I place, *a stumbling block before him."* Here a punishment — when God demonstrates his vengeance against apostates — is called a stumbling block. But the "actual warning," as they say, can also be called a stumbling block; because that would be too subtle, however, I take it simply as, *"if a righteous man turns away; but I will render the reward that he deserved,* he will die, *because you did not warn him."* Thus I separate "in his own unrighteousness he will die." Some interpreters seem to me to have joined together improperly, "He will die, in his iniquity he will die." Then he repeats the threat that we just saw, that all prophets who quit their post will be guilty before God. Their sloth is no different from faithlessness, for God dignified them with the highest honor when he committed to them the souls that he holds very dear and precious, as we said.

If they abandon such a trust, we see that they not only harm people but are also ungrateful to God. Their sloth is not only joined with faithlessness but also with sacrilege, because they allow Satan to snatch from God what is his, like a watchman who deserted his station and surrendered it to enemies. When they see some wander off and others slip away, it is certain that this does not happen out of ignorance, as we said. But those whom Christ redeems by his blood are exposed to the snares and desires of Satan. Such dereliction is completely inexcusable, as we said.

Almighty God, you appoint ministers of your teaching and make them watchmen over us on condition that they diligently care for our salvation. Grant that we listen to them so attentively that we do not perish through the double fault of error and stubbornness. But if we chance to err, grant at least that after we have been reproved, we repent and so return to the way that we never stray again but persevere to the end, that at last we may enjoy the eternal blessing that is kept for us in heaven, through Christ our Lord. Amen.

16. Mg., 1 Jn. 3:9.
17. Mg., Rom. 6:12.

101

Lecture 11

21 *"And if you warn him* [namely, the righteous] *that the righteous should not sin, and he does not sin, he will surely live, because he was warned. But you have acquitted your soul."*

We saw in the last lecture that the duty of pastors is twofold: to gather the scattered sheep and to contain those already in the fold. Human nature is so inclined to many faults that in its weakness it frequently happens that those already gathered in God's sheepfold are scattered here and there, unless they are made strong. Therefore repeated warnings are necessary, and so God asserts that pastors would be guilty if through their negligence the righteous fall. He now pursues the same thought but adds a different clause: *"if the righteous person has been warned, the pastor would be innocent."* The point is that, as one called to the teaching office, Ezekiel must be intent on recalling those who have erred back to the path and also containing the others. At the same time, we should note that even those who seem to have entered the right path can be snatched away every day, unless God retains them through his servants and urges them to press on. Now it follows:

22 *And there the hand of Yahweh was upon me, and he said to me, "Rise and go out to the plain, and I will speak with you there."*
23 *And I arose and went out to the plain; and behold, the glory of Yahweh stood* ["standing"] *there, like the glory that I had seen by the river Chebar. And I fell on my face.*

God seems to play with his prophet when he leads him around and appears to change his plan. Earlier the role of teaching was imposed on the

102

holy man; now he is ordered to go out, and afterward God commands him to shut himself in at home. This variation appears to be a change in plan; first God enjoins on him the duty of speaking but then commands his servant to remain inactive. But there is no doubt that the prophet's authority is strengthened this way, when God directs his tongue in both respects. Although appointed a teacher, he restrained himself until God assigned him something to say. Afterward he was ordered to be silent, and he obeyed God; at last when God dictated words and ordered him to speak in public, he began to carry out his duty.

If he had begun to speak immediately when first called, he could be accused of being very superficial. But when he was moved in his soul to prepare himself and then remained silent as long as it pleased God, greater weight was given to his teaching. Now we understand why the *hand of the Lord was upon him.*

Hand of God indicates "power." As I mentioned before, to say that "hand" means "prophetic office" is a colorless interpretation. He sensed that he was moved by the secret power of God. The hand of Yahweh is none other than the stirring of the Spirit so that the prophet realizes that he was not moved by anything human or some senseless impulse.

Therefore he says that *the hand of Yahweh was upon me, and he said to me, "Rise and go out to the plain so that I may speak with you there."* The only thing Ezekiel could assume was that he was being led out to present immediately God's commands to the people. But he was greatly deceived in this opinion because, as we will see, he was brought out in public so that he might immediately be shut up at home!

But before he tells about this, he says that *he went out.* We see that wherever God sent him, he was submissive. This is worth noting, because unless the call of God is acceptable to us and our mind subscribes to it, we run away or at least delay. Yet the prophet had a valid excuse, in human eyes, for vacillating, with some plausibility. God had often spoken to him but without result. Even now, although still held in suspense, God did not proclaim what he wanted him to do; *nevertheless, he goes out into the plain,* because that was what God commanded. Let us learn from this example that even if the outcome is hidden from us, we must obey the moment God commands us to do something. Even if it contradicts our understanding, we ought to obey him and follow wherever he calls, even if doing it seems not only useless but foolish.

God did not deceive him, however, because he did appear in his glory. The vision of God's glory ought to satisfy a holy man, even though everything else fails. Therefore *he saw the glory of God as he did by the river Chebar.* We can see that this vision was not linked to a specific place. Thus God appeared at one time by a riverbank, and then in the middle of a plain.

We have explained elsewhere what he means when he says that *he fell on his face*. It is inevitable that the faithful who are touched by a sincere fear of God should tremble at his sight. The wicked too are compelled to fear God, but they quickly become hardened; and although they are left almost lifeless, a stupor follows that extinguishes all understanding. But that fear which the faithful experience at the sight of God is joined with reverence. *Thus Ezekiel fell on his face,* and he could not arise until the Spirit of God lifted him up, as it says next.

24   *And the Spirit came into me, and stood me on my feet, and spoke with me, and said to me: "Go, shut yourself up in the middle of your house* [that is, 'within your house'].*"*

Here Ezekiel confirms what I said, that when the faithful are terrified by the vision of God's glory, they cannot recover unless the Lord supports them by his power. But there was a special reason in the prophet's case, because he should acknowledge that he was as dead and then sense God's Spirit living in and invigorating his soul. Therefore to have the Spirit restore him from death to life is a confirmation. Thus, he says, *the Spirit came*. In sum, just as the soul animates a human being, so God's Spirit is supernatural life in a person. We live as human beings because power is implanted in our souls, which have their own faculties. The seat of understanding is in the soul, as well as the will and the senses. It diffuses its power throughout all parts of the body. But the life that the soul breathes into the body is earthly; the Spirit of God brings supernatural life to the soul.

This distinction must be maintained because the profane glory so much in external appearance, as they say, that is, in splendor that is nothing more than a mask. Thus with great bombast they celebrate free choice and the natural faculties, because they have never tasted what the supernatural life mentioned here would be like. Ezekiel certainly was filled with God's Spirit to an unusual degree, to be capable of carrying out the prophetic office. But as far as spiritual life is concerned, this is common to the faithful.

He says, *he was placed on his feet;* because he was lying prostrate, he could not, as I said, raise a finger unless God raised him up. He refers next to God's command, which could seem absurd. Why did God make Ezekiel a prophet except to prepare himself for the teaching office? But now he orders him not only to be quiet but to hide at home. He uses the phrase *"shut yourself up,"* as if to say, "remain at home like a prisoner." If he had been a private citizen, he would have been free to go out. But now when God lays on him the prophetic office, he is held captive. This is completely contrary to his calling. But God first wanted to test his servant's obedience; then, most importantly, he wanted to affirm his calling even more strongly.

This was no ordinary confirmation, so that more authority might accrue to him. Although he excelled in extraordinary virtue, he did not leap into public view; he remained silent at home and was a willing captive, because that pleased God. Since he had often remained silent at God's command, all the people could recognize that he was not a prophet by chance and that he did not emerge by some sudden impulse. Next:

25 *"And now, son of man, behold, they will put on you chains* [or, 'ropes'; they mean twisted and tangled ropes, **עבותים** *(ᵃḇôṯîm)*]; *and they will bind you with them* [that is, 'with which to bind you']; *therefore you will not go out into their midst.*
26 *And I will make your tongue cleave* [or, 'I will affix'] *to the roof of your mouth, and you will be silent, and you will not be to them as a reproachful* [or, 'rebuking'] *person, because they are a house of rebellion* [or, 'bitterness']."*

Now God explains why he wants his prophet to stop for a time and to remain at home as if he were mute. *"They have placed,"* he says, *"on you ropes with which to bind you."* The interpretation of those who explain this metaphorically makes good sense; the people's stubbornness prevented Ezekiel from being able to carry out his duty as effectively as if they had bound him with ropes.

To make this clearer, let us remember what Paul said to the Corinthians:[1] he was constrained because he found no access to them, and his teaching did not penetrate their hearts. But he casts the blame on them. "Our mouth," he says, "is open to you Corinthians; our heart is opened wide." That is, "I am ready to work among you in good faith, as much as I can. But your hearts are closed." Since people impede the course of teaching by their depravity and reduce God's servants to anxiety, it is quite appropriate to compare their malice to ropes that bind faithful teachers so that they cannot freely persevere in the course of their calling.

If someone prefers to take what is said here strictly and literally, the discourse must still be interpreted to mean that the Israelites were at this point not ready to be taught. If the prophet immediately carried out God's commands, they would become furious and seize him and bind him with ropes. This interpretation also fits very well. One is free to choose. But as far as the main point is concerned, God's meaning is clear; the prophet should not be impatient if he lies useless for a time, since he has still not found listeners and fit disciples.

We see that this was said to console the prophet, so that he would not grumble or be annoyed that God wanted him to remain shut up at home. The

1. Mg., 2 Cor. 6:11.

time was still not right; as if he had said: "If you hurry to approach these furious people, they will immediately assault you and bind you with ropes. Because you see that they are not yet ready to learn, wait awhile until I prepare ears that will listen to you; or at least I will send you to render them more inexcusable. Although they remain obstinate, they will not be able to rise up in violence against you; whether they want to or not, they will be compelled to listen to the commands that come from my mouth." He confirms this immediately, as we will see.

But now he adds, *"I will affix your tongue to the roof of your mouth,"* or, "I will make your tongue stick to the roof of your mouth, *so that you will not be to them as a reproachful person, because they are a rebellious house."* What God ascribed to the Israelites he now attributes to himself. He said, *"They will bind you with ropes"; now he says, "I will make your tongue stick to the roof of your mouth."*

These two statements are easily reconciled, because the Israelites rejected the prophecies through their own intemperance. God deprived them of this benefit because he saw their unworthiness. This passage teaches that it is a sign of God's judgment when all prophecies cease and the benefit of teaching is snatched away. Just as God illumines us through his Word and we have a certain sign of his fatherly grace and favor, so when teaching is taken away, it is as if God has hidden his face or even turned his back against us.

We must remember what it says here: *"because the house of Israel was rebellious"* the prophet was silent, and the benefit of teaching ceased among those wicked people. God stops when he sees that he is dealing with the stupid and dumb. This does not happen after one irksome occasion; God struggles with people's ingratitude, so that, as we saw in Jeremiah,[2] he continues to rise up in the morning and keep watch even in the night. He does not stop calling those who are slow and sluggish, even those who are completely rebellious. But when he finally sees that he accomplishes nothing by being long-suffering, he removes his Word, as we said. Thus the church laments that it is destitute of prophets and classes that disaster among the clearest signs of God's anger: "We see no signs, and no prophets appear among us."[3]

They realize thereby that they are alienated from God, so that no comfort remains for them when God does not give even a taste of his goodness through the prophets. The reprobate actually desire this, because nothing annoys them more than to hear God constantly calling. Therefore they try their best to hide and think there is nothing better than to slumber in their vices so that they hear no voice of rebuke. Yet nothing is more destructive to them, because as long as God urges us to repent, he at least offers himself as a physician to heal our

2. Mg., Je. 7:11; 11:7; 35:14.
3. Mg., Ps. 74:9.

106

diseases. But when he is silent, he leaves us for lost. Hence I said that nothing is more destructive than to have no warnings sound in our ears. But we delight and flatter ourselves, since in this way Satan takes away all our understanding. His ultimate poison is to soothe us with his flattery so that all the rebukes that would shatter our overconfidence cease. Next:

27 *"And when I have spoken to you and opened your mouth* [this is how I interpret it; literally, 'I will open your mouth.' But I read it as a single construction: 'When I have spoken to you and opened your mouth'] *then you will say to them: 'Thus says Sovereign Yahweh: He who hears, let him hear; and he who desists, let him desist, for they are a house of rebellion.' "*

After his silence, God sets forth the commands that he wants to give his servant, ones that will provoke the people, as we have seen. This commission was odious since the prophet would begin with this rebuke: "If you want to listen, listen! But if not, it does not matter to me." Those sent on a mission are usually commanded to use flattering and friendly speech to procure if possible the favor of those with whom they deal.

But God follows an entirely contrary course. What do these words mean: *"He who hears, let him hear: he who desists, let him desist?"* They mean that the Israelites would understand that the prophet was not sent to them because there was any hope of repentance, since they had testified by far too many experiences that they were completely beyond hope. The Lord sent the prophet to disturb them even more, to wound them, and then to inflict a mortal wound on them.

Now we see confirmed what the prophet related before, that the office of teaching was bestowed on him not because his labor would be useful or beneficial as far as the masses were concerned, but to incite the Israelites to rage if they refuse to repent, to break them if they would not bend. If they refuse, they would render themselves guilty before God, who would be their judge. In the meantime, the course of prophetic teaching would run freely, no matter how stubbornly they resisted.

Now we understand the prophet's plan. We conclude from this what we mentioned earlier, that God deals with the reprobate in various ways. At times he makes an experiment to see whether they can be healed, and he appoints prophets to urge them to repent. But when they seem to extinguish all light with their ingratitude, he leaves them without any teaching. Afterward he illumines them again; but in the end the darkness that follows the light is thicker still. Therefore let us hurry while the teaching of salvation still shines on us, so that God might not darken our minds and all our senses and deprive us of the special benefit of having the image of his fatherly favor engraved on us, as we said.

Let us continue:

CHAPTER 4

1 *"And you, son of man, take for yourself a tile, and place it before your face, and paint a city on it, [namely,] Jerusalem.*
2 *And lay siege to it and build a siege tower opposite it, and pile a rampart against it, and put up a camp against it, and station battering rams against it all round.*
3 *And take an iron pan [or, 'frying pan'], and place it an iron wall between you and the city. And set your face toward [or, 'against,' 'opposite'] it, and let it be under siege, and you will besiege it. This a sign for the house of Israel."*

Here God begins to speak more openly through his servant, and not only to speak but also to stamp with an outward symbol what he wanted to express in words. Therefore he orders *his prophet to paint Jerusalem on a tile.* *"Take the tile,"* he says, *"and set it up before your eyes;* then *paint a city on it, namely, Jerusalem."* This is one order. Next, *"build a siege tower facing it."* He describes the way ancient warfare looked. At that time when they wanted to attack a city, they built ramps with which they filled up the trenches. Then they moved wooden towers in place so that their soldiers could fight hand to hand. Finally, they had other machines, too, which are no longer in use, for cannons have done away with that ancient technique of warfare.

Here God simply wants Ezekiel to besiege a replica of a city. Then he orders him to *"set up a frying pan,"* or *"an iron pan, like an iron wall."* This would be a childish spectacle if God had not ordered the prophet to act this way. From this we learn that the sacraments cannot be distinguished from empty spectacles, except by God's Word. The authority of God is the distinguishing mark whereby the sacraments stand out and have their own dignity and weight. All human contrivances are frivolous. That is why we say that all the pomp which fills the papal religion is just so much nonsense. Why? Because without God's command people have contrived whatever dazzles the eyes of the simple.

Yet if someone objects that the water of baptism cannot reach our souls to cleanse them of hidden, inner impurities, the solution is easy: baptism should not be considered solely from its outward appearance: we must consider its author. Thus the entire form of worship under the law was not much different from the ceremonies of the gentiles. On the one hand, since the profane gentiles also slaughtered victims, they had whatever could be desired for exceptional splendor. But it was all foolishness, for God had ordained nothing of the sort. On the other hand, nothing was useless among the Jews. When they offered their victims, when they sprinkled blood, even when they immersed themselves in water, they did so at God's command and with God's promise. Hence these ceremonies were not empty. So we must affirm that at first glance sacraments can appear trivial and of no consequence, but their power is lodged in God's command and promise.

If anyone reads what Ezekiel relates here, he will say that it is child's play. He took a baked brick and painted a city on it. It was pure charade. Then he even had imaginary machines to attack the city. Children can do better than this. Finally he set before himself an iron pan for a wall — a gesture no more serious than the rest. For that reason profane people would not only despise this symbol; they would even attack it. When God sends his prophet, however, let us be satisfied with his authority, which is a clear distinguishing mark and cannot deceive, as I said.

First, he says, *"Paint a city, namely, Jerusalem"*; then, *"lay siege to it and move all the instruments of war into place; also set up the* בדים *[bdîm],"* [a] which some translate "leaders"; they are rams or sheep. But the Hebrews use the term "rams" metaphorically to describe the iron devices with which they demolished walls, as the Latins did. Nevertheless, some prefer to translate it "leaders." But I do not approve of their opinion.

Finally, he says that *"this will be a sign"*; and I would like to pursue that detail. As I just said, the entire description could be regarded as inane if this testimony was not added. In brief, by itself this vision would be insipid; but some flavor is added by this spice: God says that *"this shall be a sign for the Israelites."* When God announces that his prophet will do nothing in vain, we ought to be satisfied and rest in his Word. If we debate according to our understanding, he will show that what seems foolish "surpasses all the wisdom of the world," as Paul says.[4] Sometimes God works through foolishness. That is, he has reasons for acting that to human eyes are absurd and barely appropriate. If we wish to be wise, we will think that he is foolish.

But so that this foolishness of God should surpass among us all the wisdom of the world, let this sentence come to mind; *"let this be a sign for the house of Israel."* Although the Israelites could shake their heads and stick out their tongues and pursue the prophet with unbridled violence, this was enough to overthrow them: God said that *"this will be a sign."*

We know the event of which it was a sign, however, because the Israelites who were dragged into exile thought they had been far too compliant and regretted their obedience. Then envy crept upon them when they saw the rest of the people remain in the city. So God confronted them and showed them that exile was more bearable than suffering a siege closed up in the city. Thus

---

a. The Hebrew is unrecognizable in the meaning Calvin discusses (and hence cannot be confidently vocalized in transliteration). It seems a printer's slip for the very similar כרים [kārîm].

4. Mg., 1 Cor. 1:25.

this prophecy was undoubtedly directed against the Jews who were glad that they were still at peace in their nest.

This is why God orders the prophet *"to build siege towers,"* then *"to establish a camp and prepare whatever is needed to attack the city."* Shortly thereafter the Chaldaeans were to arrive, not only to oppress the city but to storm it, as we will see at length later on.

> *Almighty God, since you so kindly invite us to yourself and do not cease, even if we are deaf, to extend your grace toward us, grant that we obey you willingly and allow ourselves to be ruled by your Word. And grant that we might obey you steadfastly, not only for a day or a short time, but until we have completed the course of our journey and are gathered together in your heavenly rest, through Christ our Lord. Amen.*

Lecture 12

4 *"And you, lie down on your left side and place the iniquity of the house of Israel on it. You will bear their iniquity for the number of days that you will lie on it.*
5 *And* [meaning, 'for'] *I have granted to you* [or, 'appointed for you'] *the years of their iniquity to the number of days, three hundred and ninety days* ['there shall be' must be understood], *and you will bear the iniquity of the house of Israel.*
6 *And when you complete them* [that is, the 'days'], *then you will lie down a second time on your right side, and you will bear the iniquity of the house of Judah for forty days, a day for a year, a day for a year I have appointed for you.* [I will continue with the whole context.]
7 *And you will direct* [or, 'set,' for כוּן (kûn) means both] *your face to the siege of Jerusalem, and your arm* [will be] *bare, and you will prophesy against it.*
8 *And behold, I have placed ropes on you, and you will not turn from your side until you have fulfilled the days of your sieges."*

First, we must consider the purpose of this prophecy, and then we will be able to investigate the individual parts more easily. It is obvious that God wanted to oppose the people's pride, for they thought that they were being punished more severely than their crimes warranted. This is the way of hypocrites: while they do not dare to absolve themselves completely, they grumble if God afflicts them severely. Then they eagerly advance some compensating factor in order to escape punishment. Although they confess they are guilty, they continue making excuses, and they think that if God should descend to some sort of equity, they would be exempt or less miserable. That was the character of the ancient people, as is well known.

111

Now we should recall what I have said elsewhere, that the Jews were all the more obstinate because God had spared them. They did not think that this was just temporary: they boasted with great license, as if they had settled with God. In the meantime the exiles complained constantly, first because God had dealt so severely with them, when in fact he showed mercy and pardoned them. Then they thought that they had been deceived and that, if they had looked after their affairs more prudently, they could have escaped the many miseries that oppressed them.

So now Ezekiel is ordered to appear in public and briefly show that the entire population is only reaping a just reward for its crimes. But since simple teaching would not have been effective in arousing them, a vision is added; and for this purpose the prophet is ordered *"to lie on one side for three hundred and ninety days, but on the other for forty days."* Now the interpretation is added: *"the days are taken for the same number of years."* The point is that the people had waged war with God for three hundred and ninety years because they had never stopped sinning. Therefore the prophet is ordered *"to assume the iniquity of so many years."* God appointed to him days for years. Then he added the forty years that pertained to the Judeans.

This passage is twisted in various ways by interpreters. I will not refer to all their inventions, for they have worn themselves out in vain by contriving subtleties that are self-disintegrating. So I will not waste time refuting them but only try to elicit the real meaning.

We must refute, however, the view of some who extend the name "Israel" to all the people. They begin the 390 years from the people's first defection, which is mentioned in the book of Judges,[1] and they put together those years in which the Israelites most often lapsed into wickedness. So they count up 390 years, subtracting the times in which religion and the pure worship of God flourished, as it did under Gideon, under Samson for a time, and under David and Solomon. They take away the years during which piety among the people was strong. What remains comes to about 390 years.

But it is absurd to include the tribe of Judah under the name "Israel," when a comparison is made between the two kingdoms. We know that all the descendants of Abraham were named after their father Jacob. Therefore, when the name "Israel" is used, we understand the twelve tribes — or thirteen if no exceptions are made. But when a comparison is made, "Israel" denotes only the ten tribes, or that adulterous kingdom which Jeroboam raised up after Solomon's death.[2] Therefore, since we are dealing here with Israel and Judah, it does not make sense for the prophet to speak of the whole people and mix the tribe of Judah in with the rest.

1. Mg., Jdg. 2:2.
2. Mg., 1 Ki. 12:20.

But then the subject matter itself dispels all the clouds and removes what otherwise might be controversial. If we count the years from the defection that came about under Rehoboam, we will find 390 years up to the sack of Jerusalem. What could be easier? What need is there for conjectures? I am surprised that Jerome boasts of marvelous wisdom when he had nothing but nonsense to offer. But he says that he did not do it out of pride. There was certainly no reason for him to be proud! If anyone reads his fictions, he will find nothing but childish ideas.[3]

But as I just said, since the name "Israel" everywhere indicates the ten tribes, what is said here fits perfectly, namely, that the obstinacy of the ten tribes was constant throughout 390 years. As is well known, Jeroboam erected two altars to turn the people from the worship of God.[4] He thought that he was still not well-enough established in his kingdom to keep the people obedient unless he turned them away from the house of David. Therefore he used this scheme. In this way the worship of God among the Israelites was corrupted.

By idolatry the prophet designates the people's other sins, for other iniquities flowed from this source. Once the people had deserted God, they forgot the entire law. So the prophet included all their corruptions under one heading; that is, by edict of the king the people threw off God's yoke, for which Hosea also rebuked them.[5]

Now we understand the 390 years of Israel's iniquity, because at that time the people cast aside the law and followed foreign superstitions concocted by Jeroboam with no other purpose in mind than to strengthen the power of his reign. Worldly kings are led by no other interest, even though they pretend otherwise and grandly profess to be seeking God's glory with the utmost devotion. Nevertheless, religion for them is only a game to keep people obedient and dutiful; it does not matter to them which God is worshiped or how.

Such was Jeroboam's astuteness. But his descendants lapsed even further, so that the worship of God could never be restored among the Israelites. Circumcision did continue to be practiced, and of course they imitated what Moses taught in the law. But meantime they had two altars for the one true altar — and profane ones at that. Finally, they were not afraid to adopt openly the idolatries of the gentiles. Thus they so mixed God with their own inventions that whatever they valued under the pretext of piety was an abomination. This is the reason that God says, *"The iniquity of the people of Israel lasted for three hundred and ninety years."*

3. *Commentary on Ezekiel* 4:4-6.
4. Mg., 1 Ki. 12:28.
5. Mg., Ho. 5:11.

There is a greater difficulty in the second part because the numbering does not quite fit. After the death of Josiah, there are only twenty-two years to the sack of the city. Yet we know that this king, with exceptional piety, took care that God would be worshiped in sincerity, for he cleansed the entire land of all iniquity. So where are the forty years? It is necessary to include part of the reign of Manasseh,[6] because at that time not only did Jerusalem abandon the teaching of the law but that tyrant cruelly raged against all the prophets, and the city was defiled by innocent blood. But it will be necessary to omit the reign of Josiah, and part of the reign of Manasseh will have to be discounted, because he did not lapse into wickedness immediately. He despised the worship of God and the examples of his fathers and fell into foreign and spurious cults only after he had grown up, but he did not persist in his wickedness until the end of his life.

Therefore eighteen years must be included and added to the twenty-two, to constitute the number set down by the prophet — unless perhaps someone prefers to take part of Josiah's reign. Although that pious king was zealous in protecting the worship of God,[7] we know that the people of that time struggled in their wickedness against God's goodness. Although the law had been found, no correction followed. All memory of teaching dimmed. But when the law was produced, the people ought to have been renewed. But those who earlier had been alienated from God were so far from repenting that they revealed increasing stubbornness.

Since the people's wickedness was disclosed at that time, it will not be surprising if the people of Judah are said to have sinned for forty years. This latter explanation is certainly more acceptable to me; that is, the prophet counts without a break the years that followed the captivity of the ten tribes. But I do not reject the other view that takes into account those years when Manasseh played the tyrant against the servants of God and attempted to abolish pure worship as much as he could and to pollute it with all the impurities of the nations. So now we have the forty years of the iniquity of the tribes of Judah.

I am afraid the view of interpreters that the 430 years refers to the siege of the city — as if God's revenge came to a halt then — is not well grounded. It does not make sense to me. He only means that it is not strange if the enemy besieged the city for as many days as there were years when they had constantly provoked God. The city was besieged for a full year and two or three months. To be sure, there was a year and a half between the beginning and the end of the siege, but it was interrupted for three or four months when Pharaoh led his army and tried to liberate the Jews, who were his allies and confederates at the time. Then Nebuchadnezzar went out to oppose him, and the city recovered for a short time.

6. Mg., 2 Ki. 21.
7. Mg., 2 Ki. 22.

Now if we take 390 days, we will find, first of all, a full year, that is, 365 years.ª At that time, however, there was an intercalary month; they did not have the year fixed as we do today. Anyway, there will be 365 days to make up an entire year. Then two months will make 60 days, and so we will have 420 days. Now a month and a half passed before Nebuchadnezzar returned. Then the count will reach 430 years. Interpreters are satisfied that the siege lasted as long as the time corresponding to that attributed to Abraham, for God made his covenant with Abraham 430 years before the law was promulgated.

But I do not see why they should be so satisfied with that parallel, for this is not our prophet's intention. When he speaks of the siege, he is certainly referring primarily to the storming of the city. So I do not think the days when the city was under siege are being numbered, as if they were a just punishment; but only that the years are compared to days to establish that although the siege would be long, they should not hope for the end until all the people were destroyed.

Furthermore, as we continue, we will see that the prophet lay on his side for 390 days without any mention of 40 days; that part appears to have been omitted. This much remains certain, however: because Israel and Judah were obstinate in their sins, the city would be besieged until it fell. Certainly the punishment of Israel cannot be considered in the sacking of Jerusalem; the ten tribes had already migrated out of their homeland, and they would not know what was taking place in Jerusalem except by hearsay. Whatever the case, their condition was completely separate from all the miseries of the people, for they were at peace in exile.

Therefore the fact that the prophet was ordered *"to bear the iniquity of Israel for three hundred and ninety days"* does not have to be restricted to the siege. Rather, God simply means that since so many years had passed during which the Israelites and the Judeans continually sinned, their final destruction was near.

We know that the kingdom of Judah was abolished at that time, and exile was tantamount to the destruction of the ten tribes. They had perished, and the prophet was not bearing their iniquities as if they were then suffering the penalty for their sins. But we know that it is common in the Scriptures for God to postpone punishing sins to the third and fourth generations.[8] Therefore, when God decreed that the ten tribes be carried off into exile, he then exacted punishment for the sins of 390 years.

Afterward he sustained the city of Jerusalem for some time; and he tolerated similar wickedness in that tribe, lest he completely erase all memory

a. I.e., days. The translation is taken literally from Calvin's text.
8. Mg., Ex. 20:5; Dt. 5:9.

115

of that people. Nevertheless, the Jews did not repent; but as we see when Isaiah compares them to the Israelites, they were worse.[9] Micah rebukes them for following the statutes of Omri.[10] From this it is not at all surprising if the punishment they pay corresponds to the sins in which they were involved. We will see in chapter 16 that our prophet repeats the same point.

In sum, God wanted to show that the people had abused his tolerances far too long in continuing to sin for as many as 430 years. The Israelites began to fall away from the pure worship of God while the temple still remained pure. Finally even the tribe of Judah degenerated into similar wickedness and became guilty, too. Now we see the mind of the Holy Spirit.

Now I come back to the text: *"you,"* he says, *"are to lie on your left side."* We should note that this was not carried out literally, because Ezekiel did not lie on his side for 390 days. But he lay on his side in a vision, so that he might convey to the people what God had made known to him. Some interpreters think that the ten tribes are designated by the left side because Samaria is located to the left. I do not see how this makes sense.

I have no doubt that God wished to show preference for the tribe of Judah over the kingdom of Israel. Even though the ten tribes excelled in population, wealth, and strength, nevertheless God always made more of the kingdom of Judah. The throne of David was there, and the ten tribes were the posterity of Abraham only according to the flesh. The promise to Jerusalem remained, and there the lamp of God shone forth, as we are told in many passages.

Therefore the right side signifies the dignity with which God always wished to honor the kingdom of Judah. But the ten tribes are designated by the left side because, as I have said, they were not equal in glory to the kingdom of Judah — even if they were more numerous, stronger, and excelled in every advantage.

Now we must note that the burden of iniquity was not placed on the prophet because God transferred to him the people's iniquities. Some have devised an allegory here, saying that the prophet was a type of Christ because he accepted the iniquities of the people. But this is not a description of expiation. We know that God used his servants for various purposes. So in one sense the prophet is being ordered to attack Jerusalem as though he were the king of Babylon. He played the role of Nebuchadnezzar when he besieged the city of brick, as we said yesterday. Now he plays the roles of the ten tribes and of the kingdom of Judah, *"when he lies on his left side for three hundred and ninety days, and lies on his right side for forty days."*

That is why it says, *"I have appointed for you the years of their iniquity*

9. Mg., Is. 28:1, 7-8.
10. Mg., Mi. 6:61, i.e., 6:16.

according to the number of days," etc. That is, "When I order you to lie on your side for so many days, I am indicating the number of years to you." It would be absurd to command the prophet to lie on one side for four centuries! God accommodates himself in these figures to our meager capacity. It would be monstrous for a man to lie on his side for four centuries, and since that is absurd God changes years into days. This is the reason that days are said to be substituted for years.

Next he adds: *"when you have fulfilled those years, then you will lie a second time on your right side, and you shall bear the iniquity of the house of Judah for forty days."* Here God shows that, although the tribe of Judah should have been terrified by the punishment of the kingdom of Israel, it persisted in its evil ways. For that reason it was inevitable that the Judeans would be ravaged by the same punishment as the Israelites.

It is added: *"you will set* or fix *your face on the siege of Jerusalem."* Either of two meanings can be drawn from that: either "you will direct or order" or "you will establish or make firm." I prefer "direct" or "order" in this passage. Earlier he said, "you will direct your face," that is, until Jerusalem is sacked. But in my judgment, God simply orders the prophet to be intent on the sacking of the city. *"And let your arms be bare,"* which is to say, "unimpeded." We know that the orientals wore sleeved tunics and long robes and therefore could not carry out their duties unless they took off their robes. The prophet is ordered *"to bare his arms,"* exactly as if one would undo part of his cloak and throw it to the other side to free one of his arms. Such was the prophet's garb, but in a vision, as we said.

Next it says, *"and you will prophesy against it."* God repeats what we saw yesterday. Nothing would have been more futile than for the prophet to bare his arm and set his face to the siege of the pictured city. If it were only an empty picture, the spectacle could have been scorned. But God adds that the intent of this figure was to grant the prophecy greater authority, as if to say: "I recognize that these signs in themselves would be of little importance, and you might object to me: 'Why should I trouble myself with these ridiculous matters?' What you are doing will be a clear seal of the prophecy." Now we see why God adds the phrase about prophesying.

Finally he adds, *"Behold, I will put ropes on you so that you do not turn from side to side, until you have fulfilled the days of your sieges."* God signifies that his decree concerning the sack of Jerusalem is inviolable. By binding his servant so tightly he shows that the decree, which the Judeans thought they could escape by trickery, was firm. We know they always flattered themselves whenever the prophets threatened them. God therefore indicates that there would definitely be a siege of the city until it was sacked, because the prophet will be bound by ropes, as it were, so that he would not move or shift from side to side.

117

We can conclude that this figure showed that the Judeans are subject to the same punishment as the ten tribes, as if God were saying that the time which he established for the destruction of the kingdom of Israel had come; and it would be the same end for the Judeans, for wherever they might flee, to this region or that, in the end God's judgment would certainly be carried out against them — as if the matter were confirmed once and for all. Next:

9 *"And you, take for yourself wheat and barley and beans and lentils and millet and spelt* [zeas, כסמים *(kuss^emîm)* is plural, just as he also said 'barleys' in the plural; but there is enallage[11] of number]; *and you shall put them in one vessel, and make them into bread for yourself* [that is, 'make bread for yourself out of them'], *according to the number of days on which you will be lying on your side; for three hundred and ninety days you will eat it."*

This verse undoubtedly refers to the siege, because God indicates that the city would be subject to deprivation. He immediately adds another vision, from which we gather that he is referring not just to the siege of Jerusalem but in general to God's vengeance against all the tribes that was inflicted also on the Judeans because of their association with them, and that finally occurred in the sack of the city.

Here God shows what the condition of the city of Jerusalem would be, for mixed bread is a sign of want. We make bread out of wheat. But if an area is barren, barley or oats is eaten instead. Even where there is a moderate supply of wheat, wheat bread is usually made. When lentils, beans, millet, and zea (which they call spelt) are mixed in, however, a more pressing need is revealed. In Jerome's time the term "spelt" was used for zea, since he says that word was native to the Italians. For some reason it suited Jerome to translate the term *vitia;*[12] in the commentary he says it was zea and gives it the name "spelt," which was the usual term.[13]

Whatever the case, when beans are mixed with wheat, and barley and spelt too, it is obvious that normal food was not in adequate supply. It is as if Ezekiel announced to the Jews a shortage in food supplies at the time that they were reaping, when they were still free. This vision was offered to the prophet before the city was besieged. He threatened shortages and famine while they were still eating bread made of pure wheat.

Moreover, God orders him *"to put all these things into one vessel."* We infer from this that it was a mixture that would have little taste for delicate palates. We know that beans and lentils are coarser than wheat and cannot be

11. Substitution of one grammatical form for another.
12. I.e., *vicia,* vetch (Vulgate).
13. *Commentary on Ezekiel* 4:9-12.

made into a mixture of proper proportions, since wheat and beans are so dissimilar. This is why God expressly mentions *one vessel*.

Then he adds: *"You will make bread for yourself from them according to the number of days."* Only 390 days are counted here; there is no mention of the 40 days. But it could be included by synecdoche. Now follows:

10 *"And the food that you eat will be twenty shekels in weight for a day* [that is, 'on each day,' or, 'for each day']; *you will eat from the time to the time* [that is, 'from the beginning to the end'; that is, 'from the first day to the three hundred and ninetieth'].
11 *And you will drink water by measure, up to the sixth part of a hin; you will drink from the time to the time."*

He confirms what I have already said, that the need would be so great that the prophet would not dare to eat as much bread as he wanted. *"You will eat,"* he says, *"bread by weight, namely, twenty shekels."* That is not even a full pound. So this means the same as if God ordered his prophet to eat meagerly. When the city was under siege, bread was distributed in pieces to individuals. God is saying that the Judeans would be hungry when the city was besieged for a long time, so hungry that they would have only a measured weight of bread, and just a little at that.

What follows is even worse, for there would also be a shortage of water. To be driven by thirst is the worst calamity. It is exceedingly harsh and difficult to have no wine, but when water fails, as I said, that is the worst need. Nevertheless, that is what the prophet announced to the Judeans, when he says that water was not given to him during the siege, *"except by measure."*

I will leave the rest until tomorrow.

Almighty God, since you have sustained us until now with your inestimable clemency, may we neither abuse your goodness nor provoke your vengeance against us with our stubbornness. May we forestall your judgment and so subject ourselves to you that you take us into your trust and protect us from our enemies, and then supply us generously with whatever we need. And although you want us to live sparingly according to the flesh, may we never lack spiritual food so that we might constantly be refreshed, until at last we enjoy that fullness promised us and kept in heaven through Christ our Lord. Amen.

Lecture 13

We saw in yesterday's lecture that the same number of days was fixed for the siege of the city of Jerusalem as the years in which they provoked God's wrath. As we said, God did not exact punishment for their vices by a long siege, because Israel in this way would have been immune from punishment. The point is that since they for 430 years did not cease bringing on themselves God's vengeance, so now the end had come and they paid the price they deserved. Now follows:

12 *"And you will eat a cake of barley* [that is, 'a barley cake'], *and you will cook it on the dung of human excrement before their eyes."*
13 *And Yahweh said: "Thus will the sons of Israel eat their defiled bread among the nations to which I will drive them."*

This vision pertains specifically to the ten tribes. For that reason I said that we should not regard God's punishment as consisting solely of the siege of the city but as extending further. Therefore after the prophet spoke of the sack of Jerusalem, he then adds that God has prepared a reward for the sons of Israel, because God is a just judge of both peoples. Just as he finally exacted punishment from the rest who still remained in Jerusalem, so he punished the sins of the ten tribes in the Babylonian exile.

For this reason the prophet is ordered *"to cook a cake on dung,"* that is, he is ordered to use human dung instead of coal. He does not simply say "dung," but adds *"dung of human excrement."* The application soon follows: *"thus will the children of Israel eat their defiled bread among the nations."*

Now we see that the Judeans are finally dragged into the judgment because the ruin of their brothers had not moved them to repent. At the same time, God's vengeance against the ten tribes was obvious, because those wretched exiles were forced to eat their defiled bread among gentiles.

We know that cakes are made of finely ground flour. A purer meal is preferred to make the bread more delicate. But the prophet is ordered *"to make cakes out of barley."* Then he is ordered *"to cook them on dung."* But such uncleanliness was condemned in the law.[1] Thus God shows that the Israelites were so abandoned that they were no different than the defiled gentiles. As we know, the Lord had separated them from the rest of the world, but from that time they took part in all sorts of vices of the wicked. Finally, after much patience, God completely rejected them, as it says here.

Widespread pollution is indicated under this figure, as if to say that nothing was pure or holy in Israel any more, because they were mixed up in the iniquities of all the nations. Also the unclean bread indicates any kind of uncleanness. When he says *"among the nations,"* he means that they would be inhabitants of the lands to which they had been driven, not just as fugitives but as exiles from the land of Canaan, which had been their birthright. In sum, disinheritance is meant, since the Jews are said to have been driven from one place to another to prevent them inhabiting the land promised to them. Next:

14 *And I said, "Ah* [or, 'Alas'], *Sovereign Yahweh, behold, my soul was not defiled, and I have not eaten of a carcass or a mutilated animal from my youth until this day; and rotten flesh* [or, 'abominable'; they call פגול *(piggûl)* decaying, rancid, or putrid flesh. But by transference it denotes the flesh of a detested animal, that is, an unclean animal] *has not entered my mouth."*
15 *And he said to me, "Look, I have given you cow dung for human dung, and you will make* [that is, 'you will cook'] *your bread on it."*

Here the prophet asserts an objection by which he obtains a partial remission of God's severe command. It was abominable to eat meat cooked on human excrement, not so much because of the filth as because religion forbade it. The prophet was not considering the taste to his palate, but he objects that he was not allowed to do this, and he tells how carefully he had abstained from all defiled foods his whole life. If, before this time, he had brashly dared to eat whatever he wished, he could not have pleaded, as he does, not to be forced to eat defiled bread. But he makes it known that he has abstained from all unclean foods his entire life: *"My soul,"* he says, *"has never been defiled."* "Soul" is often understood as "stomach." Then he says, *"I have never tasted a carcass or a mutilated animal."* By synecdoche he means all unclean foods that it was sacrilegious to eat according to the prescriptions of the law.[2]

1. Mg., Lv. 5:3; 7:21.
2. Mg., Lv. 11.

Since meat from a carcass is mixed with blood, God forbade them to touch the meat of an animal that died by itself, because it had not been slaughtered. If a wild beast mangled a sheep or a cow, its hideous corpse ought to be detestable to people. Since carcasses, as well as torn or mangled flesh, were unclean foods, the prophet says that from boyhood to the present he had kept God's precept with the greatest care. For that reason he obtained some mitigation, as I said. Nevertheless, he is forced to eat bread cooked on cow dung. This was done in a vision, as I pointed out yesterday. But in the meantime, God did not change what he appointed concerning the people, namely, *"that they would eat their bread defiled among the nations."* Cakes cooked over cow dung were also unclean according to the law. So God shows that his decree was fixed, that the Israelites would be mixed in with the nations to become defiled by their filth. Next:

16 *And he said to me, "Son of man, behold, I am breaking* [or, 'crushing'] *the staff of bread in Jerusalem* [or, 'at Jerusalem'], *and they will eat bread by weight and in fear* [or, 'fright,' or, 'trepidation'], *and they will drink water by measure and in bewilderment;*
17 *that they may lack bread and water* [that is, 'that bread and water may fail them'] *and be bewildered* [others, 'be desolate'; שׁמם *(šāmam)* means both], *a man and his brothers, and they will vanish* [or, 'melt away'] *in their iniquity."*

God turns again to the citizens of Jerusalem and proclaims that they will be so weakened by hunger that they will be reduced to the breaking point and consumed by starvation. But he states this two ways. He says that *"he would break the staff of bread;* then, *they will have a meager supply of bread"* because they will be forced to eat their scraps of bread *"by weight and in fear, and drink water by measure and in bewilderment."*

I said that the punishments were different, because even if there is plenty of bread, God often "breaks the staff," as he puts it. This is clear from Leviticus 26, from where our prophet borrowed this saying. There Moses explains what it means to break the staff of bread. "Ten women," he says, "will bake bread in one oven, and then in good faith they will restore the meal given them. The bread will be weighed, you will eat, and you will not be satisfied."[3] God said in that passage, "I will break the staff of bread"; but a clearer explanation follows: he supplied the wheat for baking bread, and the women kept an eye on one another so that no one stole any part of it. They returned by weight whatever had been given them. Nevertheless, there was no nourishment.

Hence we see that the staff of bread is broken by God when there is a

3. Mg., Lv. 26:26.

sufficient supply of food but those who eat are not satisfied. To make this clearer, this principle must be assumed: "people do not live by bread alone, but by every word that proceeds from the mouth of God."[4] There God indicates that we are not nourished by the power of bread, strictly speaking. How could bread give life when it lacks understanding and vitality? So we see that bread has no power to nourish us apart from the hidden grace of God. We live by the Word of God.

The issue here is not the Word of teaching, and not even spiritual life. Moses means that we are not sustained by bread and wine and other foods or any kind of drink, but by God's hidden power, as he inspires the bread with power to nourish us. Bread nourishes us, but not by its own intrinsic power. It has power from elsewhere, namely, God's grace and decree.

Just as a small portion of bread can suffice for us, so one who gorges himself will more likely groan than be satisfied, unless God inspires the bread with his power. That is why Christ hurled this passage at Satan: "Man does not live by bread alone";[5] it shows that human life depends on the secret power of God, and that, whenever he pleases, God does not need these external supports. God is able to sustain us on his own; he occasionally uses bread, but as an external instrument. Meanwhile, nothing detracts from his power. The staff, then, is taken metaphorically for a prop. Old men, whose legs are shaky and every limb broken with infirmity, lean on a staff. In the same way, bread is said to have a staff because we lean on it for nourishment. Strength declines, and one taking nourishment for that reason is said to restore himself with food.

Thus God breaks the staff of bread when he makes people hungry even if they have an adequate supply of bread. No matter how much they gorge themselves they are not satisfied, because the food weighs down rather than restores them. This is the first punishment with which God threatens the Jews.

A second is added: *"they will be deprived of bread."* We see then the twofold way in which God punishes us with hunger. Although he gives a liberal supply of bread, he breaks and crushes its staff so that it cannot support us or reclaim our lost vigor. Second, he also takes bread away from us, because he strikes the crops with either blight or hail, or afflicts the fields with other calamities. Barrenness brings want. Thus God inflicts us with hunger, and both kinds are included. He says, *"Behold, I will crush the staff of bread in Jerusalem."*

Then he adds, *"They will eat their bread by weight and in fear, and they will drink water by measure and in bewilderment,"* because they will be reduced to such straits that they scarcely dare touch bread. When they look ahead to the next day, they will be afraid and dumbfounded.

4. Mg., Dt. 8:3.
5. Mg., Mt. 4:4; Lk. 4:5, i.e., 4:4.

He confirms this thought in the next verse: *"so that they will be without bread and water,"* he says, *"and they will be bewildered."* This explanation makes more sense: *a man and his brother will be bewildered;* that is, they will both look at each other in amazement. This is how those who lack purpose and perceive nothing but despair usually act.

Finally, *"they melt away in their iniquity."* Again God repeats that the Jews cannot complain when he afflicts them so heavily, because they will receive the reward for their own iniquity. Next:

CHAPTER 5

1 *"And you, son of man, take for yourself a sharp sword, a knife for cutting hair; take it for yourself and make it* [or, 'draw it'] *over your head and over your beard; and take for yourself a balance for weighing* [that is, a 'true balance'] *and divide them* [that is, 'the hairs cut from your head and beard'].
2 *You will burn a third part with fire in the middle of the city, as the days of the siege have been completed* ['will be completed'; literally, 'according to completing the days']; *you will take a third part, you will strike all around it with the sword; and you will scatter a third part to the wind; and I will unsheathe the sword after them.*
3 *And then you will take a few in number* [that is, 'a part small in number'], *and you will bind them* [that is, that part] *under your arms* [or, 'in the folds of your garments'].
4 *And from them you will take yet again, and throw them into the middle of the fire* ['you will hurl'], *and burn them in the fire. From there fire will break out on the whole house of Israel."*

God confirms with another vision what he taught before about the assault against Jerusalem. He orders his prophet to shave the hairs of his head and beard, and then to divide them into three parts and weigh them on a scale. But he calls the scale for weighing "true," so that equality will be preserved and one portion will not outweigh another. He most certainly understands the hairs as the inhabitants of Jerusalem, just as he understands the head to be the place where they live.

Then the application will follow, but I will omit that today, because I cannot go any farther than these verses. It is enough to affirm briefly that people are designated by the hairs, for hairs can scarcely be numbered; even the hairs of a beard are not counted. So great was the population of Jerusalem. We know that city was very populous. On the other hand, we know that this was cause for pride. When they realized that their strength lay in the size of their population, they assumed that they were equal, and even superior, to all their enemies combined — hence that foolish confidence which destroyed them.

Therefore God commanded the prophet to cut all his hairs, on his head as well as his beard. So he taught that not one person would be exempt from destruction, because he says, *"make the sword pass over,* or *draw it across,"* he says, *"your head; then your chin,"* so that nothing at all remains. We see that the razor's crossing over means that not even one hair would remain untouched on his head or beard. From this it follows that God intends to take vengeance against the entire nation so that not one would remain alive.

To order *"three parts to be weighed out"* and a proportion *"preserved"* between them indicates what we often saw in Jeremiah: "whoever escapes from the sword will perish from hunger; whoever flees from hunger will perish by some other means."[6] Here God expresses clearly how all the Judeans will be destroyed, although they will be divided into various categories. Since some escaped and fled, and others went to Egypt, their condition could seem to vary. But in this variety God shows that nothing detracts from his power to destroy every single one.

Let us come to the words *"make it pass across over your head and over your beard";* and then, *"take the scales."* מאזני [*mō'z^enê*] is properly called a balance because of its two pans. *"Take a balance,* or *weighing scales,"* and divide *"the hairs."* I have already briefly explained the point of this division, namely, that not all the Jews were destroyed by the same punishment. Those who evaded one destruction boasted that they were saved. Therefore they raged against God. But this foolish confidence is taken from them when the prophet is commanded to divide the hairs cut from his beard and head: *"divide them,"* he says, and he adds next, *"a third part."*

God did not divide the people into three parts without the best of reasons. Part was consumed by hunger and starvation before the city was attacked. Because by *fire* God designates all misery, he orders a third part to be cast into the fire and consumed. Now because there were two parts left, everyone assured himself he would live. Those who escaped immediate death assumed they were out of danger, and their confidence increased — because we assume that we have been acquitted when we have overcome one kind of death.

This is the reason he adds, *"After you have burned a third part with fire, take another third and cut it with the sword."* Moreover, he orders that third part to be burned in the center of the city. At the time, Ezekiel was in Chaldaea, and so did not enter the city; but we have said that this was all done in a prophetic vision.

Nevertheless, what is said here fits God's vengeance, because before the

6. Mg., Je. 15:2.

sack of the city a third part was consumed by plague, famine, and starvation, and other evils and disasters. All these miseries are indicated here by "fire." After the city had been sacked, God ordered a third part to be struck by the sword. We know that this was fulfilled when the king and his entire entourage were apprehended as they fled through the plain of Jericho.[7] The hostile army attacked them, and many were killed. The king himself was abducted, and his sons were strangled before him; then his eyes were gouged out, and he was dragged off, bound in chains, to Babylon. This is the third part that *he ordered the prophet to strike with the sword,* because that slaughter was in addition to the destruction of the city.

Now he adds that *"he should take a third part and cast it on the wind."* Then follows the threat, *"I will unsheathe the sword after them."* This is said of both the fugitives who fled into various regions and the poor people who were scattered after the destruction of the city and prolonged their lives for a brief time thereafter. We know that some hid in the land of Moab and others in the land of Ammon, some in Egypt and still others fled to various hiding places. This scattering was like someone throwing shaved hair to the wind. But God proclaims that the flight and scattering would not benefit them, because he would draw the sword against them and pursue them to the end. Although at first glance the citizens of Jerusalem differ, as if divided into three classes, we see that God's judgment, which would destroy the entire multitude, threatens them all.

Now is added, *"But you will take a small number and bind them,"* that is, that "number"; he changes to a plural. That is, *"you will bind those hairs of which the number will be small in the folds of your clothes."* Either he removes any confidence they might have conceived because of a temporary escape, or he means that very few would be saved amid the destruction of the entire people, as amazingly happened. If we accept the latter, a correction has been added, so that God might grant some hope of grace, because the people were so extensively consumed that it became imperative for God's covenant to abide. Some remnant had to be preserved. They would have been reduced to nothing, like Sodom, if God had not preserved that small seed.[8]

So in that sense the prophet is ordered to bind and hide a part of the hairs in the folds of his garment. To be precise, that is only a part of the third group, because those who had escaped imagined that they had obtained safety by fleeing — especially since they gathered in groups.

Next, it follows, *"you will take yet again of them and throw into the middle of the fire and burn in the fire."* Out of that small number God still wants some to be burned and consumed; he indicates with these words that,

7. Mg., 2 Ki. 25, i.e., 25:4-7.
8. Mg., Is. 1:9; Rom. 9:29.

even though only a small portion remains, it would be consumed in a similar manner, or at least that many of the few would be rejected. Those who seem to have had the good fortune to escape and survive unharmed were cut down by various disasters a little later or gradually wasted away and perished slowly.

If we accept that a promise is implied in these words, we understand that it happened by God's wondrous mercy that a few of the people survived. Because he remembered his covenant, he wished to preserve a small part; and thus that correction was interposed that the prophet should bind a small number in the folds of his garment. Nevertheless, from that flower God seized one part and threw it in the fire. If there was such filth in the remnant that they had to be purged and part thrown into the fire, what would be found in the whole people, that is, including the very dregs? The portion that the prophet bound in his folds was certainly the flower of the people; if there was any integrity, it ought to be seen there.

But we have already seen that there were many reprobate in that small number. We can easily gather from this that the entire people were hopelessly wicked; *"take still,"* he says. The adverb is used so that those who remained after the destruction of the city might not assume that all punishments have been carried out. *"Still,"* he says; that is, when they imagine that every crisis has passed, *"you will nevertheless take from that part which you have saved and throw it into the fire. From there,"* he says, *"fire will break out on the whole house of Israel."*

As we saw before, he indicates with these words that the vision is not a game, as in the theater where many fictions are presented. God says that what he shows his servant through the vision would be affirmed, as the outcome itself finally proved.

But he goes further: *"the whole house of Israel will be burned in this conflagration,"* because the final destruction of the city brought despair to the miserable exiles who promised themselves a return to the city as long as it was standing. But when they saw such destruction of the city, they were consumed at the same time, as if the fire from Judea had spread all the way to them. At the same time, a remnant whom the Lord miraculously preserves is always exempt, although he appears to destroy the entire people.

Now we see the purpose of this vision. I will go no further, because I would be forced to stop and disrupt the prophet's teaching. It is enough to understand that although the people were divided into many parts such that each was in a different condition, all would perish because that is what God determined. After that, the confidence of those who assumed they would be safe in Jerusalem was broken; and the ten captured tribes ought also to acknowledge that God's final judgment was still not fulfilled until the city itself, the seat of kingship and priesthood, was wiped out.

LECTURE 13

Almighty God, since you have published in your ancient people such proof of your terrible vengeance, grant that today we might learn wisdom from the misery of others, and so subject ourselves to you in obedience that you will receive us into your favor and show yourself so well disposed toward us that through your pardon we may be restored from death to life, until we enjoy that eternal blessing which your only-begotten Son, our Lord, has won for us. Amen.

Lecture 14

5 *Thus says Sovereign Yahweh, "This is Jerusalem; I have placed her in the middle of the nations, and the lands around her.*
6 *And she has changed my judgments into wickedness* [or, 'she has transgressed my judgments'; or, 'she was rebellious,' for strictly that is what מרה *(mārâ)* means. Thus 'she was rebellious against my judgments'] *more than all the nations, and my statutes* [or, 'she was rebellious against my statutes'] *more than the lands around her. They have rejected my judgments and have not walked in my statutes."*

Now God shows why he determined to act so severely and harshly with the holy city that he had selected as his royal seat. Because he had adorned that city with so many benefits, their ingratitude was even more shameful and wicked. God recounts his benefits toward Jerusalem in order to rebuke her. If the Jews had embraced God's benefits, there is no doubt that he would have enriched them more and more with his gifts. But because he saw his grace repudiated, his indignation was kindled even more. Contempt of God's benefits is profanity and sacrilege.

Now we understand the Holy Spirit's plan in saying that Jerusalem had been placed as if in a theater on high, so that its dignity would be visible everywhere. This is not said in praise of Jerusalem but with great reproach. All that God had conferred on her had to be taken into account, since they corrupted themselves so unworthily and deliberately defiled God's glory.

In this connection he says that *"Jerusalem was in the middle of the nations,"* but I do not take this as subtly as Jerome[1] and several others. They

1. *Commentary on Ezekiel 5:5-6.*

imagine that Jerusalem was the navel of the earth, and they twist other passages to mean the same thing. When it says, "God has accomplished salvation in the middle of the earth,"[2] they explain it literally as the "very middle," as they put it.

In my judgment that is childish. The prophet simply means that Jerusalem was located in the most celebrated part of the world. That area contained on every side the most noble, and certainly the wealthiest, nations, as is well known. It was not far from the Mediterranean Sea. Asia Minor lay in one direction, and it had Egypt for a neighbor; and to the north was Babylon. This is the prophet's genuine meaning: Jerusalem was furnished with the highest dignity among the other nations, as if God had placed it at the highest level.

Every city has nations and lands surrounding it, but here God calls them *"lands and nations"* κατ᾽ ἐξοχήν [*kat' exochēn*],[a] not just any whatever but those which excel in productivity as well as wealth and other assets. When he says, *"This is Jerusalem,"* the demonstrative pronoun is emphatic, for he extols that city with magnificent praises to make its ingratitude more obvious. Therefore *"it was placed in the middle of the nations and the surrounding lands"*; since it was bounded by many wealthy regions, God's grace shone there most brightly so that it would be the most beautiful part of the theater, draw all eyes to itself, and move the spirits of all in admiration.

Now he adds that *"they changed his judgments."* I said the word מרה [*mārâ*] occasionally means "to change," but more often "to transgress" or "reject." This sense fits better because the Jews rebelled in wickedness against God's judgments. He increases their guilt by saying that *"his precepts were condemned"* in their addiction to wickedness. If there had been some appearance of virtue, their guilt could have been extenuated; but when they throw themselves into flagrant wickedness and spurn God's commands, it is inexcusable.

Let us learn from this passage that unless we use God's blessings purely, our ingratitude will not go unpunished. Whatever goodness God confers on us, he consecrates to our salvation and to the glory of his name. We are sacrilegious when we corrupt the things appointed for his glory. We are three and four times perverse when we turn to our destruction what God has devoted to our salvation. We must remember that Jerusalem's ingratitude was extreme, *"because she rejected God's commands."* When God deposits the treasure of heavenly teaching with us, we must be diligent and careful not to turn aside to wickedness. There is no excuse for error when we have been taught once and for all what is right — from the mouth of God himself. He declares the same judgment many times.

2. Mg., Ps. 74:12.
a. par excellence.

But he says, *"more than all the nations and more than the lands that surrounded them."* He indicates with these words that the Jews were worse than all the others because they knowingly and willingly threw off God's yoke. The other nations did not conduct themselves any better, for we know that the worship of God was corrupted everywhere. But the wickedness of the elect people was more shameful because they transformed light into darkness. The nations went astray in their darkness as though blind. But there was another explanation for the people whom God personally instructed. Therefore since the teaching of the law shone among the Jews, the prophet rightly says that *"they were more wicked than all the nations and lands."*

Then he explains how they changed the judgments of God or rebelled against them: *"because they rejected my judgments,"* he says, *"and did not walk in my statutes."* First of all, he does not say that they fell through ignorance, but through pride and contempt. When the will of God has become known to us, there is no place for ignorance. We do not sin through superficiality, but our minds are inescapably infected with pride and contempt for God. Now he adds that they *"did not walk in his precepts";* these words indicate that the contempt of which he spoke was blatant, because its results spread throughout their whole life. Next:

7 *"Therefore, thus says Sovereign Yahweh, 'Because of the multiplying of you* [or, "because of your multiplication"] *more than all the nations around you, so that you did not walk in my statutes and keep my judgments, and did not act according to the judgments of the nations around you';*

8 *therefore, thus says Sovereign Yahweh, 'Behold, I, even I, am against you; and I will carry out judgments in your midst in the sight of the nations.' "*

This verse is explained in various ways because of the word המנכם [h^amonkem]. Some read this together as a single construction: "because they multiplied, they did not worship God." They reveled, as it were, in their opulence, as horses run wild because of rich food and overeating. That passage of Moses is noted, "Israel became fat and kicked."[3] They assume that this passage is similar, and they construe it this way: "Because you have multiplied more than all the nations around you, you have despised my judgments." That is, they were blinded or inebriated by their prosperity. But for me, that interpretation is not proved, and it is certainly too forced.

Others derive it from המה [hāmâ], which means to be disturbed or stirred up, and draw this interpretation: "Therefore, because you have made more disturbance than all the nations, that is, because your licentiousness and intemperance have surpassed all the peoples, while your desires have left you

3. Mg., Dt. 32:15.

131

out of control, as if unbridled." But I am afraid that exposition is farfetched. Thus I simply take it as "to multiply" or "multiplication." It could be a noun, or the verb *"machor,"*[b] but the meaning is the same.

Moreover, I do not refer this to the number or multitude of people, or to their abundance of goods, as most do. They say that the number of people was multiplied, but we know that does not fit. If it is referred to riches, it is certainly true that God acted more than generously toward that city. But I take the word in an active sense: " *'they had multiplied more than all the nations.'* " Jerome has not rendered it badly, in my judgment, "because you have surpassed the nations."[4] But he has departed from the proper meaning of the word, and it will be more satisfactory to retain the verb "multiply" or the noun "multiplication." But it should be taken actively: "they have been so immoderate and reckless in their superstitions that they have exalted themselves above all the nations in doing evil."

Therefore, " *'on account of the multiplying of you,'* " or "because of your multiplication beyond all the nations," means, "you were not content with moderate wickedness, but heaped up every kind of shame so that your wickedness attained the highest point." Threats follow accordingly. But before he comes to that, he confirms what he said before: " *'they did not walk in his statutes and did not keep his judgments.'* " *To multiply* means that when the law was given to them, they held it in contempt and emulated the wickedness of the other nations and lands around them. These statements mean the same: they rebelled in wickedness against God more than any other nation, and they multiplied more than all the nations and lands.

The reason must be noted again: " *'because they did not walk in God's statutes.'* " The nations held to no particular path; thus it is not surprising that they wandered in their distorted ways. But since the way had been shown to the Jews, Moses did not say in vain: "I call heaven and earth to bear witness that today I have set before you life and death. Therefore choose life."[5] Since God entrusted the teaching of salvation to the Jews, their stubbornness in not walking in his statutes was all the more unworthy and shameful. Life was set before them, as Moses said; it was up to them to walk in it — something that could not be done by other nations.

Now he adds, " *'and according to the judgments of the nations around you.'* " Here the prophet seems to turn into a fault what is praised elsewhere — and in many places, too. It was necessary that the Jews be separate from the nations in order to worship God purely. The prophets often criticize them because they followed the judgments or statutes of the nations. I have said nothing here about these words because they occur often, and many passages

b. It is not clear what Hebrew verb Calvin means in this context.
4. Vulgate.
5. Mg., Dt. 30:19.

make it clear why God calls his judgments laws. Some distinguish between judgments and statutes, because judgments pertain to morals and statutes to ceremonies. But that distinction is not observed everywhere.

In many passages, however, God commands the precepts of his law to show nothing was omitted from this perfect pattern of teaching. But sometimes this word is transferred to perverted rites and flawed morals; the phrase "to walk in the judgments of the fathers" means to follow their superstitions. In the same way, "to walk in the judgments of the nations" means to corrupt themselves by their perverse morals.

Now as I said, the prophets often condemned the Jews for being so addicted to the corruptions of the nations. But here the prophet says that *" 'they did not act according to the judgments of the nations.' "* But he understands this in the sense that they surpassed the madness of the nations, because they did not embrace God's law and steadfastly obey him.

We saw in Jeremiah 2 that the "nations were obstinate in their ravings."[6] Although that was not laudable, nevertheless God justly blamed his people because they honored him less than the nations honored their idols. We know how stubbornly the nations were set in their superstitions, for religion did not change except by some violent impulse, just as if heaven and earth were shaken together. Therefore, since each nation's religion was fixed and firm, God justly accused the Jews of superficiality, because they turned aside to the errors and foolishness of the nations.

Now Ezekiel means the same thing when he says that *" 'the Jews did not act according to the judgments of the nations.' "* "At least," he says, "they might have observed the nations, and as they saw them obstinately worship their idols, they should have stood firm in my law and pure worship. Although the stubbornness of the nations was so great that they could not be torn away from their illusions, my people," he says, "faithlessly abandoned me and my law by some rash impulse and without cause."

Now we understand why the prophet emphasizes this crime, *" 'that the Jews did not act according to the judgments,' "* that is, according to the customs of the nations. They could have realized that what we have once embraced must not be lightly rejected, because when we are diverted so suddenly and easily, it is certain that we had never put down living roots in the worship of God. Since the nations dictated to the Jews what ought to be done, their crime was even more detestable.

Now follows the threat that God was prepared to pursue vengeance: *" 'Behold, I, even I, am against you.' "* The particle גַּם [*gam*] is used as we in French say, *"Oui, ou Voire,"*[c] that is, "even I," *"voire moi."* We see that the

6. Mg., Je. 2:10-11.
c. Literally, "yes" or "even."

133

repetition is emphatic, as if God exclaimed that a horrible judgment awaited the Jews. He wanted to inflict fear on them by confirming that he would be their avenger.

But I do not accept the comment of Jerome.[7] He says that angels and other ministers of God's wrath are excluded because God determined that he himself would destroy the Jews. But we know that is false, for he used the Assyrians and Chaldaeans. Since those peoples were his whips, it follows that God does not exclude either angels or humans when he pronounces that he himself will be the avenger. Rather, he amplifies the gravity of the punishment when he says, " 'I, I am he with whom you will deal.' "

Now he adds that " 'he will carry out judgments' "; by this word he means the "administration of justice," as they say. What Jerome and others who followed him affirm is flimsy, that this word denotes God's justice; as if he said that he would not be cruel, unjust, or excessively strict in exacting punishment. To carry out judgments means the same as to administer justice. An earthly judge carries out judgments whenever he presides at the tribunal, even if he perverts justice and equity. This certainly cannot be applied to God but is a figure of speech. Moreover, there is a subtle antithesis between judgments of teaching and "actual judgments," as they put it. God complained that the Jews had not carried out his judgments; now he threatens that he will carry them out, because he will vindicate his law by punishments.

The whole point is that " 'he will carry out judgments in the middle of Jerusalem,' " because he will ascend the tribunal to compel sinners to defend themselves and to give an account of their lives. God exercised his judgment when he carried out his vengeance through the Chaldeans. Famine was part of the administration of justice, and also sword and plague. As long as he remains hidden, he seems to abandon his responsibility, and then the wicked indulge themselves as if he had forgotten to execute judgment. To counteract this he proclaims that " 'he will carry out judgments' "; as if he said, "I will appear as judge, even though you assume that I am asleep."

He says that " 'he will carry out judgments in the middle of Jerusalem in the sight of the nations.' " This passage means that the punishments would be extraordinary and easily seen by all the nations. We know that the nations were blind at that time, for they assumed that good and bad occurred by chance. But God affirms that the judgments which he will carry out would be so obvious that even the blind would be eyewitnesses. Now follows:

9   " 'And I will do to you what I have not done, and what I will not do likewise again, because of all your abominations.

10   Therefore ['because,' or 'for that reason'] fathers will devour their sons

7. Commentary on Ezekiel 5:7-9.

in your midst, and sons will devour their fathers. Therefore I will carry out judgments against you, and I will scatter to every wind all of you who remain.'"

God now adds that the punishments would be so terrible that nothing like it would be found in the world. *" 'I will do what I have not done, nor will do'";* that is, "I will avenge contempt of my law in a portentous and extraordinary way." From time to time God castigates people without going beyond what is normal. But because punishments are trivialized and treated with contempt when they are so general, God is forced to exceed the ordinary and to inflict punishments that are striking and ominous, as Moses said.[8]

Now when he says that *" 'he intends to do what he has not done before, and what he will not do after this time,'"* he indicates a horrible vengeance that has no parallel. Thus he means exactly what we quoted from Moses: "that judgment would be striking and ominous." To take this, as interpreters do, in a metaphorical sense is completely unacceptable. According to them, history does not record that this was fulfilled, and for that reason they resort to allegory or metaphor.

But first of all we know that Josephus records that mothers went mad and strangled their own children and served them for food,[9] although here an earlier siege is referred to, in which God indicates that he will cause fathers to devour their own children. I admit that. But if we accept their interpretation, it did not happen at that time. Hence Jeremiah lied when he says that the miserable women cooked their own children.[10] Jeremiah's testimony is certainly sufficient. To claim that one can nowhere find that this happened is to reject Jeremiah's testimony.

Besides, God had threatened the same thing through Moses; and that passage cannot be avoided because the words are so imposing: "The delicate men among you and those accustomed to luxuries," he says, "will eat their sons; a man will begrudge the wife of his own bosom and refuse to share with her that illicit food. Then he will sneak away and eat the flesh of his son without sharing any part of it with another."[11] When Moses speaks this way, it is certain that he does not mean internal dissent, such as disciples rising up against their teachers, or even teachers oppressing their disciples, as Jerome imagines.[12]

Rather, it is necessary to take the words as they are, that God would not be content with common and ordinary punishments when the Jews had run to

8. Mg., Dt. 28:46.
9. *Jewish Wars* 6:3:4.
10. Mg., La. 4:10.
11. Mg., Dt. 28:53-55.
12. *Commentary on Ezekiel* 5:10.

the limits of wickedness and sin. He will turn against them in ominous ways. This is what Ezekiel threatens against them now. It is not surprising that the prophets take such expressions from Moses, because by speaking the language of Moses rather than new words their prophecies would not be rejected. Now it must be affirmed that the prophet literally (as they say) threatens the Jews with what we read here.

But if someone objects that what God denies would happen often does happen, we must seek a solution. We said that when the Jews were besieged by Titus, such madness spread among some of the women that they secretly ate their children. But God proclaims that " 'he would never do this again.' " I reply that this kind of vengeance is not restricted to one day so that God could never again take vengeance against the Jews in the same way. But we read nowhere else that this was done.

Although the cruelty of children being fed to their parents is recounted in the tragedies, the barbaric act of a father knowingly and willingly eating his own son never occurs. That happened uniquely among the Jews. But that God carried out his vengeance through the Chaldaeans at one time is no obstacle to his vengeance raging again in a similar way when he wanted to punish the extreme treachery of his people. Although in Ezekiel's time everything was thoroughly corrupt, we know that when God's Son was finally rejected, the Jews cut off all hope for themselves with no place left for God's mercy. Hence it is not surprising if he once again allowed children to be eaten by their fathers, just as he threatens now that fathers would be so maddened as not to spare their own offspring.

I do not know why Jerome devised a completely useless distinction at this point. He says that when something honorable and proper happens, it is ascribed to God; but when the matter is base, God turns that infamy away from himself.[13] Since an outrageous action is at issue here, God does not say, "I will cause the people to eat their children," but, "Fathers will eat their own children, and children their own fathers." But there is nothing solid in this fabrication. Although the cruelty that the Chaldaeans carried out against the Jews was certainly not something honorable and proper, nevertheless God ascribes to himself whatever the Chaldaeans did.

What is more shameful than the incest of Absalom, who defiled his father's wives? Not only that, but at the sound of the trumpet, he wanted the entire people to witness his outrage.[14] But how does God speak? "I will do this in daylight," he says.[15] We see that this man[d] was not practiced in the

13. *Commentary on Ezekiel* 5:10.
14. Mg., 2 Sa. 16:21-22.
15. Mg., 2 Sa. 12:12.
d. I.e., Jerome.

Scriptures but still flourished his inventions with excessive license. There was certainly no true religion in that man. I am warning you for good reason, for there is danger that many might be deceived unless they are warned that his genius was full of ostentation and arrogance.

He says, " *'fathers will eat their sons in your midst.'* "This has certainly been fulfilled. Jeremiah speaks of the women, but he includes the men. He says that women were merciful;[16] he does not simply mean "the mothers" but those more humane than others. We know that maternal affection is more tender. But when mothers, and merciful mothers at that, devour their children, that was the gravest portent.

Now he adds, " *'Therefore I will carry out'* " (here the copula ought to be taken as emphatic). " *'Therefore I will carry out judgments against you.'* "That is, "in this way I will truly show myself to be the judge." " *'And I will scatter all of you that remain to every wind.'* " Here he indicates that the scattering would be so great that no community of people or name would remain. Hope could somehow support and sustain the Jews if some name or community remained for the people. But when God proclaims that they would be like refuse that " *'will be scattered to every wind,'* " he removes all hope of restoration, certainly in the present. We know that a number were left, but God had to threaten such destruction before giving some hope of his mercy. When he says " *'to every wind,'* " he means "in every direction." When this wind or that blows up, the dust is carried away, and the refuse is scattered in different directions. Next:

11 *"Because I live,"* says Sovereign Yahweh, *"if not because you have defiled my sanctuary* [that is, 'as you have defiled my sanctuary'] *with all your detestations and all your abominations.*
12 *"I will crush* [others translate it, 'I will shatter']; *and my eye will not spare, and I will show no mercy* ['I will not pardon']."

Here God expresses again, and more clearly, that he was burning to take vengeance because the Jews corrupted religion and violated his temple, as we will discuss tomorrow.

> *Almighty God, since you have today made yourself known to us so intimately in the gospel of Christ our Lord, grant that we might learn to lift our eyes to the light set before us, and keep them there fixed, so that we may be directed ever to hold to the path and struggle to reach the goal to which you call us; until at last, having completed the course of our calling, we attain to you and enjoy with you that glory which your only-begotten Son has won for us by his blood. Amen.*

16. Mg., La. 4:10.

Lecture 15

Yesterday, after Ezekiel had prophesied the destruction of Jerusalem, he expressed one reason why God was so furious with the city he had earlier selected as his dwelling place. He says that his *"sanctuary had been* violated or *defiled by them."* We see now how important true and pure religion is to God, when he avenges its pollution so severely. The well-being of the city certainly depended on God's being worshiped there in purity. To profane the temple was just like rejecting God himself and renouncing his aid.

Finally, that wickedness shows clearly that they rejected whatever God had promised them. We should note those expressions when he says, *"I will crush you, and my eye will not spare, and I will not pardon,"* for nothing is more precious to God than the worship that he himself has prescribed. When his sanctuary is defiled, it is not surprising if he burns so fiercely. Now follows:

13 *"A third part will die by plague, and they will perish from hunger in your midst; and a third part will fall by the sword round about you; and I will scatter a third part to every wind, and I will unsheathe the sword after them."*

Now without using any figures he explains what he earlier put in figurative terms. He had been ordered to shave with a razor the hairs of his head and beard, and to divide them so that a plague would consume one part, the sword another, and famine the third. Now he repeats the same thing but in another way. God explains why he offered a vision of this kind to his servant. He more briefly restricts what we saw earlier, because he omits the fourth part.

He was ordered to take another portion and hide it under his arm or in the hem of his garment. There is no mention here of this part, but it was not mentioned earlier without reason. God speaks in various ways, and that is his

138

right. At the same time, both the figures and the application agree, namely, that God will consume the whole people with famine or plague or sword. What was said about the fourth part was not superfluous, but it was not necessary to repeat it. The prophet's purpose is this: since there would be some survivors, they could seem to be exempt from the common destruction. To take that hope away, he said that they too, or many of them, would fall in the conflagration, so that a fire would be kindled among all the people of Israel.

The stubbornness of that people had become so uncontrollable that the wretched exiles were hated even more. Those who had been lenient with them began again to rage cruelly against them, because that people's name was detested among everyone. Those citizens of Jerusalem who were left perished, and hence it happened that the conflagration reached the ten tribes and the miserable exiles who were held captive in remote lands. But now our prophet is silent about the whole issue.

Meanwhile, he includes all that we saw earlier, although more briefly; the only thing lacking is that explanation which was useful earlier but need not be repeated. *"A third part will die by plague, and they will die from hunger in your midst.* Then *a third part will fall by the sword around you;* and *a third part will be scattered to every wind."* God claims for himself, however, that *"he will scatter a third part and unsheathe the sword after them,"* so that they will also perish while they are being scattered. That scattering was miserable in itself, but God proclaims that he would not be content with that moderate punishment until he had completely destroyed them. Next:

14   *"And my anger will be fulfilled, and I will make my fury dwell with* [or, 'rest on'] *them, and I will take consolation; and they will know that I am Yahweh, who have spoken in my zeal* [or, 'my jealousy'], *when I have fulfilled my fury against them."*

In this verse the prophet merely teaches what he said before, but by way of confirmation; that is, God's vengeance would be horrible, and there would be no end until the people were extinct and wiped out. Some think that this verse was interposed for God to lessen the rigor of his vengeance, and so according to them it contains a promise of pardon. Instead, it is a threat.

Their affirmation that God will make his anger subside cannot stand, for it says next: *"they will know that I am Yahweh who have spoken, when I have discharged my wrath,* or fury, *against them."* The context, which we will look at later, refutes that notion. Hence it remains settled that the prophet is not promising the people a mitigation of their punishment but persists in pronouncing the vengeance that he mentioned before.

First, he says, *"it will be completed."* כלה [kālâ] sometimes means "to finish," but it also means "to be accomplished." It means "to be consumed," but also "to be consummated." In this passage God indicates that there would be no limit to punishment until he was satisfied. This analogy is taken from human desires for vengeance whose ardor does not cease until they have avenged themselves fully. When God speaks of the limit or fulfillment of his anger, he likens himself to humanity.

Now he adds, *"I will make my fury rest on them";* that is, "my fury will be fixed against them." Here "rest" is not taken for "stop." Anger is sometimes said to rest when it is stilled. But God means no such thing through his prophet; rather he denotes the tenacity, the unrelenting course, of his vengeance. *My anger will rest on them;* that is, it will not go away or be moved. God is said to withdraw his hand when he stops pursuing us. But here the "resting of his anger" is its perpetual continuation.

He adds, *"I will take consolation."* Here God transfers to himself what, properly speaking, is inappropriate for him. He does not, in human fashion, delight in taking vengeance on wickedness; but we know that God's judgment cannot be grasped unless he puts on a human face and in a manner transforms himself. Therefore he is said *to take consolation* in approving just judgments. This consolation indicates that God cannot tolerate contempt of his law and abandoned wickedness without finally appearing as judge in accord with his nature. This is not because any passions affect him, as is well known, but because we cannot conceive of him as a just judge unless he proclaims himself pleased with vengeance when he sees people so lost and senseless that they can be called to repent in no other way.

Next he adds, *"and they will know that I Yahweh have spoken."* Here God indirectly censures the people's dullness, because not only did they esteem all prophecies to be worthless but in their pride ridiculed the threats. Whenever the prophets proclaim God's vengeance and judgment, they give the wicked and impudent people something to ridicule. Their obstinacy so blinded them that they did not think it was God speaking to them. They imagined that their adversaries were mere human beings. That is the source of such madness against the prophets. If they had realized that God was speaking to them, they would never have dared to rear up so violently. But because they thought the prophets offered only their own inventions, they ignored God and quarreled with the prophets. The Jews had no understanding.

But let us note the source of this ignorance: they willingly turned their minds away from God, just as today many do not think God is speaking when his truth in the Scriptures is publicly made known. Why do they not realize this? Because they do not want to. That blindness among the ancient people was voluntary and "premeditated," as they say, since they imagined that nothing would come of these prophecies.

This is the reason why the prophet says, *"then they will know that I have spoken,"* because, as they say, "experience is the teacher of fools." Since they repudiated every threat, it finally happened that, taught by evil, they realized too late that God had spoken. So there is an antithesis between experiential knowledge and the blindness that arose from evil, from contempt of God. Since he says *"they will know when he has completed his fury,"* their knowledge and instruction will be too late and useless. Finally, God proclaims that he will wreak just punishment on their willful ignorance, so that the Jews will recognize, whether they want to or not, that the prophecies they ignored with closed eyes proceeded from him alone.

He says that *"he has spoken in his zeal,"* or jealousy, because the prophets were thought to be almost wild when they sounded forth against the wicked. God therefore absolves those who were commonly considered, as we know, to be possessed. He says, *"I have spoken in my zeal,"* because when the wicked want to oppress God's servants with hostility, they object that God is clement and kind, and that it is out of character for him to speak so harshly and sharply. Hence God says that he is also jealous and angry, to prevent the Jews assuming that the prophets are carried away with thoughtless zeal and fervor (an error that we know was widespread). Next:

15 *"I will make you into a wasteland and a reproach among the nations that are around you, in the sight of any passerby* [or, 'traveler']*."*

He uses more words to explain what we have already seen, and from this we easily conclude that the rigor of God's judgment is not mitigated in the next verse. Instead, he has proclaimed the nation's final destruction. He says that *"the Jews would be a desolation,"* as they translate it; it means an arid place, from which the word "desert" comes. But in this passage it makes good sense to say *"the Jews would be a wasteland and a reproach among the nations."*

Earlier the Jews were a celebrated nation; God had dignified them with many extraordinary gifts so that in the eyes of every nation they excelled in dignity. Now he says they *"would be like a vast desert, or a collapsed ruin; and then they would be a reproach."* Not only would their reputation be well known, but he says that whoever passed through that land would be witnesses of its reproach. He pursues the matter more fully in the next verse.

16 *"And you will be a disgrace and a taunt, a reproof and a shock to the nations that are around you, while I am carrying out judgments against you in anger and fury, and in rebukes of fury. I Yahweh have spoken."*

He explains more fully how the Jews would be a wasteland and a reproach to the nations. Now he does not speak of a "wasteland" but uses two words in place of that one. He uses חרפה [*ḥerpâ*], which means "reproach"; he adds גדופה [*gᵉdûp̄â*], which means an "insult" and a "taunt." But these could be true only

141

because of the nation's destruction. Unless the profane nations had been given a cause, there would be no reason for them to spew insults and taunts against the Jews. Therefore this desolation and final destruction are included in the words *"disgrace and taunt,"* or insult. This sentence depends on the previous verse, where it was said, *"I will make you,"* and now, *"you will be."*

Moreover, the certain execution of God's vengeance is noted. When God casts disgrace on us, it necessarily follows that we lie under the power of his hand because we will try to fight back in vain. We will struggle, to be sure, as the reprobate do; but in the end the force of his power will break us unless we willingly fall back. Hence we must note that these go together: *"I will make you a reproach and you will be,"* because God means that his threats would not be empty or ineffective.

He adds, *"you will be a correction."* מוסר [*mûsār*] means discipline and instruction; but it often refers to a corrective example that comes from an awareness of God's wrath. When God castigates his own, they are said to progress under his discipline if they repent, because they learned that they sinned by the penalties that he inflicted. He says that the Jews *"would be a correction to the profane nations"* because they will learn at the Jews' expense. When we apply examples to our benefit the correction is timely, that is, when we do not wait until God strikes us. When he takes vengeance at a distance on the despisers of his law, if we are moved by such examples, that is a timely correction, as I said. Now the prophet attributes that correction to the nations — but not without shaming the elect people. He said in effect that the punishments would be so notable that even the blind would acknowledge them and tremble as they understood their meaning.

Next he adds, *"a shock."* That the Jews will be *"a shock and a correction"* does not seem to harmonize well. But the prophet does not simply mean that whoever considers the judgment of God would be shocked or teachable. Rather, he means that in God's severity both a cause of shock and an example would be set before everyone, so that they would be horrified when they see God act so harshly with his own elect people.

He also adds, *"when I carry out judgment against you in anger and fury, and in rebukes of anger."* He confirms what we saw before, that God's judgment would be extreme, because he had overlooked the reprobate people for so long. After patiently tolerating their wickedness, he finally broke forth in a single assault and at that time carried out the frightful judgment of which he spoke. This is why he says *"the nations will be shocked when I carry out judgments against you."* What kind of judgments? *"in anger, in fury, and in rebukes of fury."* It does seem that the prophet is verbose, but he could not be excessive in this matter since the people's madness was so great that no prophecy moved them.

As we saw before, there is no doubt that he had been scorned in Chaldaea by the Jews who still remained at home in their tranquil nests: "That miserable exile threatens us! Let him be content with his own kind. Since God has spared us, he seems to be seized by envy and desires to harass us. But we have no reason to fear the jealousy of a fugitive and captive."

Since the prophet knew that he was contemptible to the Judeans, it was necessary to pile up these expressions to give his teaching more weight, in regard not only to the Judeans but also to his own people who were dragged off in the same exile. He must be concerned about them for the reasons we explained before. Now we understand his intention when he speaks *"of anger and fury,"* and also adds *"rebukes of fury."*

He adds, *"I Yahweh have spoken,"* which he repeats in the last verse of the chapter. This confirmation was exceedingly useful because when both the Israelites and the Judeans saw in him a mortal and downcast man who was a captive and a slave of wicked people, they would undoubtedly despise all his prophecies. He therefore sets God before them to show that he was not the author of the threats but spoke only what God said, as an instrument of the Spirit, as we saw before. Next:

17 *"When I send* [or, 'shoot'; שלח *(šillaḥ)* means 'to send,' but here it is taken as 'shoot.' The context requires it] *the evil arrows of famine against them, which will be for destruction* [or, 'ruin'], *which I will shoot at them to destroy them. And I will add a famine against them, and I will break the staff of their bread."*

He illustrates a point that we have seen, but does not do so in the manner of rhetoricians who affect brilliance and adorn their speech. His single purpose was to penetrate the people's hearts, which were like stone or iron. This is why he uses such variety and adorns his teaching with various figures, and hence compares God to an archer who brandishes his arrows against them. He speaks metaphorically about God's arrows, for he says that *"they are arrows of famine,"* and he calls them *"evil,"* that is, lethal or deadly. Thus: *"when I brandish evil arrows against them, they will be for their destruction";* that is, they will not escape death because the shots will be deadly.

Someone might be wounded by the sting of an arrow and later recover; but God proclaims that the arrows he speaks of would be deadly, so that anyone struck would have no hope of recovery. Furthermore, we could interpret *"arrows of famine"* to mean a drought, as well as flies or locusts and other scourges of God. Now a blight, and then mildew withers a field; now rains make the wheat waste away, and then the heat burns it up. The arrows of God that pierce people's hearts with deadly wounds are as numerous as the pests and ravages of the crops.

If such a subtle exposition is not acceptable to someone, the issue is open; if one considers it more closely, however, one will confess that God shoots his arrows whenever he causes barrenness or deprives people of food.

He adds, *"which will be for destruction."* He confirms what we just said

143

was indicated by the epithet הרעים [hārā'îm]. He says that the arrows would be fatal, *"because they will be for perdition and ruin."* Further confirmation follows: *"which I will send,"* he says, *"against them to destroy them."* God clearly affirms that he would shoot those arrows. He repeats a second time in the same verse what we have just seen. We have suggested why the prophet used many words to emphasize a matter that is otherwise quite clear.

He adds, *"I will multiply the famine against them."* Here he indicates that he is armed with various weapons, so that if people think they have escaped, they will realize that God has other weapons hidden away that he has still not brought out. The word *to add* expresses what we saw before in the arrows. The prophet spoke of the arrows in the plural, but the wicked restrict God's power as much as they can. "If God wishes," they say, "he could certainly destroy the fields with continuous rain. He could also burn them up with excessive heat. If we escape frost, hail and storm, rain and drought, all will have gone well for us."

That is how the wicked harden themselves in their complacency. Why? Because they limit God's arrows to a specific and definite number. This is the reason why he says, *"I will add the famine against them";* that is, "When they think to themselves that the harvest is safe because they have evaded both drought and rains, blight, storm and hail, I will find," he says, "other ways unknown to them to force famine on them."

He expresses one way when he says that *"he will break the staff of bread";* we discussed this expression before. I do not subscribe to the judgment of those who say that the staff of bread is broken when God sends scarcity of wheat. Even in the greatest abundance the staff of bread is broken, as we pointed out before in Moses, when God takes away the intrinsic power of bread and causes it to vanish. "Man does not live by bread alone,"[1] but by the secret power that God confers on bread. We could eat four times as much bread as usual and still not be filled. The prophets often use this expression from Moses: "You will eat and not be filled," they say.[2] Thus the prophet repeats in this passage what we saw in the previous chapter, that God will break the staff of bread; that is, he takes away the power of bread so that those who have stuffed themselves still do not feel that they have received any new power. Next:

18   *"And I will send famine against you[a] and an evil beast* [or 'evil wild animal'] *and they will leave you[b] childless* [earlier he used the plural]: *plague and bloodshed will pass through you, and I will make a sword come against you. I Yahweh have spoken."*

---

1. Mg., Dt. 8:3.
2. Mg., Lv. 26:26; Is. 9:20; Ezk. 7:19; Ho. 4:10; Mi. 6:14.
a. *vos* — plural.
b. *te* — singular.

Here God speaks in general about several adverse events; *"I will send evil against them,"* he says. Immediately afterward he adds the kind of evil, about which he had not yet spoken. Under the name of evil he includes all adversities, as if saying it was in his power to enforce punishment on the wicked not only in one way or another; as the adversities which surround us and to which we are subjected are innumerable, so there is no limit to his vengeance, if people continue to provoke his wrath. This is the reason why he speaks in general terms about evil; but as we said, he does add the kind. He says, *"an evil wild animal will come on you and thus I will leave you childless."* Although only one kind of evil is mentioned, there is little doubt that God presented it as an example to make them realize that all punishments are in his hand.

But these punishments are countless. If we lift up our eyes, how many deaths hang over us? If we consider the earth, how many poisons are there? How many wild and savage beasts? And how many serpents? How many swords, pitfalls, stumbling blocks, precipices, collapsing houses, throwing of stones and spears? We cannot move one foot without ten deaths opposing us! But here God speaks only of wild beasts to indicate that they are ready at hand, as if he would carry out his judgments through them. Now we understand why Ezekiel mentioned the general type and then touched on one particular kind.

Finally he adds, *"I will leave them childless,"* or "I will deprive them"; that is, because he will take away children from their fathers and parents from their children. And not only through cruel and wild beasts but through other means as well. He repeats again, *"plague and bloodshed will pass through you."* He had not spoken about bloodshed, except in terms of the sword, which he repeats again; but he piles up, as we said, various expressions so that those who were excessively slow and willfully repulsed all awareness of God's vengeance might finally be aroused. Therefore he says *"both plague and bloodshed will pass through you."*

Then he says, *"I will bring a sword on you."* When he spoke about blood, he certainly meant a sword; but as we have said, it was incapable of making both the Israelites and the Judeans tremble immediately at such threats. It was consequently necessary to drive home in many ways what was sufficiently clear and easy in itself. What he repeats is pertinent here (he had already mentioned it before): *"I Yahweh have spoken."* Ezekiel turns the Israelites and Judeans away from considering himself and shows that he was not the author of the threats but faithfully passed on what he received from God's hand and was ordered to present to them.

Almighty God, since we are so slow and dull, grant that we may yet awake in time to your threats and submit ourselves to your power, lest we experience by our destruction how frightful is that

145

power. May we progress under your rod of fatherly chastisement, and may we so repent as to strive for steadfast zeal and meditate on true repentance during the whole course of our life. And having put off the vices and filth of our flesh, may we be reformed in true purity, until at last we come to that communion in heavenly glory which is kept for us in Christ Jesus our Lord. Amen.

Lecture 16

CHAPTER 6

1 *And the word of Yahweh was to me, saying,*
2 *"Son of man, set your face to* [or, 'against'] *the mountains of Israel, and prophesy to them;*
3 *And say, 'Mountains of Israel, hear the word of Sovereign Yahweh. Thus says Sovereign Yahweh to the mountains and hills, to the streams* [some translate it "torrents," others "waterfalls," and others, "cliffs"] *and valleys. Behold, I bring a sword against you, and I will destroy your high places.' "*

Now the prophet turns to the kingdom of Israel, since before he had spoken only of the Judeans. He says that *"he was sent by God to the mountains of Israel."* First, the question of time could be raised, for the kingdom of Israel was cut off at that time, and the ten tribes had been dragged into exile. That kingdom had ceased by Ezekiel's time. The time sequence does not seem to fit, since the prophet proclaims as future what happened many years before. But it is not absurd to say that it is part prophecy and part teaching so that the Israelites would understand why they had been deprived of their homeland and scattered among the nations.

I am saying that God's plan had been explained in part to the exiles to ensure they knew why God had driven them into distant lands. The punishment would not have benefited them if they had not also been admonished about the cause. Furthermore, although the kingdom had collapsed, it is a likely conjecture that many remained behind. The Assyrian did not lead away all those many thousands, and his management would have been taxed by such a multitude. Doubtless he gathered the flower of the people and allowed the

147

common folk to remain there. Moreover, he sent people from his own kingdom to inhabit the deserted land.

But the change was massive, and injurious to the king himself, and also troublesome to everyone in common. The kingdom was no more, and the name "Israel" was almost extinct because there was no community of people and they dwelt in their homeland as foreigners and guests; however, a multitude still remained. Now we understand from the prophet's words their obstinacy, because they were not moved by the exile of their brothers or their own calamity to abandon their superstition and embrace again the true and pure worship of God.

Since rebuke did not benefit them, the prophet was ordered to prophesy *"against them."* We gather from the first chapter[1] that Ezekiel accepted this mandate after the destruction of the kingdom of Israel, for he said that God raised him up in the thirtieth year, that is, after the Jubilee and in the fifth year of the captivity of Jechoniah or Joachim.

Therefore it is clear that after the ten tribes had been scattered, the prophet spoke against the land of Israel. From this it is easy to deduce again that many of the people were still there, because it would have been difficult for the Assyrians to receive all the exiles. But all who remained in the homeland continued in their abominations, so that it was necessary to proclaim another judgment against them. We will look at that judgment next.

Now then this principle remains: the prophet speaks about the destruction of the kingdom of Israel in predicting for a time yet to come what those left in the homeland feared not at all. They were persuaded that they were finished with all dangers. The prophet shows, however, that God's vengeance was not yet complete; whatever evils they had endured were merely a prelude, and heavier penalties awaited them because they had become so hardened against God's hand. The prophecy had greater forcefulness when the prophet spoke to the mountains themselves than if he directed his speech to the people.

Ezekiel is not ordered to exhort the Israelites to repent or to threaten them with the punishment that still remained; he is ordered to direct his speech *" 'to the hills and mountains and valleys.' "* God is indirectly showing that the Israelites are first deaf and then unworthy of the effort that Ezekiel would expend in teaching them.

In the same way, the prophet who was sent to Jeroboam[2] did not condescend to address him but spoke to the altar itself: "Altar, altar," he says "thus says the Lord, 'Behold, a son of the house of David will be born, whose name shall be Josiah, and he will slaughter upon you the priests of the high places, burn the bones of the dead, etc.' " The king was burning incense on the altar.

1. Mg., 1:1-2.
2. Mg., 1 Ki. 13:2.

The prophet did not look at him, but, as I said, directed his speech to the altar; that was far more forceful than if he had sharply upbraided the king. It was no ordinary rebuke to overlook the king, as if he were merely a human shadow, and to admonish the dead altar about the coming event. It is the same in this passage, *"Son of man, set your face against the mountains and be a prophet, or prophesy, to them."* The prophet could object that this was ridiculous, for mountains have no ears. But he understood God's design and so he calmly obeyed. He saw that the people were condemned and rejected by God because they were deaf and even incurable.

Meanwhile, he knew that his efforts would not be useless, although he was addressing the mountains. We know that the earth was created for human benefit. God gives us examples of his wrath in the wild animals and trees, in the air itself and the heavens, to ensure we know that admonitions which pertain to us are engraved there, even though he turns his eyes and face elsewhere.

It is therefore a sign of the Lord's indignation that he shows his judgments above and below but is silent toward us. We gather from this that we are unworthy of the effort he expends to instruct us. This is undoubtedly the prophet's thinking.

A clearer expression follows in the third verse: *"You will say, 'Mountains of Israel, hear the word of Yahweh.'"* Here the mountains are required to listen, which they cannot do; but this is done for human benefit, as I recently mentioned. God demands to be heard by the mountains to make people realize that an inanimate thing would be somehow furnished with understanding compared with their senselessness.

In the end, God carried out his judgments against the mountains of Israel. Even though they could not hear the prophet speak to them, they received his teaching because it was effective in them, and in the end God proved by events themselves that he did not speak in vain. Thus events themselves made it well known that the mountains were somehow attentive, for they could not escape the judgment he openly pronounced.

He continues, *"'thus says Yahweh to the mountains and the hills.'"* But Ezekiel does not address only the mountains, as he was ordered. He seems to exceed his prescribed mandate, for he was sent only to the mountains and hills. But now he says, *"'listen, mountains; listen, hills; listen valleys.'"* We said yesterday, however, that sometimes the prophets speak more briefly and sometimes explain with more words what they had briefly touched on. At the beginning God spoke only of the mountains, but no doubt he included valleys and waterfalls, because the prophet was only explaining what he had said in one word.

Thus, *"'he speaks to the mountains and hills and then to the waterfalls or torrents.'"* Jerome translates this as "cliffs,"[3] and whatever is violent they

3. Vulgate.

149

call אפיק [*ʾāp̄îq*]. When there is a violent course they use אפיק [*ʾāp̄îq*]; and thus we can understand this passage as either "cliffs" or "waterfalls" or "torrents." It is not of great importance. But since he adds valleys, to me the most likely exposition understands the prophet to mean torrents or waterfalls.

Now we must note that he designates the regions where the Israelites erected perverse and adulterous forms of worship. We know that mountains are associated with superstitions, and the same is true for valleys but for a different reason. When they erected their altars in the mountains, they thought they were close to God; but when they descended to the valleys, religion there was shadowy and obscure. They thought that in this way they were hidden as in a shrine. It is enough to note that their idolatries were carried out on the mountains and in the valleys. In this way the prophet shows that the entire land of Israel was polluted by iniquities.

" 'Behold,' " he says, " 'I am bringing a sword against you.' " We gather from this that when the prophet addressed the mountains he did so for the people's benefit, for a sword could not harm mountains in any way. One stone will break a hundred and a thousand swords, and still be in one piece. Did God threaten the mountains' destruction in vain? Not at all! When a sword is mentioned, we know that death is understood, for the cause stands for the effect. God indirectly addresses the people; but when he directs his words to the mountains, he shows that the people themselves were deaf, and therefore he turns his face away from them and speaks to dumb elements and lifeless objects.

" 'And I will destroy,' " he says, " 'your high places.' " Now he explains what I taught earlier, that the mountains and hills and valleys and waterfalls are named because that is where perverse and impure forms of worship flourished. Undoubtedly by " 'high places' " the Spirit signifies whatever the Israelites had concocted out of their imaginations to corrupt the worship of God. Properly speaking, they call " 'high places' " the altars that were erected in lofty and elevated places. But here the specific stands for the general.

At the same time, God indicates that he so abhors all contrived worship that he cannot bear the sight of such places. We know that the stones of which the altars were constructed were innocent. Moreover, places do not will to be defiled by idolatry, for inasmuch as the world has been created by God, it always retains its own nature. But those places were defiled by their human associations, and the contagion renders them hateful to God. Therefore this was put as a condemnation of idolatry. Now follows:

4 " 'And your altars will be abandoned, and your idols shattered, and I will make the slain fall* [or, "I will throw them down"] *before your idols.' "

He pursues the same line of thought and proclaims first that the altars would be reduced to nothing. This makes it apparent how much obedience pleases God and how true is its superiority to any sacrifice.[4] There is no doubt the Israelites greatly extolled their images as if they were worshiping God aright. At first Jeroboam astutely concocted those new rites in order to alienate the ten tribes from the family of David.[5] But in the end error became so strong that they assumed God approved of their wicked forms of worship. But we see that God abhors them.

We must always uphold the principle that however much people think that they are obeying God when they impose their own inventions, they accomplish nothing except to provoke God's wrath against themselves. This judgment against the altars would not have arisen if God had not been gravely offended by that unholy mixture.

Therefore, " 'your altars will come to devastation and desolation' "; and then, " 'your idols will be shattered.' " Some translate this as "idols of the sun," because the word is derived from "heat," which is repeated later. But that conjecture seems too forced. I have no doubt they are called idols because of the frenzied love that seized the superstitious people. Throughout the prophets the people are said to be like adulterers, and our prophet frequently speaks this way. Therefore it suits best that they are called idols from "burning," because superstitious worshipers burned with love for them, just as adulterers run after harlots, as we will see again.

Another word is used next when he says, " 'I will throw down your slain before your idols.' " They call idols גלולים [gillûlîm] because of their filth, as if they said "dung." Thus we see that first the prophet condemns the frenzy with which the Israelites burned when they perverted the pure and legitimate worship of God, and second their disgrace is rebuked because they involved themselves in sordid acts, as in dung.

Furthermore, we are taught how strongly God rages against all superstitions when he not only cites the agents themselves before his tribunal for profaning true piety but is angered by their apparatus — stones and wood. In a manner he links the apparatus of idolatry with their makers. Next:

5 " 'And I will put the corpses of the sons of Israel before your idols, and I will scatter before their [it is a third-person relative] idols; I will scatter your bones [he returns to the second person] around your altars.' "

The prophet uses these words to indicate that God's vengeance will be manifest, because he will mark it with clear signs by which one could judge that the Israelites had provoked God's wrath by turning away from the genuine and pure pattern of the law. Therefore he says, " 'I will put the corpses of the

4. Mg., 1 Sa. 15:22.
5. Mg., 1 Ki. 12, i.e., 12:27-28.

sons of Israel before their idols.' " When corpses were mixed with the idols it is obvious that God was gravely offended. We know that it was detestable in all sacrifices to add human bones or corpses to the victims. Thus the Israelites' religion was openly condemned in this sign. Unless they were completely blind, they could recognize that their worship was wholly abominable.

Thus we understand God's intention when he says that " *'he will cast the corpses of the sons of Israel before their idols'* "; in effect he said, "I shall defile all the forms of worship that seem holy to you; and I will make them smell even among unbelievers." Why? An altar is defiled by contact with a corpse. Yet corpses will be cast forth so that the contagion reaches every altar.

" *'And I will scatter,'* " he says, " *'your bones around your altars.'* " Finally, he indicates that he will profane with their corpses the sacred things that the Israelites fabricated for themselves. This means that their shame would be doubled because they will defile what they considered beautiful. The prophets persistently claimed that these were foolish and abominable, but meantime those accustomed to these superstitions were satisfied with them. Since God's servants accomplished nothing by these sacred warnings, actual tangible proof occurred when the altars were defiled with their own stench. God's remarkable judgment was visible in this event, as we said before. Next:

6 " *'In all your dwelling places* [that is, "in every habitable region"], *cities will be abandoned* [or, "will be deserted"; we have spoken about this word]; *and the high places will be reduced to devastation, so that your altars may be devastated and abandoned* [or, "be destroyed," "perish"]; *and your idols shattered and be no more* [or, "be abolished"]; *and your idols* [again it is the word derived from "heat"] *cut down, and your works destroyed.'* "

The prophet now indicates with different words that God will take vengeance on the ten tribes for all their superstitions. It is clear from this that no corner was free from corruption. In naming all the abominations, he indicates that they defiled every inhabited place. Where they lived, they erected their altars and foreign cults, as another prophet rebuked them: "Your gods are as numerous as your cities."[6]

True, Jeremiah was addressing the Judeans in that passage, but the meaning is the same. The prophet indicates that not merely some part has been defiled by idolatry, but that filth had spread through the whole land, wherever there were any inhabitants. " *'In all your dwelling places the cities will be deserted.'* " When he threatens the cities with destruction and devastation, he indicates, as I have already said, that those places had been corrupted by wicked superstitions.

He adds, " *'and your high places will be destroyed,'* " or abandoned.

6. Mg., Je. 2:28; 11:13.

Here he explains himself more clearly; that is, the cities must be reduced to nothing because religion had been corrupted and the inhabitants had turned aside to their inventions and idolatries. He links the high places with the cities to designate the reason why the cities would be destroyed.

He adds, " 'that they may be abandoned,' " or reduced to wasteland (again it is the word חרב [*ḥāraḇ*]), " 'and your altars may perish.' " He confirms the same teaching; that is, he was so disturbed by the cities of Israel because all were defiled by profane and foreign altars. God had selected that land for himself, as we said, and in this sense all the cities were dedicated to his glory. This could make us wonder why he would threaten them with devastation. One could easily protest that God had changed his plan. But the prophet shows that although the cities in themselves were pleasing to God, they were an offense because of the corruptions with which they were contaminated.

He mentions altars and high places together, and from this we can plausibly conjecture that the Israelites did not sacrifice wherever the high places were erected. They had their high places where they worshiped false gods, but they also had altars elsewhere. Furthermore, because the worship of God was corrupted in both places, the prophet put the two together, as I said.

Finally, he adds, " 'and your idols will be shattered and be no more,' " or be abolished. Again he uses that shameful word (we have already discussed it) which was taken from the smell of dung. In this way he indicates God's abhorrence of what is highest in human eyes,[7] especially when he is worshiped falsely.

" 'And your idols will be cut down,' " he says. I said that the word "idol" was taken from "heat." He thus indicates that the idols were the cause of their insanity, since the Israelites were so seized by frenzied love as to abandon God and look only to idols. But he compares the raging zeal of the idolators to impure and brute passion.

Finally, he adds, " 'your works may be destroyed.' " He uses this general word and designates a significant distinction between the pure worship of God and all corruptions. A long disquisition is not needed if we wish to understand how God should be worshiped, for he rejects and excludes our works. If we do not inject our own works but follow only what God commands, worship will be pure. If we add something of our own, however, it is an abomination.

Thus we see that useful teaching can be gathered from this one phrase, namely, that when people inject something of their own, all their worship is perverted and condemned by God. By "works" he does not mean only idols fabricated out of wood, stone, and bronze, or gold and silver; but he includes equally whatever human beings concoct and whatever can be ascribed to them, in their failure to derive it from the mouth of God and the prescriptions of the law. Next:

7. Mg., Lk. 16:1, i.e., 16:15.

7   *" 'And the slain will fall in your midst, and you will know that I am Yahweh.' "*

Here the prophet appends a brief line to the earlier threats, that God will consume the entire people by destruction to force them to recognize that he is Yahweh. *" 'The slain will fall in your midst' ";* that is, enemies will come to bring destruction everywhere throughout the land. But his saying that *" 'he is Yahweh' "* is related to the prophecy. The Israelites did not simply deny God; because they did not have confidence in the prophet's words, God appears and confirms or establishes the authority of the prophet's teaching by showing that he would be their judge if the teaching is rejected — as we know it was. He develops this more clearly a little later. Now follows:

8   *" 'And I will make remnants* [it is a single word: "I-will-make-a-remnant"] *so that there be for you some who escape the sword among the nations, when you are scattered throughout the lands.' "*

Here an important promise is added to temper the harshness of such a sad prophecy. Up to this point God is showing that he burns with indignation against the land of Israel; he decided to destroy it because it was defiled on all sides and in every corner. There was nothing to hope for if Ezekiel had spoken so absolutely. Therefore a promise of moderation is added: *" 'I will make,' "* he says, *" 'some remnant so that there be for you* (that is, "that there may be some of you surviving") *who escape the sword.' "* But how? God does not simply promise a pardon that would leave the Israelites at rest and unharmed. He says that exile would be their salvation. We conclude from this that they were so depraved that they could not be pardoned, because God saw that they despised and even rejected his patience. Although he gave some hope of grace to the Israelites, he also warns them that they could not attain salvation except through a kind of death, that is, through exile.

He says, *" 'I will make remnants out of you who may escape the sword.' "* How? Will the enemy spare them so that they do not have to move to another land? But he says, *" 'when you are scattered among the nations.' "* He promises life to them, but a miserable life, because it will be a life of exile. Furthermore, God's grace could still not be recognized from these words, if he did not add what immediately follows:

9   *" 'And those of you who have escaped will remember me among the nations, among whom they will be captives there* [the adverb of place is superfluous]; *because I am broken by their heart that fornicates* [or, "has fornicated," that is, "their heart that burned for adultery"], *which departed from me; and by their eyes playing the harlot* [or, "lusting"] *after their idols.*

And they will be ashamed before their face for the evils that they committed in all their abominations. [I see that I cannot finish; I think the clock is incorrect.]' "

Almighty God, since you have desired an abiding memory of the signal judgments you once wrought on your people, grant us today to keep ourselves to your pure worship. Grant, I say, that we may present ourselves teachable to you and never seek to adulterate your worship with our inventions. And because you have clearly disclosed your will to us through your only-begotten Son, may we abide in his obedience, and so call on you as Father in his name, as long as we sojourn in this world, until at last we arrive at that blessed inheritance which is kept for us in heaven, through the same, our Lord. Amen.

Lecture 17

In the last lecture I merely read the ninth verse: I did not explain it. The Lord says that " *'after he made a remnant of some part of Israel,'* " some good was to be hoped for from their castigation. " *'Then,'* " he says, " *'those who remain will remember me.'* " With these words he criticizes indirectly the sluggishness of the ten tribes because they could never be brought to any sense of God's wrath except by actual experience. There is an antithesis between remembrance and forgetfulness. When he says that they will remember after they have been afflicted, he means that in their prosperity and tranquillity they were immersed in neglect and contempt.

Let us therefore learn that the scourges of God are more useful to us, because when God indulges us, we abuse his clemency and flatter ourselves and so grow hardened in sin. It is essential, let alone useful, to castigate those who are so self-satisfied in their vices. Although the Lord can recall us to himself by other means, yet as our feebleness persists, we will sleep in our sins until his castigations bring us back to the way.

Furthermore, we should also note that repentance was not granted to everyone castigated by God's hand. The prophet does not speak generally but designates the survivors or those who were saved. פליטיכם [*pᵉlîṭêkem*], he says, that is, those of you who were saved. But that was a small portion, as we have seen. If a distinction is sought between the few allowed to escape and the rest of the multitude who were destroyed, none can be found except that it pleased God to preserve a seed. All deserved to be destroyed; he almost consumed the entire body of people. He wanted to save a small number.

Hence we see that the salvation of those whom the prophet now describes flowed from the mercy of God alone. Furthermore, what I have said must be remembered: only those repented to whom it was granted. From this it follows

156

that repentance is uniquely the gift of God. We see that many fall lower, even rage madly against God when he castigates them. First they murmur, then they agitate, and finally they rush into unbridled madness, prepared even to wage war on God if they could reach as far as heaven.

Although scourgings are common to reprobate and elect alike, some continue to rage increasingly against God; it follows that repentance is not granted to everyone when God admonishes them, cites them before his tribunal, and demands punishment for their sins to make them vexed with themselves. This is why the prophet restricts this promise to those of all the people who were saved. He said they would be saved because the Lord did not want the entire church to be extinguished; otherwise the covenant, which ought to be perpetual and inviolable, would be abolished.

He says, " 'among the nations' " among whom or where " 'they were captives.' " The prophet indicates that exile would benefit the Israelites, because as long as God allowed them to occupy the holy land, they deliberately provoked him. Since they defiled the worship of God in the holy land, they had to be banished far away. The prophet indicates this when he says " 'among the nations where they were captives' "; then they would return to a sound mind, even though they had been stubborn while in the region dedicated to God.

Next: " 'he was broken, or crushed, by their heart.' " The words could be interpreted two ways. The first is that God was finally overcome by their malice after learning from experience that he was accomplishing nothing by patiently bearing with them. When he sees that his grace is mocked, he burns with ever greater anger — and rightly so. It is appropriate to explain the passage, that " 'God was broken by the Israelites' promiscuous heart,' " this way: although God allowed them to sin with impunity for a long time, when he finally saw that they would not stop, he came to the point of punishing them — in effect overcome by their stubbornness.

But we can also refer this to pardon. That is, they would recognize that God was broken by their heart because he wished to forgive them. A person who voluntarily forgives injustices is said to be broken, as many are sympathetic and merciful who freely pardon their enemies even the gravest offenses. This exposition fits quite well, too, because a sinner cannot truly contemplate God without experiencing some taste of his goodness and hoping that God would be propitious to him.

But the first interpretation seems to fit better. When they are dragged into exile the Israelites will begin to take to heart that just punishments are meted out to them, because God had patiently sustained them and had not immediately dealt with them with utmost rigor. But finally he was compelled to descend to take up punishments after he had been ground down or broken by their hopeless evil. Now we understand the prophet's meaning.

157

We also gather from this that those who seriously repent do not merely acknowledge their faults, but also contemplate how many ways and how long a time they have provoked God's wrath with their stubbornness. The prophet expresses this with the word " *'broken.'* " God did not deal this harshly with the Israelites as soon as he was offended by their sins but in the end was broken by their harshness.

He says, " *'because of their promiscuous heart that departed from me, and by their eyes promiscuously whoring after their idols.'* " This image occurs throughout the prophets, and because I have explained it often, I now mention it briefly. The superstitious are said to play the harlot with their idols so that all idolatry is rendered more detestable. Those who adulterate the worship of God with their own inventions nevertheless think they exhibit acceptable obedience. Since the blind and unbelieving are so self-satisfied in their corruptions, Scripture compares them to adulterers.

The word "devotion" is praised so much among the papists today that it buries all light of sound teaching. With this one word they reject whatever is presented from the law and the gospel; it is the same with what they call "good intentions." Since unbelievers are so drunk with their own inventions, God correctly calls them harlots and says that all who abandon the pure rule of the law contaminate themselves with lust. At the same time, as has often been said, the prophets allude to the sacred and spiritual marriage by which God binds his church to himself. Chastity of soul is the pure worship of God.

When people forsake that sincerity, they are like a woman abandoning her husband and turning to any adulterer who comes along. Now to express this mad desire more forcefully, the prophet gives the heart eyes. These words indicate a raging desire, because they were not only drawn to their idols with their whole heart but were also attracted to them with their eyes — as if the eyes were torches to inflame the soul. He continues his image, in that harlots kindle the flames of desire by their wandering glances, and so their hearts are enflamed. This is the reason he says " *'they were adulterous in heart and eyes.'* "

Next he adds, " *'and they will be ashamed,* or downcast, *in their faces'* "; that is, "shame will come over their face." Others translate it, "they will be nauseated"; but that translation seems harsh. But because קוט [*qût*] means "to refuse," those who use the word "abhor" have faithfully rendered the prophet's meaning. Thus, " *'they will abhor themselves,'* " he says. Those who translate it "downcast" take the word in a metaphorical sense; that is, those who harbor so much shame that they scarcely dare look at the sky and others are said to be "downcast." But others translate it, "they will quarrel, or contend, before their own eyes." Because that meaning is quite rare, I dare not subscribe to their judgment, primarily since the earlier interpretation — "they will abhor themselves" — fits so well.

" *'They shall be rejected in their own sight'* "; that is, they will not wait until people condemn them or others rebuke their perverted worship. They will detest themselves on their own. The prophet now shows that it would be a genuine repentance. It can happen that someone senses that he is dealing with God but still not be humbled — just as Cain was forced to tremble at the sight of God but never changed.[1] It is common for the same thing to happen to all the reprobate. To acknowledge God's judgment is part of repentance, but only half. Therefore to show that the Israelites would remember God in a beneficial way when they were struck by his hand, the prophet adds that they would abhor themselves. This displeasure is the second part of repentance.

He says, " *'for the evils that they committed in all their abominations.'* " The prophet describes more clearly that the veil which covered the Israelites' eyes for so long would be removed when they confronted God. Impunity makes people connive at their sins, as if there were a veil over their eyes; and they imagine that what God both repudiates and detests is splendid. But when God inflicts punishments and extorts this realization from the wretched, so that they no longer turn darkness into light and light into darkness, then they begin to be displeased with themselves. Now follows:

10 " *'And they will know that I Yahweh have not spoken in vain toward doing this evil to them* [that is, "to inflicting this evil," or "this destruction," or "punishment." Here evil does not mean unjust violence, but merely adversity].' "

Now he mentions the fruit of repentance, that the Israelites finally will begin to honor the prophets properly. We know they boldly mocked the prophets when they threatened them. Because it was customary for them to demean all of God's servants and in a way reduce his truth to nothing, the prophet says that when God punishes them they will realize that God had not spoken in vain.

When they scorned those threats, they did not think they should be considered in contempt of God. Attentive only to human beings, when they heard Jeremiah or Ezekiel they assumed they were dealing only with them and were acting with impunity against mere mortals. In opposition to this, God testifies that he is the primary author of what the prophets said. As error is born of error, people rejected in pride whatever the prophets said, since they determined that all of it was frivolous and meaningless.

God says, however, " *'they will know at that time that I have not spoken in vain, that is, that I would inflict this evil on them.'* " This knowledge that arises from extreme displeasure is most useful. I said it is the fruit of repen-

1. Mg., Ge. 4:9.

tance; but when unhappy people remember their ingratitude, it also helps to humble themselves in earnest before God. Then they realize what did not enter their minds before, that God is truthful both in threats and promises. Hence it even happens that they reverently embrace his Word, which they had treated contemptuously.

He proclaimed earlier the same thing about the reprobate, when we said that they experience God's hand without any benefit. But because he is now speaking about those few whose conversion he praised earlier, he undoubtedly includes the fear of God under their recognition or awareness of him. If all God's threats had been buried, the people could not be considered to have returned to the way. Their conversion would have no validity before God. We know that contempt, which is the issue here, is always sacrilegious. For a sinner to subject himself to God in sincerity, he must recognize how unworthily and shamefully he earlier repudiated or neglected God's Word.

At the same time the prophet reviles the arrogance of those who rashly condemned the teaching of all God's servants, when he says that " 'they will realize,' " or they will come to know, " 'that I Yahweh have not spoken in vain.' " When the prophet portrays for us their belated repentance, let us learn in time to tremble at God's threats. Although God is not yet executing his judgment against us, let us realize that he does not speak in vain, and let us fear as soon as he shows some sign of his indignation.

God testifies to the Israelites that he would be propitious, although their repentance was late. But as for ourselves, let us be forearmed (as I just warned), and as soon as God unveils his threats, let us treat them as ready for execution. There follows:

11 *Thus says Sovereign Yahweh, "Strike with your hand* [that is, 'clap with your hands'] *and spread your feet* [or, 'extend'; literally, 'extend in your foot'] *and say, 'Woe* [or, "Alas"] *to all the evil abominations of the house of Israel, because they will fall by sword, famine, and pestilence.' "*

He confirms what we saw before about the destruction of the ten tribes. The kingdom of Israel had already been overthrown, but those who remained in the homeland assumed they were finished with everything and prostrated themselves increasingly before their idols. It was consequently necessary to pronounce complete destruction on them. But because words moved them so little, God adds a sign. This is the way he usually deals with refractory spirits. He orders the prophet to show that the land is cursed by clapping his hands and spreading his legs and feet.

" 'Spread your feet.' " This is what people customarily do when they make a serious pronouncement, or burn with indignation. They extend their legs in opposite directions. I have rendered it in one word: *"spread (your feet)."*

Clapping hands has the same import. God wanted to confirm his Word with this gesture, not for the prophet's sake but on account of the obstinacy of those who were deaf to every word, as we have said. We can tell from this how great was the stupor of the people who remained secure and continued to pursue their own desires even when God thundered from heaven. When God inflicts terror on people and they do nothing but ridicule him, it is monstrous. We see, however, that it is an ancient illness. If only we did not experience today what Ezekiel experienced then!

Finally, he was in effect ordered to lead the Israelites to the present issue. Since he was ordered to cry out, " 'Alas, or "woe," *on all the abominations of the house of Israel,' "* the gesture as well as the exclamation undoubtedly ought to have been effective. Moreover, the reason is added, " *'because all will perish by the sword, famine, and pestilence.' "*

We have said that these three kinds of punishments are everywhere advanced. It is not that God prosecutes those who condemn his law only with pestilence, sword, and famine, but because this way is more notable and common. God has countless hidden ways of exacting punishment from transgressors. But since these scourges, as I said, are more customary, the prophets mention them more often.

The point is that destruction of the kingdom of Israel — which they never imagined would happen — was at hand; God avenges the sins of that people not only with war but also pestilence and famine. Meanwhile, he includes other punishments by synecdoche. We know how many miseries war brings! Once people begin to take up arms, the door is wide open to robberies and seizures, burnings, killings, rapes, and all kinds of violence. In the end humanity and equity are buried in war. As far as famine is concerned, we know that it makes people almost mad. In pestilence a married man deserts his wife; every home is dismal; loss of parents afflicts one home, and loss of spouse another.

Since these scourges of God bring unending misery, it is not surprising if the prophets briefly speak only of war, pestilence, and famine when they indicate that those who have provoked God too long would be destroyed. Now a clearer exposition follows:

12 " *'He who is far off will die of pestilence, and he who is near will fall by the sword* [others translate it, "will fall on a sword," but too harshly. In the previous verse the prophet used the same word in a different sense. So I change nothing: "He who is near will fall by the sword"]; *and he who is left behind and besieged will die of famine. And I will fulfill my indignation* [or, "fury"] *against them.' "*

Now the prophet explains how all the Israelites are to be destroyed by famine, sword, and pestilence. " *'Those who will be far away will die of* *pestilence.' "*That is, after thinking themselves so well secluded in their hiding places that no danger or trouble hung over them, they will die by pestilence. Having been dragged off into distant exile, they thought they were at least removed from all trouble. But pestilence, he says, will move against them although the sword has stopped. Then those who are near, that is, those who remain at home, will be consumed by the sword. Those who were left behind, or besieged and confined, will die by famine.

In this way he confirms what we saw before, that there would be no reason why the Israelites should sleep in their sins when God spared them; if they do not all perish by the sword, God has other means of punishment. He holds pestilence and famine in his hand to destroy those who are far away, because pestilence pursues them wherever they are. Those who remain will perish even in the midst of peace because God will consume them with famine and starvation.

Finally he adds, " *'I will fulfill my fury against them.' "*With these words God indicates that hitherto he tolerated that wicked people; even if at times he seemed to be very strict, he still did not punish their sins as justice demanded. God therefore reproves them because up to now he tolerated them, and although now and then he cracked the whip, he had not been a rigorous judge. Instead he admonished them in a fatherly manner to return to the way. Since God's tolerance had been so stubbornly abused, he proclaims that his final action is at hand. That is why he speaks about " *'the fulfillment of his fury.' "*In this way the prophet clears God of all ill-will, to prevent the Israelites from accusing him of cruelty. Then he indicates that whatever evil they endured was merely a prelude to the horrible destruction that threatened them and that they still scorned. Next:

13   " *'And you will know that I am Yahweh when their wounded* [or, "slain"] *in the midst of their idols* [there is a change of person, but it does not obscure the meaning], *around their altars, on every high hill, on the heads* [that is, "peaks"] *of every mountain, and under every leafy tree, and under every thick oak* [others translate it "elm," but it is all the same], *in the place where they offered incense of pleasing fragrance to all of their idols.' "*

Now he proclaims again that they will come to know what they so long neglected. But here he seems to indicate a different kind of knowledge from that above. Earlier he said that they would remember and acknowledge with shame that the prophets had not predicted destruction in vain. But here he mentions no such thing but only the experiential knowledge that is common to the reprobate. This teaching certainly seems carelessly extended to the whole multitude. Although the majority did not benefit at all, they all realized that God was the judge; the demonstration of his vengeance was so clear and

162

obvious that they were forced, whether they wished or not, to admit that they were justly punished.

Let us realize, then, that the prophet takes what this verse says, " *'then you will know, etc.,'* " quite broadly, because he addresses all the Israelites without exception, even those about to perish. We said, however, that the knowledge was the kind that merely frightened but did not humble them. What follows certainly shows that God's vengeance is terrible: " *'when their slain will be,'* " that is, will lie, " *'before their idols.'* " We said that when God subjected the false gods to such ridicule, his vengeance could be more clearly recognized.

The prophet uses a word of reproach when he speaks of the idols, as we said before. The people fell before their idols, under whose trust and protection they assumed they would always be safe, and in this way the idols themselves came under condemnation. Hence God's vengeance is more visible. This is the reason, as I have mentioned elsewhere, why the prophet described these circumstances. What comes next pertains to the same point: " *'around all their altars.'* " Every altar was profaned when it was defiled by contact with dead bodies and sprinkled with human blood.

Furthermore, he describes the places where they worshiped false gods. We said that they sought out high places; here he puts " *'high hills,'* " and then " *'mountain peaks.'* " But the idolators accumulated numerous different games, and so when they had had enough of their high places, they turned to shadowy valleys. They also had their altars under trees where they offered incense. Hence the prophet proclaims that God would condemn every place to shame.

When he says that " *'the incense was of a pleasing odor,'* " there is undoubtedly antithesis, because to God that incense was foul. This is like a shameless woman whose desire to please her lover makes her husband angry. In the same way God quietly complains that he was provoked by that odor with which the Israelites wished, or desired, to gratify their idols.

Almighty God, today you not only present us with ancient examples of your wrath to keep us within your pure and perfect worship, but also have so clearly disclosed yourself to us through your only-begotten Son that we cannot err unless we are wholly senseless. Therefore grant, I say, that we may always be not only teachable and compliant but also attentive to the teaching contained in your gospel, so that we may be directed by its perfect light until at last we attain to the full and complete communion of the sun of righteousness, Christ your Son. Amen.

Lecture 18

14 " *'And I will stretch forth my hand over them, and I will make the land a wilderness and a waste* [or, "astonishment," for as we saw before, שמה (šammâ) also means that] *worse than the desert of Diblathah, in all their dwelling places. And they will know that I am Yahweh.' "*

Ezekiel pursues the same theme, but he was obliged to persist in confirming the prophecy with more words, for otherwise the prophecy would be difficult to believe, especially among people so secure and hardened against God by long-standing custom. This is why he uses many words to express something that is quite clear in itself.

Now he speaks about " *'God's stretching forth his hand,' "* a very familiar way of speaking in Scripture. God is said to extend his hand when he puts forth clear examples of his vengeance. The metaphor is taken from human beings who, wanting to undertake something great, stretch forth their arm. We know that God accomplishes all things with only a nod, but because of our dullness we do not comprehend his judgment. To cater to our backwardness, Scripture represents God's hand as stretched forth.

Then he says that " *'he will make the land into a wilderness and an astonishment.' "* These are two different words, שממה [šᵉmāmâ] and שמה [šammâ], but they come from the same root. שמם [šāmam] means to "destroy" and "lay waste"; it also means "to astonish." Hence some interpret it quite properly as "I will make the land into a wilderness and an astonishment." But because the comparison to a desert follows immediately, I readily subscribe to the opinion of those who translate it as "desolation" or "solitude," and "dereliction" or "wilderness." Although these two words are synonymous, as they say, the prophet does not needlessly join "abandoned" or "solitary" to

164

"wilderness"; he often asserts something more than once, not to explain it but to confirm what he knew would otherwise carry little weight with the Israelites.

Some translate the next phrase as "from the desert as far as Diblathah." There are also some who think that Riblatha should be read for Diblathah; and it could have happened that an error crept in because of the similarity between ד [d] and ר [r]. But I conclude that nothing ought to be changed. I also repudiate an interpretation that is completely absurd: "from the desert as far as Diblathah or Riblatha." Instead, the מ [m] indicates a comparison: " 'the land of Israel will be reduced to a wilderness worse than the desert of Diblathah.' " Why would the prophet say "from the desert as far as Diblathah"? He threatens the land of Israel, but Diblathah was in Syria outside the kingdom of Israel. They suppose that this is Antioch. Hence the true meaning, which fits with the prophet's purpose, could not be deduced therefrom.

It makes the best sense that the desert was set before the Israelites' eyes because it was not far from their region. Syria lay between them, but because there was frequent traffic, it is impossible that desert was not well known to them. Besides, when they were dragged into exile, they passed through that desert. The differences in the regions could arouse their awareness even more, for all of Syria was a fertile region, and Antioch had an outstanding location, as the geographers tell us.

When the Israelites journeyed through that pleasant land, filled with all kinds of riches, and then came to a vast and sad desert, that sight would arouse them even more, as I said. This seems to me to be the reason why the prophet says that the desert of Diblathah was not as vast and solitary, or arid and squalid, as the land of Israel would be.

He says, " 'in every dwelling place,' " so that they would know that there would be no corner immune from the devastation he predicts. It often happens that a land is ravaged and spoiled in part, but here the prophet includes every dwelling place.

" 'And they will know,' " he says, " 'that I am Yahweh' "; that is, "they will know that I have spoken through my prophets." But God proclaims this vexatiously because the authority of our prophet ought to have been sanctioned and established among the people. His calling was attested so well that they could not contend against him without opposing God. So Ezekiel is omitted and God comes forward, as if he himself had spoken. " 'They will know' " my trustworthiness and power, he says. Furthermore, this recognition extends to the reprobate who in no way profit from God's rebukes. Although God compels them by experience to acknowledge that he is the judge, they remain obstinate, as we will see again a little later and then a third time. Next:

CHAPTER 7

1 *And the word of Yahweh was to me, saying:*
2 *"And you, son of man, thus says Sovereign Yahweh to* [or, 'concerning'] *the land of Israel: 'The end, the end is coming on the four corners of the land.' "*

It seems that Ezekiel is too verbose here, for he repeats the same judgment and uses the very same words. The reason that I offered should be noted: if he had referred only briefly to God's commands, his mission would have been ineffective and made no impact because the people were not only slow to believe but of such a stubborn nature. With this intention he stresses with further words what we have already seen. At first he repeats the same words, but then he makes some changes, because that lethargy, or rather sluggishness, under which the people labored must be stimulated with every means.

Another thing to be noted is that he was ordered by God to prophesy among the people not only once but was sent frequently in order to arouse them more forcefully. If he had related God's commands in one sentence, the Israelites might think about God's judgment for that moment alone. But a prophecy recited only once would easily have eluded them. Furthermore, when Ezekiel testifies that he was sent by God, but afterward returns and affirms that he offers new commands, this touches their souls more effectively.

Now we understand his meaning when he says that the *word was given by Yahweh*. This prophecy is distinguished from the earlier one; nevertheless, the subject is the same thing. There is nothing different, so that he seems to construct the same statement. This is certainly true, but it was necessary that he be sent twice to enable the people to understand that what he heard from the mouth of God had to be repeated not only once but twice and then constantly. Since he never stopped exhorting them, it was perfectly clear that God was concerned about their salvation.

"Thus says the Lord Yahweh concerning the land of Israel. 'The end is coming, the end on the four corners.' " It seems that God is considering the moderate punishments that he had already inflicted on the kingdom of Israel. We know that they often experienced God's hand, but when some relief was granted, they assumed they had escaped. They forgot their sins and confidently continued in them, so that it became quite clear that they despised God except when he oppressed them with his frightful power.

This seems to be the point of the word *end*, which is repeated emphatically, *" 'The end is coming, the end over all four corners of the land.' "* He gives the word "wings" but uses it metaphorically for the four different regions. God is reproaching the Israelites for their stubbornness; although they were often rebuked, they did not stop sinning because they assumed that nothing serious could happen to them.

He uses the word *end,* as if to say, "Up to this point I have dealt leniently with you." Certainly God offered a remarkable example of clemency by striking the Israelites lightly when he could have cut them off completely. Since he thus tempered his punishments, the people's sluggishness was less tolerable in assuming that everything was settled as soon as God withdrew his hand.

" *'The end is coming, the end,' "* he says; that is, "after this you may hope for no moderation. I see that there is no hope of repentance in you, and therefore I will completely consume you." He adds, " *'on the four corners of the land,' "* as a little earlier he said, "among all their dwelling places." He is teaching again that no part of the land would be free from the destruction he prophesied. Next:

3   " *'Now the end is upon you; and I will send my anger upon you, and I will judge you according to your ways, and I will put all your abominations on you.' "*

For the third time he uses the word *end,* and repeats it a fourth and fifth time. We gather from this that, although they had been warned more than enough in teaching and even in experience, those miserable people were like wild animals in always promising themselves some remnant and repelling the alarm with which the prophet now strikes them. They did not think that the end could be near. "Oh, some will remain; some will escape." Such was their pride.

So the prophet does not insist on the same word so often for no reason. " *'Now,' "* he says, " *'the end is coming.' "* When he says that " *'the end has now come,' "* he indicates that the Israelites were vainly and foolishly confiding in the future because they had not yet experienced extreme harshness. As I have said, God had been lenient with them in dealing out punishments. But what did they do? Having experienced such tolerance from God, they assumed that it would always be like that.

The prophet therefore marks a distinction between the future and the past, as if to say that God's vengeance, as known to this point, was moderate. But now nothing else remained except for God to tear them out by the root and destroy them. " *'Now,' "* he says, " *'the end is upon you.' "* He had spoken in the third person, but he directed his words to the entire land of Israel: "on the four corners of the land," he said. " *'Now the end is coming on you,' "* he says.

Then, " *'I will send my anger against you.' "* God certainly had given signs of his wrath, but he had not been so severe that the Israelites stopped flattering themselves. Therefore when he speaks of his anger, he undoubtedly means that now he was so offended that he would not restrain himself as he had done before.

What follows pertains to the same point: " *'I will judge you according to your ways.'* " They had been judged before but only in part, for God had given them time to repent if they had been curable. But now when he compares his judgment to their sins, he indicates that there would be nothing short of extreme severity. He explains this more clearly at the end of the verse: " *'I will put all your abominations upon you' ''*; that is, "I will cast your own burden on you."

Although God began to exact just punishments for their superstitions, they still did not endure as grave a burden as they deserved. Therefore God now proclaims that " *'all their abominations would come on their own heads,' ''* so that they would be completely overwhelmed. Next:

4 " *'And my eye will not spare over you, and I will have no mercy, because I will put your ways on you, and your abominations will be in your midst. And you will know that I am Yahweh.' ''*

He uses other words to confirm his judgment that " *'God will not spare' ''* and will not be swayed. When hypocrites hear the praises with which God is dignified in Scripture, that he is merciful and long-suffering,[1] they seize them and fabricate for themselves therefrom a foolish and perverted confidence. God proclaims here that his mercy would not be shared with the reprobate who had not ceased to drive God's mercy far away.

This point is worth noting because nothing is more natural than to be drunk with false hope when we hear that God is merciful, if we fail to know to what purpose he thus testifies of himself — sinners may come to him and boldly pray and beg for his mercy, of which they have such illustrious testimony. But hypocrites always slide downhill and at the same time want God to be propitious to them. So when he says that " *'his eye would not spare, and he would not be merciful,' ''* his meaning must be noted; namely, that the depraved and utterly reprobate should not assume that the clemency they shut out before awaits them now.

" *'Because I will put your ways on you,' ''* he says; that is, "I will cast your sins against you." We see that the people's sins were set aside and, so to speak, lay dead as long as God spared them. But now he indicates, first, that they would have no reason to quarrel or complain, because he will merely throw back against them the iniquities that they inflicted on him. Then he also tacitly accuses them of excessive confidence, because they could never be led to repent when God endured or tolerated their sins.

1. Mg., Nu. 14:18; Ps. 103:8.

" '*And your abominations,*' "he says, " '*will be in your midst.*' " Indeed, the abominations were there before as far as guilt is concerned, but God had not yet vented his wrath. Therefore he says that " '*the abominations would be in their midst,*' " because events would make it clear that they were not so stubborn against God with impunity.

He repeats again, " '*You will know that I am Yahweh.*' " Undoubtedly their impudence forced God to speak this way, that is, since they were so contemptuous of Ezekiel. Although they pretended to be pious, beyond doubt they scorned God himself. Their wickedness is clearly exposed because they denied that God was God whenever they undermined the trustworthiness of the teaching of this holy man. Next:

5 *"Thus says Sovereign Yahweh, 'One evil* [others read אחר *('aḥēr), and thus it would be "another evil"];* behold, evil will come.' "

Whether we read אחת [*'aḥat*] or אחר [*'aḥēr*], the meaning seems to me the same: " '*an evil, another evil, comes*' "; that is, "one evil after another." Or, "one evil comes and evil"; that is, when one evil has come, another quickly follows. Others offer an exposition that seems to me harsh and completely foreign: "one evil comes"; that is, an evil so serious that one blow is enough to destroy everything. This is their subtle explanation. But the prophet's meaning seems to me to flow best this way: " '*one evil will come upon another.*' " That is, there would be no limit, but God would pile evil upon evil until the people's name was completely extinct.

It seems to me that this was said to prevent the Israelites thinking, as they usually did, that they had escaped, as if God made a truce with them. When some little break occurs, the wicked strut about and encourage themselves to think that God is pleased with them. Since hypocrites take every respite to mean that God has spared them, the prophet says that " '*one evil will come upon another.*' " Next:

6 " '*The end has come, the end has come. It has awakened upon you; behold, it has come.*' "

This entire section makes the same point: even though the Israelites may be deaf, they will be compelled to pay attention to God's unrelenting threats. The prophet pounded their ears because he was not immediately heard; he spoke again about the end: " '*the end has come,*' " he says, " '*the end has come.*' " Ezekiel did not employ stylish figures of speech; rather he was compelled by necessity to use the repetitions that we see. The *end* that he proclaims could scarcely penetrate their souls, for they always imagined that God could be placated by various means. Since they promised themselves

169

some remnant and tossed aside whatever the prophet taught about the end, he could accomplish nothing except by threatening them many times with something they doubted would ever happen.

" *'The end has come, the end has come' "*; and then: " *'it has awakened upon you; behold, it has come.' "* When he says *awakened,* he indicates haste; he does not mean that God suddenly avenged the sins of the ten tribes. But he is considering the lethargy of those who indulged themselves in vain confidence while they dreamed that God's judgment remained far away. To this day that devilish proverb flits about on many lips: *la terme vaut l'argent* ["there's plenty of time to settle accounts"];[a] and such wickedness has been widespread in all ages.

Therefore, when God suspends his judgments, the reprobate boast without limit, as if they had gotten away with something. This is why the prophet says that the " *'end is awakening,' "* that is, "is coming quickly." In other words, if God has hesitated in the past, he will delay no longer in destroying the Israelites. Next:

7   " *'Morning[b] has come on you, O inhabitant of the land, the time has come, the day of tumult* [or, "thunder"; others translate it "slaughter," but I do not know why] *is near, and not the sound of mountains* [others translate it "glory," as if the word were הד *(hōḏ)*].' "

Now he uses another word. He says, " *'morning has come' "*; others translate it "kingdom," but that is forced. Although צפירה [*ṣᵉp̄îrâ*] is sometimes "crown," or the "crown of kings," nevertheless the prophet's meaning is twisted when they say that the kingdom has been brought back or transferred to the Babylonians. But the sentence flows best as " *'morning has come.' "*

By morning he indicates what he mentioned before, the hastening of God's vengeance. As he had said that the end awakens as God hastened to take up vengeance, so he also says " *'morning has come to them.' "* In this way he drives out the drowsiness that left them senseless. We know that hypocrites allow themselves everything, as if they were in darkness. As long as God is silent and quiet, they romp about without shame or fear.

The elect and the faithful also dwell in darkness, but the Word of God always illumines the way before them, as Peter says: "You do well when you attend to the prophetic word, which is like a lamp burning in the darkness."[2] Although the faithful are surrounded by darkness, they look to the light of heavenly teaching; and because they are vigilant, they do not become "sons

a. Literally, "the term (deadline) is worth the money"; cf. R. Cotgrave, *A Dictionarie of the French and English Tongves* (London, 1611), fol. Gggg iv[r].

b. Reading *mane* (as in the following exposition) for *manus* ("hand").

2. Mg., 2 Pet. 1:19.

of the night or darkness,"[3] as Paul says elsewhere. But the wicked are immersed in darkness and assume they will enjoy perpetual night. But just as the dawn arises and drives away the darkness of the night, so also the judgment of God, when it suddenly appears, brings unexpected terror to the reprobate. But then it is far too late.

The prophet says " '*morning has come to the Israelites,*' " because they promised themselves a perpetual night, as if they would never be called on to render an account of their life. We see that he refers aptly to that torpor as the cause of their stubbornness, when they assumed they were safe in their darkness. Hence he derides their perverse confidence in promising themselves impunity because they were dwelling in darkness.

Morning, he says, will suddenly surprise you. " '*Morning has come on you, O inhabitant of the land.*' " Then, " '*the time has come.*' " עת [*ʿēṯ*] properly indicates a stated or agreed upon time. The prophet means that the time was coming that God had determined in his judgment. In this way he deprives the wicked of all grounds for pride. They always think God is asleep when he does not attack them right at the start. Therefore he speaks about a fixed time, like the prophets who frequently speak in other passages about the "year of visitation."

He indicates the same idea in other words when he says " '*the day of tumult,*' " or thunder, " '*is near.*' " This clause corresponds to the earlier one; he said that the end was awaking; he said judgment would come in the morning. Now he says straightforwardly and without any figures that the day is קרוב [*qārôḇ*], " '*near*' "; it is " '*a day of thunder, and not the sound of the mountains,*' " he says. That is, it will not be an empty sound, like the sound caused by a crash among mountains. Because the sound that emerges is trapped by nearby mountains, it returns to its source and a louder resounding is born. They call this an echo. The prophet is saying that the clamor he speaks about would not be an echo, or an empty sound, because everyone will cry out in earnest.

Some think הד [*hēḏ*] means "summons"; however, it is properly הידד [*hêḏāḏ*]. It is certainly from the same root, but הד [*hēḏ*] is read in the same sense. If that explanation is acceptable, the prophet will mean the mountains were not lofty but filled with vines, as many were in the land of Israel. Another exposition fits better, however, namely, that it " '*would be the sound of a tumult*' "; not because of an echo, as they call it, but because everyone will cry out until mourning and sadness spread everywhere. Next:

8 " '*Now I will shortly pour out my anger on you, and I will carry out my wrath against you; and I will judge you according to your ways; and I will put all your abominations on you.*' "

3. Mg., 1 Thes. 5:4-5.

Now he drives home almost the same words. We said that his purpose is that the Israelites should determine with certainty that God threatened them not just to terrify them but because he was ready to carry out his vengeance. " 'Now,' " he says, " 'I will shortly pour out my anger.' " He said that the day was near. This refers to the time. To apply this to the place would be inept. " 'I will shortly pour out my anger on you; and I will complete my wrath against you.' " *Complete* explains what he said earlier about the end. God had carried out his vengeance against the Israelites earlier, but not entirely. Therefore this completion of God's wrath means the same as the "final destruction."

I have already explained the words, " 'I will judge you according to your ways, and I will put all your abominations on you.' "

Almighty God, as we have been warned by such extraordinary examples of your wrath, grant that we might learn to walk carefully in your sight and so to constrain ourselves to obey you willingly that a clear testimony of your gracious adoption may be visible in our lives; and may we so prove to be your children that we can truly call upon you as Father, until we attain to that blessed inheritance which has been secured for us by the blood of your only-begotten Son. Amen.

Lecture 19

9 *" 'And my eye will not spare; nor will I have mercy. According to your ways I will put upon you, and your abominations will be in your midst. And you will realize that I, Yahweh, striking.' "*

This verse contains only repetition, except that at the end the prophet designates more clearly what that knowledge would be like which he had mentioned before; that is, they would experience God's power against their will because they refused to trust the prophet's teaching. He has already said two and three times, *" 'you will realize that I am Yahweh.' "* Now he adds a participle *" 'that I am striking.' "*[a]

The knowledge with which God makes himself known to reprobates forces them, like it or not, to experience him as judge of the world. The faithful prosper under the scourges of God, and now and then, because they do not willingly comply with his Word, are humbled under his hand. But we said that here the prophet reviles the pride of the people who dared to mock every threat as if God were asleep in heaven. Therefore he says that in the end, when God strikes them, they will experience what they would not believe — but it will be too late. Next:

10 *" 'Behold the day, behold, it has come. Morning has come* [or, "has arisen"]; *the staff has blossomed; pride has budded.' "*

Now Ezekiel uses another figure of speech, but for the same purpose. He repeats what he said before: *" 'the day has come.' "* But he also adds another

a. *ego sim percutiens.*

part: " '*morning has come.*' " We have said that when God shuts his eyes to the sins of the wicked, they exult without fear or shame as if they were in the dark. Since they run so wild, as if they had obtained the license of night, the prophet proclaims that morning is at hand when God will suddenly bring to light what they thought would always be hidden.

Since God delays and they allow themselves everything, as if in darkness, the prophet calls them to consider the daily sequence. The light of dawn emerges without fail. Thus he derides their foolishness, because they surmise that God has closed his eyes since he disregards them for the time being. This is the reason, as we explained yesterday at length, why the prophet calls a sudden change "the morning."

" '*Morning has arisen*' "; then, " '*the staff has blossomed, pride has budded.*' " There is no doubt that by "staff" he means Nebuchadnezzar. But interpreters vary in understanding the context. Many refer what follows in the next verse to the king of Babylon. But others, more correctly in my opinion, take it as referring to the Israelites themselves. When he says " '*the staff has blossomed,*' "he is considering God's tolerance; since the Israelites sinned with impunity for a long time, they thought, as I said yesterday, that they would have perpetual peace with God.

But Ezekiel proclaims in opposition to this that God had, as it were, a hidden root. As someone plants a tree and waits for the time when it reaches its proper size, so he compares Nebuchadnezzar to a staff, but to a staff that was growing. God could destroy the Israelites apart from human efforts. He could also compel others to obey him, for all creatures stand ready to carry out his commands. But here Ezekiel commends God's tolerance, because he plants a tree for himself from which comes a staff to strike the Israelites. In this way he criticizes their stupidity in not realizing that God determines his time of visitation according to his secret plan.

In sum, when he says " '*the staff has blossomed,*' "he refers to the steps God takes in carrying out his judgments. He does not act precipitately as people customarily do, but like a farmer when he sows or plants. God appoints ministers of judgment for his own use, but allows them to grow and to mature. So if God does not hurry according to our wishes, let us know that he has staffs ready; and if they are not yet mature, it is because the time which God has determined is still not fulfilled.

Next, " '*pride has budded.*' " I mentioned earlier that some refer this to the Babylonians, but it is better to understand it of the Israelites themselves. Hence God is showing that although the staff with which the Israelites were struck grew in Chaldaea, its root was among them. The word "pride" is used in a bad sense as usual. It does not designate mere haughtiness or arrogance but the license to sin that arises from contempt of God.

This does not fit the Babylonians, however, insofar as God governed

174

them with his own hand when he wanted to inflict vengeance on the Israelites. There is nothing forced in this understanding: *"'the staff, with which the Israelites were to be struck, grew.'"* But the place where it arose was their own sinfulness; therefore the root of this staff should be sought here and here alone. *"'The staff has blossomed'"*; but whence did it arise? From pride. Therefore, *"'the bud of this staff'"* was the Israelites' pride. This pride is the companion of wickedness, however, and we know they were so blinded by their confidence that they scorned God and counted all his threats as worthless. The prophet denotes the fount of all evils under the word "pride." A clearer explanation follows:

11   *"'Violence has risen into a staff of wickedness; not from them, and not from their wealth, and not from their clamor; and no mourning among them.'"*

This is an explanation of his statement that *"'pride has budded.'"* Now he adds to pride the violence that is its fruit. Contempt of God always breeds of itself cruelty and violence, robbery and other injustices. As I said, however, he speaks of the Israelites. He says *"'that violence has risen up into a staff of wickedness.'"* This confirms what he mentioned, that the root of God's vengeance is to be sought only among the Israelites. God raised up the king of Babylon to punish them, but that staff sprouted from the root of their sins that provoked God's wrath against them. Thus he adds that *"'there would be nothing remaining from them; there will not remain anything,'"* he says, *"'saved from them,'"* or *"'from their wealth.'"*

This is the way I interpret הָמוֹן [hāmôn]; and then, "no noise or mourning among them." Either "noise" or "mourning" fits quite well: *"'and no mourning among them.'"* Jerome reads נֹחַ [nōaḥ], and thus he translates it that there "would be no rest for them."[1] But the prophet means that there would be no mourning or lamentation, because the destruction of all will be complete. We saw the same thing in Jeremiah. When one house has been defiled with death, friends and family come together and conduct the funeral of the dead. But when the plague attacks the whole city and no house is immune from death, and when fathers are mingled with children and the corpses are so numerous they can scarcely be dragged away, then all mourning stops.

This is what the prophet means when he says that there *"'would be no mourning'"* or lamentation. נָהָה [nāhâ] is also taken for lamentation, but our explanation of the prophet's intention is that all the Israelites were destined for destruction with none surviving to mourn the dead. Even if there were survivors, they would be so overwhelmed by the mass of death that all the duties of humanity would cease. Next:

1. Vulgate.

12 " 'The determined time has come, the day has come near when the buyer
will not rejoice and the seller will not be moved by sadness, because anger on
its entire multitude.' "

Now the prophet takes up another way of speaking. He teaches that there
would be such change that everything would be mixed together, and there would
be no distinction between rich and poor. Such change does not occur, however,
unless God has been so gravely offended that he executes extraordinary punishment, as he warned before. Indeed, Paul urges all the pious to pass through this
world like sojourners.[2] Thus he says that our faith is approved, if a buyer is just
like a seller, a married man like an unmarried. This general teaching is prescribed
for all the children of God; because the form of this world is passing away, they
should be sojourners and not fix their souls on these fleeting things.

But our prophet means something else, namely, that God will upset
everything among the Israelites so that no distinction obtained between buyer
and seller. The one who acquires something rejoices, and the one forced to
sell experiences sadness. When someone is stripped of his fields and possessions, it is like tearing out his intestines. It is natural for the buyer to rejoice,
but for the seller to be sad. God shows that there would be such confusion in
the kingdom of Israel that neither poverty nor wealth would be the cause of
sadness or sorrow. Now we understand the prophet's thinking.

He says, " 'the time has come and the day has drawn near when the
buyer will not rejoice and the seller will not be sad, because anger is on the
entire multitude thereof.' " He does not allude to Paul's idea that the form of
this world is passing away. Instead, he notes the shattering, or rather the ruin,
of that land, so that nothing remains unharmed. While we sojourn in the world
we should always lift our souls and senses to heaven; but the political order
abides and flourishes even among the faithful. Although the children of God
may be poor in spirit, they possess what God has conferred on them as if they
did not possess it, just as Paul exhorts them. Nevertheless, they do enjoy their
good things. But here the prophet indicates that when the kingdom of Israel
has been overthrown, there would be no use for money or fields, because
everyone ejected from his homeland will be reduced to poverty.

He continues the same idea:

13 " 'Because the seller will not turn back to selling [or, "what he sold"];
and their life is still among the living [that is, "although they survive"].
Because the vision is over all the multitude thereof; it will not turn back, and
a man in his iniquity will not strengthen his soul [or, "will not strengthen his
life"].' "

2. Mg., 1 Cor. 7:29-31.

This verse is twisted in various ways, but the prophet's mind is not at all obscure. At the beginning he says that those who sell have no cause for sadness because they will not return to their fields. Somehow this does not seem to fit. But in one clause the prophet includes all I said above, that everything would be so upset that fields would be abandoned by their owners and those who possessed the fields before would be refugees and exiles and utterly destitute; and they would find no place where they could plant their feet on their own land.

This interpretation does not conflict with Jeremiah's prophecy. When Jeremiah was in prison, he was ordered to buy a field from a relative.[3] This was done so that the faithful might hope with quiet confidence for the promised restitution. But the speech is now directed to the reprobate, who were excluded from all hope of liberation. Our prophet does nothing but thunder in God's name and inspire pure terror. There is no mention of grace, because they had abandoned themselves to despair. This is why he speaks of complete destruction.

Therefore, he says that " *'they will not return to the things they sold, although their life is among the living.'* " This section is explained in various ways, but I am not willing to take the time to refute the errors of others. I will follow what seems correct to me. First, this clause is to be read in an adversative sense. He does say " *'and their life is still among the living,'* " but the copula ought to be translated as: "although their life is still among the living."

The prophet seems to allude to an accepted custom of that time. No sale of a field was in perpetuity among the sons of Abraham. It was forbidden in the law because they were only sojourners in the land.[4] Since God claimed for himself dominion over the land, he permitted fields to be sold only for a limited time. In the fiftieth year people returned to their possessions. If they sold them in the twentieth year, they were restored after thirty years; if they were sold in the fortieth year, the sale was for only ten years, according to the calculation of the Jubilee.

Then the prophet says, " *'although they survive, they will not get back.'* " Why? Captivity will prevent them. Now we understand the prophet's meaning: " *'those who sell will suffer no loss.'* " If they remained at home, they would be deprived of their possessions. But this will not happen, for they will be dragged off to a faraway place and there will live and die as exiles. If their life dragged on for a hundred years, their land will remain deserted, because their conquerors will not allow them to return to their homeland.

This is how he describes the exiles' miserable condition: even if God extends their life, they will still be compelled to spend it in want and poverty since they have been deprived of all their fields and could not return to them.

3. Mg., Je. 32:7-9.
4. Mg., Lv. 25:13-15.

LECTURE 19

He adds, " *'because the vision over the whole multitude will not turn back.'* " Interpreters disagree over this too. Some separate this into two parts: the vision was for the whole people, but no one was converted or repented. This interpretation is plausible because it contains a useful and fruitful teaching that occurs throughout the prophets. We know that nothing is more intolerable to God than when those warned by the prophets still do not return to a sound mind but persist in their sins. Since such obstinacy provokes God's wrath more than anything else, this interpretation could seem to fit quite well. That is, the vision was for the whole multitude, but no one repented. God exhorted everyone, from the least to the greatest, to repent, but all were deaf and hopelessly lost in their vices.

Although this exposition seems persuasive, I do not want to pursue it; I have no doubt that the prophet means something else: " *'the vision over the whole multitude will not turn back.'* " That is, it will not be in vain. Isaiah speaks in the same way when he says, "My word shall not return to me empty."[5] He means that prophecies are always bound up with their result.

Some twist this to refer to the fruitfulness of teaching, that God will always have some disciples who embrace the prophetic Word. But that idea is foreign to this text. Instead, the prophet means that hypocrites are completely deceived when they think that God's Word is an empty sound that merely disturbs the air. Hence he says that God's Word will not be ineffective, because God fulfills whatever he proclaims, whether he promises salvation to the faithful or pronounces destruction on the reprobate.

As Isaiah says that the Word of God will not return without results but will prosper, so our prophet denies that God's Word will return after it has been promulgated against the whole multitude. Therefore " *'vision'* " refers to the prophetic teaching. But undoubtedly he restricts the vision to God's judgment. Thus, " *'the vision was for the whole multitude; it will not turn back'* "; that is, it will definitely be carried out.

He adds next: " *'and a man in his iniquity will not strengthen his soul.'* " Others translate it, "in the iniquity of his soul." But because the possessive pronoun is repeated, that opinion cannot stand. Others take it differently; but I do not want to hold you in suspense here, and it seems to me that nothing is more useful than to investigate the prophet's genuine meaning. I have no doubt that the prophet confirms what we have just explained, that those who scorn God hope in vain for some escape, because when God brings forth his judgment he will hold them bound.

Others say, "they have not fortified their soul because of their iniquity"; that is, they are so bound by their evil that they will not raise up their souls and affections to hope for salvation. But that is far too forced. The prophet is confirming what we have just seen, that the threats will not return empty

5. Mg., Is. 55:11.

178

because God will deprive hypocrites and scorners of his teaching of every ground for confidence.

The wicked struggle against God and oppose him in their stubbornness and hardness, as if by acting violently they could break and shatter his Word. Since the reprobate are so aggressive and bold, the prophet says that *" 'they will not fortify themselves for their life by iniquity.' "* That is, they will endeavor in vain to obtain life through their iniquity, which is not adequate to resist God. I do not take it to mean "on account of iniquity," because he is simply proclaiming that their stubbornness would be ineffective. Profane people oppose God, using their stubbornness like a shield to reduce his power to nothing.

" 'They will not fortify themselves in life,' " or for their life, *" 'by iniquity' ";* that is, by the obstinate malice whereby they think they will prevail. Let us learn from this passage to tremble at God's threats and to have their outcome always before us, as the apostle says: "Noah saw by faith the flood that was hidden."[6] While others indulged themselves, for 120 years he constantly considered how horrible God's vengeance would be. When God has spoken, let us immediately recognize his judgment, as if it were displayed before our eyes. Because we hear what the prophet now proclaims, let us diligently avoid that stubbornness which will always fail. Next:

14 *" 'They have sounded the trumpet and prepared everything* [or, others translate as imperatives: "sound the trumpet and get everything ready." But I prefer the past tense: "they sounded and they prepared everything"], *but no one has gone out to battle, because my anger is on all the multitude thereof.' "*

Here the prophet adds that, although the Israelites equipped themselves with every aid, prepared everything needed for waging war, and in short omitted nothing for their best defenses, nevertheless, when the time came for action, their hopes would be vain, and all the support that they prepared would be of no importance. Therefore, *" 'However much they sound the trumpet and prepare everything, nevertheless no one goes out to battle.' "* We must note the reason: *" 'since God's anger is on the whole multitude thereof' ";* that is, because God decided to destroy everyone. Next:

15 *" 'The sword is outside, pestilence and famine are inside; the one in the field will die by the sword; the one in the city will be consumed by famine and pestilence.' "*

He drives home again what we saw before, although this sentence fits with the previous verse. He had said that God's anger was on the whole people;

6. Mg., Heb. 11:7.

179

now he shows that when God puts forth his hand to avenge their sins, none would be saved. He says that " *'he has in his hand a sword and pestilence and famine. If they go out,' "* he says, " *'into the field, the sword will confront them; if they keep themselves at home and in the city, there pestilence and famine will consume them.' "*

He says in effect that God could summon numerous destructions from everywhere, because he will arm foreign enemies to devastate the whole land. If those enemies are silent, he has others, namely, " *'famine and pestilence.' "* He thus indicates that although the Israelites close their homes and seek or endeavor to drive every danger far away, God's vengeance can reach any hiding place. Next:

16 " *'Their escapers will escape* [i.e., "those of them who have escaped will escape"], *and they will be on the mountains like doves of the valleys, all by mourning* [or "murmuring," or "moaning"], *a man* [that is, "each one"] *in his iniquity.' "*

The prophet seems to contradict himself, because earlier he proclaimed that all were devoted to destruction. How can he say now that some will go here and there to hide in the mountains? But what seems contradictory fits together in the best possible way, because he indicates that the life of those who escape will be more miserable than if they had been killed by the sword or consumed by pestilence and famine. Why? " *'They will be,' "* he says, " *'on the mountains.' "* There is hardly any doubt that by "mountains" he means dry and deserted places. Those who seek hiding places in the mountains are so anxious to save their lives that they do not think about food. The prophet means that nothing would be more miserable than exile, because they will be in dry and deserted places; " *'like doves of the valleys' "* they will not dare to cry out.

He means that they will be so apprehensive and anxious about everything — their poverty, squalor, and hopelessness — that, facing a heap of miseries, they would moan " *'like doves,' "* and doves " *'of the valleys' ";* that is, they will hide out of fear and not dare to expose themselves to view. But perhaps the contrast magnifies the evil, as if he said they would be more astonished because the unaccustomed appearance of the places will strike them with greater fear.

Now we understand the prophet's intention: " *'if any of the people escape,' "* nothing could come of their flight except to prolong their miserable lives in extreme distress. We know that it provides great consolation in evil times for people to complain freely and console themselves by crying and mourning. But when someone is miserable and still does not dare complain, he must be doubly dead among the living. Next:

17   " '*All hands will be loosened, and all knees will go waters* [this note must be understood as an analogy: "will flow like waters"; here "to go" is taken as "to flow"].' "

He confirms the previous sentence, that the trepidation will be so great that those who are pressed by all kinds of evil will not dare to speak openly. He says that " '*all hands will be loosened and all knees will flow like water.*' " We know that this teaching frequently occurs among the prophets. Through it God shows that peoples' hearts are in his hand. But since the profane rage against God and confide in their own ability or strength, God proclaims to the contrary that they will be fearful and anxious. They will almost melt away and have no life — as if their knees turned to water and their hands fell loose. Next:

18   " '*And they will gird themselves with sackcloth and fear will cover them; there will be disgrace* [or, "shame"] *on all faces* [or, "countenances"], *and baldness on all heads.*' "

He continues the same thought. He says that the destruction of the people would be so great that everyone would put on sackcloth. Somehow it hardly seems consistent that those who are too shocked to mourn the dead would put on sackcloth. But the prophets thus vary their speech because otherwise they could not arouse stubborn hearts. At first sight these two points do not appear to fit together satisfactorily — " '*that all will gird themselves with sackcloth, and baldness will be on all heads,*' " and then that all will perish without grief or sorrow. Nevertheless, they fit together quite well because the prophet does not express what they plan to do but what the event itself will bring about.

Since there will be slaughter everywhere and God will consume some by pestilence and others by famine, he adds that there will be cause for grief; because of the abundance of evils, however, people will be numb and show no signs of grief, as if they were lifeless.

" '*They will gird themselves with sackcloth.*' " We know that this was a special sign of repentance, but it was often used of common sorrows. Moreover, profane people covered themselves with sackcloth even though they failed to acknowledge God as the author of their evils. So when the prophet says that " '*all will take sackcloth to clothe themselves,*' " he does not mean that they would realize that the punishments were inflicted by God and then repent. He only depicts the accepted rite of mourning and sorrow as common to the reprobate and anyone who despises God.

Now he adds that " '*fear will cover them, and disgrace,* or shame, *on all faces*' "; and then " '*baldness will be on all heads.*' " Shaving the head was

181

forbidden in the law,[7] as we know that God prohibited excessive and immoderate grief by forbidding people to cut their face or to shave their heads. That was distorted affectation. We know how ostentatious people are in expressing sorrow. To impose a limit to grieving, God ordered them not to cut their skin or shave their heads. Thus we see that the prophet is not speaking of true signs of repentance, but only indicates, as I said, that God's vengeance would be so horrible " 'that fear would overlay them,' "and then " 'that shame and disgrace would overwhelm their faces' "; moreover, they would cut their skin according to the custom of the nations and put on sackcloth like desperate people.

Almighty God, whenever you call us back to yourself, grant that we might not sleep in our evil deeds or be hardened to your scourges, but may forestall in time your final judgment; and may we so humble ourselves under your powerful hand that we seriously attest and genuinely prove our repentance. And may we so desire to dedicate ourselves to your obedience that we advance more and more in newness of life, until at last, having cast off all the iniquities of our flesh, we attain to the enjoyment of that blessed rest which your only-begotten Son has won for us by his blood. Amen.

7. Mg., Dt. 14:1.

Lecture 20

19 " 'And they will throw out their silver into the streets and their gold will
be for scattering [others translate it "uncleanness"]; their silver and their gold
will not be able to liberate them in the day of Yahweh's fury. They will not
satisfy their soul, and they will not fill their bellies, because their iniquity has
become a stumbling block.' "

Now the prophet proclaims that the people would be so desperate that they
would forget their silver and gold. We know that people are more concerned
about such possessions than their own lives. Unless gold is adapted for use, it is
not precious in itself; nevertheless, we see the majority burn with such desire for
gain that they put themselves in danger of certain death. How many risk their
lives for gain? Therefore, when people scorn gold, it is clear that they have been
so shocked by fear and anxiety that they are deprived of all their senses.

This is what the prophet means when he says that " 'they will throw their
gold into the streets.' " If they thought they would survive and if some hope
of life remained, they would undoubtedly hide their gold and silver. But when
they throw away their gold, it is certain, as I said, that despair is everywhere.

" 'Their gold,' "he says, " 'will be for throwing out.' "I prefer to interpret
it this way rather than " 'will be unclean.' "נדה [niddâ] indicates uncleanliness;
it also indicates menstruation and separation. If someone prefers to translate
it "separation," I will not argue; only let us understand that the Jews will
regard their gold as worthless and gladly separate themselves from it. We know
that people are so attached to gold and silver that it grieves them when
something they love so much is taken away, no less than if someone snatched
their vital organs from them. The word "throw out" is clearer, however, and
also corresponds to an earlier clause.

He adds, " *'their gold and silver will not be able to save them in the day of Yahweh's fury.'* " The prophet is deriding the perverse confidence of those who suppose they would be protected because they have been fortified with great riches. As long as people see themselves protected by guards, they fear nothing; and it is not easy to drive such confidence from them. This is the reason Ezekiel proclaims that gold and silver would be useless to the Jews when God's fury burned against them. At the same time he indirectly criticizes their foolishness in spurning God's judgments when he spared them for a time.

For that reason he reminds them that " *'the day of God's fury will come' "*; then he says that " *'they will not satisfy their souls or fill their bellies.'* " Here he indicates that all of the richest people would also be starving. Even if great need oppresses the multitude, those who have money at home never go hungry; and, for the most part, the rich have all kinds of provisions hidden in their storehouses and granaries. But the prophet says that the need would be so great that it would involve even the rich, who would not have food to renew themselves.

Finally, the explanation is added: " *'because their iniquity has become a stumbling block.'* " Some take this clause in a general sense, that the Jews then will stumble on account of their iniquity; that is, then the time will come to receive their due. God seemed to overlook them and not consider all the iniquities with which they provoked him. But he says that " *'there will be a stumbling block in that day,'* " if that interpretation is agreeable. But, along with others, I prefer to restrict it to the money itself, namely, that their gold and silver will come to nothing, " *'because it will be a stumbling block of iniquity.'* " That is, it will be the cause or occasion of sinning; and the next sentence confirms this view, when he says:

20   " *'And he has turned the very beauty of his adornment into pride; and out of it they made images of their abominations and their impurities; therefore I have set for them* [or, "given to them"] *for throwing out.'* "

I have no doubt that Ezekiel is using different words to confirm what he has already taught, that the people's money would be thrown out because they used it in an unworthy manner for both luxury and vanity as well as superstitions. They expound צבי עדיו [*ṣᵉḇî ʿedyô*] of the temple, and I certainly acknowledge that the temple was the highest glory of the Jews. They could boast of the temple if they properly and purely worshiped God there. God adorned the Jews with exceedingly great glory when he decided to erect a temple among them for his earthly dwelling place.

But I do not see why we apply these words to the temple when the prophet's own words provide the context. He spoke about gold and silver; he said that there will be no use for gold and silver because everyone will throw them to the ground when they give up all hope of life and salvation.

Now he continues the same idea; he shows the legitimate use of gold and silver: " 'it was,' " he says, " 'the glory of its adornment.' " Whatever God bestows on us is a testimony of his paternal favor. God's liberality shines forth in us when he enriches us with his gifts. In this sense, riches are the beauty of wealth, as health is to the body, and honors and other such things.

Since God wanted his grace to be visible in all the gifts with which he adorns and dignifies human beings, the prophet says correctly that the Jews were adorned with silver and gold. But he accuses them of ingratitude because they twisted such glory into a source of pride. Here I take גאון [gā'ôn] in a pejorative sense, as in many other passages. Sometimes it indicates excellence, but I do not doubt that here the prophet is rebuking the Jews because they became proud of their riches, which were really testimonies of God's favor. Therefore, " 'he turned it,' " he says, " 'that is, the beauty of their adornment, he turned it into pride.' "

Next: " 'and the images of their abominations and their impurities,' " or their idols. This is how the Hebrews frequently speak of idols: " 'they made out of it.' " Here ב [b] is used in place of מ [m], as it often is in other passages. This is the way he designates the material. He is saying that the Jews " 'made their images,' " which were nothing but abominations before God, " 'of gold and silver.' "

This was the second way they profaned God's gifts. The first was in their pride when the Jews were inebriated with an abundance of everything and began to grow haughty toward God; in this way they profaned the glory with which they were adorned. But another defilement was added when they produced idols for themselves out of gold and silver and offered them gifts and sacrifices. God complained similarly in Hosea that they twisted whatever he conferred on them into wicked forms of worship: "I gave," he says, "my grain and wine and oil. But they adorned their idols. This was their way of giving thanks; blinded by my liberality, they offered sacrifices to their idols from my grain and oil and wine."[1]

Ezekiel will treat this same issue more fully in chapter 16, but for now he says that " 'they made images of abominations out of that glory with which he had distinguished them.' " At the end of the verse he confirms what we saw above: " 'on account of this,' " he says, " 'I will give it' "; that is, " 'I will give' " that glory, or I will make " 'it for them for throwing out.' " We see the same idea repeated that he presented earlier; but here he mentions the reasons why the Jews would consider gold and silver to be worthless in the day of God's fury; that is, they unworthily defiled these gifts that radiated God's grace and paternal favor.

Therefore he says, " 'I will put your gold, or glory, for throwing out.' "

1. Mg., Ho. 2:8.

185

He said the very same thing earlier, but the reason for God's vengeance was still not expressed. Next:

21 " *'And I will put it* [or, "give it over"] *into the hands of strangers as plunder and of the wicked of the land as spoil; and they will profane it.'* "

Interpreters also twist these words to apply to the sanctuary, but I have said that this is not credible. The prophet is undoubtedly still speaking of the people. He did change the number in the earlier verse; at the beginning of the verse he spoke in the singular, and now he returns again to the singular and designates "the people." " *'I will put it into the hands of strangers.'* " This was more serious than if they had been oppressed by some domestic tyranny. I have no doubt that by "strangers" the prophet indicates distant and barbarous nations; we know how those with whom we have no communication rage more fiercely and brutally.

First, he says that they " *'would be slaves of strangers'* "; he adds, " *'the wicked of the land.'* " He indicates that their enemies would be so cruel and vicious that there would be no hope of mercy and equity from them. The point is that God's vengeance would be terrible since he had endured the people's iniquities for so long. We gather from this that the wicked and shameless are God's scourges and are ruled by his judgment and hand.

Since this is so, we infer that God works through the wicked such that he is pure of any association with guilt. He so executes his judgments through them that in them he appears blameless. They deserve to be blamed, however, because they are moved only by avarice or ambition or other desires.

Thus, " *'I will give them into the hands of strangers as spoil'* "; and then, " *'to the wicked of the land as plunder, and they will profane them.'* " Perhaps it is this word that leads interpreters to take this verse as referring to the sanctuary. But we know that חלל [*ḥillēl*] is also taken in another sense as "to kill." This phrase therefore could be interpreted as, "the destruction of the people will be everywhere"; that is, not content with plunder and spoil, the enemies will murder their captives when they have obtained victory.

But I willingly keep the rendering "to profane," which means the same as "to vilify," because it seems to me that the prophet alludes to the common abuse of failing to consider why things are appointed for us. Instead, we waste them — rashly, indiscriminately, and contemptuously, even insultingly. He is indicating that the enemies' arrogance would be so great that they would waste and squander not only the people's substance but even the people themselves. This could refer, however, to the substance itself. It is said that a robber steals from a man when he takes away whatever he has and leaves him naked. It would be appropriate to explain in this way what the prophet says. But the simple explanation that God will scatter the people so thoroughly that they will no longer be distinct is quite satisfactory. Next:

22   *" 'And I will turn away my face from them, and they will profane my hiding place; and intruders* [or, "destroyers"] *will enter it; and they will profane it.' "*

There is nothing ambiguous about the beginning of the verse. God proclaims that the Jews would be miserable, *" 'because he will turn away his face from them.' "* Their happiness was based on the fact that God, as he had promised, was concerned about their salvation. Hence as long as God condescended to care for them, their salvation was certain and there was nothing dangerous to fear. But when he set aside his concern for them, these miserable people were exposed to every calamity. Thus they were also said to be stripped of all protection when they alienated themselves from God.

This is one point. Interpreters expound also what follows to refer to the sanctuary; if someone is convinced by this view, I do not contest it strongly. But I take it more broadly. In my judgment God calls *" 'his hiding place' "* the land that was preserved through his protection. He said that he had spread his wings to hide the people,[2] and David prays that God would receive him in the hiding place of his tabernacle.[3] Since therefore the people are protected by God's power, it is proper to call the land *" 'God's hiding place,' "* as if it were a sanctuary. It is quite proper to interpret it this way.

" 'The destroyers will profane my sanctuary, because they will enter there and profane it.' " He uses the same verb twice. Those who take this as referring to the temple restrict it to the Holy of Holies. That is what they called the shrine or oracle where responses were given. They called it the oracle not because they prayed there, but because that is where they inquired about secret matters. But as I have said, that seems to me to be forced.

I do not want to quarrel about this, however, but show what is more acceptable to me. The point is that God had spared the Jews for a long time; he had even hidden them, as it were, under his wings, and their land was like a sacred sanctuary where they hid and so experienced no harm from outside enemies. Yet in the end this will not benefit them because God will destroy every wall and give easy access to their enemies to break through and then profane or confound everything. Next:

23   *" 'Make a chain, because the land is filled with the judgment of bloods, and the city is filled with violence.' "*

Interpreters refer the prophet's being commanded to make a chain to captivity, for we know that captives are usually bound with chains and

2. Mg., Ex. 19:4; cf. Ps. 17:8.
3. Mg., Ps. 27:5.

187

manacles, or locks for their feet. They explain that God threatens the people with exile. But it seems instead that the Spirit is alluding to criminals who plead their case in chains. The Jews had reveled in their faults for a long time, and impunity made them very bold. Now the prophet says that the time has come when they would be dragged before God's tribunal where they would be treated with the strictest justice like common criminals.

Since they bound criminals with chains so that they had to defend themselves in disgrace, criminals, I say, are, as it were, already half condemned. Hence the prophet is ordered " 'to make a chain' " so that the people are not only cited to render an account of their shameful acts but also dragged — like it or not — before God for judgment. He explains what he means by saying " 'since the land is filled with the judgment of bloods.' " The Hebrews call "the judgment of bloods" the material cause of death, when it is a capital case and a criminal has been convicted of a crime that cannot escape the ultimate punishment. Every capital judgment is similarly called a "case of blood."

Then he says that " 'the land is filled with the judgment of bloods.' " That is, the land is guilty of so many sins that it cannot escape ultimate judgment. Next he adds " 'the city,' " which ought to retain at least some purity in the midst of the widespread corruption of the land. But he says that " 'the city also is filled with violence.' " There is no doubt that he includes in this word all unjust oppressions, seizures, plunderings, illicit gains, robberies, and whatever denies justice and equity.

The sum is that the people's wickedness and sin had reached such depths that God could no longer tolerate them. Thus God ascends his tribunal to exact punishment from them. This is the point of the chain of which he spoke. Next:

24 " 'I will cause the wicked of the nations to come [that is, "those who are evil and perverse among the nations"], and they will take possession of their homes; and I will cause the pride of the strong to cease, and their sanctuaries will be defiled.' "

He repeats what he said, that the enemies who are coming will be the ministers of God's vengeance. We learn again from this passage that the wicked are also impelled by the secret direction and hand of God so that they do not move a finger except according to his will. He said first that he would give the Jews into the hand of strangers. But what does he say now? " 'I will cause them to come,' " he says, as if he would extend his hand and lead them.

We see that God has the wicked as mercenaries to carry out his judgments. But we must maintain the distinction I made above, for God works through them in such a way that he nevertheless has nothing in common with them. They are borne along by a depraved disposition, but God has a wonderful

188

plan, incomprehensible to us, according to which he impels the wicked here and there — without becoming involved in their guilt.

He calls them *"'the perverse of the nations'"* so that the Jews would know that ultimate destruction was at hand because they would be dealing with the cruelest enemies. He says that *"'they will take possession of their houses'";* and because the people's pride might seem an obstacle to prevent God exacting the punishment that they deserve, he adds: *"'I will cause the pride of the powerful to cease.'"* As long as the Jews were swollen with contempt and pride, the prophet could not accomplish anything with them. God says he will bring to an end that contempt with which they were puffed up all the time God bore with or tolerated them.

Finally, he adds: *"'their sanctuaries will be defiled.'"* This passage confirms the view that I approved earlier. Ezekiel speaks, as it were, of something new: *"'sanctuaries will be defiled.'"* He takes away from them the empty hope with which they deceived themselves in boasting that they were under God's protection and the temple would protect them and the city. Jeremiah rebukes them because they confided in lies when they proclaimed, "We have the temple of the Lord, the temple of the Lord, the temple of the Lord."[4]

Our prophet does not speak so bluntly, but he undoubtedly shows that their security is false when they oppose the temple to God himself, as if the temple actually would be a shield to repel his vengeance. God did indeed dwell in the temple, but on the specific condition that there he should be called on in purity. But when the temple was defiled, God withdrew from it, as we will see later. This is why the prophet says that *"'enemies will come to defile and contaminate the people's sanctuaries.'"*

Up to this point the prophet has not spoken of the temple, but now he adds *the temple,* so that the Jews would not rashly display the Lord's name as an excuse, as if God were obligated to them. Next:

25 *" 'Destruction has come, and they will seek peace, and not* [that is, "and there will be no peace"].' "

He confirms the same teaching. He says that *" 'destruction has come.' "* Now he adds that *" 'there will be no peace.' "* This confirmation was not in vain. People always hope to accomplish something by making excuses, and so they run and hide when God drags them into the light. Then they constantly fabricate hope of deliverance while God keeps them confined. Since people are so deceptive as to think they have eluded God and his judgments by seizing an opportunity to escape, the prophet says that although they seek peace, they

4. Mg., Je. 7:4.

189

will have no peace. They should have no doubts about the destruction or slaughter that he mentions. Next:

26   " *'Calamity upon calamity will come, and there will be rumor upon rumor; and they will seek a vision from a prophet* [or, "because there is no prophet"], *and the law will pass* [that is, "vanish"] *from the priest, and counsel from the elders.' "*

Here the prophet explains in more detail the nature of the destruction that he intimated before. Again he robs the Jews of all ground for hope, and shows that they will look around here and there in vain, because God will leave them destitute of all help. This is the point. Hence he says that " *'ca-lamities' " will come,* and indeed such that one follows right after another. In this way he warns the Jews that they are seeking security in vain, as if when one evil is passed, they would be finished. As soon as God withdraws his hand, the wicked imagine that they have escaped from all trouble; and therefore they boldly despise God.

They somehow imagine that they have a contract with God, like a debtor who pays off a very small amount to his creditor, gets a reprieve, and thinks he is secure. In the same way the reprobate become hardened when God grants them any kind of truce. They think they have a deal with him so that he is no longer disturbed with them. But the prophet proclaims that there would be such a heap of evils " *'that one calamity would have many companions,' "* because God would keep adding evil upon evil.

He adds, " *'rumor upon rumor.' "* This refers to the cause of their fear, when rumors of wars and the enemies' cruelty become common. Since the Jews were deaf and dumb, the prophet proclaims that God will constantly carry out his vengeance so that one calamity would simply be a prelude to another, until they perish a hundred times rather than God allow them to escape without punishment.

Next he adds: " *'they will seek a vision.' "* The prophet shows again that the Jews would be completely stripped of all help. Although they boldly despised God, we know they shamelessly abused his name. They set aside all sense of shame so that they did not hesitate to deride God and all his gifts. The final refuge in their evils was " *'to seek a vision,' "* that is, to inquire about what God would do. Thus he says, " *'they will seek a vision from the prophet.' "* The expression " *'that they will seek a vision from the prophet' "* seems to me too harsh, because nothing is added except concerning the priest and the elders. Occasionally when מ [*m*] is joined to words it is taken negatively; I do not know whether proper use of the language would allow us to say that " *'they will seek a vision, but there will not be a prophet.' "* The meaning would flow better, however, if Ezekiel denied there would be any prophets. This is a sign of abandonment when there is no consolation to sustain us in evil times. Thus the church in the Psalms complains that it was reduced to extreme anxiety because no prophet appeared: "We see no signs; and there is no prophet among us."[5] Certainly Ezekiel meant that the Jews would seek a prophet in vain because God would take that gift away from them.

As far as the issue is concerned, there is no ambiguity; but the expression, as I said, is slightly obscure. The point is that when they regard God as so bound to them that he would never leave them without preparing visions to console them, they would already be deprived of this gift. When they were destitute, nothing remains for them except that destruction of which he has spoken.

Let us defer the rest until tomorrow.

Almighty God, thus far you have condescended by your power to keep us safe and have driven from us every violent attack, and also overturned so many perverse plans of our enemies and snatched us from countless injuries. Grant, therefore, so to continue your benefits to us that we are grateful to you in return and so dedicated to you in obedience that your holy name will be glorified throughout our lives, in your only-begotten Son, our Lord. Amen.

---

5. Mg., Ps. 74:9.

191

Lecture 21

Yesterday we began to explain the sentence where the prophet proclaimed something to the Jews that they were not fearing at all: the time will come when God would deprive them of prophets. Since God was accustomed to rule that people through counselors, priests, and prophets, he says that " 'counsel would perish from the elders and the law from the priests.' " Concerning prophets, he says that the Jews would seek God's will from them in vain. The point is that since God had always governed that people, their scattering will be wretched because the light of teaching will no longer shine; instead they will be immersed in the darkness of ignorance.

This was the most serious threat of all, because in extreme evil it is a great consolation to have God shine on us with his Word. Thereby we are encouraged to be patient, and sorrows are lightened when we taste some hope of pardon and God testifies that he will be propitious to us. But when this consolation is taken away, it is easy to be overwhelmed by even the slightest evils. Being in the deepest afflictions is like being in a vast sea, but God sustains us by his Word. As long as we still have teaching, we have a plank in our shipwreck to carry us all the way to port.

But when God never appears, the slightest temptation can overwhelm us like the deepest abyss. Thus it was a sign of God's horrible vengeance when the gift of prophecy became extinct among the Jews, and the priests and the elders had no counsel to offer. But we know how greatly they boasted that they were strong in wisdom, for when Jeremiah rebuked them in chapter 18, we see how they rose up against him, relying on the boast that the law could not depart from the priests, or prudence from the wise men or counselors, or vision or word from the prophets: "Come, let us plot against Jeremiah and attack him with the tongue; for counsel will not perish, etc."[1]

Aroused by diabolical fury, they dared to strut about in God's presence and boldly arrogate to themselves what God declares he would take from them: "It can never happen that no vision would remain with the prophets or teaching of the law with the priests." But we see that God overturns that perverse boasting when he intimates that there would be no counsel among the elders, no teaching of the law among the priests, and no vision among the prophets.

From this we also gather that the papists today are refuted by the same arguments. With what weapons are they equipped to rage in pride against the clear and explicit teaching of the law and the gospel? The claim that they are the "representative church," as though protesting openly to God that it was impossible for teaching to perish among the priests? I make nothing of their priesthood not being from God, since they are created priests to sacrifice Christ, with no mandate at all. But let us grant that they are pastors ordained to serve the church; what does that title give them, since God took all light of teaching from the Levitical priests who were appointed by him and not by human suffrage.

Let us learn from this passage that the gift of prophecy and all teaching are the unique gifts of God. Let us also learn that the gift is taken away when God wishes to exact punishment for human ingratitude. If teaching is received with less reverence than is proper and God himself is scorned, as often happens, he casts people into darkness and makes them wander as though blind with no spark of light shining upon them. When even the priests themselves forget their office, God infatuates them, as we see has happened in the papacy.

Nothing is more despicable than these beasts, and yet they claim for themselves the spirit of revelation. But God recompenses them with the just reward of their madness, because they have ruled like tyrants and greatly abused the holy name of "pastor." They have mixed their fabrications with the law and gospel and thereby thoroughly corrupted pure teaching with their inventions. Therefore God has avenged their pride, as we see.

But God shows us the way through his servants and enlightens us with heavenly teaching so that we who are so blind might not wander in darkness; then let us realize that this inestimable treasure must not be scorned, lest we ever be deprived of it. Next:

27   " 'The king will mourn, and the prince will be clothed with desolation [or, "devastation"], and the hands of the people of the land will be disturbed; I will deal with them according to their ways, and I will judge them according to their judgments, and they will know that I am Yahweh.' "

1. Mg., Je. 18:18.

193

In this verse the prophet affirms that God's vengeance would be so widespread that it would strike the greatest and the lowest. It begins with the king and then descends to the counselors, and finally includes the entire people. " 'The king will mourn,' "he says; but it is the king's duty to encourage others and to offer a remedy for all evils.

It is a sign of desperation when nothing remains for the king except struggle and sorrow. He speaks metaphorically and describes the leading men as clothed in desolation. We know that clothing has two uses: we clothe ourselves to keep out the cold and to cover what is shameful. In the opposite sense, the prophet says that shame would be like a garment for them, that is, for the leading men. Finally, he comes to the common crowd.

He also assigns a reason: " 'I will deal with them,' "he says, " 'according to their ways.' " מ [m] is taken here in a causal sense: " 'therefore, I will deal with them according to their ways.' "In the same sense he adds: " 'I will judge you in their judgments.' " The word "judgment" is used here improperly and contrary to its ordinary meaning, for judgment means the same as rectitude. But it is often applied to corruptions, as though he said: "they will know that I am a just judge because I will avenge their sins." Hence he understands "their judgments" to mean "perverse abuses"; it includes not only superstitions but every iniquity whatsoever.

With these words Gods indicates that although he will punish the Jews quite severely, nevertheless he would not be cruel, because they deserved such a reward. Confirmation follows in the next vision. It is a separate vision, but the prophet asserts briefly in God's name that the punishments to be inflicted on the Jews would be just, and then he confirms this teaching with the vision that follows. He was seized by the Spirit of God and taken to Jerusalem where he saw the temple filled with various abominations; every corner was defiled and violated by their idols.

But let us get to the text.

CHAPTER 8

1 *And it was in the sixth year, the sixth month, on the fifth day of the month; I was seated* [literally a participle, "sitting"] *in my house, and the elders of Judah sitting before my face. And the hand of Sovereign Yahweh fell on me there.*

There is no doubt that he is recounting a prophetic vision. The prophet has not been taken to Jerusalem, and he has not changed place. There were no elders of Judah with him. But it seemed to him that he had been taken away by the Spirit of God to observe the defilements with which the Jews had profaned the temple. He says that *he was at home when this vision was presented.* Nevertheless, he could have been walking in a field. So he is not telling something that actually happened; he simply teaches how God appeared to him and then adds the circumstances.

I do not understand *elders of Judah* to mean the captives, but those who were living at the time in Jerusalem so that they could be witnesses to this prophecy and so be deprived of any excuse or pretext of error. He even mentions the exact time at which this vision was offered, that is, *the sixth year,* which he counts from the exile of Jechoniah, as we saw in chapter 1. There was a year and two months, then, between the first vision that he described earlier and the one with which he is now dealing. After fourteen months had passed, God appeared again to his prophet.

The time is not at all irrelevant, for this shows that the people's stubbornness was very great. As I have said, the prophet is counting the years from the exile of the king. They were accustomed to counting the years from the Jubilee, but now he recalls the mourning for that defeat when the king was ignominiously dragged off like a lowly captive and harassed by his enemies like a slave. When the prophet humiliates the Jews by this counting of the years, it shows how indomitable was their stubbornness; that is, they did not repent even though they were so harshly castigated.

But we will see that they were seized by an unnatural madness; as a result, after they had set aside the worship of God, they heaped up new idolatries from everywhere, and the temple was infested with their abominations. In Jeremiah[2] we saw that the worship of God was overturned in Jerusalem itself and in the temple. They were pouring libations to the "works of heaven"; others translate it "queen of heaven." But we explained that those passages should be understood as referring to all the stars.

They were burning incense to the "works of heaven," and they gathered idols for themselves from everywhere and defiled themselves with all the superstitions of the nations. Our prophet shows that they were so far from being moved by any sense of punishment that they sank even lower when God began to stretch out his hand against them. It was as if he showed himself from heaven to be an avenger of those superstitions.

We have, then, the reason why the prophet designates the years and months — and even the fifth day of the month. The Jews would be convicted even more of their stubbornness, because no punishments called them back to the way; instead, they fought against God with diabolical tenacity.

He says, *the hand of God fell.* By *hand* I do not think he means "prophecy," as others think, but "power." The idea that the "prophecy fell" seems too

2. Mg., Je. 7:17; 44:17-19.

restricted, and the expression itself is colorless. But it is appropriate to speak this way about the power of God. He professed in effect that he presented nothing of his own, because he somehow set aside his humanity while the power of God ruled him. This power of God is set against all human abilities. Next:

2 *And I looked, and, behold, a likeness* [or, "image"] *as the appearance of fire; from the appearance of the loins down, fire; and from its loins upward, as the appearance of brightness, as the semblance of hasmal*[3] [or, "electrum"].

Others translate it "angel," but incorrectly in my judgment. עין [*'ên*], properly speaking, means "color," and I already refuted that error in the first chapter. I am not sure what color *hasmal* was, and so I follow the usual view that it was something like electrum.

Now the prophet says that *he saw a likeness,* or an image, composed of two parts. *From the loins down it was like fire, but above it was brightness.* I have no doubt that by the word דמות [*d^emût*] he means the image of a human being. God appeared to his servant in some kind of image. It is not unacceptable to say that it was a human figure, for if it had been a different figure, the prophet would certainly have said so.

But we have already seen that God put on human form, and has thus represented himself in the person of his only-begotten Son, as we said and as we will see again in chapter 10. This is the likeness, then, of which the prophet speaks, but he uses this term deliberately to let us realize that it was not a real and solid, or what they call "substantial," body. What the prophet saw was a figure or likeness. What happened was purely a vision; it was not God putting on a body at that time. I discussed this matter more fully in chapter 1, and I will mention it again a little later.

Now he says, *one part of the figure was like fire,* while the other *was the appearance of brightness.* This seems to express what the Jews should hope for when they finally recognized that God was near. They thought they were very far removed from him, since they boldly defied his law and all his prophets. As far as the brightness is concerned, it indicates God's majesty and incomprehensible glory. If the splendor of the sun dazzles our eyes, what will happen if we attempt to penetrate to that boundless light, compared to which the sun is but a tiny spark?

Therefore, when Ezekiel says that *in the likeness there was brightness above the loins,* he no doubt shows how terrifying the majesty of God should be to us. God dwells in light, but an "unapproachable light," as the apostle says.[4] *Below,* he says, *was the appearance of fire,* because of course this was

3. Here *chasmal.* See above on 1:4.
4. Mg., 1 Tim. 6:16.

not at all to be expected while the Jews experienced some joy from God's presence.

We know that hypocrites always rashly boast in God's name, as Amos rebukes them: "What is the day of the Lord to you? It is a day of darkness, not light."[5] In their miseries they boasted that God would hear their prayer and could not possibly fail to help them because he had taken them under his protection. The prophet refutes this arrogance and says that the day of the Lord would be darkness. Hence even in this passage God appeared in the form of fire against the earth, so that the Jews would tremble when they saw God's vengeance flare up to consume them.

The majesty of God was manifested in that brightness in order to humble the prophet and all the pious, so that they might reverently accept the vision. God's vengeance was manifested in the fire so that the Jews would no longer make a shield for themselves out of God's name, behind which they falsely and deceitfully hid. Next:

3 *And he put forth the likeness of a hand and lifted me up by a lock of my head; and the Spirit erected* ["raised"] *me between earth and heaven and led me to Jerusalem in visions of God, to the entrance of the inner gate that faces north, where the seat of the idol of jealousy causing jealousy.*

Now the prophet tells that he was transported to Jerusalem to see the filthy superstitions with which the Jews had defiled the temple. But first he says that *the likeness of a hand was put forth.* From that we infer again that the prophet did not see a solid or substantial body, but only a figure was presented to symbolize God's presence. So much for the term "likeness" or "figure." It was not a real hand that seized the prophet by the hair, or the locks of his head, but the likeness of a hand. That is why he adds, *this happened in visions of God.*

He says that he was carried off between heaven and earth. But to prevent anyone imagining that this was fulfilled literally, he explains himself, saying, *in visions of God.* By *visions of God* he no doubt means a revelation. But there is a tacit antithesis between these revelations of God and the specters that often deceive human senses. Those who interpret "visions of God" simply as "prophecy" weaken what the prophet wished to emphasize. But those who think God's name is used as an epithet (the Hebrews call anything extraordinary "divine") deviate from the prophet's genuine meaning. Undeniably he opposes *visions of God* to every apparition. As we know, Satan deludes human senses with his illusions and has miraculous devices to fascinate unbelievers. It even happens on occasion that the children of God are deceived. Therefore to

5. Mg., Am. 5:18.

197

remove all doubt from his teaching, the prophet says that *he was carried to Jerusalem in visions of God.*

Now he adds that *he was transported to the entrance of the north gate.* We know that there were several gates to the court so that people could enter more easily. If only one gate had been open for them all, there would have been a riot, as often happens with a crowd. The court had an east gate, a north gate, and other gates to give easy access to the people as well as the priests. The priests had the inner court, which was separate. But when they offered sacrifices at the altar, they had to mingle with the people. This is why the court was divided by several gates. Now the prophet says, *he was transported to the entrance of the gate,* so that he did not enter directly into the more secret part of the temple. Instead, it seemed to him that he was standing before the doorway until God advised him about what was happening inside.

He says, *there was the seat of the idol.* What the idol was is not known, except that the prophet teaches that it was abominable. At first, he calls it an *idol of jealousy;* then he adds a participle that means that *it provoked God to jealousy.* Both the noun and the verb are often taken in a bad sense; God attributes the emotion of jealousy to himself, however, and in this sense says in Deuteronomy 32, "They provoke me." It says there, "They caused me to be jealous with what is no god; I will also cause them to be jealous."[6] He alludes to the jealousy between husband and wife. If a woman prostitutes herself, the husband burns with indignation, in a blazing outburst of fury. Likewise the wife, when she learns that her husband is an adulterer, is seized by extreme outrage.

To show how much he values his glory and worship, God compares himself to a jealous human being when we deviate into idolatry and adulterous forms of worship. In this sense the idol in the forecourt or entrance to the court is called an *idol of jealousy* and an *idol that causes to be jealous.* But we can translate it: "there was the seat of an idol that causes jealousy," so that the noun קנאה [qin'â] would be taken in the ablative case. He says that the idol provoked jealousy in the sense that when the Jews set up that idol, they in some way stomped on God with their feet, or at least attempted to overthrow his glory. Next:

4   *And, behold, the glory of the God of Israel was there, according to the vision that I had seen on the plain* [but strictly it is "valley," because בקעה *(biqʿâ)* is derived from "cleave." An intervening valley seems to split up mountains, which otherwise would be joined in an uninterrupted expanse. But it is also taken generally of any plain, and the first vision presented to the prophet was near the river Chebar, where there were no mountains].

6. Mg., Dt. 32:21.

198

Now he merely says that *he saw the glory of God as he had earlier seen it near the riverbank.* This was like the seal of the prophecy. The holy man had to be strengthened so that he might hold up boldly under the people's fury and audacity, and their stubbornness. He had to contend with hardheaded people; it was for good reason that God armed him and that a new vision was offered again for this purpose. He knew it was the glory of God. It was exactly as if he was assured again that all of this was directed by God. There was nothing human, nothing contrived, nothing false, and nothing doubtful. Next:

5 *And he said to me, "Son of man, come lift up your eyes to the way of the north"; and I lifted up my eyes to the way of the north and, behold, from the north at the gate of the altar, that idol of jealousy in the entrance.*

Here the prophet is shown one way in which the temple was profaned; an idol was set up in the entrance to the court, near the altar. Now and then it may happen that the worship of God is spoiled, but so slightly that the corruption scarcely appears. Yet while the prophet repeats that *it was an idol of jealousy,* he indicates that the crude and disgraceful shame of that spectacle was such that they could not conceal their wickedness under any guise since they had so openly and admittedly deviated from God's law.

But when *he is ordered to "lift up his eyes to the way of the north,"* that also serves to confirm the teaching. If the prophet had turned his eyes thither of his own accord, his looking would have been less serious. But when God expressly commands him to direct his eyes, the reprimand that follows has greater weight. This is why the prophet does not voluntarily cast his eyes upon the idol, which he could have done, but was commanded to do so by God. Meantime it is clear that he obeys God's commands with great teachableness. He places these two together, that *he was ordered to "lift his eyes"* and that *he lifted them immediately.* We see then he was so obedient to God's command that he made no delay but complied immediately.

He says, *that idol was near the gate of the altar.* This circumstance makes the crime worse. If the idol had been set up in some remote corner, it would certainly have been an intolerable sacrilege, but the Jews would have shown a sense of shame by placing it there. But when they erect the idol in front of the altar, it is like spitting in God's face.

If an impure woman runs after her lover, the husband is justly offended. But if she brings her lover home and flirts with him before her husband's eyes and prostitutes herself in all kinds of disgraceful acts to arouse his anger, her insolence and lust are utterly intolerable. Yet that was what the people's audacity was like when they set up an idol near the gate of the altar, as if they wanted to force God off his throne and defile the altar itself with the sight of that idol.

199

6 *And he said to me, "Son of man, have you seen what these are making? the great abominations that the house of Israel is making* [that is, 'committing'] *there, that I should withdraw far from my sanctuary? And yet turn yourself* [that is, 'turn around'], *and you will see great abominations."*

Now God complains to his prophet. We must always note the purpose, or consider God's plan, because at the end of the chapter we will see how God was to inflict heavy vengeance on the people. He anticipates the raucous words they hatefully heaped on him, when he castigated them as they deserved. Then too, no doubt, he wanted to persuade the exiles of something they could hardly imagine, that the destruction of Jerusalem was at hand.

We said that those taken into captivity were discontent and hoped to return to their homeland. Since their condition seemed excessively severe and grave, God wanted it to be clear to them that the final destruction of Jerusalem was at hand. He did this by showing what great abominations were flourishing in the temple itself. It was inevitable that God appear as the avenger of his glory and worship.

The rest tomorrow.

Almighty God, until now you have treated us so indulgently, and although you have been provoked by our many offenses, yet you have revealed yourself to us as a gracious father. Therefore, grant that we may no longer abuse your patience but promptly return to the way and submit ourselves to you. In a true spirit of repentance may we be so humbled and displeased with ourselves for our sins that with wholehearted zeal we devote ourselves to you and follow the direction of your holy call, until the race of life has been completed and we arrive at that blessed rest which your only-begotten Son has won for us by his blood. Amen.

Lecture 22

We stopped yesterday at the sentence where God asks his prophet *"whether he saw the abominations that the children of Israel were committing"* in the temple itself. With these words he not only cites his servant as a witness but in a way appoints him as judge, so that all would know that the impending punishment was not only just but could be deferred no longer. This is the reason God asks the prophet *"whether he has seen the abominations."* If a mortal is forced to pass judgment, surely God, who sees far more clearly than any human eyes, will not be able to forgive sins when they have reached such a level of stubbornness that his patience achieves nothing.

Now he uses an adverb of place that seems to be used emphatically, to designate the temple from which all filth and iniquity ought to be removed. When God complains that abominations are being committed there, he underscores the people's crime because not even the temple remains pure.

He adds, *"to withdraw."* Some refer this to the people and draw from it the meaning that those who so pervert the worship of God withdraw from the sanctuary because they no longer have anything in common with God. I prefer instead to interpret this of God himself, because he is compelled to move out of his own sanctuary, as we will see later. Although they thus defiled the temple with their sacrileges, they still think that God is confined there. Now he renounces the temple and says that he is leaving it empty and worthless, because he will not tolerate dwelling in sordid filth.

In sum, God will leave his temple because the genuine worship he taught in the law did not flourish there. This passage is worthy of note, too, because we gather from it that God cannot bear to see his worship profaned without abandoning those who so pervert the law with their inventions, as we see the Jews had done.

Today we see how arrogant the papists are about their inventions. The more contrived practices they pile up, the more they provoke the wrath of God. Consequently they boast in vain when they think they have the Lord in their temples. This judgment will always abide: God cannot dwell in a profane place. Nothing sanctifies a place more than obedience and sincerity of faith. Therefore, when people introduce their own contrivances, in effect they drive God away from them. That is his point.

Now he adds, *"turn yourself, and you will see great abominations."* Others translate it "greater." But from that interpretation the question might arise: "Why should he call the following abominations and others 'greater'?" I interpret it simply to mean that the prophet would see other great abominations.

Later[1] he puts it another way. He will say תעבות גדלות מאלה [*tôʿēḇôṯ gᵉḏōlôṯ mēʾelleh*]; but even in that place, in my opinion, there is no comparison of larger and smaller. I interpret מאלה [*mēʾelleh*] simply as "after these," and this simplicity is more acceptable to me. Other interpreters anxiously toil to make the final abomination more serious than all the rest. There is certainly no obvious reason for doing so. But there is no need for us to seek these difficulties, because the prophet speaks only of "great abominations." Let us continue:

7 *And he led me to the gate of the court; and I looked and, behold, there was one hole in the wall.*

8 *And he said to me, "Son of man, go ahead and dig the wall." And I dug in the wall, and, behold, one gate.*

9 *And he said to me, "Go in and see the evil abominations that they are making."*

10 *And I went in and looked and, behold, every likeness of reptile and animal, an abomination, and all the idols of the house of Israel, painted* [there is a change of number; "painted" should be plural] *on the wall all around.*

11 *And seventy men out of the elders of the house of Israel, and Jaazaniah, the son of Shaphan, was standing in the midst of those who stood before them* [that is, the idols], *and to a man* [that is, "each"] *a censer in his hand; and a thick cloud of incense was rising.*

The prophet is led to another place where he is shown a different type of abomination. If an idol had been set up only in some recess of the temple, the impiety — along with the sacrilege — would have been intolerable. But when every part of the temple has been contaminated by such filth, we infer that the people are completely hopeless.

1. Mg., v. 15.

The prophet says that *he was led down to a more secret place,* and since there was a hole there, he was ordered by God to dig a doorway through which he could enter. This is the only thing the vision could mean. The prophet did not take anything with him with which to dig through the wall. But since he was only allowed to see that hidden abomination through the crack, God opened the wall. But it seems that the prophet made for himself, with his own hands, the doorway through which he could enter.

He says, *There were birds, reptiles, and animals portrayed there.* Then he adds, *an abomination, and all the idols of the house of Israel.* We see that there was not just one idol but a crowd of them. Certainly as soon as the true worship of God is neglected, people set no limits for themselves. They are not happy with one or two errors but from these pile up countless delusions. Thus from one idol the children of Israel lapsed into a huge multitude. We should note that the idol of which he spoke was more detestable than the others. It was called the *idol of jealousy* for good reason, because it provoked God to jealousy. It is therefore likely that that idol was more prominent than the others and held in higher esteem and veneration, as unbelievers have greater and lesser gods. But now the prophet refers to the ordinary idols, of which there were a great many, but not so high in honor.

He says, *that part of the court was filled all around with pictures.* There was certainly always a liberal use of pictures, but God wanted his temple to be free of images, so that people would not be captivated by such enticements and directly turn to superstition. If we see a picture of a human being or animal in some unconsecrated place, no religious feeling affects our souls. Everyone acknowledges it to be a picture. Even idols themselves are not worshiped as long as they are in studios or workshops. If a painter's studio is filled with images, everyone walks by; if they delight in looking, they still show no sign of reverence for the pictures. But as soon as a picture is moved into another place, its sacredness blinds people and transports their minds into a stupor. They do not stop to think that they just saw that picture in an ordinary studio.

This is why God would not allow any pictures in his temple. Certainly when a place has been consecrated, it is inevitable that an image bemuses people, as if some arcane divinity lurked therein. The prophet does not simply say, however, that the walls were filled with pictures; he says, *there was an abomination and the idols of the house of Israel.* We see, then, that the walls had not been painted merely for decoration but because the people desired all these gods, whose names they knew were celebrated among the profane nations.

Now because the prophet is ordered *"to dig through the wall,"* we infer that superstitions are sometimes so hidden in secret places as to escape our eyes even when we are looking at them. The weakness of the human mind is such that it does not easily discern how abominable it is to corrupt the worship of God. The prophet merely looked through a crack and hence could not make a definite judgment about those defilements. So he is ordered to *"dig the wall,"* as if God was warning him that a scant and darkened view was not enough, but a door should be opened for him to peer in and consider in detail what otherwise could be hidden beneath the surface.

Now when he says that *he went in and saw every image,* we must remember what I just mentioned, that the Jews are being condemned here for adopting a numberless crowd of gods from all over. It was thoroughly shameful to worship reptiles and brute animals. There is an outward show of beauty in a human likeness. The Greeks, who always thought themselves wiser than others and regarded all other nations as barbarian, were nevertheless deceived by idols that bore a human form. But to worship a bull, a dog, and a donkey as a god is too base and crude.

Hence we see how base and blind the Jews were in confusing God with brute animals and reptiles. Moreover, it is not surprising that they were so deluded, because Egypt was close by, where we know that dogs and cows — even cats — were taken as gods. Why, they even worshiped all types of herbs! Since the Egyptians imagined deity to be present even in reptiles and animals, as well as in garlic and onions, it is no wonder that the Israelites were drawn into these traps by their proximity. But since heavenly teaching had showed them the way, such blindness was inexcusable; they could not have gone so utterly astray without suffocating and extinguishing the light placed before their eyes. But we see how human impudence erupts when they do not keep themselves obedient to God's teaching.

He says that *these images were painted all around* on the wall to confirm again what we said, that the Jews were so inflamed by desire that they left no spot empty. They wanted those figures to meet their eyes in every direction to inflame their superstitions ever more ardently.

Then he says that *seventy out of the elders of the house of Israel made incense for those idols.* I do not think that he means the seventy who had been chosen to rule the people. But the prophet was undoubtedly alluding to that number. We know that in the beginning seventy were at the head of the people and were chosen from each of the tribes to unite in one. But as for the present passage, I think the number of men is put at seventy, even though they were not those rulers who, properly speaking, were called "elders" in respect of office and not only age. Meanwhile, we must remember that the prophet is looking at that pattern, because from the beginning God wanted seventy men to be in charge at the helm.[2] So the prophet means that the people's leaders who ought to have the responsibility of ruling others were like standard-bearers in ruining the worship of God.

2. Mg., Nu. 11:16.

He mentions *Jaazaniah, son of Shaphan,* who was probably a man of unusual esteem. Since he excelled in his reputation for prudence as well as piety, the prophet wanted to exaggerate his disgrace in that he too offered incense to idols along with the others. What integrity could remain among the people when one who was considered holy profaned himself along with the rest? Hence we see the prophet's point that the entire people, from the least to the greatest, were so corrupt that the finest among them prostituted themselves to idolatry.

Moreover, he says that *they were standing before them, and there was a censer in the hand of each.* At that time incense was a sign of the highest veneration, and it was used for this purpose almost everywhere. That is why, in the beginning of the gospel era, when the wicked wanted to force Christians into idolatry, they would simply give them two or three grains of incense. That was a sign of apostasy. They did not order them to bend the knee before idols or offer sacrifice, but only to burn a few grains of incense.[3] So the seventy men are said to have carried censers or incense boxes as a sign of veneration.

The prophet adds, *and a thick cloud of incense was rising.* Here I detect a particular likeness: *the incense was rising like a thick cloud.* He is undoubtedly indicating that they were so extravagant, or rather prodigal, in their madness that they spared no expense. Idolators thus rashly squander everything when excessive zeal seizes them. This point was not sufficiently prudently considered. Hence the prophet says that the incense was not ordinary but was like a thick cloud since they threw in a great quantity of incense to make a richer and fuller offering. He said in effect that they were so excessive in their superstitions that they threw in quantities of incense and considered all the expense as nothing, as long as their idols were satisfied. Now it follows:

12 *And he said to me, "Son of man, have you seen what the elders of the house of Israel are doing in the darkness* [or, 'gloom'], *each one in the secret places* [or, 'inner recesses'] *of his imagination? Because they say, 'Yahweh does not see us; Yahweh has deserted the land.'"*

Again God questions his servant. We have mentioned that the purpose is that he offer his verdict as the judge of his people. It should be clearer from this that those who have provoked God in this way are unworthy of any pardon. *"Do you see,"* he says, what the elders are doing? He does not call them *"elders of the house of Israel"* to honor them but rather to censure their ingratitude because they drew others with them into their fellowship of wickedness. Elders

3. Mg., Pliny the Second, *Letters* 10, Letter to Trajan concerning the Christians, i.e., Pliny the Younger, *Letters* 10:96.

ought to show others the way. Since the profaning of God's worship originated with them, the outrage increased and they became deserving of greater rebuke.

"Do you see," he says, *"what they are doing in the darkness?"* I infer from these words that the place was out of public view, for there were many cells and cubicles near the court, as we saw in Jeremiah.[4] Since the nobles had their chapels there, it is not surprising that the place so defiled by their pictures was shown to the prophet. He says, however, that they were doing this *"in the darkness,"* because they held their rites in secret, as profane nations celebrated mysteries not open except to the initiated. Therefore, since the masses were not thought indiscriminately worthy of these mysteries, it is probable that among the Jews, too, the place described by the prophet was like a chapel that the nobles with any authority among the people kept to themselves.

He adds, *"each one in the inner recesses";* some translate this as "in the dens of their paintings." But I take **משכית** [*maškît*] metaphorically for the imagination, as in other passages. Properly speaking, it means "picture," but it is also applied to human thoughts. When he speaks of innermost recesses or hiding places, I do not understand "dens," although I do not deny he alludes to the recesses that separated them from the crowd out of reverence. At the same time he criticizes the twisted and perverse counsel that the elders of the people inwardly cherished. Those who think they are wiser than the common people have something hidden and are puffed up with concealed disdain; hence those who deceive God are said in Isaiah to dig hiding places for themselves while they think they are being clever.[5]

Now we understand what the prophet means when he speaks of *"the inner recesses of their imagination";* that is, they considered it a matter of the highest and most profound wisdom to have such pictures. But again, it was almost unnatural when the elders thrust themselves into these repulsive defilements.

Among the profane nations, the rulers and heads of state affirmed no religion. We will not find among the Greeks or Latins any of the outstanding figures and leading rulers involved in the errors of the masses. Rather, they pretended they were religious in order to keep others obedient. They displayed great pomp in public and pretended great reverence. But when they behaved privately at home with one another, they scoffed at all that nonsense. Hence since all the rites of the nations had been held up to ridicule by perceptive people, it was a completely detestable portent *"that the elders of the people of Israel fabricated idols for themselves in a secret place, even in the inner recesses of their thoughts."*

Now he explains the reason why they acquired for themselves that heap

4. Mg., Je. 20:2; 1 Ki. 6:5.
5. Mg., Is. 29:15.

of gods: *"because they supposed that 'God no longer watched them.' "* This passage is poorly explained when interpreters think that those elders were Epicureans who dream that God cultivates idleness and amusements in heaven. They introduce other passages that appear to be similar, but only in word, as in the book of Job where the wickedness of the multitude is described: "They think God is walking on the dome of heaven."[6] But the prophet is speaking in a more restricted sense. Taking the passage in a general way diminishes the force of the teaching that should be drawn from these words.

Why then did the Jews devise so many gods for themselves? Because they thought that God no longer observed them, as I have already explained. But this was a sign of horrible depravity. God rebuked them in various ways; they ought to have returned to the path. They were so far from repenting that instead they champed at the bit and persuaded themselves they should seek other gods. This wickedness has spread in every age. Today it is clearly apparent in the papacy; even the blind can feel it with their hands! Whenever God punishes those wretches, at first they humbly beg for pardon. But when God presses them more heavily, they begin to rage and look this way and that. They have a common proverb: "I know not to which saint I should make my vow." Boys in the papacy learn this proverb; old men always have it on their lips in difficult circumstances.

This is the vice that Ezekiel mentions now in explaining that the reason the elders amassed a monstrous number of gods was their belief they were not observed by God. *" 'Yahweh does not see us,' "* they say. They are not speaking simply of God's providence but complain indignantly of God's indifference, because he does not help them in their misery and has deserted the land, as they explain a bit later. After that they clamor that *" 'God has abandoned the land.' "*

We see that they were not simply speaking against God's providence, as if he were contemptuous of human affairs; but they were incensed with rage because God's hand pressed them more harshly, and they did not feel that he was of any further help. Because of this they drifted away to brute animals, to reptiles, to a variety of pictures, to all types of abomination; they thought that they were worshiping the one, true God in vain. Next:

13 *And he said to me, "Turn again, and you will see the great abominations they are making."*
14 *And he led me down* [or, "led me through"] *to the opening of the gate of the house of Yahweh that faces north, and, behold, women were sitting there mourning for Tammuz.*

6. Mg., Jb. 22:14.

207

Now he mentions the third type of idolatry with which the Jews contaminated the temple. This was a vice unique to women. We know that they were always more addicted to such deceptions. Satan has certainly deluded men more than enough, but the insanity of superstitions has always reigned more fully in women. They had a cult of women to mourn Tammuz.

It is not certain who Tammuz was. Jerome translates it as "Adonis."[7] Adonis was the lover of Venus, according to the nonsense of the poets. He was mutilated by a boar and changed into a flower of the sweetest aroma; in gratitude to Venus, women would mourn the death of that handsome young man every year with solemn lamentation. But I do not think it likely that this rite had spread into Judea, because we do not read that this lamentation was observed in the surrounding regions but only in Greece and Asia Minor.

Therefore I refer it instead to Osiris. As I have said, the Jews were neighbors of the Egyptians, from whom they consequently borrowed various rites. We know that Osiris was mourned every year among the Egyptians, but it was even more foul than that. They carried private parts on a bier in a parade and called it "Phallus." The women displayed their private parts to the idol as if they were offering themselves to be defiled. That was a thoroughly shameful spectacle. I conjecture, then, that the Jews had borrowed that rite, since the women were mourning Tammuz.

From this we see that once Satan is in control and people have been cast into a reprobate mind, they become fools in everything, even reduced to a more than animal-like stupidity. Who would think it possible that women would sink to such disgrace after being trained in the teaching of the law from earliest childhood? But since the temple was open to such filth, we see that the Jews were so blinded by madness that God showed them signs of his severest vengeance in allowing them to slip that far.

Almighty God, since you have given us a certain and unfailing rule by which to worship you, and since your Son was made our perfect teacher of all wisdom and true piety, grant that we may obediently follow whatever he prescribes us and turn not aside to the right or to the left. Grant that, contented with the simplicity we have learned from his gospel, we may continue in the course of your holy calling, until at last we complete this race and attain to the perfect state of your glory. And may we so enjoy it that we may be transformed into it, as you have promised us through the same Christ our Lord. Amen.

7. Vulgate.

Lecture 23

15   *And he said to me, "Son of man, turn again; you will see great abomi-nations before these"* [or, "besides these"].
16   *And he led me into the inner court of the house of Yahweh; and, behold, at the gate of the temple of Yahweh, between the vestibule and the altar, about twenty-five men, their backs toward the temple of Yahweh, and their faces toward the east, and they were worshiping the sun in the east.*

Here the prophet recounts how the temple was profaned in another way. The foremost citizens of Jerusalem, who ought to be showing others the way, were prostituting themselves to wicked forms of worship. He says, *he saw about twenty-five men;* and it is likely that they were all from the highest rank of citizens. But a definite figure is used for an indefinite number. I think that the prophet — or rather the Spirit of God who showed him this number in his vision — was not precise in this matter.

Whatever the case, they worshiped the sun not only in private chapels but in the temple itself, and they did so in blatant and crass contempt of God. When they turned their backs to the sanctuary, it was like holding God up to ridicule. They were obviously so arrogant that they were openly glorying in their superstitions, as if they were deliberately defiling God's temple. It was horrible to see leaders of the city, trained in the teaching of the law and in worship, so completely alienated from piety that they would worship the sun.

This could not have happened by error or ignorance. When God forbids us to worship the sun and the stars in his law, he also adds the reason: the entire heavenly host were created for our use.[1] The sun is our servant and the

1. Mg., Dt. 17:3; cf. 4:19.

moon our handmaid, and even the stars were created to serve us; therefore it is utterly preposterous that the divinely established order should be overthrown so that the sun, given us to work on our behalf, should take the place of God for us. Since God clearly witnesses to this in the law, there was no excuse for error when the Jews worshiped toward the east.

Now comes a second, even cruder disgrace to God, when *they turned their backs on the sanctuary.* They could, as I said, defile themselves with such filth at home or in secret. But when they come into the temple of their own accord, it is like provoking God to battle. Now when they turn their backs, it is not just a foul rejection of God but an insult, as if God was unworthy of their respect. Now we get the point of this passage.

He says, *"Turn again, and you will see great abominations."* Others translate it "greater," as I explained before. But I do not know if it fits. I do not quarrel about this, but if a reason is sought why this abomination is called greater than the others, it is not clear to me. I prefer to take it simply in the positive sense. It does not matter that מאלה [*mē'ēlleh*] is added, for the מ [*m*] is not always taken as a comparative. But in my opinion it is tantamount to God's saying, "You will see other abominations besides those," that is, the ones already mentioned.

He designates the place where they worshiped the sun, that is, *between the court and the altar.* It was a sign of great perversity to break into the holy place and despise God there. We already know that it was a sign of proper adoration when the faithful turned their eyes on the sanctuary and the ark of the covenant. But when these men turned their backs, there is no doubt that they deliberately wanted to glory in their contempt of God and the law.

It is already apparent that they had borrowed various, almost countless sorts of superstitions from everywhere. They did not see the sun worshiped in Egypt, and we do not read that such a cult was active among the Chaldaeans. But since they heard that the Persians and other Eastern peoples worshiped the sun as God, they imitated their ways. We see whence they piled up these cults, into an enormous collection. Next:

17 *And he said to me, "Have you seen, son of man? Is it a trifle to the house of Judah to do the abominations they have done there? For they had filled the land with violence and have turned to provoke me; and behold, they put a branch* [others translate it 'stench'] *to their nose* [this is acceptable to many, but to me it is more convincing as 'to their wrath,' that is, taking it passively for God's wrath that they inflamed against themselves]."

God complains, as he did before, about the people's sins, especially about their heinous defection, through which they contaminated the temple that ought to be sacred to God alone. He goes on to add a further complaint: they would not be content with the sins that resulted in the violation of human society and common law and the neglect of mutual equity, unless their religion was also overthrown. The word חמס [ḥāmās] includes whatever is contrary to the second table of the law. Therefore, by synecdoche חמס [ḥāmās] says in effect they were addicted to fraud, robbery, murder, cruelty, perjury, and rioting.

Therefore, since they refrained from no injustice, God says, "Now they have obviously provoked me as well!" It is as if he said, "After their injustices to humanity, now they dare to level their horns at me." We know that the law of God is comprised of two tables. As for the first table, it prescribes what true and pure worship of God is like. The Jews had violated the second table when they neglected all the duties of love, when no equity and uprightness flourished among them. Then the phrase, *"after they had filled the land with iniquity";* there was intolerable wickedness, because after despising humankind, they attacked God himself. Now we see the point of this passage.

"Is it a trifle?" he says. After he has spoken about the seriousness of the sin, "simply and of itself," as they put it, he expands on it with a comparison when he says, *"They had earlier filled the land with violence, but now they have turned to provoke me." "Behold, they. . . ."* The adverb of place, "there," must be noted, as I mentioned before. Their wickedness was more detestable since they broke into the temple to fornicate with their idols. At least that place ought to have remained untouched and unimpaired, even though the whole world was infected with many iniquities. But when not even the temple is spared, it is a sign of a desperate and furious boldness — or something worse. That is why he repeats, with the same intent, the adverb he used before.

As far as the last part of the verse is concerned, some take הזמורה [hazzᵉmôrâ] as "stench," which I have already mentioned. I do not know what prompts them to do that. I do not know whether this word is read in that sense anywhere else. But since nothing better occurred to them, they think that this is probable. Some concocted the absurd story that they would break wind in honor of the sun, as if the noise of the bowels was an obeisance acceptable to the idol, since in this way they openly scorned God. But these are fabrications.

Others more correctly think that this is used metaphorically. They were accustomed to make incense for their idols, and hence, on this view, God is alluding to the pleasing sweet aroma by calling it "stench." He said, as it were, "Although the Jews were pleased with their superstitions, nevertheless the smell of incense was worse than foul; and in the end they would realize that." If he is speaking about the nose, it ought to refer to punishment.

There are some who suppose, however, that a third-person possessive pronoun is used for a first person, as if God were saying "to my nose" or "to my wrath." They fabricate the foolish notion that the passage was changed by the rabbis out of reverence for God, as if there were not countless passages where God proclaims in very clear words that he was abused and despised.

211

But, in the first place, since this word strictly speaking means "branch" and is used in several passages with this meaning, and since the noun אף ['ap] can be taken in a passive or an active sense, the construction runs very well if we say, *"they put forth a branch to their wrath"; that is, to their destruction, because they provoked God. What then does "put forth a branch" mean? They heaped evil on evil. They had violated, I said, the second table of the law; they were thieves, plunderers, perjurers, and violent. Later, their madness attacked the first table of the law, so that they completely overturned the worship of God.

Therefore, *"branches were put forth"* fits quite well. The singular is frequently used for the plural. When they had put forth branches or sprouted, God says that this would be to their ruin; that is, after sparing them for so long he would consume them when the appropriate time for their punishment arrived. Now we understand what the prophet means. But if another opinion is more acceptable, each person is free to judge. I do not want to argue, but show what seems most probable to me. Next:

18 *"I even* ['I too'] *in turn will act in my anger. My eye will not spare, and I will have no mercy; and when they cry in my ear with a loud voice, I will not hear them."*

This seems to me to be a confirmation of the previous verse. He said that they had put forth or sprouted their branches, but to their ruin. Now he repeats the same thing using other words: *"And so I too will act in turn."* That is, "As they now boldly amass their superstitions and constantly provoke me, *I will finally act,"* he says. There is a tacit antithesis here; God was at rest for a long time because when he desists from his judgments, there is a sort of calm. God appears to be at rest when he does not avenge human sins, when he indulges them and shuts his eyes for the moment. Since he suspended his judgments against the Jews, he seemed to be at leisure in heaven. It is in this respect that he says *"he will act in his wrath."* He adds that his vengeance would be so terrible that there would be no place for mercy.

When God proclaims that he would be implacable it ought to shatter us completely. What is more frightening than to have God hostile with no hope of pardon? Whenever God removes his mercy, he gives us reason to tremble. It is not surprising that he threatened the Jews so harshly, for he had learned from every sort of experience that they were hopelessly wicked. Certainly nothing had been omitted to heal them, if they had not been so incorrigible and more than obstinate in conduct. Since such they were, it is not surprising that God was so extremely incensed with them that he left no hope for pardon.

This should be referred in general terms to the entire community. At the same time, there is no doubt, as we will see shortly, that God exempts his elect

212

from the common crowd. If anyone objects that God always hears prayers, I answer that prayers which are born of faith are never rejected. But here it is a matter of cries of confusion that necessity forces from unbelievers. Although they flee to God, as common sense dictates, they do so not with a settled mind, confident of God's promises. Because their tortured souls do not allow them to be at peace, they run to God and cry out to him. This is natural, but they do so without faith and insincerely.

Hence he speaks of the kind of wailing described for us in the person of Esau,[2] and for that reason says, *"with a loud voice."* The faithful raise their voices, even crying out with all their force, as David testifies about himself.[3] But it particularly belongs to unbelievers to spew forth their cries with great bombast, even though their souls are void of faith and constricted by wickedness. Their hearts are not open when they cry out to God in that way. So it is not surprising that God rejects them and is deaf to their complaints. Now follows:

CHAPTER 9

1 *And he cried out with a loud voice in my ear* [that is, "in my hearing"], *saying, "Come near* [others translate it in the past tense: 'they came near.' But I think the other version fits better, that God ordered them to come near. So, 'Come near'], *prefectures* [others translate 'visitations'] *of the city; and each one* ['let each one have' must be understood] *the instrument of his destruction* [that is, 'instrument of war with which to destroy'] *in his hand."*

He now expresses the way he would take the vengeance that was mentioned a little earlier. The prophet says that *God cried out* so that his command reached the Chaldaeans to become the executors of his vengeance. For that reason, the imperative mood is more acceptable to me: *"Come near."* Those who read it as a finite verb in the past tense translate "visitations"; they could not do otherwise, because no meaning can be elicited from "The prefectures of the city have come near." But if we read it in the imperative, the meaning will be most suitable: *"Come near, prefectures."* Moreover, the office is taken for the person; or it is possible for the word "men" to be understood, and then פקדות [*pᵉquddôṯ*] will be taken in the genitive case.

As far as the point is concerned, God commands his ministers, whom he appointed to destroy the city, to *"come near,"* or to prepare themselves, or

2. Mg., Ge. 17:34, i.e., 27:34.
3. Mg., Pss. 3:5, i.e., 3:4; 22:3, i.e., 22:2; 32:3; and frequently elsewhere.

to be ready to carry out their task. *"And let each one,"* he says, *"have the instrument of his destruction."* "Destruction" is taken in an active sense. God did not mean that the Chaldaeans would be armed for their own destruction but to destroy the Jews and to overthrow the city itself. Next:

2 *And, behold, six men coming from the way of the upper* [or, "high"] *gate, which is toward the region of the north; and to each* [literally, "man"] *an instrument for his hammering* [or, "shattering"] *in his hand. And one man in the midst of them was clothed in linens* [or, "a linen garment"], *and a scribe's ink holder was at his side. And they came and stood near the bronze altar.*

Now the prophet recounts that God's command was not uncertain or useless, because its results appeared immediately through a vision. So six men are brought forward. Why he mentions six rather than more or fewer I have not figured out. Some cite Jeremiah 39, which refers to eight leaders who were in Nebuchadnezzar's army and whose authority was foremost.[4] But first they face a difference in number, and second, their interpretation is contorted in many respects.

I am not too anxious or curious about this; and it does not seem to me to deal with the main issue, unless perhaps God wanted to show his servant that only a handful is sufficient and a large army unnecessary. Or he designates in a rather confusing way an entire army in the six men. It is certain, however, that Nebuchadnezzar came equipped with unlimited forces to destroy the city. God wished to break the people's pride and stubbornness by showing his servant only six men who could destroy the whole city.

Then he says that they *came from the gate, or, from the way of the high gate,* or the upper gate that faced north, because Babylon lay in that direction in relation to Jerusalem. It is apparent that the Chaldaeans are denoted here, for whom there was a direct route through that gate when they arose[a] against Jerusalem from the north.

He says that to *each man an instrument for hammering,* or crushing. This word is taken from נָפַץ [*nāpaṣ*], which means "to destroy" and "to grind down." Therefore it can be taken as "a hammer" as well as the act of hammering. Doubtless the prophet indicates that God's command brought quick results, because as soon as he called out, the six men were ready to obey without hesitation. He then expresses this more clearly when he says that *they stood near the altar,* for their standing before the altar was a sign of their readiness to carry out God's commands.

Moreover, this passage is worth noting because it warns us how necessary it is to take seriously God's threats, which are so often slighted among

4. Mg., Je. 39:3.
a. reading *ascenderent.*

us. The joining of God's vengeance with threats is set before us like a mirror so that we learn to be aroused from our torpor. As soon as he spoke, we see that six men appeared before him, armed and prepared to overthrow the city.

God wanted to show this vision to the prophet because he was dealing with a hard and stupid people, as we saw before. The voice of God was like a final denunciation, as if someone sounded a trumpet and proclaimed that there would be no hope of pardon unless the enemy immediately gave up. Thus *God cried out with a loud voice.* But this was no empty cause of terror, because he also added its execution when the six men appeared before the altar. He says, however, the *altar* was made of *bronze,* though Solomon had constructed it out of fitted stones. The bronze altar was not adequate; the reference is to its original form.[5]

Now he says that among them *was one man clothed in a linen garment.* He is not placed with the group, like one of the rest; he is separated because his nature was different. This *man* undoubtedly has the role of an angel; it is quite common in Scripture for angels, when they take on visible form, to be called human. This is not because they were really human, but because God clothed them in that form whenever he pleased. Some restrict this to Christ, and I do not reject their judgment out of hand. But because the prophet adds no distinguishing marks, I prefer to take it generally of any angel.

Thus he says that among the Chaldaeans prepared to carry out God's vengeance there was *one man clothed in linen garments.* Some mark is always attributed to angels to distinguish them from human beings. A linen garment was an unusual adornment at that time. Like apes, the papal sacrificers have improperly imitated that custom in what they call their "surplices." But since priests were usually dressed in linen garments, the angel was presented to the prophet in that attire.

Now let us continue, because the next verse will make clear why that angel was mentioned.

3 *And the glory of the God of Israel went up* [or, "was taken up"] *from the cherub over which it dwelt* [literally, "which was over it"] *to the threshold of the house; and he called out to the man clothed in linen garments, who had a scribe's ink holder at his side.*
4 *And Yahweh said to him, "Pass through the midst of the city, through the midst of Jerusalem, and make a sign on the foreheads of the men who mourn and cry out over all the abominations that are carried out in its midst."*

Now the prophet shows that the angel was yoked to the Chaldaeans as a bridle to prevent them raging blindly and indiscriminately against the elect

5. Mg., 1 Ki. 8:64.

and the reprobate. This is a notable passage. First we learn from it that God effectually threatens the wicked in that he always has ministers ready to obey, and second that even unbelievers fight under God's direction and are ruled by his nod and do nothing except according to his will.

It is not said in vain that the Chaldaeans came to the temple to stand before God's altar. This is not mentioned in their praise, as if they willingly obeyed God; and it was not declared of them that they dedicated their works to his command. But the issue here is his secret providence. Although the Chaldaeans loosened the reins of their desires and did not imagine they were governed from above, God proclaims that they were in his hands, as if they were his mercenaries — just as Satan is said to have appeared as one of the sons of God.[6] Satan did not obey voluntarily, but nothing he devised could harm the holy man Job, except by God's command.

The sons of God are completely different; they offer obedience freely in their desire that God alone should rule. But however great is the distinction between the sons of God and Satan and all the reprobate, it is entirely true that Satan and the reprobate obey God. This is the second point to be learned.

Third, we are taught that God never carries out his vengeance so carelessly that he fails to spare his elect. This is the reason he had an angel in the destruction of Jerusalem who would set a shield, as it were, against the Chaldaeans, to prevent their cruelty exceeding what was acceptable to God, as we will see again a little later. I said that this passage is noteworthy because when God brings forth signs of his wrath, heaven is clouded over and even the faithful are alarmed, indeed panic-stricken, and lose courage no less than the unbelievers. In outward condition they differ in no way from each other.

Terror is hurled against the children of God to obscure all sense of God's grace in the face of adversity. We must therefore diligently affirm the teaching that when God loosens the reins for furious men to scatter, overthrow, and reduce everything to nothing, angels are always present to restrict their excesses with a hidden bridle; otherwise they would be uncontrolled.

Then he says that the *glory of the God of Israel went up from the cherub to the threshold*. He uses God's glory for God himself, as we can easily see from the first of these two verses, for he says that Yahweh himself spoke. This expression fits very well, because we cannot comprehend God except insofar as he accommodates himself to the meager measure of our understanding. God in himself is incomprehensible and does not appear to his prophet as he is (since not even angels can bear the boundless magnitude of his glory, much less mortals), but only insofar as he knew was expedient. The prophet uses God's glory for God himself. That is, the vision was a sign or symbol of God's presence.

6. Mg., Jb. 1:6.

He says that it *went up from the cherub*. There is also a change in number, because it says everywhere that God sits among the cherubim.[7] Here only one cherub is mentioned, but this figure is widely accepted because of its common use. Thus God dwelt among the cherubim. It says that *from there he came to the threshold of the temple*. This was a prelude to the departure that we will see later. It was necessary that this be made known to the Jews because they imagined that God was confined to the visible temple. The prophet therefore shows that God was not fixed to a place and so forced to remain there. This is the reason why it says that he *came from his seat to the threshold of the temple*.

Now he adds that he *called out to the man who was clothed in linen garments and who had an ink holder on his thigh*. However, others translate it "writing tablets." But because it says later, *"write on their foreheads,"* it is likely that the ink holder was on his belt so that he could mark all the elect of God to prevent the Chaldaeans touching them. He again calls the angel a human being, but because of the form he assumed, as I said before.

I cannot continue any longer.

Almighty God, since you have condescended to approach us so intimately, grant that we in turn may eagerly approach you and abide in firm and holy communion. While we continue in the legitimate worship that you prescribe for us in your Word, may your benefits to us also increase, until you lead us to their fullness when you gather us together into your heavenly kingdom, through Jesus Christ, our Lord. Amen.

7. Mg., 2 Sa. 6:2; 2 Ki. 19:15; Is. 37:16.

217

Lecture 24

We began to explain the command given to the angel before God sent out the Chaldaeans to demolish the city and destroy the people. In sum, the angel was ordered to mark the foreheads of all the pious. But the word תו [tāw], which means the same as "sign," is taken by many for the last letter of the Hebrew alphabet. But there is no compelling reason to do so. To the Hebrews תו [tāw] is "sign." It is childish to invent some clever notion that the foreheads of the pious were marked with that letter because the word תורה [tôrâ], which means the teaching of the law, begins with the same letter.

Jerome offers another speculation: he says that during his time among the Samaritans the letter ת [t] was in the form of a cross, with which Christians usually marked themselves at that time.[1] But everyone sees how trifling this is. It was not the figure used today among the papists but the sign that the Antonine Brothers[2] employ. I omit that, however; it is not worth relating.

If subtleties appealed to us, a better reason why the faithful were marked with the last letter would be that they are the last among mortals and the offscourings of the world. Since the beginning, the world has esteemed the sons of God as nothing, like castoffs. That is why I say that they could be marked with the last letter.

But let us be content with the simple and genuine meaning of the prophet. God commands the foreheads of his own to be marked. Yesterday we explained the reason, and we said that the most useful teaching to be gathered from this passage is that when all things seem to be confused on

1. *Commentary on Ezekiel* 9:4-6.
2. Calvin may be referring to the congregation founded by Gaston de Dauphine in 1095, the "Hospital Brothers of St. Antony." Their Genevan Hospital was established in 1453.

218

earth and turned upside down, God never fails to care for his own and protect them from all harm.

God always directs his judgments so that events themselves prove that the salvation of his own is dear and precious to him. We also understand that angels are the ministers of his grace, because they watch over the salvation of the faithful, as Scripture testifies everywhere.[3] Now if someone asks what this sign was like, the response should be simply that this vision was presented to the prophet for the common understanding of all. If we want to distinguish a few people in a crowd, some sign will be necessary. God borrowed from human customs what we read about a sign. Otherwise, the faithful, when mixed in with unbelievers, might not realize that they were beyond the range of weapons.

Because everyone's condition seems to be the same, the faithful could be terrified as soon as God raised a hand to punish sin. Therefore he says here that they were marked in some manner. Indeed, it is true today that we bear a sign by which God distinguishes us from the reprobate, for the blood of Christ reconciles us to the Father, as is well enough known. But perhaps that is too subtle. It is also true that when God struck the land of Egypt, the Israelites were passed over by the angel since the blood of the lamb was splattered on the doorposts.[4] Every house that had the mark of blood was safe and unharmed when God's vengeance attacked all the Egyptians.

But as for this passage's purpose, I interpret it to mean that when God grants freedom to unbelievers so that they seem able to overturn the whole world, he sends angels at the same time to curb their passions to prevent them touching the children of God. This is sufficient for us.

Now the prophet adorns the faithful with various qualities, when he says: *"on the foreheads of the mourning and weeping."* These two words, אָנַק [*'ānak*] and אָנַח [*'ānah*], rhyme. One is written with a final ק [*k*], and the other with a ח [*h*].[a] He says that *"the faithful mourn over the abominations,"* and then *"cry out."* This is how people translate the last clause. It could be taken as "to grieve," provided we understand it of outward sorrow that is openly visible.

We gather from this how God receives us into his protection and sends angels to us as guardians. Even if mixed in with the wicked, we keep ourselves undefiled by their sordid acts. When we cannot correct their offenses, yet we witness to our displeasure by sorrow and sadness. When the apostle commends to us the patience of Lot,[5] he says that his heart was grieved as long as he lived in Sodom. One man — and a foreigner at that — could not recall to a sound mind those lost souls who abandoned themselves to all iniquity. Yet he

3. Mg., Ps. 91:11-12, and frequently elsewhere.
4. Mg., Ex. 12:22-23.
a. The verb Calvin cites as אָנַק [*'ānak*] should be אָנַק [*'ānaq*].
5. Mg., 2 Pet. 2:7.

did not become hardened to the filth of so many sins but constantly mourned before God and was continually sorrowful.

The prophet testifies to the same thing about other believers. Whatever the case, God shows here what he wants his children to be like. Thus if we pretend to approve of the sins of the wicked and applaud them while we curry their favor, we boast in vain that we are God's children. God does not reckon among his own those who fail to mourn over abominations.

It is certainly a sign of excessive heartlessness when we see the sacred name of God subjected to mockery and all order overturned, and yet no grief possesses us. It is no wonder if we are involved in the punishment of sins that we nurture by our conniving: so far are we from being tormented by them. We must affirm this exhortation: "May zeal for the house of God consume us, and may the reproaches of those who reproach God fall on us."[6] As it says in another passage: "Let my tongue cleave to the roof of my mouth, if I do not remember you, O Jerusalem, in my highest joy."[7]

We see on the one hand God's name trampled underfoot and righteousness totally violated, and on the other hand the church of God cruelly and miserably afflicted; if then we laugh in our security, we make it clear and plain that we have nothing in common with God, and we call him "Father" in vain.

So we must note these qualities with which the prophet marks out all the elect of God when he says: *"whoever mourn over the abominations."* Then he adds the words *"cry out"* to express more effectively vehemence and burning zeal, as if he said: "Mourning alone is not sufficient, since many mourn in a corner when they see God's entire order perverted. But when they come out into the light and in public view, they do not dare to give even the slightest hint of suspicion, because they do not want to be hated or cursed." The prophet demands more from the children of God than a secret mourning; he wants them to mourn and cry out in public in order to testify that they abhor what God has condemned in his law. Now it follows:

5 *He said to them in my ears: "Pass through the city after him, strike; and let your eye not spare and have no mercy.*
6 *Strike to kill the old, the young, girl, boy, and women. But you will not go near every man on whom there will be the mark* [or, 'you will not touch whoever bears the mark']; *and begin from my sanctuary." And they began with the older men who were in front of the house.*

Now the prophet adds that the Chaldaeans were sent to destroy the city and its inhabitants. But we must remember the sequence, that they were ordered

6. Mg., Ps. 69:10, i.e., 69:9.
7. Mg., Ps. 137:6.

"to follow behind the angel." So God's grace goes first in order to save all the pious. Then he opens the door and exposes a path far and wide for his wrath after removing the faithful from all danger. This is why he says, *"pass through the city, but after him."*

Paul indicates the same thing when he says, "After your obedience has been completed, then we will be quick to take vengeance against all the rebellious and proud."[8] Thus God takes special care of his own. After taking them under his protection to hide them under his wings, he allows the fire of his vengeance to be kindled against all the reprobate. In sum, we see that whenever God avenges human sins, he is concerned for his church and dignifies with his special care all endowed with a true and earnest zeal for piety.

He commands them *"to strike so that their eye does not spare."* What God himself has undertaken he transfers to the Chaldaeans; there must be agreement between God and all his ministers, even those who do not voluntarily obey but are bent this way and that by God's secret impulse. Then he explains more clearly that *"they should not spare either the old or youths,"* *boys* or girls — as if he said that they must act violently and indiscriminately against everyone, with no choosing between age or sex. Here he contrasts women with men, because women move even the cruelest to be merciful. We know that when men are slain, the women are nevertheless preserved. Girls seem to hold a favored position; boys, too; moreover, decrepit old men, because there is nothing to fear from them, are also kept unharmed. But God wants the Chaldaeans to attack the entire city without regard for age or sex.

At the same time, he exempts the faithful, of whom he said: *"you shall not come near anyone on whom will be the sign."* Here it may be asked whether all good people will be untouched by the destruction. We know that Jeremiah was dragged into Egypt, but it would have been better for him to be exiled in Chaldaea. Before him, Daniel was taken away with his friends; many faithful people were in that crowd.

In contrast, we have seen that many who scorned God either escaped or remained in the land, as if Nebuchadnezzar wanted the dregs of the people to remain there. We saw in Jeremiah what kind they were.[9]

It follows that God did not spare all the elect or maintain a distinction in accord with the sign, because the reprobate were kept safe like the faithful. But it must be noted that although God appears to afflict his own in common with the reprobate, they are nevertheless distinguished so that nothing happens that does not finally lead to salvation.

So when God forbids the Chaldaeans to attack the faithful, he does not mean them to be immune from all trouble or inconvenience. But he promises

8. Mg., 2 Cor. 10:6.
9. Mg., Je. 39:10; 43:2-4; 44:15-16.

that they would be so separated from the reprobate that in the end they would know clearly from experience that God never forgot his faithfulness and promise. Now we understand how that knot is to be untied. Although God does not spare his own without exercising their faith and patience, nevertheless he spares them to prevent anything deadly befalling them; he spares them, in short, as their undying guardian.

Moreover, when he seems to pardon the wicked, this results in their destruction because they are rendered more and more inexcusable. Experience also teaches the same today, for we see the very best so afflicted that God's judgment begins with them. At the same time we see many reprobate exulting and rejoicing even when they boldly rise up against God. But God cares for his own as if they were marked with a sign and distinguishes them from the reprobate. Waiting for the reprobate is their destruction, in which they are already bound, even though it is not yet visible.

Next: *"begin at my sanctuary."* By the word "sanctuary" he no doubt means the priests and Levites; their guilt was even more serious. Indeed, some small number worshiped God purely and persevered in their duties; but the majority had fallen away from the worship of God. So this passage should be understood of the wicked priests who had scorned God and his servants.

It is no wonder that God's vengeance begins with them, for their sin was double. If some private person falls, he does not do as much harm by his example as the prominent, who drag everyone into the same ruin. We know that the eyes of the crowd are fixed on the nobles. Since the priests sinned more seriously than all the rest, it is no wonder if God drags them away for punishment first.

Those who expound this sentence in a general sense, as if God ordered the Chaldaeans to begin with his church, stretch the prophet's meaning too far. The comparison here is not between the church of God and the foreign and profane nations. Rather, God compares the ministers of his temple with the common people. A clearer exposition of this follows immediately: *the Chaldaeans began with the men, the elders who were in front of the house;* that is, the leaders of the temple. Now follows:

7 *And he said to them: "Defile* [or, 'contaminate'] *the house, and fill the altars with the slain. Go forth." And they went forth and struck in the city* [that is, "they wrought slaughter or destruction in the city"].

Here God repeats what he touched on briefly and obscurely some time earlier, that the Jews trusted in the visible temple in vain, because he no longer dwells there. As we will see later, he had departed. He promised that it would be his perpetual dwelling place,[10] but that promise did not stand in the way of

10. Mg., Ps. 132:14.

his deserting that station for a while. Now he begins to deal with this judgment when he orders the Chaldaeans to *"defile the temple itself."*

I admit that someone might say the temple was already defiled; but these words concern the prevalent view among the people. Although the Jews stained God's sanctuary with their sins, they boasted that the worship of God and his sacred name still remained there. Thus he now speaks of another kind of pollution, that *"the Chaldaeans should fill all the courts with the slain."* If the corpse of a human being, or even a dog, was seen in the sanctuary, it was an intolerable sacrilege. All would cry out that it was an omen.

Although they brought their sins before God whenever they entered the temple (for they came defiled by blood, robbery, fraud, perjury, and a great pile of sins), nevertheless they considered all these pollutions as nothing. God indirectly ridicules their foolishness when he says that they boast in vain of the temple's sanctity, because in the end they would see it filled with corpses and would actually recognize that it was no longer sacred. Now we understand the mind of the Holy Spirit.

Now he adds that they *went forth and destruction was inflicted by them in the city.* Here again the prophet shows that the Chaldaeans would be ready to strike terror among the Jews, as soon as God commanded them to wipe out the city and murder all its inhabitants. Perhaps the city was still not under siege at that time; that seems likely. The Jews consequently thought that Ezekiel's threats were fantasies. For this reason he says that the Chaldaeans appeared before him, to hear or receive God's command. Then they *returned from the slaughter* to prove their obedience to God.

In sum, he means that God's threats were not empty; as soon as the right time comes, the Chaldaean army will be ready to obey. Next:

8 *And it happened that when they struck, I was left; and I fell on my face and cried out and said: "Ah* [or, 'Alas'], *Sovereign Yahweh, will you destroy whatever is remaining of Israel* ['all the remnants of Israel'] *by pouring out your wrath on Jerusalem?"*

The prophet is not very anxious to preserve the historical sequence in the construction of his statement, for he says *the Chaldaeans returned,* and then adds later that *when they struck the city he fell on his face.* We know it is common for the Hebrews to recount later what happened earlier. It seems that the prophet *fell on his face* a little before the return, that is, when he learned that the city was already nearly destroyed. But he says that *when they struck, he was left.* Some think that the verb is composed of past and future tenses, because a grammatical account cannot explain how it might be one, simple verb. But the verb seems to be compounded also of the first and third persons, as if he said that he was left alone when all the others perished.

There is no ambiguity in the meaning, however, for he indicates that the Chaldaeans attacked everywhere and left nothing. Since they raged so cruelly against the entire multitude, it seemed to the prophet that he alone was left, as if God snatched him from the horrible fire in which he wanted to consume and destroy the entire people.

Now if someone objects that not everyone was slain, the response is that a destruction occurred that almost wiped out the people's name. Those who survived were as dead, because exile was worse to them than death itself. Finally, it must be noted that although God connives for a time or punishes the reprobate only moderately, this prophecy extends to the ultimate punishment that in the end awaits them. In sum, in the destruction of the city shown to the prophet, it seemed that all the citizens were completely destroyed. In this way God wished to show what a terrible destruction threatened the people, even though no one feared it.

That the prophet *fell on his face* is a testimony to the human affection with which he pursued the people, for all its unworthiness. Thus, *he fell on his face* like an intercessor, for we know that when the faithful beg God to pardon them, they fall on their face. They are also said to pour forth their prayers in lowliness, because they are not worthy to direct their prayers and vows above.[11]

Thus Ezekiel shows that he interceded for the people's salvation. Certainly God did not want his servants to lose all sense of humanity under the pretext of zeal, treating the people's destruction as a joke or game. We saw how anxiously Jeremiah interceded for the people and in the end was wholly consumed in sorrow. He desired, as we saw in chapter 9, his tears to flow like fountains.[12]

Therefore, although the prophets were God's heralds to make known his vengeance, they were not entirely devoid of all care and concern. They pitied the people, whose enemies they might easily appear. This is why *Ezekiel fell on his face before God.*

This was certainly a severe testing that he did not conceal. He did not complain that the populous city would be destroyed and women and boys killed indiscriminately with the men; but he set the covenant before God, as if to say: "Even if the entire world perish, it is absurd that God would completely destroy his church, because he promised that as long as the sun and the moon shine in the heavens, there will be some seed of the pious in the land." He says, "They will be my faithful witnesses in the heavens."[13]

The sun and the moon remained in place. Therefore God might appear

11. Mg., Ps. 102:1.
12. Mg., Je. 9:1.
13. Mg., Ps. 89:37-38, i.e., 89:36-37.

to deny his faithfulness when he destroyed the entire people. This is why the prophet is shocked and falls down on his face and vehemently cries out: *"Oh, Lord Yahweh, will you destroy the remnants of Israel by pouring out your wrath?"* That is, "while you thus pour out your wrath against Jerusalem?" That city remained as a witness to God's covenant. They could still hope for some salvation. Although it was later destroyed the faithful struggled with that testing, and the struggle was arduous and hard. No one would think that any memory of God's covenant could flourish with that city gone. He chose it to be his seat and dwelling place; he wanted to be worshiped in that place alone.

So when the prophet sees the city destroyed, he cries out: "What will happen in the end? When you pour out your anger against Jerusalem, nothing will be left in the city." From this it would be easy to conclude that God's covenant was utterly obliterated and ineffective. Now follows:

9 *And he said to me, "The iniquity of the house of Israel and Judah great beyond measure* [that is how I interpret מאד במאד *(bim'ōḏ mᵉʼōḏ)*], *and the land has been filled with bloods, and the city has been filled with perversity* [some take it as 'judgment,' but it means simply 'defection'], *for they have said: 'Yahweh has abandoned the land, and Yahweh takes no notice.'"*

God responds to his prophet in order to restrain his excessive fervor and at the same time to assert his own righteousness. The prophet might be driven this way and that; he might doubt whether God is true. His faith could also have been struck by another assault, that God raged with excessive cruelty in destroying the innocent. Tossed as he was between these waves of temptations, he had to be settled down — which is what God does. So, as I have already said, God calms his prophet's emotions, and at the same time asserts the equity of his own judgments against all the false opinions that commonly impinge on us when God's judgments do not correspond to our liking.

Meanwhile, it must be noted that the prophet complained submissively about the destruction of the city, and although he seemed to argue with God, he subjects all his feelings to God's rule. Hence a response was given to calm him. Whenever God does not seem to work as our fleshly reason dictates, let us nevertheless learn from the prophet's example to restrain ourselves and subject our reason to God's will; if we do this, it will be enough for us that God wills it so, for his will is the perfect rule of all justice.

We see that sometimes the prophets complain and seem to allow themselves excessive freedom when they debate with God, as we saw in the memorable example of Jeremiah.[14] We read of a similar example in Habakkuk:

14. Mg., Je. 12, i.e., 12:1-4; 20, i.e., 20:7-18.

225

"How long?"[15] The prophets appear to argue with God himself, but they immediately come to their senses and bring to order all the erratic opinions that they sense are improperly disturbing them.

Our prophet on the one hand wonders at the destruction of the city and vehemently cries out; on the other hand at the same time *he falls on his face,* and in this way testifies that he would comply as soon as God answers. This is the reason why God seeks to calm his servant; we would undoubtedly experience the same if only we would learn in modesty and sobriety to inquire of God when his judgments do not correspond to our opinions.

Therefore if we approach God in this manner, he will assuredly show us that whatever he does is right and furnish us with reasons to be at ease. Hence we comprehend God's priceless indulgence toward his own in condescending to give them an account, as if wanting to satisfy them.

It is certain that people are carried away with excessive boldness whenever they question God. "Who will dare to oppose God's judgments? and who will answer against him?" as Paul says.[16] But in his limitless goodness, God condescends to the point of rendering an account of his deeds to his servants in order to calm their minds, as I said.

> *Almighty God, since you once chastised your people so harshly, grant that we may profit by their example and so restrain ourselves in fear of your name and in obedience to your law that you do not pour out your fury against us. Then if you do chastise us, may it all turn to our salvation; and thus may we realize that you have sealed us and numbered us among your children, until at last you gather us into that blessed inheritance which has been won for us by the blood of your only-begotten Son. Amen.*

15. Mg., Hab. 1:2.
16. Mg., Rom. 9:20.

Lecture 25

Yesterday we began to explain God's response when he restrained the prophet's emotions as he complained about the destruction of the entire nation. The prophet's reasoning was somewhat plausible, because he assumed that God's covenant would become void as a result. But God simply responds that he is not exceeding the limit in this punishment.

But the issue is not thus resolved, for the prophet could always doubt how God's covenant would remain firm while the people are slain. But God does not always loosen the knots that bind and perplex us. He leaves us in suspense. In doing so, he wants to test our modesty, for if he completely satisfies us, there will be no test of our obedience. But when he orders us to rest in his judgment, we then behave with proper modesty toward him if we reach no further.

So when God proclaims that *"the sin of Jerusalem and Judah is serious,"* he is giving his prophet only a partial response. He does say *beyond measure,* however, so that the prophet understands that both city and nation are to be destroyed completely, because there was no limit to their sin. When he says that *"the land was filled with bloods and the city with perverted judgments,"* we can take "bloods" to refer to murders, or in general for all kinds of sin. Sometimes Scripture uses "bloods" to describe atrocious sins that deserve death, but at other times simply unjust murders. But because God includes all the sins of the people, I readily interpret *bloods* as the sins that provoked his wrath so many times and brought destruction on themselves.

Next: *"for they said, 'The Lord has abandoned the land, the Lord sees nothing.'"* We had a similar sentence a little earlier,[1] and I warned at the time

1. Mg., 8:12.

that it was taken coldly by interpreters, in assuming that the Jews were Epicureans who imagined God as enjoying his leisure and not caring about human affairs. They think that Jews were so drunk with brutish contempt of God as to imagine they were allowed whatever they wanted with impunity, because God was far away. It is the same today when the profane allow themselves such great license because "they do not keep God before them," as Scripture often says.

But we said that the prophet means something else. Since the Jews were· rebuked very often, they became hardened in their evils; and when they ought to have acknowledged that those penalties were justly inflicted on them, they imagined that everything happened to them by chance. This is how unbelievers refer the outcome of everything to fortune. That is how foolish those people were!

"God visited them," as it often says. He wanted them to acknowledge him as their judge. Although they sensed God's hand was near, they said he was far away because he did not aid them in their miseries or shield them from their enemies. Their fathers had experienced God's helping hand in all their dangers. Therefore when God set aside his care for them and showed himself the enemy rather than the defender of their salvation, they said he was far away.

But as we have seen, he raised up the Chaldaeans and proved the reliability of all the prophecies when he fulfilled all he proclaimed through his servants. Now we see in what sense they said, " 'God has abandoned the land' "; namely, he gave not even a taste of his grace. But they experienced his power in another way when he inflicted punishment on them.

Why did they not consider him a just judge in chastising them in this way? They grasped at this one thing, that God did not care to help them in their miseries. But this passage is worth noting. When God not only invites wretched souls to himself but even draws them by exacting punishments for their sins, they are often rendered more obstinate and imagine God is far way. As a result, they are seized with rage and do not hesitate to provoke him more boldly.

This stubbornness is now described when Ezekiel represents the Jews as saying that " 'God has abandoned the land.' " They conclude that God no longer sees, for once the profane assume that they are abandoned by God, they also think that whatever they do escapes his knowledge. This is extreme godlessness, and God therefore shows that it is impossible for him to spare any longer such utterly lost souls. He also confirms this in the next verse when he says,

10 *"Even I — my eye will not spare* ['them'], *and I will have no mercy. I will turn their ways back on their heads."*

Now God proclaims that the Jews were so obstinate in their evil that they cut themselves off from all hope of pardon. When he says that *"he would be hostile to them without mercy,"* he shows that inflicting judgment was inevitable; their wickedness had reached as far as heaven, and he could not spare them without denying himself. The abrupt expression increases the vehemence, as if God proclaimed that he will get his due. Now we understand the point of this response: the Jews were bound by so many and such shameful offenses that they shut the door on God's mercy; they even forced him to the ultimate vengeance, by not ceasing to provoke him with increasing brazenness.

Let us learn from this passage not to weigh God's judgments on our scales, because we are mostly accustomed to extenuate our sins and to make minor errors out of the most serious offenses. We do not offer God his due honor as the only judge.

Now when God orders his prophet to be quiet and silent, he also undoubtedly restrains our recklessness in erupting into protest when he seems to us excessively rigid. But as I have already said, we do not grasp how serious our sins are. It is God's prerogative alone to proclaim what constitutes sins, so that no mortal judges the quality of this or that deed. When we do that, we seize for ourselves what is proper to God alone. Next:

11 *And behold, the man clothed in linen garments, who had the ink holder on his side, returned and reported, saying, "I have done as you instructed* [or, 'commanded'] *me."*

This sentence confirms what we said yesterday about God's paternal care for the faithful. The prophet taught that before God permitted the Chaldaeans to destroy the city, the angel was sent ahead to aid the elect and oppose the harshness of their enemies. We said that we were shown, as in a mirror, God maintaining this order in his judgments, that his paternal love always goes before the faithful, allowing nothing to happen to them except what in the end results in their salvation.

This is the reason why the angel now says that *"he did what was commanded."* The angel's obedience is surely being reported to us because he responded to God's will. We gather from this that the salvation of the faithful is always precious to God; they will always be protected and unharmed even when we think heaven and earth are mixed in confusion. This is the point. Now follows:

CHAPTER 10

1 *And I looked and, behold, above the expanse that was over the head of the cherubim, like a stone of sapphire, as the appearance of the likeness of a throne, which was seen above them.*

Here the prophet relates another vision that has a great affinity with the first vision related to us in chapter 1. But this one has another purpose, as we will see later. Since we examined the individual parts of the vision in chapter 1, however, I will now be more brief. I will only touch on what was said before, and I will also note the differences.

But before I come to this, we must understand God's purpose in this vision. God wished to make it clear to the Jews that there would no longer be anything in common between them and him, because he intended to abandon the temple and consume the entire city in a blaze. God's terrifying majesty, which would strike even the senseless with fear, was manifested to the Jews so that this threat would not be ineffective.

Now I come to the text. He says that *he saw again a throne over the heads of the cherubim, whose color was like sapphire.* Now he uses "cherubim" in place of "creatures"; there is no doubt, however, that the creatures he spoke of before were cherubim. But because the vision is now presented in the temple, God begins to make known to his servant in a more familiar way what before was too obscure.

He saw four creatures near the river Chebar, that is, in a profane region. Since the Jewish and Israelite exiles were far from the temple, it is not surprising that God did not appear to his prophet as distinctly then as he does now after being led into the temple. Although the prophet did not change places, not in vain did he appear as though transported to Jerusalem to behold what was happening in the temple. This is why he now uses the word "cherubim" for what he simply called "creatures" before.

We said that although there were only two cherubim in the sanctuary, four were seen here because the Jews were so hardened in their crass ignorance. They had long ago fallen away from a desire for sincere piety and had almost completely extinguished the light of heavenly teaching. Since the ignorance of the people was so crass, something must be allowed for their rudeness, because otherwise they could not grasp what they must learn.

There is also no doubt that God wanted to rebuke indirectly their shameful ignorance. It was not his fault that they failed to perceive in the law and the temple whatever was beneficial to know for salvation. So when God changes the pattern of the law — as if he had changed himself — he is no doubt showing how degenerate the people were.

But we must also remember what I said then, that the four cherubim were presented to the prophet to show that God embraced the whole world under his rule. A little earlier we saw that the Jews became thick-skinned and imagined they were outside God's care; they were so blind as to conclude that God had no concern for the world. Since they used their perverted imaginations to enclose God in heaven, he shows that he governs the whole earth and that nothing moves except by his hidden power.

Therefore, when four cherubim are put in place of two, God is, as it were, showing that he reigns throughout the four regions of the world and that his power extends everywhere. Thus it was exceedingly wicked for the Jews to imagine that he had abandoned the earth.

Third, we should note what we also stated at that time, that four heads are attributed to the cherubim so that God might show that angelic motion flourishes in every creature. But I will repeat this last point in its place; now I merely mention it.

Now we must see why the prophet says *there was a throne whose color resembled sapphire, and that throne was over the four cherubim.* The reason is that God's angels are ready to obey. They are positioned under his feet so that we might know they are not independent but under God and always wait for his nod and move wherever he orders. This is the reason *why they were placed under the expanse, where God's throne was.*

As far as the expanse is concerned, it is the word that Moses uses when he narrates the creation of the world.[2] The Greeks[3] translated it στερέωμα [stereōma], but improperly, and the Latins followed them with the word translated "firmament."[4] It is used for heaven and the entire space between us and heaven, yet it stands out above this world.

It is not irrelevant that God shows his throne above the expanse of heaven, to prevent the prophet conceiving of anything earthly. We know how prone human minds are to imagine earthly things. But when God is mentioned, we cannot conceive anything correctly unless we raise all of our senses above the entire world.

The expanse was therefore interposed between God's throne and the earth so that God might raise up his prophet's mind and show that he was near, and the prophet would consider the oracles with reverence and with proper humility look to God's heavenly glory. Next:

2   *And he said to the man who was clothed in the linen garments, he said: "Go [or, 'enter'] in ['into'] the middle of the wheels ['wheel'] under the cherub; and fill your palms with coals of fire [that is, 'burning coals'] from*

2. Mg., Gn. 1:6-8.
3. Septuagint.
4. Vulgate.

*the midst of the cherubim, and scatter against the city." And he entered in my
eyes* ["before my eyes"].

Now he recounts the goal of the vision, which I mentioned a little earlier:
that God had decided to destroy the city completely. This is depicted under a
visible and outward symbol. God is said *to have commanded the man who
was clothed in linen garments "to fill his palms with coals and throw them
against the city,"* that is, to start a fire everywhere.

The name of God is not used here, but a little later the prophet will refer
more clearly to what he now mentions briefly and thus obscurely. It is certain,
however, that the words concern the one sitting on the throne; and from the
context it is also easy to infer that this command could refer to none but God.

We must note that the angel who earlier was commanded to mark the
elect now takes on a new role. We can tell from this that the angels are ministers
of God's grace to the faithful and also carry out God's vengeance whenever
ordered to do so. They are like a steward in charge of a great family; he not
only has the duty of nurturing the family, that is, supplying them with food
and clothing, but he also disciplines the badly and improperly behaved. That
is the explanation of the angels' duty.

When God wishes to brand sinners with a double shame, he often assigns
that role to the devil as his executioner. To be handed over to the devil is a
sign of extreme vengeance. But God often carries out his judgments against
the reprobate through his angels. Examples of this occur everywhere, but the
example more memorable than all the others is when the angel destroyed many
thousands of Sennacherib's army to relieve their oppressive siege against
Jerusalem.[5]

The same thing is now related by the prophet. We saw that the angel
clothed in linen garments was the guardian of the faithful to keep them from
any harm. Now, however, he is sent *"to scatter coals throughout the entire
city,"* thus to consume both stones and wood, along with the people. These
things seem to contradict one another, but we have shown that there is no
absurdity in God imposing a double role on his angels. Thus, *he said to the
man who was clothed, "Enter into the middle of the wheel under the cherub."*
There is a change of number, because the singular "cherub" is used for
"cherubim." But earlier I mentioned that this was common, and God's purpose
was only to note where the coals were taken from to burn the city.

The altar is never without fire.[6] It was not permitted to take fire from
anywhere else, since the sacrifices would have been contaminated thereby. But
the purpose of that perpetual fire which God wanted burning on the altar was

5. Mg., 2 Ki. 19:35; Is. 37:36.
6. Mg., Lv. 6:12-13.

to reconcile God, for sins are expiated by sacrifices. The altar fire was like the soul of the people. But now God indicates that he has the fire hidden among the wheels that were near the cherubim or the four creatures. We said, and it must be repeated again, that all the motions, or changes as they are commonly called, which we observe under heaven, are represented *"by the wheels."*

He saw *"the wheels under the angels."* When a wind arises, when the sky is covered with thunderclouds or fog, when rain falls from the sky, when the air is disturbed by lightning — when all these things happen, we suppose that such motions and agitations happen naturally. But earlier God wanted to teach us that those disturbances are not blind but directed by a hidden power. Angelic motion or inspiration is always active.

Now, when God orders his angel *"to take fire from the middle of the wheel that was under the cherub,"* this is the same as teaching that he has various ways of destroying the city. As we saw before, the wheels were moved in different directions so that they flew about through the whole world. Since the fire was in the middle of the wheels, and the angels moved the wheels by their own secret motion, we conclude that the burning of the city was in God's hand and at the same time in the temple. The wheels appeared now to the prophet not by the river Chebar but in the temple itself. As I mentioned, there is a tacit antithesis between the fire that reconciled God by its incense and whose sacrifices emitted an odor pleasant and gratifying to God, and the fire that would destroy the whole people.

Moreover, he says that *the angel had entered,* to let us know, as I taught before, that as soon as God has pronounced what he wants done, it is promptly carried out. In short, the prophet here commends to us the outworking of God's authority when he says that the *angel entered immediately,* as God ordered. Next:

3 *And the cherubim were standing at the right of the house when the man came* [that is, "when he entered"]; *and a cloud filled the inner court.*

Here the prophet tells where the cherubim were when the man went in; this concerns only the certainty of the prophecy. We should not seek clever speculations about why they were on the right. He only wanted to show that the way was clear for the angel to approach God directly and that the cherubim were there as if posted to offer their services.

The angel who picked up the fire to hurl against the city had to correspond to the cherubim who represented all the angels. The prophet shows this correspondence in that the cherubim were directed to the right side when the angel[a] entered, in such a way that God was preeminent. The cherubim were

a. *ille.*

ready, and the wheels also supplied the fire. Now we understand his purpose in interposing what we have just read.

By saying that *the inner court was filled with a cloud* he no doubt indicates that God confirmed the vision in every way, lest any suspicion sneak in about the prophet's being deluded by some empty specter. This is the reason why God not only appeared on his heavenly throne but also filled the temple with a cloud.[7]

As we said before, however, this cloud was a symbol of God's alienation.[8] We know that the sanctuary had been filled with a cloud, although God then wanted to testify to his fatherly favor. But in this passage and many others, such as Psalm 18[9] and other passages, a cloud seems to indicate that God's face was turned away, as if the temple was filled with darkness. This will be confirmed better in what follows, for he says:

4 *And the glory of the Lord was raised from over the cherub* [that is, "which was over the cherub"] *to the threshold* ["over the threshold"] *of the house* [that is, "the temple"]; *and the house was filled with the cloud. And the court was filled with the brightness of the glory of Yahweh.*

In this verse the prophet confirms what he touched on above, that the temple was filled with darkness because God had transferred his glory from that place. He says that *the brightness of the glory of God appeared above the threshold.* As God's glory resided in the sanctuary and in the very ark of the covenant, when it moved to the threshold, in effect he extinguished the splendor of his glory that adorned the temple and transferred it elsewhere.

Moreover, he says that *the glory of Yahweh was raised from its place.* These words indicate his departure. Everywhere God is said to dwell among the cherubim; that is where he wanted to be called on. But now his glory is said to be transferred elsewhere. It appears from this that the temple was emptied of God's presence and somehow devoid of his adornment. Apart from God what remained? Darkness, as was mentioned before and is now repeated.

The glory of Yahweh was taken away. From where? From its place and station where it dwelt among the cherubim; then it came to the threshold of the temple. Then, he says, everything changed. God's glory shone in the temple before, but then it was darkened. Nonetheless, the threshold of the house, which was almost profane, was filled with splendor — but not because God dwelt on the threshold.

This vision means something far different: God abandoned his temple

---

7. Mg., Ex. 40:34-35; Nu. 9:15.
8. Mg., 1 Ki. 8:10-11.
9. Mg., Ps. 18:12, i.e., 18:11.

and appeared outside it. By "threshold" he means a place visible to everyone. Now we understand the intention of the Holy Spirit when he says that the *glory of Yahweh was raised up from that seat* which he selected for himself to dwell between the cherubim. *And it was seen above the threshold;* the result was that the temple itself became dark. But God's splendor was seen in the court itself. Next:

5 *And the voice of the wings of the cherubim was heard as far as the outer court, like the voice of God Almighty when he speaks.*

The prophet also confirms the vision in this verse, because God gave signs of his presence everywhere. But it also seems to have another purpose, because the cherubim, by the sound of their wings, show that there has been an unusual, unaccustomed, even incomprehensible, change. He says that *there was a sound that shook that place, as if God were speaking.* The prophet is saying that when we hear God's voice it is like God thundering from heaven or making the whole world tremble. No sound could be more awesome than that of the cherubim's wings.

Since God filled his prophet with such terror that he became a messenger or witness to all the others, we can conclude that a miraculous change had occurred.

Almighty God, since you place before our eyes evidences of your wrath, grant that our perversity may not provoke your wrath, as did your ancient people. But rather let us so advance in this teaching that we might repent in time and strive to reconcile yourself to us, and at the same time to cast away all our depraved desires, until at last we are gathered into that blessed rest which your only-begotten Son has obtained for us by his blood. Amen.

Lecture 26

6 *And it happened, that when he ordered the man who was clothed in linen, saying, "Take fire from the middle of the wheel, from the middle of the cherubim," he went ahead and stood near the wheel.*
7 *And the cherub extended his hand from the middle of the cherubim to the fire that was in the middle of the cherubim; and he took and gave it into the palms ["hands"] of the one who was clothed in linen; he took it and went out.*

Here the prophet teaches about the purpose of the vision. The Jews thought they would always be protected and unharmed in God's presence. They thought that the sacred fire of the altar was able to expiate all their sins. But God shows that he resided in the temple and was filled with vengeance against them, and that the cherubim were like guardians of the arms that would finally destroy the people. Here we see shattered that false and perverse boasting which intoxicated the Jews, imagining that God was somehow bound to them.

The angel is ordered to take up fire and scatter it throughout the city to destroy it by burning. This was necessary because the Jews had abused God's tolerance so long and so obstinately that they could not sense God's wrath and repent. This is why the vision was shown to the prophet. It says that fire was given to him. From where was it taken? *It was*, he says, *in the middle of the cherubim*. When David prayed to God,[1] he mentioned the cherubim by which chosen access was opened, and rightly so, because in inviting the faithful to himself — as if reaching out his hands to them — God had available his angels to unite himself with humankind.

1. Mg., Ps. 80:2, i.e., 80:1.

236

Now, however, the prophet teaches that God's presence would not benefit the Jews at all, because he was armed to destroy them. The cherubim who earlier were ministers of grace are now at hand to execute vengeance, because they passed fire from hand to hand to burn the whole city.

He says that *the one who was clothed in linen garments came and stood near the wheels;* these words indicate that the angels were so prepared to obey God that they did not halt in the least. Hesitation — even listlessness — is common with human beings; but the prophet warns that the angels are ready and alert to do their duty. As soon as God shows what he wants done, they extend their hands and are ready to act. This is why he says they *stood near the wheels.* Next:

8 *And the cherubim seemed to have the likeness of a human hand under their wings.*

Now I will mention briefly what I explained more fully in chapter 1, so that I do not burden you with needless repetition. I said *hands appeared under the wings* to let the prophet understand what great power the angels had to act. At the same time he notes the harmony between their movement and the obedience that they offered to God. No doubt the wings represent direction in the angels; thereby God testifies that the angels possess no motion intrinsic and proper to themselves but are governed by God's secret power. The wings indicate something beyond the earthly or human. Giving wings to the angels certainly symbolizes God's secret governance, for they are called not only principalities but also powers.[2] Since God governs the angels by his own will, he wanted them depicted in the sanctuary with wings.[3]

Now because there is no action without hands, the prophet says that *human hands appeared under the wings;* as if to say that the angels' alacrity was not ineffectual, because it was combined with action. Moreover, we know that functions of all kinds are designated by this word in Scripture. In effect, he said that "the angels have wings" because, borne along by the secret power of God, they have no motion of any kind of their own. By possessing hands they are ready and prepared to carry out the functions imposed on them.

But he says that *those hands were concealed under the wings;* this is because the angels did not hastily undertake this or that, like human beings active too eagerly and indiscriminately. Hence he says the *hands were covered by the wings,* because the angels tackled nothing rashly without consideration. All their actions depend on God's hidden governance, as I said. Next:

2. Mg., Col. 1:16.
3. Mg., Ex. 25:20; 37:9.

9 *And I looked and, behold, four wheels near the cherubim; one wheel near one of the cherubim, another wheel near another of the cherubim. And the appearance of the wheels was like stone of Tarshish.*

Here, as in chapter 1, the prophet says that the wheels were added to each of the creatures. I have fully explained the significance of the wheels; now I will repeat myself only in passing. The creatures will be treated more fully a little later.

The wheels are images of all the transformations that are discerned in the world. A more appropriate figure could not be found, for there is nothing stable in the world, and "revolutions," as they commonly say, are unending. Since things are suddenly changed, everything turned upside down in confusion, profane souls cannot be convinced that the world is ruled by God's set plan. Instead, they fabricate for themselves "blind fortune." Therefore, as a concession, God depicted all the transformations, all the "accidents," as they are called, all events, under the form of wheels — as if everything in the world was turning and changing; not only all the elements but especially human affairs are turned upside down.

At the same time he corrected an error while making a concession to human simplicity. We see multiple transformations presented to us in the form of a wheel. Meanwhile we indulge in excessive license when we conceive of blind fortune. The prophet accordingly *saw the wheels near the creatures;* that is, he saw those changes that disturb human minds, as if everything happened in the world by chance. He saw, however, that those wheels are not turned by their own motion but are joined to the angels. Hence the outcome of everything depends on a first cause, namely, God's hidden direction and inspiration that moves the angels and also gives them their power. There is nothing forced in this explanation, because without doubt — as we will quickly see — he represents angels by the creatures.

Let us continue this section:

10 *And their appearance was one likeness* [that is, "they had a single likeness"] *to the four, as if a wheel was in the middle of a wheel.*

We have explained this part as well. He says that *all had the same appearance;* not that God always tempers the outcome of things in a uniform manner. That contradicts our experience. But he means that their appearance was the same, because the diversity that darkens our eyes does not diminish the even tenor and well-tempered tone of God's works. Therefore *the four wheels had one likeness,* because all God's works agree with each other; and although their wondrous variety draws our eyes here and there, nevertheless God knows how to direct to his own purpose things that seem so diffused.

Once again there is a type of concession, when he says that *a wheel was in the middle of a wheel.* We perceive things to be so blended together that no distinction strikes us in considering God's works according to our carnal sense. So if we would pass judgment about God's works, *a wheel was in the middle of a wheel;* that is, there will be a wondrous complexity holding us so enthralled that our minds will not be able to extricate themselves.

This is a concession, then, that *a wheel was in the middle of a wheel.* But right after that a common error is corrected, when the prophet adds that the *wheels had eyes.* There follows:

11 *When they set out, they moved to the four sides; they did not turn back in going* ["in setting out"], *because to that place which their head faced, toward that they walked, they did not turn back in going.*
12 *And the whole flesh of them, and their backs, and their hands, and their wings, and finally the wheels themselves were full of eyes all around the four wheels.*

Now as I mentioned, after the prophet conceded that the outcome of everything is, as it were, contorted and twisted and that God acts enigmatically, he finally shows that nothing happens randomly of itself. The events that we assume are tumultuous and confused have the greatest and most definite direction. For this reason he says first that the *wheels set out in such a way that they did not turn back, since they each one followed its head.*

Interpreters do not agree on these words. The word I translated "head" others translate "first," meaning that the direction in which the first cherub faced, the other cherubim set out after him. But I prefer to think that the wheels are linked with the cherubim themselves, and the singular "head" is used for the plural "heads." Earlier we saw that wheels were joined to each of the cherubim. Therefore each wheel had its own head; that is, it had a creature that directed it. The prophet means that the wheels were not turned in this or that direction by some extrinsic or alien force but were governed by the cherubim themselves, as he will explain more clearly in the next section.

He adds that the *wheels had eyes.* From this we gather that although the outcome of things might make it appear that God plays games, as it were, and executes varied and erratic turns, yet everything is governed by his incomprehensible wisdom. This is why the *wheels* are said *to be filled with eyes.*

The prophet improperly uses the word *flesh* for the body of the wheels; but we know that his speech was not entirely fitting because he lived in exile. So it is not surprising if it is too crude and smacks of barbaric harshness. But the meaning is not ambiguous: *the entire body of the wheels, in the back, in the hands,* that is, every part had eyes.

Next he adds *the wheels themselves;* this is not as if he indicated some-

239

thing different. But after speaking of the body, the backs, and the hands, he simply mentions the wheels, as if to say they had eyes in every part. Now we see how things apparently quite contradictory can be reconciled very well. The way events fall out is as unstable as turning a wheel, and they are also bound up with one another, like one wheel in the middle of another wheel. Furthermore, everything that seems confused to us is so ordered by God that he obviously perceives best what must be done. Events themselves have eyes. How is this so? This seeing depends on angelic inspiration; that is, the wheels do not turn spontaneously hither and thither, but each one follows its leader and head.

But he says something that I omitted: their *appearance was like stone of Tarshish.* Jerome thought the sea of Cilicia was meant and therefore translated it as dark blue.[4] But because we know that Tarshish is the name of a precious stone, I keep that simple meaning. Now follows:

13 *To the wheels themselves, he cried "Wheel" in my ears.*

In this verse the prophet confirms more thoroughly what I have already said, that events have "eyes," since they depend on the secret commands of God. Because nothing happens except according to God's rule, it follows that, in relation to God, there is still a consistent tenor in the complex transformations of things. Therefore he says that *God,* or the angel, *cried out, "Wheel!"*

We know that wheels lack understanding, properly speaking; but here the prophet indicates that all creatures hear God's voice, so that not even the slightest motion happens without that hidden power. When the air is serene and peaceful, we do not reckon that God's voice rules there but imagine some natural cause. Even when the sky becomes cloudy, when it rains, when storms arise, and when other changes occur, we exclude God, as it were, from these happenings.

In contrast the prophet says that *he heard the voice of God when he cried out, "Wheel!"* God did not cry out in jest; he wanted to witness to that hidden inclination which moves all creatures to comply with his rule. The reason why God cried out, *"O, wheel!"* was to prevent us supposing that events move or disturbances arise at random, or that the elements are too brutish to obey God. Indeed, God's voice gives efficacy and vigor to everything. Next:

14 *And four faces to one, to each of the creatures; the face of one was the face of a cherub, and the face of the second was the face of a human being, and of the third the face of a lion, and of the fourth the face of an eagle.*

4. Vulgate of Ezk. 1:16; and Jerome, *Commentary on Ezekiel* 1:15-18.

Now Ezekiel comes to the creatures themselves, which he states were cherubim, but in another form than they had in the sanctuary. We stated in chapter 1 why he saw four cherubim, when only two surrounded the ark of the covenant. This variation could seem absurd, for God usually accommodated visions to the pattern of the law in order to hold the people to its simplicity.

There is no reason to repudiate the account I offered in chapter 1; that is, the people were so crass and dull in that age that it was necessary to deviate from the original and fundamental institution of the law. God was content with two cherubim; and in that number he no doubt represented all the angels. He was surrounded on left and right to show that he in no way lacked the power to bring the people help.

The Jews were so foolish as to enclose God in heaven, because, as we saw before, almost no knowledge of his providence remained. Since the Jews excluded God from governing the world, a new form, differing from that of the law, had to be granted them, so that they would acknowledge God's power as extending to the four corners of the world.

Without doubt through the four creatures God was admonishing them that nothing happens in the world except in accord with his will. Moreover, when the world is described, four regions or quarters are ascribed to it, so now we understand why the prophet saw not only two cherubim but four. The same pattern of diversification occurred in the shape of the cherubim. They were like boys with wings; but the prophet says that each creature had four heads. Without doubt this too was like an aid to arouse the people from their torpor, because otherwise the Jews could not have grasped the power and effectiveness of that angelic inspiration whereby God governs the entire world.

After the four creatures were presented to the prophet, four heads were also given to each of the creatures, namely, the *head of an ox, the head of a human being, the head of a lion, and the head of an eagle.* We said in chapter 1 that all creatures are represented for us in those heads. Although trees, the sea, rivers, plants, air, stars, and the sun are also parts of the world, nevertheless there is in living creatures something close to God, where his power can be seen. There is motion in a human being, an ox, an eagle, and a lion. Hence by synecdoche these creatures embrace all individual parts of the world. In addition, since the creatures are angels, we must see how God attributes the head of a lion, the head of an eagle, and a human head to the angels themselves. This hardly seems appropriate. But he could not have better expressed the inseparable connection that exists between the motion of the angels and all the creatures.

We said that angels are not called "powers of God" without reason. When a lion roars or exerts its strength, it seems to move by itself. This is also said of other living creatures. But here God says that the creatures themselves are somehow parts of the angels but not of the same substance — it refers not to nature but merely to effect.

241

Thus let us realize that when people run about and direct themselves and their concern this way and that in discharge of their duties, and when wild beasts do the same, angelic motion is present; neither humans nor other creatures move themselves. All their power depends on secret inspiration.

A difficult question remains, because Ezekiel says that the first head was a cherub, when he said in chapter 1 it was an ox.[5] Some devise this way out: at a distance it appeared to be an ox, but a closer look showed it to be a cherub. But that is very forced. So I have no doubt that there is some difference in this vision. What he adds immediately afterward is no obstacle to this — that it was the creature he saw at the river Chebar. Things that are related and have an identical purpose are called "the same." Paul says that the fathers in the wilderness ate the same spiritual food and drank the same spiritual drink,[6] and yet we know that the symbol of manna and water flowing from the rock was very different from the holy supper that Christ left us. But as I just said, there is an affinity between these symbols, and they have the same purpose. Hence Paul says it was the same drink and the same food, and Ezekiel says *it was the same creature*.

Moreover, there is nothing absurd in saying there was a change in the vision. When God made himself known at first, it was in a profane land; now the vision comes closer to the form of the sanctuary, because the prophet was seized by the Spirit to see the abominations with which the temple of the Jews was defiled, as we said before. The face of an ox had been presented to the prophet near the river Chebar; now he is shown the face of a cherub that he might understand that the creatures were angels or cherubim, and that the four heads might not distract him. Alerted by that sign, he would determine that each of the creatures was none other than an angel, or a cherub, even though it differed from the usual form, an example of which God placed before Moses on the mountain.

Now we understand that God departed from his prescribed law in presenting this vision to his prophet because the people had so degenerated from all sense of piety as to be unteachable by the simple pattern or rule of the law. They needed crude aids. That is one thing. Next the four creatures are used by God to indicate that his power is diffused throughout the whole world. Four heads are attributed to each of the creatures to let us know that no part of the world is exempt from his providence and secret inspiration that is carried out by the angels.

Now concerning the last clause: earlier the face of an ox was seen by the prophet, but now the face of a cherub appears to help him understand that those creatures were nothing other than angels. God clothes his angels in a

5. Mg., 1:10.
6. Mg., 1 Cor. 10:3-4.

new form because the people's intense dullness could not grasp what they ought to have learned in a personal way. It certainly was not God's fault that they failed to imbibe the teaching of piety from early childhood. Now follows:

15 *And the cherubim went up: this is the creature that I had seen at the river Chebar.*

We will explain later, in its place, why he says that the *cherubim went up.* The purpose and chief point of this vision was that God would no longer dwell in the temple; he decided to depart from there because of the wickedness and sacrilegious profanities that contaminated the temple. This is the reason he says that the *cherubim went up;* but he adds: *that was the creature that he had seen near the river Chebar.* This increases the certainty of the vision, because if it was offered only once, the Jews could vacillate, and its very obscurity would deaden its appeal and render the prophetic teaching tasteless.

But when the vision is repeated, God confirms and ratifies what otherwise was not sufficiently sealed on the people's hearts. Experience teaches that we advance in faith and make greater progress as long as God speaks with us again and again. Even if we think that we are following what we have learned from Scripture, yet if we come across the same verse again, we reflect on it more thoroughly. Moreover, if we read the same idea in two or three of the prophets, God employs several witnesses to establish its truth more firmly. Since we know how great is our propensity to doubt, we always waver; and although God's Word has sufficient power in itself to strengthen us, we continually falter unless our minds are supported by various aids.

God therefore deliberately put before his prophet's eyes the same thing on two occasions so that the prior vision would have more certainty, not only with the prophet himself but also among all the Jews. As we said, although there was some difference, the prophet's saying that it was one and the same creature nevertheless fits quite well. Next:

16 *And when the cherubim set out, the wheels set out from over against them* [or, "next to them"], *and when the cherubim lifted up their wings on high from the earth, the wheels did not turn back, even those over against them.*

The prophet confirms again what he said before, that there was no motion intrinsic to the wheels, which were drawn by a secret impulse as soon as the cherubim moved. We gather from this that events are not fortuitous, moved this way or that by some blind impulse. Instead, they are directed by God's hidden power through the angels.

He says first that *when the cherubim set out, the wheels also set out at the same time;* and then, *when the cherubim lifted up their wings on high, the wheels followed the same course and did not turn back.* That is, they were not distracted from that harmony of which he has already spoken. But we will explain more clearly tomorrow how the wheels did not turn back.

> *Almighty God, since we are the work and creation of your hands, grant us to realize that we do not live and move except in you alone. And grant, we pray, that we would be so subject to you that we are not only ruled by your hidden providence but also give such evidence of our willing obedience and submission to you, as children should, that we zealously glorify your name on earth, until we attain to the enjoyment of that blessed inheritance which is laid up for us in heaven, through Christ our Lord. Amen.*

Lecture 27

Yesterday we began to expound the sentence where the prophet says that the *wheels were lifted up at the same time as the creatures.* We briefly taught that whatever we discern in created things so depends on the motion and inspiration of the angels that they are inseparably connected. Now the prophet adds that the *wheels did not turn back,* which indicates a constant course. For a time some coordination might have been apparent, but a change might suddenly occur. The prophet says, however, that the wheels were raised up with the creatures so that they never departed from them. Now we understand his thinking.

Before this he asserted the same about the creatures; and there we had to resolve a kind of contradiction that might raise a difficulty. He said that the creatures turned back and did not turn back. We reconciled these two statements by saying that the creatures never turned aside until their course was completed and their allotted space was finished. They did turn back, however, in that they dashed about like lightning, hurrying from one activity to another. Therein the prophet wanted to teach that there is nothing abrupt in God's works, nothing cut short, nothing mutilated. The angels direct all actions and the outcome of all things, so that whatever God determines reaches completion. But this does not prevent God working in various ways; after he arrives at one goal, he begins a new course. Now follows:

17 *And when the creatures stood, they also stood; and when they were lifted up, they lifted themselves up, because the spirit of the creatures in them.*

As he said earlier, the wheels complied with the actions of the creatures. Now he says that they also stopped together. It might appear there is something

245

absurd here, for it does not seem fitting that the angels should ever stop moving. We know that their quickness and promptness in carrying out God's commands is celebrated,[1] and as powers of God they consequently never cease carrying out their duty. God never rests. He sustains the world by his power; he governs every little thing so that no sparrow falls to the ground without his decree.[2] That famous saying of Christ is well known: "My Father and I are still working."[3]

So since God never stops working, how should we understand this cessation that the prophet mentions — *when the angels stood, the wheels also stood?* I respond that it relates to human understanding. Although God works constantly through his angels, he seems at times to rest. He does not direct his works uniformly, as the sky is sometimes peaceful and sometimes turbulent. In the same way, variety also appears in God's works, and hence we can easily imagine that sometimes God moves vigorously and other times stands still or rests. This is the stopping that the prophet speaks about when he says that *the creatures stood, and the wheels at the same time with them.*

Experience confirms the same. Sometimes God seems to confound heaven and earth and arouses us to unaccustomed tasks. Other times the course of his works seems to flow like a peaceful river. Therefore it is not absurd that *the wheels stood with the creatures, and at the same time they set out or were lifted up.*

He adds that the *spirit of the creatures was in the wheels.* I explained this portion in chapter 1, but it must be touched on briefly again. Here I take "spirit" as a secret power or force. Properly speaking, wheels are not animated; we said that they represent the outcome of events and whatever seems to happen in the world. But their incomprehensible power and action derive from God's rule such that all creatures are animated by angelic motion. It is not that an angel changes into an ox or human being, but God exerts or diffuses his power by hidden means, so that no creature is directed by its own power alone but is animated by the angels themselves. Now it follows:

18 *And the glory of Yahweh went out from the threshold of the house and stood above the cherubim; and the cherubim lifted up their wings and went up from the earth in my eyes. When they went forth, the wheels also before them; and he stood above the threshold of the eastern gate of Yahweh. And the glory of the God of Israel above them on high.*

Here the prophet teaches the principal meaning of the vision: that God left the temple. We know how confidently the Jews boasted that they would

1. Mg., Ps. 103:20-21.
2. Mg., Mt. 10:29.
3. Mg., Jn. 5:17.

always be protected and safe under God's guardianship. Because of that promise, that "the temple would be the resting place of God where he dwelt,"[4] they did not think it possible that God would ever leave them. So they sinned with abandon. Although they utterly banished God by their sins, they still wanted to hold him bound, as it were.

Isaiah derides this foolishness: "Heaven is my throne; the earth is my footstool; what house will you build for me?"[5] God ordered a temple to be built for himself and wanted to have his earthly dwelling place there. Yet he says it is worthless. In what way? When he promised to dwell in the temple, he wanted his name to be invoked there purely and dutifully. But the Jews defiled the temple in every way. So in vain did they imagine God was enclosed there, for the purpose of his liberality was not to abandon himself captive to the Jews but to have them obedient to him.

Thus Isaiah rightly says that the house was not fit for God's use because it was profaned. We also see this in Jeremiah: "Do not confide in the words of liars: 'The temple of the Lord, the temple of the Lord, the temple of the Lord.' "[6] He uses that repetition because the Jews continually were carried away in their stubbornness and resisted the prophets. Whenever some threat was hurled at them, they immediately fled to that refuge: "The temple of the Lord."

This is why the prophet now relates that *God's glory went out from the sanctuary.* Otherwise what we saw earlier, that "he was sent to scatter fire throughout the entire city," would be absurd; he would burn the temple at the same time and thus God would be consumed by his own fire. I am speaking loosely. When the ark of the covenant is called the "God of hosts,"[7] how could that fire also destroy the ark along with all the other parts of the temple?

But God himself appears and shows that the temple would be emptied of his glory while being destroyed by its enemies. The temple was subsequently destroyed. The Psalms describe its lamentable ruin;[8] with what cruelty and pride, with what barbarous spite their enemies reviled it. This was completely shameful, and it disturbed unsettled minds. Hence it was essential for the faithful to be persuaded that God no longer dwelt in the temple; all that remained was an empty spectacle, and God removed his glory when that place was corrupted by so many iniquities. Now we understand the prophet's purpose when he says that the *glory of Yahweh went out from the threshold of the house and stood above the cherubim.*

He has already said that the cherubim lifted up their wings, which he

4. Mg., Ps. 132:14.
5. Mg., Is. 66:1.
6. Mg., Je. 7:4.
7. Mg., 2 Sa. 6:2.
8. Mg., Pss. 74 and 79.

247

confirms again. It follows that God, along with his angels, in abandoning the temple deserted the Jews; they boasted in vain that in the future they would rest under his protection. Therefore he says that the *cherubim lifted up their wings and went up from the earth before his eyes.*

This clause is not redundant, because it was difficult to persuade the Jews of what he said concerning God's leaving. That saying was famous: "Here will I dwell because I have chosen it."[9] When they seized on this, they thought it more likely that the sun would fall from the sky than God would abandon that temple. But the prophet says that *he saw clearly,* so that no doubt remains.

If someone asks how the promise I just related is consistent with the departure that the prophet now mentions, the response is easy, provided we understand that God does not always work in human ways nor according to our fleshly capacity. It often seems that God breaks off his works so that the beginning lacks its completion. It also seems sometimes that God playfully withdraws his hand so that the outcome does not correspond to its happy beginning.

Since such frustration appears in God's works, according to our carnal sense, it is necessary to speak this way. Otherwise, we might never understand how God departed from the sanctuary that he nevertheless had chosen as his perpetual seat. But he so departed that the place still remained sacred, and the temple that was overturned in human sight still stood before God. The form of the visible temple was destroyed, but since the temple was founded on God's promise, it stood among those ruins, as I said. Although the desolation and devastation ought to have turned Daniel's eyes and senses away from Judea, he still prayed in that direction as if the temple remained intact.[10] Why? Because he had regard to the promise.

For the same reason, the prophets said after the return that "the glory of the second temple will exceed the glory of the first," as the prophet Haggai says in chapter 2.[11] We know how magnificently and profusely Isaiah discoursed about the splendor of the second temple and its inestimable glory.[12] We will see a similar teaching at the end of this book. The temple remained standing in the presence of God because it was founded on his promise; therefore, this temporary departure could not abolish what I said before about God's perpetual abode.

The same thing must be said about the kingdom. It is true that the kingdom ought to stand as long as the sun and the moon shine in the sky;[13] nevertheless, there was a sad interruption for many years. We know the last

9. Mg., Ps. 132:14.
10. Mg., Dn. 6:10.
11. Mg., Hag. 2:10, i.e., 2:9.
12. Mg., Is. 60:7.
13. Mg., Ps. 89:37-38, i.e., 89:36-37.

king was treated with great disgrace, and how all his dignity collapsed so that nothing could be seen except God's horrible vengeance. Nevertheless, that promise always remained in effect, "As long as the sun and the moon stand, they will be my faithful witnesses of the everlasting kingdom."

Now we understand how God left his temple and yet did not retract anything from the promise of his faithfulness. He says, however, that the *glory of the God of Israel stood at the east gate, but above it, such that it was lifted up* from the earth. The point of this ascending is that the Jews should know to seek God no longer in that dwelling of stone and wood; he not only abandoned his seat there, but he ascended above so that they should have no more dealings with him. Now follows:

19 *This is the creature that I had seen beneath the God of Israel at the river Chebar; and I recognized that they were cherubim.*

He repeats what we saw before, that one vision was presented twice because God wanted to emphasize what otherwise could have been ambiguous. The prophet was sufficiently persuaded that he had seen God, but because he had to face great struggles this confirmation was not useless. At the same time we must note that the vision was confirmed a second time not only for the private benefit of one man but so that this sealing testimony would benefit the entire people — or at least render inexcusable those who spurned God's grace, which was so obvious and clearly revealed. Hence he says that *this was the creature that he had seen beneath the God of Israel.*

In chapter 1 he recorded a throne in the expanse of heaven where sat one like a human being in outward form but nevertheless not human. There we saw that he spoke of the one, true God, but those words could not be expounded of the Father; they necessarily applied to the Son.

We must therefore affirm these two things: the prophet removes all doubt when he designates the *God of Israel* as *like a human being.* That could not apply to the person of the Father. The meaning of that likeness ought to be acknowledged among all the pious. There should be no controversy about this, for Sabellius,[14] who removed the distinction of persons, and his madness have been sufficiently refuted. Since the Father never assumed human form or likeness, and since we never read in Scripture that he is compared to a human being, this must be expounded of Christ.

But now Ezekiel testifies, *that is the God of Israel.* We see how absurdly those frauds babble today when, in their eagerness to upset the church, they make Christ a God, as it were, transfused from the substance of the Father.

---

14. A third-century "Modalist Monarchian," who claimed that Father, Son, and Spirit are merely three "modes" or names for the single God.

They confess that he is God; but that is pure deceit, since they say that God the Father is the God of Israel and that this title cannot be applied to Christ or the Spirit. So the Spirit lied through the mouth of the prophet when the Spirit says that the *God of Israel appeared in the form of a human being.* This notable passage refutes that madness with which those frauds weary themselves and others. They confess that Christ is God in such a way that they undermine his true deity by claiming that he was deified from the Father.

He says that *he also recognized that they were cherubim.* Thus he made progress in this second vision, for although he knew before this that God appeared to him, there was no clear recognition of the creatures. So to a degree he remained in suspense about the creatures. But now after God has so directly unveiled to him the vision in the temple, he says that *he was taught that they were cherubim.*

What we said yesterday is confirmed: the face of the ox was changed into the face of a cherub so that the prophet would understand that angels were represented by the appearance of the cherubim who encircled the ark of the covenant. Let us continue:

20 *Four, four faces to one* [that is, "four each"] *and four wings to one; and under their wings the likeness of human hands.*

The prophet seems to be verbose in matters that are not at all in doubt. He has already spoken about the four heads. Why does he repeat this? Because he was dealing with a slow — even recalcitrant — people. They were slow to grasp the prophet's teaching; but their vice became worse because they almost deliberately tried repeatedly to detract from the authority of all the prophets.

The reason the prophet says there were *four heads and four wings for the creatures* is to prevent the Jews from mocking and joking, saying that the prophet was deluded by an empty specter in imagining he saw something that never existed. That is why he stresses frequently what would have been clear in itself, if the Jews had been teachable and compliant. Next:

21 *And the likeness of the faces to them the face that I had seen by the river Chebar; their appearance and they themselves* ["the creatures," or "the cherubim themselves"], *each* ["cherub"] *set out to* ["toward"] *their face.*

He pursues the same theme, that there was nothing perplexing or obscure in this vision since everything was consistent. The memory of the vision that the prophet had received flourished in his mind; now when he was borne into the temple, he recognized the same God and the same forms by which he had been taught before. We see him oppose the audacity of those who would otherwise have boasted that he was advancing his own inventions and had learned nothing. Hence the prophet restrains their petulance and shows that God definitely appeared to him a second time.

Now when he says that *each creature set out toward its face,* without doubt he refers to its movements. He indicates that the angels did not wander from their course, as usually happens if one looks to this side and that or abandons the track and turns aside to the left or right. The prophet says that the creatures set out with each one intent on its goal or purpose. If there were unruly motions in the angels, they would not be God's ministers. In short, the prophet indicates that the angels were not only prompt and ready to obey but also were composed and disciplined according to a definite regimen, so that they would not deviate even a little from the rule and command of God. Now follows:

CHAPTER 11

1 *And the Spirit lifted me up and led me through to the east gate* ["which looked east"] *of the house of Yahweh, and, behold, twenty-five men at the threshold of the gate. And I saw in the middle of them* [that is, "among them"] *Jaazaniah, the son of Azzur, and Pelatiah,*[a] the son of Benaiah, leaders of the people.
2 *And he said to me, "Son of man, these men are devising treachery and offering perverse counsel in this city."*

The prophet warns the entire people that perverse leaders will be the cause of their ruin. "If the blind lead the blind, both will fall in the pit."[15] Since the nobles of the city were evil apostates, they dragged the entire citizenry with them into ruin. Now the prophet shows that the condition of the city is so corrupt that there is no hope of pardon left. Those who ought to have been the eyes of the people had enveloped them in darkness.

He mentions *twenty-five elders.* That number was probably chosen in the confusion, or a definite number used for an indefinite. I prefer the second interpretation. Whatever the case, he means that the governors of the people were impious scorners of God. That is why it was not surprising if their impiety and defection from God and his law had long ago begun to spread among the entire population.

But we must note the prophet's intention. Groups of people are always

a. Here and below Calvin gives this name in various forms — Pelthiah, Phalatias, Phaltias.
15. Mg., Mt. 15:14; Lk. 6:39.

251

accustomed to set up their leaders as shields, as we see being done today in the papacy. Their last refuge is to plead that they are conscious of no guilt in obeying holy mother church. Such was the stubbornness of that ancient people.

Under the excuse of error or ignorance people always gladly reject any blame. Now the prophet shows that the city would not be immune to God's vengeance, since it had been corrupted by its own leaders and rulers. In fact, the reason for the city's destruction was the people's excessive receptivity to perverse examples.

Meanwhile, we must note the prophet's freedom in boldly assailing all the noble leaders. He was, to be sure, beyond danger, since he was in exile; but he thought he was in Jerusalem when he delivered this prophecy. So he displayed a courageous spirit in not sparing even the nobles.

We can infer from this a useful teaching, that people of outstanding reputation or status are not free from blame if they conduct themselves wrongly and badly, as we see the papacy doing. As for the pope himself, it is in his power to condemn the whole world, while he exempts himself from all blame. As for the bishops, first twenty and then thirty witnesses are required; afterward, it went up to seventy. One of those horned beasts cannot be convicted unless the entire population rises up. That is how it was in times past.

Here the prophet shows that no matter how eminent those imbued with power among the people become, they are not sacrosanct or exempt from the law by special privilege. On the contrary, God freely judges them through his Spirit and reproves them through his prophets. Finally, if we would fulfill our duty properly when the role of teaching has been enjoined on us, let us put aside all προσωπολημψία [prosōpolēmpsia],[b] and let those who boast of their superiority over others subject themselves to God's correction. Therefore it says next:

3 *"They say, 'It is not near; build houses* [that is, "let us build"]. *It[c] is the pot* [or, "cauldron"], *but we are the flesh.' "*

Here the prophet explains more clearly what might be obscure about their perverse counsels. He brings into the open what those wicked people thought could be covered up by many deceptions. We know that hypocrites attempt to keep God's eyes shut, and when they scatter their clouds they think that somehow even God has been blinded. This is why Isaiah says that God too is wise, and he laughs at their cleverness in thinking they can besmear God's eyes and conceal their sins with various cover-ups.[16]

b. "respect of persons."
c. *ipsa,* i.e., the city.
16. Mg., Is. 31:2.

Since those people were so defiant, the prophet removes their masks. They might have made excuses about their perverse counsels and denied that they deserved any such punishment. The prophet cut off that opportunity, for their godlessness was more than crystal clear when they boasted that the time was not yet come and that houses could be built in Jerusalem in leisure and peace. The time of the final destruction was at hand, as we saw in Jeremiah, and Jeremiah ordered houses to be built in Chaldaea and those distant regions because they were to spend a long sojourn — seventy years — as captives.[17] Since that predetermined time was at hand, it was monstrous stupidity to oppose God, make fun of God's threats, and boast that it was still time to build.

Now we see that the prophet convicts and condemns the twenty-five men who were leaders of the people because they hardened the people in their stubborn malice and induced in them an insensitivity that rendered the prophet's threats ineffective. They stupefied the people with their flatteries, removed all sense of repentance, and drove away all fear of the vengeance of God that had been announced. This is the depravity in their counsels that the prophet condemns.

But in the second clause, their contempt appears more detestable when they say, *"Jerusalem is the pot, but they are the flesh."* No doubt they are alluding to the prophet Jeremiah. In chapter 1 he was shown a pot; but the fire came down from the north.[18] At the time the Spirit wanted to teach them that the Chaldaeans would come like fire to consume Jerusalem. If a pot is placed on a large and steady fire, even if filled with water and meat, everything in it is consumed. The juice of the meat is burned up by long cooking. God had demonstrated this through his servant Jeremiah. Here the Jews derided and facetiously mocked what should have struck great fear in them, if they had not been so foolish. *"Behold,"* they say, *"we are the flesh and Jerusalem is the pot."* They seem to assail the prophet Jeremiah with their wit, as though he contradicted himself. "What? You threaten us with captivity, and at the same time you say that this city will be a pot and the Chaldaeans the fire. If God wants to cook us, then let us remain in the city. Then we will be free to build houses."

Now we understand why they were looking for some appearance of contradiction in the prophet's words. Reprobate and profane people always try to find subtleties to disparage and demean any faith in heavenly teaching — even to reduce it to nothing, if that were possible.

Therefore the prophet applies a remedy to this evil, as we will see. But before he goes on to that he mentions their wicked joke that *"Jerusalem will be the pot but they the flesh."* They turned what he said into its opposite

17. Mg., Je. 29:5, i.e., 29:5, 10.
18. Mg., Je. 1:13.

LECTURE 27

meaning. The prophet was saying that they would be burned up, since the Chaldaeans would be like fire. But they were saying, "Well, we will be boiled, but it will be done lightly so that we will survive, even to the last old man."

On the one hand, we gather from this how diabolical is the boldness of those who are blinded to God's just judgment; they do not hesitate in their impudence to assail God himself and to overturn the authority of his teaching with their mockery. On the other hand, we see how faithfully Ezekiel performed his role. He was made a prophet; he was not content, however, to carry out his duty on his own but was Jeremiah's helper.

The only way we can devote our efforts to God and his church is when we extend a hand to one another and when ministers join together and strive to help each other. This is what Ezekiel means when he professes to be Jeremiah's associate and helper.

Almighty God, we know from your ancient people how hardened we become unless we are molded by your Spirit and completely renewed in obedience to your teaching. Whenever we hear your threats, grant that we might be terrified in earnest and not for just a moment, but that we strive in a constant spirit of repentance to restore ourselves to you in true and perfect obedience, until at last we are gathered into that blessed peace which has been obtained for us by the blood of your only-begotten Son. Amen.

Lecture 28

4 *"Therefore, prophesy against them; prophesy, son of man."*

Yesterday we saw how the Jews mocked and ridiculed Jeremiah's prophecies, but especially when he threatened them with God's vengeance. He said that he been granted a vision in which Jerusalem was likened to a cooking pot and a fire had been lit in the north. They said in jest that they could rest safely in the city, because they were not cooked yet but still raw. "Even if that prophecy is true," they said, "we will still not leave the city quickly. God predicted that we would be meat to be boiled. If this city is a cauldron, we must stay here until we are cooked. But that has not happened yet. It is meaningless for Jeremiah to proclaim that we will soon be dragged into exile. It is contradictory to say that God wants us to remain quietly in this city and to drag us off to a distant place. Since this is the case, Jeremiah's prophecy is false." That is how they ridiculed him.

But God ordered his second prophet to rise up against them. The repetition of the verb is emphatic: *"Prophesy, prophesy against them."* Nothing is more intolerable than for people to scorn so impudently the wrath of God, which ought to strike fear in everyone. If mountains melt at his presence, if angels tremble before him, how could a vessel of clay dare to contend with its maker?[1]

We see how incensed God becomes against such stubbornness, especially when he proclaims through the mouth of Isaiah that such sin would not be expiated: "I have called you," he said, "to sackcloth and ashes. But you have taken up the opposite: 'Let us eat and drink.' You take my threats as a joke.

1. Mg., Is. 64:1, 3; Jb. 41:16, i.e., 4:17-19.

This was your saying: 'Tomorrow we will die.' As I live, this iniquity of yours will never be forgiven."[2] God affirms under oath that he would never be placated by these wicked and profane despisers of his judgments. That is why he repeats, *"Prophesy, prophesy."* Let us continue:

5 *And the Spirit of Yahweh fell on me and said to me, "Say: 'Thus says Yahweh, "Thus you have spoken, house of Israel; and the risings[a] of your spirit, I know it* [the number is changed].*" ' "*

The prophet changes the meaning of the people's wicked mockery, for they had corrupted what Jeremiah said. They knew what the pot and fire meant for them but thought they could divert God's vengeance by their wit. Here the prophet offers another meaning, not Jeremiah's and not the one the people contrived, but a third. In chapter 24 he will declare again that they will be like meat, because God will cast them into a pot to be boiled so that he might consume their very bones.

But in this passage the prophet's only purpose is to rebut their wicked joke in thinking they had Jeremiah trapped in the inconsistency of his prophecies. What then does he say? First, he says that *the Spirit fell on him,* in order to create confidence in his prophecy. If his words had been based on his own understanding, he could be repudiated with impunity. One who speaks must present the words of God and be the instrument of God's Spirit. The pope and his followers boast of this, but faithful and upright servants of God must exhibit this in deed, that is, not vaunt their own inventions but accept from God's hand what they pass on to the people and thus faithfully fulfill their commission. This is the prophet's purpose in saying, *the Spirit fell on him.*

Although he had been endowed with the gift of prophecy, whenever he appeared in public that gift must be renewed; it is not enough for us to be imbued once with the illumination of the Holy Spirit, unless God works in us every day. Since he continues his gifts in his servants for as long as he uses their labors, Ezekiel does not say needlessly that the *Spirit was still granted to him;* this gift was necessary for each deed.

Then he explains more clearly what he had said, by saying *the Spirit spoke.* He means that whatever he will add thereafter had been dictated to him. He is therefore warning the Jews not to be so foolish as to promise themselves impunity in despising his prophecies. He is not speaking on his own but conveying only what the Spirit prompted and dictated to him.

" ' "*Thus have you spoken, house of Israel,*" ' " he says, " ' "*and I know the risings of your heart.*" ' " Here God presses the Jews sharply lest they hope

2. Mg., Is. 22:12-14.
a. *ascensiones.*

to accomplish something by their shiftiness. We know how audaciously and confidently hypocrites reject all teaching. They do not hesitate to dispute with God, while they find many pretexts to excuse themselves.

There would be no end to this if God did not intervene and with all the power and authority of a judge show that their evasions were in vain and the objections they offered empty and useless. This is the thrust of the prophet's intention when he now says that " ' "whatever arises in their hearts is known to God." ' " These words mean that they seek in vain for an audience[b] in the world, as if they could accomplish something by proving their case before humankind. He says that is useless because their case must finally come to the heavenly court where God alone will be judge. Now, since our thoughts are known to God, it is vain to bring up this or that objection since God will not permit our evasions and allow himself to be mocked by our wit and subtlety.

Now we understand the prophet's point in saying that " ' "God knows what arises in the heart of the Jews." ' " Otherwise they would never stop contending and quarreling with their fallacious arguments and undermining trust in every prophecy. The benefit of this teaching is clear: we grasp at ingenuity in vain, thinking we can escape by means of our devious thoughts. But God sees people's cleverness, and when they try to be ingenious he catches them and shows that whatever they consider to be the highest wisdom is vanity. So let us be eager to prove ourselves to God and not value our works and plans according to our own understanding and judgment. Now follows:

6 " ' "You have multiplied your slain in this city, and you have filled her streets with the slain."
7 Therefore, thus says Sovereign Yahweh, "Your slain that you have put in her midst, they will be the flesh; and she will be the pot [or, 'cauldron']. And I will cast you out of her midst." ' "

Now Ezekiel attacks in hand-to-hand combat the jesters who make light of God with their witty sayings; and he presents the interpretation that I mentioned before, that Jeremiah's prophecy was fulfilled in a way that differed from what they imagined. " ' "You," ' " he says, " ' "have slain many." ' " The city was filled with many corpses. The pot was filled with flesh — cooked flesh. Now there is no room in the pot. "You must be thrown out like scum or stinking meat." No pot can be found for them to be boiled in.

We see the prophet here dealing cleverly with them and mocking them with matching humor. He gives them, however, a deadly wound when he shows that their impudence and jesting in gloating over Jeremiah's supposed contradiction led to their own destruction. Therefore he confirms Jeremiah's prophecy

b. *theatrum.*

257

yet does not give an interpretation of it, because Jeremiah had spoken precisely and clearly in saying they would be meat. The force of this was as if God announced that he would consume them in the center of the city. It happened, as we saw before, but he scattered some of the people to the four winds; others he slew by the sword, and others by famine.

Whatever the case, Jeremiah's prophecy[3] will always be found to be true, for God did cook the Jews with the fire of Chaldaea. But since they twisted that teaching, the prophet now does not pay attention to what Jeremiah meant but shows that they accomplish nothing when they try to evade God. "You," he says, "will not be meat: rather, your slain will be meat. *You have filled the pot.*" That is, "you filled the city with the slain; now there is no place for you. What remains, except for God to throw you out like foul meat? He will not cook you," he says, "or boil you in the pot. But when he has dispatched you into a distant land, there he will consume you."

Now we see how great a disaster the Jews summoned for themselves when they assumed so much freedom in joking that they facetiously ridiculed the prophecies. Therefore, he says, " ' *"they have filled the city with the slain."* ' " He did not mean that people had been openly murdered in Jerusalem, but in expressing it that way he included all types of injustice. We know that all who oppress wretched people, turn them out of their possessions, and suck the blood of the innocent are considered murderers before God. Since all violence is killing in God's sight, he says correctly, " ' *"the city has been filled with the slain."* ' "

The Jews could object that they had used force against no one; they certainly could not be convicted in human eyes. But since iniquity had spread among them to the point where they did not spare the wretched the cruelty of their depredations, he says, " ' *"the city was full of the slain."* ' "

Now he adds that since the city was full of flesh, there was no longer room for them. He shows that although Jeremiah had predicted they were to be cooked by a Chaldaean fire, they had advanced so far in their sins that they were not worthy to be cooked in the city. "A more severe judgment of God remains for you," he says, "since you do not stop provoking his wrath increasingly." Next:

8 " ' *"You feared the sword, and I will bring a sword on you,"* says Sovereign Yahweh.*
9 *"And I will throw you out from her midst and give you into the hands of foreigners; and I will carry out judgments against you.*
10 *And you will fall by the sword. I will judge you to the border of Israel, and you will know that I am Yahweh.*

3. Mg., Je. 1:13.

11 *It will not be a pot for you, and you will not* [the negative must be understood] *be flesh in her midst. I will judge you at the border of Israel." ' "*

We must join all these verses together because the prophet uses several words to pursue one issue. First, *he proclaims that they are " ' "to perish by the sword, since they were frightened of the sword." ' "* He warns them with these words that even if God dragged them out of the city, Jeremiah's prophecy would not be invalid; the Chaldaeans will consume them, like a pot boiling on a fire. In short, he shows how frivolously they mocked in saying, "If we are meat, then we will remain in the pot." The prophet shows that none dare mock God so childishly. When he showed a pot to his servant Jeremiah, he meant this only — that the Jews would perish because the Chaldaeans were coming to consume them. But they twisted the meaning of the prophecy — and did so deliberately. They thought they were sharp and witty when they corrupted heavenly teaching in this way. Therefore the prophet says first, *" ' "You feared the sword, and you will fall on the sword." ' "*

Next he adds the means: *" ' "I will bring on you the sword that you feared." ' "* He says, *" ' "I will drag you out of her midst." ' "* He declares how he will do this — he will lead them out into an open plain to slaughter them more easily. If someone objects that in this case they would not be boiled in the city, the answer is easy: God did not confine his vengeance to one type of punishment when he spoke this way through Jeremiah. We know how the prophets present God's judgment in various ways, and in so doing frequently employ novel figures. The prophets do not always teach in the same way; hence it is not surprising that when he shows briefly that God's revenge on the Jews is near, he employed that illustration.

" ' "You will fall," ' " he says, *" ' "by the sword, and I will judge you at the border of Israel." ' "* He now expresses more clearly what I just mentioned. It certainly was God's judgment when the Jews were dragged out of the city where they thought they had a peaceful nest. God inflicted his judgments on them when he violently dragged them into exile. He began to be their judge at the time when he deprived them of their homeland.

But here he speaks of a more serious judgment. God had already begun to castigate the Jews in driving them out of the city, but he treated them even more harshly at the borders of Israel, because when they came within sight of the Babylonian king, the king of Israel saw his sons being slaughtered. In the end, he too was blinded and taken to Chaldaea. All the nobles were murdered.[4] We may deduce from this that the people's blood was spilled indiscriminately.

Now we understand what God meant when he threatened that *" ' "he would judge them at the borders of Israel," ' "* that is, outside their homeland.

4. Mg., 2 Ki. 25, i.e., 25:4-7; Je. 39, i.e., 39:4-7.

In sum, he threatens a double punishment: First, God will throw them out of Jerusalem, where they were enjoying themselves and said they would dwell for a long time. So the first punishment was exile. Second, he adds that he would not be content with exile, but a harsher punishment awaited them when they were thrown out of their homeland: the land would vomit them forth like rotten meat that it could not stomach. " ' *"I will judge you at the border of Israel"* ' "; that is, beyond the holy land. "Since one curse has already appeared in your exile, a harsher and more fearful revenge will await you."

Now he adds, " ' *"You will know that I am Yahweh."* ' " Without doubt Ezekiel is rebuking them for the insensitivity that was the cause of their intense stubbornness. They would never have dared to fight against God so tenaciously if their minds had not been so numb. If we realized we were struggling with God, horror would immediately seize us. Who labors under such madness that he would dare to come into conflict with his God and creator? Ezekiel indirectly censures this stupidity when he says that the Jews would recognize too late that they were dealing with God.

Although they sinned in ignorance, it does not follow that they are excusable, for whence arose that ignorance except from being inattentive to God? It arose first from carelessness; but that carelessness and security arose from contempt, and contempt from the depraved desire to sin. Since they wanted to hurl themselves into every kind of offense, they drove away — as much as they could — all teaching. They eagerly tried to numb their consciences. So we see how depraved desire drove them to contempt, contempt generated their feelings of security, whence finally emerged this ignorance. At the time it did not occur to them that they were battling with God, but this did not diminish their guilt; as I said, they had willingly and with deliberate evil deadened their minds.

At the same time, God certainly always stung them to make them realize they were sinning. The prophet here speaks of "experiential knowledge," as they say. The wicked are said to know God when they are struck by his hand and recognize his power unwillingly. Whether they will or not, they sense that he is their judge.

Nonetheless, this recognition is of no value to them; it actually heightens their destruction. But we understand the prophet's meaning, that the Jews have been irresponsible and contemptuous of God's servants; because they imagined they were dealing only with human beings and covered themselves with darkness, they failed to perceive the light presented to their eyes. God proclaims that they would in the end recognize with whom they were contending, as Zechariah says, "They will see whom they have pierced."[5] That is, "They will know it was I whom they wounded when they so arrogantly spurned my

5. Mg., Zc. 12:10.

servants and destroyed confidence in my teaching." We infer from this that the minds of the wicked are so confused that "seeing they cannot see."

When they experience God as judge, they are forced by experience itself to confess that they feel his hand. But they continue in their stupidity because they do not profit from it, as the prophet said a little earlier: "You feared the sword." Yet they were carefree, as we have seen, and scorned every threat. What is this fear that the prophet notes? Although the ungodly flatter themselves and imagine they have "made a covenant with death," as Isaiah says,[6] and promise themselves impunity even if the scourge passes over the land, yet they tremble and are always ill at ease, because "there is no peace for them," as he says elsewhere.[7]

In sum, we see that the ungodly always remain secure and stupid; but while secure, they are anxious and tormented by their secret impiety because God's sternness oppresses them.

He concludes, " ' "Jerusalem will not be a pot for them," ' " but he will inflict their punishment " ' "at the borders of Israel." ' " But I have adequately explained that idea. Next:

12 " ' "And you will know that I am Yahweh, because you have not walked in my statutes and you have not kept my judgments. But you have acted according to the judgments of the nations that surround you." ' "

He repeats what he had said, that in the end they would realize too late how impiously and shamefully they had scorned the prophecies, which was to drag God himself down from heaven. God wants the reverence he demands from us to be paid to his Word. In their contempt of teaching, people act insanely, as if they were giants trying to drag God down from heaven.

But he explains the reason more clearly: " ' "because they have not walked in the law and its precepts but entangled themselves in the superstitions of the nations." ' " We see that God cannot be charged with excessive strictness for carrying out so severe and harsh a judgment against the Jews. He had given them the law. It was the height of ingratitude to cast aside the teaching that ought to have been so welcome, and at the same time to adopt the godless rites of the nations. That was deliberately choosing the devil over God himself!

Therefore God shows how severely he would deal with the Jews, yet his punishment would be moderate in proportion to their crimes because they overlooked nothing in piling up wickedness when they rejected the law. When he says that " ' "they did not walk in the law," ' " however, he takes as understood the principle that the law had not been handed down in vain but that the

6. Mg., Is. 28:15.
7. Mg., Is. 48:22; 57:21.

261

Jews had been faithfully and clearly trained in it as the right way. As Moses says, "This is the way; walk in it."[8] Ezekiel undoubtedly had in mind that judgment of Moses in saying, " ' *"The Jews have not walked in the law, and have not kept the judgments of God." ' "* Since God had so clearly showed the way that they had no excuse for their error, what kind of ingratitude was it to leave the way and deliberately throw themselves into error?

Now a comparison makes the crime worse, when he says, " ' *"They followed instead the judgments and rites of the nations that were around them." ' "* Although they had unbelieving neighbors, God set his law before them like a wall to separate them from the profane nations. Since they summoned detestable rites from afar and did so by abandoning and rejecting the law, should we not conclude that they deserved the worst punishment?

At the same time, let us note that if, despite God's extended patience with us, we persist in our stubbornness, there is nothing left when the light of teaching has been extinguished except for God to show in a different way that he is God. The prophetic Word is like a mirror in which we see God. When we close our eyes or even throw the mirror to the ground and smash it, then God reveals himself to us in a different way. That is, he no longer condescends to show us his face but teaches us with his hand; and as we experience his power he convicts us of our wicked stubbornness in being unwilling to submit to his teaching. Next:

13 *And it happened, when I was prophesying, that Pelatiah, the son of Benaiah, died; and I fell on my face and called out in a loud voice and said, "Alas, Sovereign Yahweh, will you work the extermination of the remnant of Israel?"*

There is no doubt that Pelatiah died at the same time this vision was presented to God's servant. We will see at the end of the chapter that the prophet was always in exile, but at the time he believed he was carried off to the temple and also believed that he saw Pelatiah's death. Yet it is likely that he died at his home rather than in the forecourt or threshold of the temple. But we know that visions are not limited in regard to place. As Ezekiel was in the temple in his vision, so he saw the death of Pelatiah in the temple. God thus began to show by way of a prelude that the destruction of the city was at hand, for Pelatiah was among the outstanding governors, as we said.[9]

Pelatiah was undoubtedly highly esteemed, and so his death presaged widespread destruction. This was the reason the prophet exclaimed: *"Alas, Sovereign Yahweh, will you work the extermination of the remnant of Israel?"*

8. Mg., Dt. 5:33; Is. 30:21.
9. Mg., in v. 1 of this chapter.

Only a small number remained out of an immense multitude. Pelatiah was snatched away, and in this way he shows that destruction of the entire population was near. Inevitably the prophet was astonished, fell to the ground, and exclaimed that it was scarcely congruous for God to consume the remnant of Israel. Some remnant had to remain, as we have frequently seen elsewhere. Even in the general slaughter of the entire people, God still creates some hope that the covenant would not be completely abolished. This is why the prophet now cries out.

> Almighty God, since today we too have not ceased to provoke your wrath, grant that, admonished by the prophecies that the ancient people did not scorn with impunity, we might be touched with a true sense of repentance, and so subject ourselves to you that we willingly humble and deny ourselves. May you not only mitigate the punishments that would otherwise hang over us but also reveal yourself as a merciful and forgiving Father toward us, until at last we enjoy the fullness of your fatherly love in your heavenly kingdom, through Christ our Lord. Amen.

Lecture 29

In the last lecture the prophet's complaint and lament over the death of Pelatiah was described for us. He learned from the Spirit that Pelatiah and his peers were wicked despisers of God who had completely corrupted his worship. Yet when he sees him dead, he cries out, as if everything were lost. But we must keep in mind that the prophet was not speaking from his own understanding. He had regard for Pelatiah's great reputation and dignity. He undoubtedly excelled among the other nobles, so that a majority of the people thought that their fortunes depended on his counsel and wisdom. Since almost everyone thought that Pelatiah was the pillar of the city and kingdom, it is not surprising that the prophet, because of the general feeling of admiration, asks whether God plans to destroy the entire remnant of the people. He alludes to the man's name, for פלט [pālaṭ] is "to escape," and hence survivors are called פלטים [pᵉlēṭîm], those who have escaped safely from some danger or slaughter. Pelatiah's very name expresses the idea that whatever hope they have of salvation resides in his person. That is why the prophet asks whether God wants to destroy the rest of his people. Now follows:

14 And the word of Yahweh came to me, saying,

15 "Son of man, your brothers, your brothers, men of your kith and kin, and every house, the entire house of Israel; to whom the inhabitants of Jerusalem have said: 'Depart far from Yahweh; the land has been given to us as an inheritance.'

16 Therefore, say: 'Thus says Sovereign Yahweh, "Because you have been cast far away among the nations, and because you have been scattered throughout the lands, therefore [the copula ought to be taken as inferential,

264

'therefore'] *I will be to them a small sanctuary* [or, 'a sanctuary of a few'] *in the lands to which they shall come." ' "*

Here God seems indirectly to criticize his servant's lack of understanding, or rather the people's error. We said that the prophet proclaimed not his own personal feeling but the generally accepted view. Whatever the case, God responds to the prophet's complaint, as we saw, and shows that even if he removes the eminent and illustrious who seem to be pillars of the city and kingdom, nevertheless the church has not perished. God has hidden reasons for preserving the church, not "great pomp and splendor," as they call it, but that in the end its preservation may arouse wonder.

The point is that even though Pelatiah and all the king's counselors and leaders of the people perish, God is able to work through weakness, ensuring that the church will still survive. So he warns them that the remnant should not be sought in those ranks that were prominent at the time but rather in the common and despised populace. Now we understand God's intention in this response.

So he says, *"Your brothers, your brothers, and the men of your kith and kin."* God calls his servant back to the exiles and captives of whom he himself was one, as though saying that they had not been cut off from the church but were still of some account. God seemed to disown them when he threw them out of the promised land; now he shows that they are still counted among his sons, even though they have been disinherited of the land of Canaan. He repeats the word "brothers" and adds *"men of your kith and kin"* so that the prophet should increasingly reckon himself one of them.

Those who refer this to the three exiles dilute the speech's vehemence; they actually divert readers from the prophet's real meaning by injecting their alien notion. Instead, as I just mentioned, God finds fault with his prophet for perversely restricting the body of the church to the citizens of Jerusalem. God said, in effect, "Do the Israelites appear as foreigners to you because they are captives? So will you leave no place for them in the church? *They are your brothers, your brothers,* God says, *and men of your kith and kin."*

So the repetition is emphatic, and its purpose is that the prophet stop measuring God's grace by the salvation of one city, as he had done. Since one man had suddenly died, he thought all were doomed. In the meantime, he failed to see that he was doing injury to the wretched exiles, whom God had so expelled from the land of Canaan that some hope of mercy remained for them, as all the prophets show and as we will see a little later.

This passage is worth considering, however, so that we learn not to measure the state of the church by common human judgment — or even by the splendor that frequently dazzles the eyes of the simple. Then we would surely think we have found the church where none exists, and despair if it does not present itself to our eyes. So today we see many struck dumb by the magnificent and glittering displays of the papacy. The word "church" is boldly bandied about by everyone, and its banners are brought out. Simple people are caught up in the empty show, and they are dragged to destruction under the name "church" because they decide that the church is present in that deceptive elegance.

By contrast, many cannot see the church with their eyes and point to it with their finger. They consequently accuse God of falsehood, as if all the faithful people in the world were extinct. We must understand that the church is often miraculously preserved in secret. Members of the church are not arrogant people who gain veneration for themselves by empty show among fools. Rather, they are common folk of no repute.

We have a memorable example of this when God recalls his prophet away from the eminent rulers of Jerusalem — and not to other leaders who could attract admirers — but to the wretched exiles whose scattering could render them despicable. So he is teaching that some remnant remains even in Chaldaea.

Now follows: *"to whom the inhabitants of Jerusalem said, 'Depart far from the sanctuary of Yahweh; the land has been given to us.'"* Here God criticizes the arrogance of the people who remained quiet and carefree at home. He quotes the words of the citizens of Jerusalem, placing themselves above the exiles and boasting that the exiles were alienated from the holy people because they had been dragged into exile or gone there of their own accord.

Their words, *" 'Depart far,' "* should not be taken strictly as an imperative but as a declaration to be explained as, "However far they depart from the sanctuary, the land will remain as our heritage." We see the self-satisfied citizens of Jerusalem flattering themselves in their ease, because they were still enjoying their homeland and worshiping God in the temple, and the kingdom — at least in name — still stood.

Although they were enjoying themselves, God shows to the contrary that they were blinded by pride, for he had not cast aside the captives forever, but exacted from them a temporary punishment. It was very stupid boasting to exalt themselves because they had not yet fallen into exile. What meantime was their situation? The king himself had certainly been covered in ignominy. We know what happened to them shortly afterward — reduced to such poverty that mothers devoured their own children, and those nourished in the greatest luxury ate dung. What was left for them to boast about even before the city was besieged? But we deduce from this how deep-seated their stubbornness was, because they had become hardened to the lashes of God. That stupor made it impossible for God to subdue them.

What sort of viciousness is it to exult over the wretched exiles as though driven far away from God? Yet Ezekiel was one of those outcasts, as were

Daniel and his companions. We know that Daniel's piety was so famous in Jerusalem that everyone acknowledged him as the special light and ornament of his age. Since Daniel was so esteemed for his outstanding piety, how could they strut in pride against him? After all, they were guilty of many offenses — profane people full of all kinds of filthiness, addicted to cruelty, fraud, and perjury, sullied by their own fornications, and also infamous for their excesses.

When we see how brazenly they insulted their brothers, we should not be surprised if today the papists also rage that they retain the order of succession and the title of "church," and claim we are outcasts, cut off from the church and consequently unworthy to occupy a place or name among Christians. If the papists are so insolent toward us today, there is no reason their haughtiness should disturb us. In this mirror we may learn that this has always been the case.

There was some ground for the citizens of Jerusalem to claim that the captives had been cast far away. Exile was certainly a just punishment for their sins. But at the same time, how did they dare to distinguish themselves from the exiles when their own lives were worse? In addition, since God had already passed sentence on them, the position of the exiles on whom the judge had also pronounced his sentence could certainly be no different. But the citizens of Jerusalem were deaf to all the prophets' warnings and spurned God; hence that arrogance which said that all who did not remain in the land of Canaan were foreigners.

This passage also teaches that if God ever punishes the sins of those who profess the same religion as we do, there is no reason for us to condemn them completely, as if they were beyond hope. A place must be given for God's mercy.

We must also diligently note what comes next. After the prophet reported the boasts of the citizens of Jerusalem, in supposing they were the only survivors, God responds to the contrary: " ' *"because they have been cast far away among the nations and scattered into the lands, or throughout the lands, therefore I will be a small sanctuary for them." ' "* We see that God claims still some place in the church for the sinners against whom he had executed his rigorous judgment. He says by way of concession: " ' *"they have been rejected and scattered," ' "* but he adds that " ' *"he will nevertheless be a sanctuary for them." ' "* Because they have endured their exile peacefully and with tranquil hearts, he proclaims that he will have mercy on them.

God's sentence is not so general that he has no regard for his elect. This promise should therefore not be extended to all the captives indiscriminately, since we will see that God did not have the generality in mind. There is no doubt, then, that this promise was special, one that God wanted to be a source of consolation for his elect.

He says, " ' *"because they had endured exile" ' "* and dispersion with calm and gentle minds, " ' *"he would be a sanctuary for them." ' "* This approval of their restraint and subjection was significant, for they endured not only expulsion but also dispersion, which is somewhat more grievous. It was a harsh enough test for them all to be dragged off to a faraway place; but they could have united again more easily if they had not been scattered. This dispersion was very grim for them, because they perceived in it grounds for despair, as if they would never again be gathered into one body.

To struggle with these testings was a sign of considerable piety. Some of the faithful do not immediately demonstrate obedience; but because "God knows who are his own"[1] and watches over their salvation, he opposes to all their miseries his protection, on which their salvation is based. Therefore, since " ' *"you have been dispersed throughout the lands," ' "* he says, " ' *"I will be a small sanctuary for them." ' "* He still speaks of them in the third person. They take מעט [*m^e'aṭ*] to be an adjective[a] and translate it as "small sanctuary," even though it can mean "a scarcity of people." It could be appropriately translated "sanctuary for a few."

The other sense fits best, however, that God would be a "small sanctuary" for the captives. This way there will be an antithesis between the splendor of the visible temple and the hidden grace of God, which had not yet been recognized by the Chaldaeans. They would rather trample it under foot, as the Jews who still remained in Jerusalem spat on it. The sanctuary that God selected for himself on Mount Zion rightly attracted everyone's attention; the Israelites were always gazing on it, and God's majesty shone there. It could be called God's "magnificent sanctuary," and there was no such sight in the Babylonian exile. But God says that " ' *"he would nevertheless be a small" ' "* or minor sanctuary *for the captives.*

This passage corresponds to Psalm 90, where Moses says, "O God, you have always been a dwelling place for us."[2] Yet God did not always have a temple or tabernacle since he had made his covenant with the fathers. But Moses teaches that what God finally represented in a visible symbol the fathers knew by experience, namely, that they were hidden in the shadow of God's wings and would be safe and sound only because God protected them.

Therefore in the name of the fathers Moses celebrates the grace of God that had been unceasing even before the construction of the sanctuary. In this passage, then, God uses a metaphor: " ' *"he will be a sanctuary," ' "* but not because he had erected an altar there. Since the Israelites were destitute of any external proof or symbol, he admonishes them that the reality had not been completely removed, that is, that God spread his wings to nurture and protect them.

---

1. Mg., 2 Tim. 2:19.

a. *nomen Tóar,* a Hebrew grammatical term, שֵׁם־תֹּאַר, *šēm-ṭō'ar.*

2. Mg., Ps. 90:1.

This passage is also noteworthy as teaching the faithful not to despair of their lives when God has not set up a standard. He does not come forth publicly with royal banners to save them, yet they should not therefore conclude that they have been completely abandoned. Let them remember what is said here " ' "*about a minor sanctuary.*" ' " Although God does not flaunt his power before human eyes, nevertheless he does not stop helping them secretly. We have a splendid proof of that in our own time.

The world thinks we are lost whenever the condition of the church wavers; the majority are as troubled as if God had deserted them. Let his promise serve as a remedy: " ' "*God is a small sanctuary for the scattered and outcast.*" ' " Even if his hand is hidden, our salvation shows that in the end he has worked powerfully through our weakness.

We see that this sense fits best and contains a very useful lesson. Nevertheless, it fits quite well to say that "God is a sanctuary for a few"; that is, in that huge multitude not many remained who were truly God's people. Most of them had fallen away. God is not considering the godless crowd outside the church but directs his Word only to his elect; it is therefore not surprising that he says they are few in number. Now follows:

17   *"Therefore, you will say: 'Thus says Sovereign Yahweh: "I will assemble you from the peoples, and I will gather you from the lands to which you have been expelled, and I will give you the land of Israel." ' "*

Now God expresses the outcome of his grace. In the previous verse he had said he would be a sanctuary. I mentioned that those words should be understood not of a visible place where God would be worshiped but of his hidden power that would sustain his people. Yet if the exile had been permanent, that promise might appear to be empty. Why would God protect his people in exile if he intended them to rot there? At the same time, the covenant would have been nullified.

Therefore, lest anyone object that God is deceiving his faithful in proclaiming that he would be a sanctuary for them, he now indicates the outcome, that he will finally restore them to their country. *"Therefore,"* he says, · " ' "*I will assemble you from the peoples, and I will gather you from the nations to which you have been expelled, and I will give you the land of Israel." ' "* Since return to their country was a sure token of God's love, he proclaims that they will finally return.

In sum, God promises the restitution of the church in order to ratify his covenant. He said to Abraham, "I will give this land to you and your seed

3. Mg., Gn. 13:15; 17:8.

forever."[3] God therefore speaks of this restitution to show that his covenant remains whole and intact, even though it has been briefly interrupted.

In order to confirm his words, the prophet emphasizes God's name many times, issues instructions in God's name, and directs his discourse to the captives. In such hopeless circumstances, it was difficult to wait patiently for the time to arrive when God would gather his own and call them back to their homeland, as the prophet taught. Hence the faithful were urged to consider God's power so that they would have faith in this prophecy. Next:

18 *"And they will come thither and remove all its idols and all its abominations from it."*

Something more remarkable is added here; when the Israelites return to their country they will be sincere worshipers of God. They will not only offer sacrifices in the temple but purge the land of all impurities. But the prophet warns how great and detestable was the impiety of the ten tribes in contaminating the land with idols. He does not mention the idols of the gentiles; rather, he reproaches the Israelites because they had contaminated the land dedicated to God with their own filth. So the prophet exhorts his fellow citizens to repent, when he shows them that they had not been cast out of the land until they had polluted it. For that reason just was the punishment imposed on their sacrilege. That is one point.

Second, it should be noted that we use God's benefits truly and purely only when we direct their use to the purpose that is here set before us — the pure and correct worship of God among us. Nothing occurs more frequently than this teaching that we have been redeemed by God to celebrate his glory, that the church has been planted for him to be glorified in it and for us to tell of his goodness. So let us learn that God's benefits only then make for our salvation and testify to his paternal favor when they arouse us to worship him.

Third, we must note that we dutifully acquit ourselves toward God only when we purge his worship of all filth and stink. Many so worship God as to corrupt by vile mixtures whatever service they think they are offering. Today even those who count themselves wise are shamefully divided between God and the devil, as if they could satisfy God with half of their worship. Let us learn from this passage that God despises such deceit. When he says that after the Israelites return they will be devoted to piety, he distinguishes them with this mark: " ' *"they will remove all abominations and all idols from the land."* ' " There follows next:

19 *"And I will give them one heart, and I will place a new spirit in their inwards, and I will take away the stony heart from their flesh, and I will give them a fleshy heart,*

270

20 *so that they walk in my statutes and keep my judgments and do them. And they will be my people, and I will be their God."*

Now God shows that what he said about the Israelites' piety could not issue from them until they were renewed and reborn by his Spirit. In the previous verse he seemed to praise the Israelites; but because human beings are too eager to arrogate to themselves what is given them from above, God claims for himself the glory of that goodness which he just mentioned. That zeal to purge the land of all filth was worthy of praise.

It is right that those of the people of Israel who were preserved as survivors be celebrated for being driven by fervent zeal to rid the worship of God of all corruption. But to prevent them boasting that they did this by their own efforts and the impulse of their own hearts, God tempers his previous judgment and shows that the Israelites would have such zeal for piety after he has regenerated them by his Spirit.

This passage alone is sufficient to refute the papists whenever they seize verses from Scripture where God either demands something from his people or speaks of their goodness. "David did this; therefore he acted with free choice." "God demands this; therefore it is within a person's power that he be equal to doing it." So ineptly do they reason! Yet we see how the prophet reconciles these two things: the faithful and God's elect vigorously apply themselves to their duty, are intent on promoting God's glory, and burn with a desire to serve him, yet they are nothing in themselves, for he immediately adds, " ' "I will give them one heart, and I will place a new spirit in their inward parts." ' "

But let us defer the rest until the next lecture.

Almighty God, since the sorry disintegration visible today in your church seems to threaten nothing less than its destruction, grant that we may learn to cast our eyes on the condition of your ancient church and then upon those promises that are common to us also today, so that we might await the emergence of your church from the darkness of death. Meanwhile, may we be content with your aid, however weak in the eyes of the flesh, until it finally becomes clear that our patience was not in vain when we shall enjoy the reward of our faith and patience in your heavenly kingdom, through Christ our Lord. Amen.

271

Lecture 30

In the last lecture, after Ezekiel heralded the people's conversion, he also taught that they would have a singular gift enabling them to repent. Once someone has left the right path, he will sink into a deep abyss unless God extends his hand. Once someone abandons God, he cannot come back to him.

We mentioned this teaching briefly at that time, but now we must add a fuller explanation. First let us consider the prophet's words, and later we will look at the actual issue. *God* promises *that* " ' "*he will give the people one heart.*" ' " Some explain this as a mutual consensus, but that does not fit in my opinion. In Zephaniah 3 the phrase "one shoulder" is understood in this sense.[1] When the prophet says that God will cause all to call upon him purely and worship him "with one shoulder," he seems to mean that they would be of one mind, and each would urge on his neighbor.

But in this passage, "one heart" is opposed to a "divided heart." The Israelites were drawn away by many errors. They ought to have listened to what God was teaching them and submitted to his law, and thus have been content with him alone and devoted themselves wholly to true piety. Their heart was divided, however, like a woman who is not faithful to her husband and wanders after her lusts. Everything is disordered within her. So, too, when the people defected from God's law, they were like a wandering harlot. We see how the hearts of all the ungodly are divided and distracted so that nothing in them is simple or sincere. Now God promises that he will cause the people to be not thus distracted by superstitions but to remain in pure and simple obedience to the law.

If anyone objects that the faithful have a perpetual battle with the desires

1. Mg., Zp. 3:9.

272

of the flesh and for that reason have divided hearts, the answer is easy: "one heart" is understood as the measure of regeneration. The faithful experience great contradiction in themselves, and their hearts are not at all whole. Yet as long as they seriously aspire to God, their heart is said to be whole because it is not two-faced or false.

Now we understand what the prophet means; and in chapter 36, where he repeats the same thought, he will write "new spirit" for "one heart," as he says a little later here: " ' "I will put a new spirit in your inwards, or inner being." ' " By the word "heart" he means the affections; by "spirit" he designates the mind itself and all its thoughts. A person's spirit is often taken as the whole soul, and then it includes all the emotions as well. But when these two words are used together, "heart and spirit," the heart denotes the seat of all the affections and in fact is the will itself. But the spirit is the faculty of understanding.

We know that there are two principal gifts of the soul; the first is the ability to reason, and the second the gift of judgment and choice. Later we will say how people have the faculty of choosing and yet lack freedom of choice. But we must affirm this principle: a person's soul excels first of all in intelligence or reason, and second in judgment, on which choice and will depend. We see, therefore, that with these words the prophet testifies to the need for complete renewal, so that people return to the way from which they once began to stray.

After this he adds, " ' "I will take away the heart of stone, or stony heart, and I will give them a fleshy heart." ' " The word "flesh" is understood in different senses. The prophet alludes to the heart, which we know is part of the body, when he says, " ' "I will remove from their flesh the stony heart." ' " When God regenerates his elect, he does not change their flesh or their skin or blood. Spiritual and inner grace has nothing to do with the body. But the prophet speaks so roughly in order to fit his speech to the understanding of a raw and stupid people. In the first passage, flesh means the same as body; but at the end of the verse, "heart of flesh" is used for a compliant heart.

We must note the antithesis between flesh and stone. Because of its hardness, stone resists even the strongest blows of a hammer. Nothing can be carved on it. But because of its softness, a heart of flesh allows something to be written or carved on it. As I said, the prophet speaks roughly, but his meaning is not at all ambiguous: since the Israelites were full of intransigence, they would be compliant and obedient only after God changed their heart. That is, by correcting their hardness he rendered their heart soft.

He adds next, " ' "that they walk in my statutes and keep my judgments, and do them; and that they be my people and I be (or, "will be") their God." ' " Now the prophet explains more clearly how God confers on his elect hearts of flesh in place of hearts of stone when he regenerates them by his Spirit.

273

That is, he forms them for obedience to his law so that they want to observe his commandments and effectively accomplish what he gives them to will.

Now let us consider more attentively the entire matter that the prophet discusses. When God speaks about a heart of stone, he no doubt condemns all mortals for their stubbornness. It is not a question of a few people whose nature differs from that of others. Instead he presents the Israelites to us as a mirror so that we might recognize our own condition when we are abandoned by him and follow our own inclinations. We infer from this passage that everyone has a heart of stone; that is, everyone is so corrupt that he cannot bear to obey God. Rather, all together are carried away with stubbornness.

It is certain, however, that this fault is accidental.[a] When God created human beings, he did not endow them with hearts of stone. As long as Adam remained whole, without doubt his will was upright and well ordered. He was also inclined to obey God. So when we describe our hearts as "stone," this derives from Adam's fall and the corruptions of nature. If Adam had been created with a hard and refractory heart, that would be a reproach to God.

But as we said, at the beginning Adam's will was upright, at least ready to follow God's righteousness. When Adam corrupted himself, however, we were also lost with him. Thus there is a "heart of stone" because we have been deprived of that integrity of nature which God conferred on us in the beginning. Whatever Adam lost issued in our loss, for he was not created solely in his own right; God showed in Adam's person what the future condition of the human race would be. Therefore, after he had been robbed of the splendid gifts with which he had been adorned, all his posterity were reduced to the same poverty and misery. Thus we have hearts of stone, but it is because of original sin. We must credit this to our father Adam, and not cast the blame for our sin and corruption on God.

Finally we see what the beginning of regeneration is like, when God removes that depravity to which we have been subjected. We should note the two parts of regeneration with which the prophet deals. God states that " ' "*he is giving one heart and a new spirit to his elect.*" ' " It follows therefore that the entire soul is corrupt, from the reason to the affections.

The sophists in the papacy confess that the soul is corrupt, but only in part. They are forced to agree with the ancients that Adam lost his supernatural gifts and that his natural gifts were corrupted. But then they mix light and darkness and imagine that some part of the reason remains sound and whole, and furthermore that the will has been corrupted only in part; hence their common view that human freedom of choice has been wounded and crippled but not destroyed.

They now define freedom of choice as the free faculty of choosing that

a. *adventitium.*

274

is joined with and dependent on reason. The will of itself, apart from judgment, does not have full and solid freedom. But when reason governs and holds supremacy in the soul, then will is obedient and forms itself to follow a prescribed rule. That is freedom of choice. The papists do not deny that freedom of choice is wounded and crippled; but, as I said, they retain something, as if people were partly right-minded through their own initiative, and there remained in the will some inclination or openness to both good and evil.

This is how they chatter in the schools, but we see what the Holy Spirit declares. If a new spirit and a new heart are needed, it follows that the soul is not only wounded in both faculties but is so corrupt that its depravity can be called death and destruction, as far as righteousness is concerned.

But a question is raised: "Is there no difference between a person and a dumb animal? Experience shows that people are gifted with some reason." I answer that, as it says in John 1, "light shines in the darkness."[2] That is, some sparks of understanding remain, but they do not lead people into the way, much less to the goal. Whatever reason and understanding we have do not lead us to obey God, much less with steadfast perseverance to attain the goal.

What then? The sparks shine in the darkness to render us inexcusable. Now see what a person's reason is worth: convicted in his own heart, he realizes that there is no excuse for ignorance or error. So human understanding is quite useless for establishing rightness of life. Perversity appears more clearly in the heart. The human will boils up in defiance, and when something upright and approved by God is thrown in our path, our emotions immediately rage and kick, like a bucking horse when it feels the spur and leaps ahead, throwing its rider. This is just how our will shows its defiance when it accepts nothing that reason and sound understanding dictate.

I have already taught that reason is blind; but that blindness is not so obvious to us, because, as I warned, God leaves some light in us so that no excuse is left for error. Therefore it is not surprising if God promises that " ' "he will give a new heart," ' " because if we examine all human affections, we will find that they are opposed to God. Paul speaks the truth in Romans 8: "all thoughts of the flesh are at enmity with God."[3] No doubt he takes "flesh" in his usual way; that is, it means the entire person, as he is by nature and as he comes from the womb.

If all our emotions are inimical to God and in conflict with him, we see how foolishly the scholastics trifle when they imagine that the will is only wounded; for them the will is weak, not dead. Paul says that he "has been sold under sin,"[4] insofar as he was a son of Adam. "The law," he says,

2. Mg., Jn. 1:5.
3. Mg., Rom. 8:7.
4. Mg., Rom. 7:14.

"brought about sin within me. I have been sold under and delivered over to sin." But what do those people say? "Sin rules in us, but only in part, for there is some integrity that resists sin." How far they are from Paul! Fabrications of that sort are refuted by this passage where God declares that " ' *"newness of heart and spirit are his gift alone."* ' "

This is why in other passages Scripture uses the word "creation," which is noteworthy. Whenever the papists boast that there is the smallest particle of righteousness in them, they make themselves creators. But when Paul says that we are reborn through the Spirit, he calls us τὸ ποίημα [*to poiēma*], his "workman-ship," his "creation,"[5] and he explains that we have been created for good works. What the Psalmist says is also relevant: "He made us and not we ourselves."[6] The issue there is not the first creation when we were made human beings, but the special grace by which we were reborn by the Spirit of God. If regeneration is creation, whoever arrogates to himself even the least part in this matter takes that much from God, as though a person were his own creator — which is detestable even to hear! This point is easily found in teachings throughout the Scriptures.

Now it follows: " ' *"that they walk in my statutes and keep my precepts and do them."* ' " The prophet removes other evasions with which Satan has attempted to obscure God's grace, since he was not able to bury it completely. We have already seen that the papists do not completely do away with God's grace, for they are forced to admit that a person can do nothing except with the help of God's grace, and that freedom of choice lacks energy or effective-ness until it becomes strong through the aid of grace. The papists therefore hold in common with us that human beings, as corrupt, cannot move even a finger to perform some duty for God. But here they err twice, because, as I said, they imagine that some right motion remains in the will and some sound reason in the mind. Then they also add that the grace of the Holy Spirit is not effective without the agreement or cooperation of our free choice. At that point their crass impiety is uncovered.

On the one hand, they agree that we are reborn by the Spirit of God, because otherwise we would be useless in thinking correctly, hindered by our weakness from effectively using our will. But on the other hand, they imagine that God's grace is impaired. How so? Because, according to them, the grace of God gives rise in us to the ability to will aright and to pursue and accomplish what we will. We see that they leave people suspended in midair when they deal with the grace of the Holy Spirit. To what extent does the Spirit of God work in us? They say, "So that we can will correctly, so that we can act correctly." So the Holy Spirit gives us nothing except ability. It is up to us to cooperate and to validate and confirm what would otherwise be of no avail.

5. Mg., Eph. 2:10.
6. Mg., Ps. 100:3.

Of what benefit to us is ability unless an upright will is added? Our condemnation would only increase. Their ignorance is ridiculous, for how could anyone stand even for a moment if God conferred upon us only ability? Adam had that ability in the first creation, and at the time he was whole. But we are corrupt. As long as the remnants of the flesh dwell in us, and as long as we carry them about in this life, we must struggle with great difficulties. If Adam fell so quickly even though he was endowed with an upright nature and had granted to him the faculties of willing and acting rightly, what will become of us? We need not only Adam's uprightness, or the faculty of willing and acting rightly, but we need invincible strength not to yield to temptations, to be superior to the devil, to subjugate all the depraved and corrupt drives of the flesh, and to persevere to the end in this struggle or battle.

We see, therefore, how childish they are to ascribe nothing to the grace of the Holy Spirit except the gift of ability. Augustine prudently examines this question and treats it quite thoroughly in his work *On the Gift of Perseverance and the Predestination of the Saints*. He compares us with the first Adam and shows that God's grace would be effective in an individual only if it brought to us more than ability.

But what need is there for human testimony when the Holy Spirit clearly declares through the mouth of the prophet what we read here? Ezekiel does not say, "I will give them a spirit or a new heart so that they may be able to walk, so that they might be endowed with evenly balanced capacity." What then? " ' *"So that they walk in my precepts, so that they keep my precepts and fulfill my statutes."* ' "

We see then that the scope of regeneration is such that the effect follows, as Paul teaches: "Work out your salvation," he says "with fear and trembling."[7] He exhorts the faithful to strive. God certainly does not want us to be like stones. Let us strive, then, let us stretch every nerve, let us devote our zeal to behaving aright. But Paul warns us that this should be done with fear and trembling, that is, by casting aside all confidence in our own power. If we are so drunk with diabolical pride as to suppose we cooperate with God, and that with the motion of our free choice we aid his grace, we will be babbling and finally God will show us the depths of our blindness.

The reason for this comes next in Paul: "because it is God who works to will and to perform."[8] He does not say that it is God who works an ability and moves us to be able to will. Rather, he says that God is the author of the right will itself. Then he adds the result, since it would not be enough to will without being able to carry it out. But Paul does not use the verb "to be able." That would cause a dispute. Rather, he says that God works in all to perform.

7. Mg., Phil. 2:12.
8. Mg., Phil. 2:13.

If someone objects that people naturally will and naturally act by their own judgment and motion, I respond that the will is inborn in people by nature, so that this faculty is by nature common to both the reprobate and the elect. Everyone wills, but through Adam's fall, it has come about that our will is depraved and rebellious toward God. The will, I say, remains in us, but it is devoted and delivered over to sin.

Where does a right will come from? From the regeneration of the Spirit. Therefore the Spirit does not confer on us the faculty of willing, for that was imparted to us in the womb; it is hereditary and a part of creation that could not be destroyed by Adam's fall. But although there is a will in us, it is by God's gift that we will aright. That is his work. Furthermore, when it is said to be his gift that we will, this is not understood in a general sense, because it should not extend to evil as well as good. When it is a matter of human salvation, Paul properly attributes to God our willing rightly. Now we understand what the prophet's words mean; and he seems to denote perseverance when he says, " ' *"that they may walk in my precepts and keep my judgments and do them."* ' "

The whole matter was made clear in one phrase: " ' *"that they walk in. my statutes."* ' " But in their wickedness human beings always devise ways to dilute God's grace and with sacrilegious audacity attempt to claim for themselves what belongs to God. Hence in order to exclude all pride, the prophet says that our walking in God's precepts, keeping his statutes, and fulfilling the entire law must be attributed to God.

In sum, let us learn to leave all praise to God and thus acknowledge that in our good works there is nothing of our own. But let us especially consider God's singular benefit in perseverance itself. This is certainly necessary when we consider how weak we are and how many violent assaults Satan continually launches against us. First, it would be easy to collapse each moment unless God sustained us; second, the assaults of Satan far surpass our strength. Therefore if we reflect on our condition without God's grace, we will confess that in our good works there is nothing of our own except what is corrupt — an exception wisely noted by Augustine.

It is well known that no work is so laudable that it is not stained by some blemish. Whatever duties we perform do not proceed from perfect love for God, but we always have to struggle to obey God. We see that our works are contaminated by that defect. There is then something of ourselves in our good works — what mars them, so that they are deservedly rejected before God. Where righteousness and praise are concerned, let us learn to leave to God what is his own — unless we deliberately wish to be sacrilegious.

It says next, " ' *"And they will be my people, and I will be their God."* ' " The prophet no doubt includes in these words the free pardon by which God reconciles sinners to himself. It would certainly not be sufficient for us to be renewed in obedience to God's righteousness unless his fatherly forgiveness were added to pardon our weaknesses. This is expressed more clearly in Jeremiah 31 and chapter 36 of our prophet.[9] But this passage of Scripture is well known. Whenever God promises that the sons of Abraham will be his people, this promise is grounded in nothing but his free covenant that includes the remission of sins.

On the one hand, it is as if the prophet added that God will expiate all the stains of his people. Our salvation is comprised in these two parts: God pursues us with his paternal favor, while he tolerates us and does not call us into judgment but buries our sins, as is said in the Psalm: "Blessed is the man to whom God imputes no iniquities."[10] On the other hand, it follows that all to whom he does impute iniquities are wretched and accursed.

If anyone objects that there is no need for forgiveness when we do not sin, the response is easy: the faithful are never so regenerated that they fulfill the law of God. They aspire to keeping his commandments, and earnestly and sincerely at that; but because defects always remain, they are guilty and their guilt cannot be wiped out except by expiation when God forgives them.

We know that rites were prescribed in the law for expiating their sins. Water was sprinkled to that end, and even blood was poured out. But we know that these ceremonies meant nothing of themselves, except to the degree that they directed faith to Christ. So whenever there is a question of our salvation, let these two principles come to mind: we cannot be counted children of God unless he expiates our sins by his grace and thus reconciles himself to us, and unless he rules us by his Spirit.

Now we must keep in mind that human beings should not separate what God has brought together. Those who depend on God's indulgence and permit themselves license to sin tear up his covenant and impiously mangle it. Why? Because God has said simultaneously that he will be propitious to his children and thus will renew their hearts. Those who seize on only one part, that is, the forgiveness by which God tolerates them, and disregard the other, act exactly like sacrilegious forgers who would abolish half of God's covenant. That is why we hold to what I said; these words denote the reconciliation through which God does not impute sin to his people.

Finally, let us note that the full perfection of our salvation is based on God's numbering us among his people. As it says in the Psalm, "Blessed is the people whose God is the Lord."[11] Full happiness is there depicted, when God dignifies a people with the honor of reckoning them his special possession. Only may he be propitious to us, and we shall not be anxious, for our salvation is sure. Next:

9. Mg., Je. 31:33, i.e., 31:33-34; Ezk. 36:25-27.
10. Mg., Ps. 32:1-2.
11. Mg., Ps. 33:12.

279

21 *"And of those whose heart goes* [or, 'walks'] *after the heart of their abominations* ['obscenities'] *and pollutions. I will pay back their way upon their heads, says Sovereign Yahweh." ' "*

The prophet certainly uses an awkward expression: " ' *"their heart will go after the heart." ' "* That is why some refer this to imitation; that is, God promises that he will be an avenger of any of the people who surrender themselves to bad examples and associate with the ungodly as if they were united in heart and soul. But that is harsh.

The repetition is redundant, for the prophet means nothing else but that God would be the avenger if the Israelites follow their own hearts and walk in their filth and abominations. The first thing to grasp is the prophet's intention in presenting this sentence. God freely poured out the treasures of his mercy, but hypocrites are always mixed in with the good and confidently boast of themselves as members of the church and with great audacity pretend to God's name. The prophet accordingly adds this threat lest all without distinction assume that the promises we hear apply to them.

There have always been many reprobates among the chosen people, because "not everyone descended from father Abraham was a true Israelite."[12] Since this is so, the prophet rightly shows that whatever he promised earlier is restricted to God's elect and to the true and legitimate members of the church. It is not for the spurious or degenerate, or those who have not been reborn of the true and incorruptible seed. This is the prophet's point.

But it might seem excessively rigorous for God to come forward armed, as it were, to destroy all who have not repented. So the prophet reveals their offense, that " ' *"their heart walks after their heart." ' "* Their heart draws itself on, and that is why the word "heart" is repeated twice. The repetition is superfluous but emphatic, when he says, "The heart of those who so insistently cling to their superstitions is repeatedly impelled by itself to new passions, so that it always pursues superstitions in an uninterrupted course. I will be the avenger," God says.

So whenever God places before us testimonies of his grace, let each descend within himself and examine all his affections. Let no one who has discovered his vices be pleased with them. Instead, let him groan and strive to renounce his own affections in order to follow God. Let him not become hardened and stubborn with his heart heading for evil and ruin in an unbroken course, as it says here.

Almighty God, as we have completely perished in our father Adam,
and no part of us remains uncorrupted so long as we bear in both

12. Mg., Rom. 9:6-7.

body and soul grounds for wrath, condemnation, and death, grant that, reborn in your Spirit, we may increasingly set aside our own will and spirit, and so submit ourselves to you that your Spirit may truly reign within us. And then grant, we pray, that we not be ungrateful to you, but, appreciating how invaluable is this blessing, may dedicate and direct our entire life to glorifying your name in Jesus Christ our Lord. Amen.

Lecture 31

22 *And the cherubim lifted up their wings, and the wheels beside them. And the glory of the God of Israel was over them above.*
23 *And the glory of Yahweh went up from the middle of the city and stood on the mountain that is east of the city.*

Here Ezekiel repeats what we saw before, that just as God had chosen Mount Zion, in the end he repudiated it, since the place had been defiled by the people's numerous sins. The Jews imagined that God was held like a captive among them, and in this confidence gave themselves immense license. Therefore the prophet shows that God was not so bound that he could not go elsewhere when he saw fit. What is more, he proclaims that he has now gone away, and the temple has been emptied of his glory.

This was almost incredible. Since God had promised that he would dwell there forever,[1] the faithful could scarcely conceive that he would leave his chosen temple and ignore his promise. But this break did not prevent the promise being permanently true and valid. God did not completely abandon Zion, since he must keep the contrary promise about the return. Since the exile would be temporary and after seventy years the temple would be restored, these two things could be reconciled: God had departed elsewhere and yet that place remained sacred. After the time that God had predetermined had passed, he would again restore his worship in the temple and on Mount Zion.

He says, however, that God *went out of the city in a visible manner, and the cherubim at the same time.* In fact, God was carried on the wings of the cherubim, as Scripture says in another place.[2] He does this because the Jews

1. Mg., Ps. 132:14.
2. Mg., Ps. 18:11, i.e., 18:10.

282

were entranced by external symbols. Since the ark of the covenant was enclosed in the sanctuary, no one would have persuaded them that God could be torn away from there. The prophet says about this, *the cherubim flew elsewhere, and at the same time God was borne on their wings.* Now he adds:

24 *And the Spirit lifted me up and took me back to Chaldaea to the captivity, in a vision, in the Spirit of God. And the vision that I saw went up from above me* [that is, "left me"; let us also add the next verse:]
25 *And I spoke to the captivity all the words that the Lord had shown me* ["that he caused me to see"].

The prophet confirms what he said at the beginning, that this vision was presented to him by God and was not some empty and deceiving specter. The prophecy was difficult to believe, and therefore all doubt had to be removed lest anyone charge that God was not the author of the vision. Therefore he says that *he was lifted up by the Spirit of God and taken back to Chaldaea.*

We mentioned that the prophet did not change his location, although I do not want to argue this point if someone is convinced otherwise. I conclude that, since the prophet remained in exile, he saw Jerusalem and the other spectacles he discussed not in a human way but through the prophetic Spirit. He was carried off by the Spirit to Jerusalem, and now he was taken back into exile the same way.

But here the Spirit is contrasted with nature, since we know our sight is limited to a definite space. If the smallest obstacle obtrudes, our vision cannot exceed five or six paces. But when the Spirit of God illumines us, a new faculty begins to flourish in us that should in no way be measured by natural standards.

Now we understand in what sense Ezekiel says that *he was led back to Chaldaea by the Spirit of God.* That is, he was like an "ecstatic." He was lifted up "outside himself." But now he is left in his ordinary state. These words *in a vision, in the Spirit of God,* pertain to the same point, for a vision contrasts with reality. If the prophet was brought back through a vision, it follows that he had not literally been in Jerusalem and did not have to be transported back to Chaldaea.

Now he confronts a question that could be raised: "How did the vision possess such great efficacy?" The prophet calls us back to the power of the Spirit, a power we are not allowed to measure on our little scale. Since we cannot understand the work of the Spirit, we should not be surprised if the prophet was taken to Jerusalem in a vision and then brought back into exile.

He adds that *the vision withdrew from him.* With these words he commends his teaching and extols it above all mortals, because he distinguishes himself as a human being from his role as God's ambassador. *The vision went away from me,* he says. The prophet wants to be understood in two ways. As a private person, as merely one of the crowd, he does not pretend to have any authority to be heard in God's place. But when the Spirit led him, he wanted to separate himself from the ranks of humanity, since he was not speaking on his own and did nothing human or act in a human way. It was the Spirit of God flourishing in him, so that everything he uttered was heavenly and divine.

He says next that *he spoke all these words to the captives,* or exiles. This account seems to have been superfluous. Why was the prophet instructed about the fall of the city, the destruction of the kingdom, and the ruin of the temple, if not to induce the Jews who still remained in the homeland to abandon their pride? But we must note that the prophet had a difficult struggle with those exiles among whom he moved, as we will see more clearly in the next chapter. As the Jews boasted that they still remained unharmed and laughed at the captives who had allowed themselves to be taken away to a distant land, so the exiles were weary of their wretchedness.

Their condition was sad indeed because they saw themselves exposed to all sorts of scorn and treated by the Chaldaeans servilely and ignominiously. Since their condition was so miserable, they grumbled among themselves and became indignant at having complied with the prophets, especially Jeremiah. Since the captives were so offended by their lot, the prophet had to restrain their insolence. This is the purpose of his words, *he recounted Yahweh's words to the captives.* This warning was just as necessary for the exiles as for the Jews who still remained safe in the city.

But he speaks of *the words that God made him see.* He speaks irregularly but most appropriately for the meaning. God did not only speak but placed the thing itself before the prophet's eyes. We see, then, why he says, *the words were shown to him so that he would examine them.* Now I said that what applies to the eyes is transferred improperly to speech. Eyes do not receive words; ears do. But the prophet means that God's words were not bare and simple but clothed with an outward symbol.

Augustine says that the "sacrament is a visible word";[3] and he speaks wisely, since God addresses our eyes in baptism when he offers water as a symbol of our cleansing and regeneration. In the supper he directs his words to our eyes, because Christ shows us that his flesh is for us truly food and his blood truly drink when the bread and wine are set forward. That is why he now says that *he saw God's Word;* it was clothed in outward symbols. God appeared to his prophet, as I said, showed him the temple, and then raised up something like a theater for him to behold the entire condition of the city of Jerusalem.

Let us continue:

---

3. Mg., *Homilies on John* 89, i.e., 80:3; *Against Faustus* 19, i.e., 19:16.

CHAPTER 12

1   *And the word of Yahweh was to me, saying,*
2   *"Son of man, you are living in the midst of a rebellious house; they have eyes for seeing, and do not see; they have ears for hearing, and do not hear, because they* [that is, 'they are'] *a rebellious house."*

Because God was going to give his servant a new command, he wanted to provide him with courage so that when he realized that he was expending his effort in vain, he would not turn back from his course. We know how seriously God's servants are tempted when they speak to the deaf and their teaching is not only spurned but also ignominiously rejected. They think that nothing is better than to be silent, because when God's Word is slighted with such impunity, prophesying is none other than exposing God's name to the reproaches of the godless. Now we understand God's purpose in warning his prophet about the nation's stubbornness.

The prophet was thoroughly aware how intractable the Israelites were; but God confirms with this judgment what the prophet learned well enough by experience. Another reason also should be noted: God not only commanded the prophet what to say but added an outward symbol, as we shall see. The prophet could object, however, that he would be ridiculed when he took up a staff, a bag, and a traveling cap like a pilgrim about to go on a journey. In their perversity, of course, the Israelites derided what he was doing as childish and ludicrous. So because the prophet might have thought what he was commanded to do absurd, God anticipates and offers a reason for his plan. Thus he says that *"the house of Israel is rebellious";* after that he *depicts the depth of* their stubbornness: *"they are deaf, even though endowed with ears; they are blind, even though they do not lack eyes."*

God shows here that the Israelites could not cover up their error as if they had sinned without thinking. He attributes their failure to hear and see to their defiance. We must note this carefully, because whenever hypocrites are convicted, they seize the excuse that they fell through ignorance or error. God proclaims the Israelites to be blind and deaf, however, and shows that their blindness was willful. Therefore when unbelievers make the excuse that they have not been enlightened by the Lord, we can concede that they were blind and deaf. Yet it is often necessary to go far beyond that because the source of this blindness and deafness is their defiance. God blinds them because they refuse to let in the light offered them. They plug their ears!

The reasons for God's judgments are not always apparent. Sometimes we will see that one nation is blinded, but no reason will be obvious to us. But as far as the ten tribes are concerned, there could be no excuse for error, since they had been instructed in God's law from childhood. Thus pride and contempt

285

caused God to give them up to a reprobate understanding. In this way they became numb, discerning nothing with their eyes and hearing nothing with their ears.

The prophet expresses this in a striking way: *"they do not hear,"* he says, *"because they are a rebellious house."* He does not say, "because their understanding does not reach the secret things of God," "because they are not sufficiently acute," or "because they were not endowed with great prudence"; but *"because they are a rebellious house."* That is, because they have made themselves numb and hence neither hear nor see. Next:

3   *"And you, son of man, make [or, 'prepare'] for yourself vessels for migration; and migrate during the day in their sight. You will migrate from your place to another place in their sight, if perhaps they might see that they are a rebellious house."*

Now God instructs his servant what he wants him to do. He orders him to take up "vessels for migration"; that is, he orders him to prepare for a long journey, even exile. Exile is the issue here. A person forced to leave home for exile in a foreign land gathers whatever he can to carry with him — clothes, shoes, hat, bag and staff, and other things of that sort if he has a little money. Thus the prophet is ordered to prepare for a journey to represent the role of those who would be dragged into exile a little later.

This is why he is ordered *"to prepare his vessels for migration."* The Latins call both clothing and other provisions "vessels." Thus the proverb "to gather your vessels"[4] is to "pack up your gear," as they say in the military, or to move your goods. He orders *"this to be done in the daytime"* so that the Israelites observe what is being done.

Then the prophet is ordered *"to transfer from one place to a different place."* As I have already said, this could seem childish. Cicero[5] laughs at those law-court rituals in which the litigants over some field used a fictitious form — so to speak — of presenting their case when they were called in. Because it was too troublesome for a praetor suddenly to get on his horse and run through different fields, from ancient custom they retained this ceremony. The plaintiff said: "The field that you say is yours, I claim for myself and say is mine. If you wish to dispute with me at law, I call you to the place." The other one responded: "I in turn summon you to the place where you summon me." The praetor rose and moved his position. It was a kind of imaginary enactment.

Cicero derides that game and says that it is unworthy of a court's dignity.

4. Cf. Seneca, *Letter* 19:1.
5. Mg., Cicero, *Pro L. Murena,* i.e., 12:26.

But such was the nature of the prophet's action; he took up his hat and coat, staff, shoes, and other things, and changed his place as if he were moving away. But he went only a little distance. God told him beforehand, however, that he was dealing with a perverse nation, and therefore such aids were necessary.

We must note this part: *"If perhaps they might see, because they are a rebellious house."* Here God seems to leave in suspense the outcome of his teaching when he says, *"if perhaps they might hear."* The explanation is appended that the people were so hardened that they could scarcely be moved to obey by any words or signs.

In addition, let us learn from this passage that although our success may not correspond to the labor we expend in our work for God, nevertheless, we must see it through. This teaching is especially useful, because when God places some burden on us, we dispute with ourselves about the outcome and then all zeal evaporates. Unless we discern a successful outcome, we are hardly willing to lift a finger. Because we are always too concerned about the fruit of our labor, let us diligently note this passage, where God sends his prophet and yet adds: *"if perhaps they might hear."* Whatever the outcome may be, God is to be obeyed; if we achieve nothing in our work, God still wants to be obeyed. Next:

4 *"And bring out your vessels, like the vessels of captivity, during the day in their sight; and you will go out at evening in their sight, according to the going out of the captivity.* [Other verses should also be linked together.]
5 *You will dig through the wall in their sight and bring them out through it.*
6 *You will carry them on your shoulder in their sight; in darkness you will go out; you will hide your face, and you will not look at the ground, because I have appointed you a portent for the house of Israel."*

Ezekiel is wordy in this account. But at the beginning of the book we said that he used a rough style because he was a teacher set over slow and almost stupid people. We also said that he picked up something of the style of the region in which he was living. The people gradually drifted away from the elegance of their own language, and that is why the prophet's speech is not so pure but smacks of a foreign element.

Concerning the matter itself, there is no ambiguity since God repeats that *"he should dig through the wall in their sight and bring out his vessels through it."* The other part of the vision comes next: the departure will not be free, but the Jews will try to escape secretly. First, the prophet was shown that the Jews who were at ease in Jerusalem and boasted that all was going famously for them would be exiles; second, that when they wanted to leave, their departure would not be free — unless they secretly escaped from the hands of

287

the enemy by undercover means, like thieves escaping through a hole dug in a wall. The application will come next, but it was worth the trouble to mention briefly what God intended in this vision.

Next, both are included: *"in their sight,"* he says, *"you will carry them on your shoulder";* that is, you will be ready and prepared for a journey, *"like a traveler, and that will happen in the daytime; but you will bring them out,"* he says, *"in the darkness; after your vessels have been prepared, wait for evening; after that you will go out in darkness."* He shows what I have already mentioned: since necessity expelled the Jews from their homeland, their departure would not be free; it will go well for them only if they sneak away out of sight of their enemy by undercover means in the dark of night.

He adds, *"you will hide your face."* The clause *"and you will not look at the ground"* pertains to the same idea. This phrase denotes trepidation and anxiety, like *"you will hide your face";* he indicates that the Jews would be so perplexed that they would fear whatever happened. It is well known that someone who fears everything covers his face. But trepidation is better expressed when he says *"do not look at the ground."* People in a hurry dare not turn their eyes even a little to one side or another; they are swept along to the place they hope to reach and see themselves arrive with their eyes, because their feet cannot hurry as quickly as they desire. They somehow speed the journey with their eyes.

This is the reason why God said, *"you will not look at the ground, because I have given you,"* he says, *"as a portent to the house of Israel."* Here God confronts the petulance of those who otherwise would deride what the prophet was doing: "What do you mean with this pretended migration? Why don't you rest at home? Why do you frighten us with this empty spectacle?"

God adds that *"the prophet is for a sign or a portent for the house of Israel"* so that the Israelites would not impudently spurn what was shown them. Here the word "portent" is used simply in its true meaning. Sometimes it is taken in a pejorative sense. We say something abominable is a "portent," but a portent, properly speaking, designates something in the future. Thus when people have a foreboding of what is hidden, it is called a portent. The same idea is also seen in Isaiah 8,[6] which says, "Behold, I and my children whom God has given me are signs and portents."

There he uses "signs," אתות [*'ōṯōṯ*], in the first place, and then, מופתים [*môp̄eṯîm*], "portents." Here the prophet speaks in the singular: *"I have given you as a portent."* But since Isaiah is dealing with the remaining faithful, he speaks of "signs" and "portents." It seems, however, that Isaiah means something more, namely, that the people are so stupid that they feared and abhorred

6. Mg., Is. 8:18.

God's servants, as if some portent threatened. Thus the people's depravity is indicated in that passage, because when they saw a pious and sincere worshiper of God, they averted their eyes as if he were a frightening monster.

But now Ezekiel simply says that *"he has been given as a portent to the house of Israel,"* because his action was a foreboding of the future captivity that the Jews did not fear and the Israelites could not believe — hence that remorse and weariness of which I spoke. If someone thinks it better to say that the prophet was called a portent because the Israelites remained astonished, I do not object. But the first interpretation fits far better. In this way God distinguishes the prophet's actions from all empty charades and thus defends what he commanded his servant from everyone's mockery. At the same time, God indicates that no matter how much the prophet is scorned, he would be true and also the avenger of contempt. Next:

7 *And so I did as I had been ordered. I brought out my vessels, like the vessels of captivity, in the daytime. And in the evening I dug through into the wall* [literally; but "I dug through the wall for myself"] *by hand; in the darkness I brought them out; I lifted them out* [or, "I bore them"] *on my shoulder in their sight.*

The prophet relates that he did what God commanded; nevertheless, it did not escape him that this action would be exposed to much reproach and mockery. But nothing was more important to him than to obey God. We must note the prophet's alacrity in obeying God's command. Since nothing is bitterer for a sincere person than disgrace, he might have rejected the burden imposed on him because he would incur everyone's ridicule. Since that would displease God, he did as he was ordered.

Therefore, he says, *he lifted out his vessels like the vessels of captivity,* or departure, and did so during the daytime. That is, he prepared whatever was necessary for travel, since he saw that a long journey, even exile, awaited him. This is the reason why he prepared his belongings during the daytime.

Now it follows: *in the evening he dug through the wall.* The point of this second part is to let the Israelites understand that all exits would be obstructed for the Jews, with no safety left except in a secret flight. He also says *by hand;* the phrase makes it obvious that this was done hurriedly and hectically.

He says that *they went out in the darkness and carried on their shoulders,* in order to confirm what we have already said so often: the Jews had no hope of safety except under cover of night. Because they were besieged on all sides, they could not go this way or that without the enemy capturing them. This is why the prophet says that *he went out in the darkness after digging through the wall.*

Almighty God, since you want us to dwell in this world as so-journers until the time when you gather us into your heavenly rest, grant that we truly meditate on that eternal inheritance and apply all our efforts to attaining it. Grant too that we might sojourn in the world without wandering or straying from the way; may we always be intent on the goal that you set before us and continue on our course, until we complete our course and enjoy that glory which your only-begotten Son has prepared for us through his blood. Amen.

Lecture 32

8 *And the word of Yahweh was to me in the morning, saying,*
9 *"Son of man, did not the house of Israel, that rebellious* [or, as we said elsewhere, 'exasperating,' or, 'bitter'] *house, say to you: 'What are you doing?'*
10 *Say to them, 'Thus says Sovereign Yahweh, "This burden* [or, 'this sad prophecy'] *of the prince in Jerusalem and of the whole house of Israel in their midst." '*
11 *You will say, 'I am a portent for you; as I have done, so it will be done to them; they will go out into exile and captivity* [etc.].' "*

We gather from the prophet's words that he was ridiculed when he girded himself to depart; then he secretly dug through the wall at night and went out with his baggage. Those who think that the Israelites were merely inquiring about something unknown to them have not adequately considered the prophet's words. That phrase *"a rebellious house"* is not repeated without reason. If this questioning had arisen out of foolishness, God would not have called them rebellious.

This epithet applies to the passage at hand, and thus it is valid to determine that ridicule led the Israelites to ask the prophet what this meant. He seemed to them to be playing, and so they scoffed. We know how bold that nation was in scorning the prophets. Hence it is no wonder that when they hit on a plausible reason they freely attacked what the prophet was doing.

We said yesterday that it was like a childish display, and so it seemed reasonable to the Israelites to reject what the prophet was doing as worthless. But God does not allow his servants to be vilified this way. He had already marked out our prophet so that his calling deserved to be accepted as holy. Although at first glance Ezekiel's action could not be taken seriously, nevertheless the people ought to have inquired modestly since he bore definite marks of the prophetic office. Whatever we know to proceed from God ought to be accepted reverently and without controversy. But if something is obscure, we can express surprise, we can inquire; but as I said, teachableness and modesty should always be foremost.

But the Israelites? They inquired about the purpose of the prophet's actions, but only to reject them as ridiculous. That is why God became irate and proclaimed that he would be a severe judge of their audacity in attacking the holy prophet. Therefore, *"'what are you doing?'"* should be read with emphasis, as if they said the prophet was silly, and pointlessly carried or prepared his baggage and dug through the wall, because all this was useless. But when he shows that God was gravely offended with such sarcasm, the response adequately demonstrates that they were not inquiring out of error or ignorance but out of pure perversity.

He says, *" ' "this prophecy is of the prince and the whole house of Israel, which is in their midst." ' "* Undoubtedly he means the king, as we will see a little later; and he does not speak indefinitely of just any king but designates Zedekiah, as will be clear immediately from the context.

He says, *" ' "this burden,* or this sad *prophecy concerns the prince and the house of Israel" ' "* who were dwelling in Jerusalem. It is probable that some had taken refuge to avoid falling into the hands of the enemy, because Jerusalem was a safe shelter for them. The captives thought themselves lacking in foresight in failing to follow those leaders, for Jerusalem had been a safe refuge for them. This made their captivity even sadder. Therefore God proclaims that the Israelites are included in the prophecy together with the king. It is true that the name was common to all of Abraham's posterity, for the twelve patriarchs were begotten by Jacob. But at the time it had become customary for the ten tribes to retain the name Israel. The tribe of Judah had its own special name.

Next he confirms his teaching *" 'that he would be a portent to them.' "* We explained this word yesterday; the prophet was set before their eyes as a sign, whereby God might represent to them what was still unknown. We call "portents" signs sent from heaven to prefigure what no one imagines will happen. God often shows by many signs what will happen, but by common signs; we call a "portent" an extraordinary sign, which could not be reckoned natural. Thus the prophet is ordered to tell the Israelites that *" 'he is a portent to them,' "* in order to shatter the defiance that, as we said, was the cause of their impious contempt.

They had no scruples about making fun of a prophet because they thought he was presenting something silly, as if he wanted to terrify children about nothing. Hence God proclaims that *" 'his servant is a portent to them' "* to awaken the Israelites at last from their stupor. From an additional explanation, we gather what the word "portent" meant to him, as we saw in yesterday's lecture, for he says, *" 'as I have done, so will be done to you.' "* That is, "What you now think to be a game will finally be fulfilled in you in earnest."

The prophet seemed to play out a story like an actor, and for that he was ridiculed. Now he proclaims that it would be no story, because the Israelites who remained among the Jews, and even the king himself, would not be playing the part of others. Then in person would God finally compel to gather their baggage and secretly take flight in the dark of night. He continues that idea throughout the entire verse: " *'they will depart,'* " he says, " *'and go out into exile.'* " Therefore, ordering the prophet to make up, or prepare, his belongings was a sign of the exile of which he is now speaking. But an explanation of the second part is also added.

12 *"And the prince in their midst will carry on his shoulder in the dark and will go out in the wall that they dug out for leading out* [or, 'for bringing out'] *in it; he will hide his face, lest he might* ['so that he should not'] *see the ground with his eye."*

We said that two things are shown here: the people's exile and their clandestine flight. Now the prophet speaks again of their trepidation. He says that not only the mass or the dregs of the people would be so anxious that they would try secretly to escape carrying their baggage, " *'but the prince himself.'* " That is, the king would be subjected to such ignominy that *"the prince himself,"* he says, *"will bear on his shoulder."* Many certainly followed him, as we have seen, and in the end he was seized along with a great throng, as the prophet will add a little later. He was dragged off to the king after being captured in the desert of Jericho.

But the king[a] alone is mentioned here, because it was almost incredible that the enemy could not be appeased. Surrender usually placates even the most hostile enemy; although slaughter is inflicted on all sides, at least kings are spared. We know that after kings have been led in triumph, they are kept alive because of their dignity. Hence what the prophet proclaims about King Zedekiah does not mean that the mass would be exempted from punishment but that the king himself, together with the common people, will be forced to slip away secretly. He still could not escape from the hands of the enemy.

"The prince in their midst." Here *"their midst"* is taken in a different sense than a little earlier when he said that the Israelites were in the midst of the people who dwelt in Jerusalem, because they were mixed in with Judeans from the time that they took refuge within their boundaries. But he says *"the prince is in their midst"* in a different sense, namely, that the eyes of all were turned on him. When a banner is erected, it is seen by everyone and keeps all the troops in their ranks. So, too, *"the king was in their midst"* so that the people would not drift away. A pathetic scattering occurs when the leader is carried off.

a. I.e., the prince.

We must note, however, the intention of the Holy Spirit, for the Jews, as we have seen elsewhere, were hardened in their malice by the deceptive claim that God would always have his dwelling place among them. It was said that the throne of David would stand as long as the sun and the moon shone in the heavens.[1] From this arose that lamentable complaint in Jeremiah: "The Christ, or the anointed of God, in whose spirit our soul lived."[2] The prophet is not speaking there in the customary way, as if he thrust in God's face (as hypocrites are accustomed to do) God's own promise, but has regard to God's plan. Since David was the image of the Christ, he was truly the soul of the people even among the nations, as that passage puts it.

They not only hoped for salvation from their king while shut up within the walls, but even though dispersed among the nations, still hoped they would be safe under the king's shadow. But that confidence was perverse, once they had wickedly departed from the true worship of God. Thus, to eradicate their pride and empty boasting, the prophet says that *"now the king is in their midst."* That would not always be the case, because God will expel him — and not only that but also compel him to flee in secret using undercover means.

He adds next: *"he will hide his face, lest he see the ground with his eye."* So it was fulfilled, just as sacred history records.[3] Zedekiah went out through the gardens in underground passages. He thought his flight could evade the enemy, but he was apprehended. Thus we see the reason for his hiding his face or countenance is that Zedekiah feared meeting anyone along the way. But it was exceedingly galling and also base and shameful for a king to cover himself and not dare to look at the ground. What follows next was sadder still:

13 *"And I will spread my net over him, and he will be caught in my snares* ['nets'; others translate it 'fishing nets' — but incorrectly; the cause of this error was thinking that the image was taken from fishing; nevertheless, it is certain that the same thing is denoted by different words; therefore, 'he will be caught in my net']; *and I will lead him out* [he says] *to Babylon in the land of Chaldaea; and he will not see it, and he will die there."*

It was no slight destruction, since Zedekiah, in desperate circumstances, finally considered escape; and when he went down into the hidden trenches, it was like seeking life in a tomb. He was thus reduced to extreme measures. Now the prophet adds that it would be useless, *"because he will still be captured by the enemy."* Furthermore, God attributes to himself what he executed through the Chaldaeans, and rightly so; the Chaldaeans laid an ambush

1. Mg., Ps. 89:37-38, i.e., 89:36-37.
2. Mg., La. 4:20.
3. Mg., 2 Ki. 25:4-5; Je. 39:4-5.

because they were warned of the king's escape. They knew what he intended, and he was caught in their ambush.

But God proclaims that he will be the instigator: *"I,"* he says, *"will spread my net."* We know that the Chaldaeans did not leave their homeland on their own initiative and wage that war in their own strength. It was not by their own efforts that the king was captured, but the entire business was directed from heaven. Human beings expend their effort and seem to accomplish something by their own labor; but unless God provides the outcome, every undertaking will certainly crumble.

Furthermore, as God raised up the Chaldaeans to exact punishment from the king and the people, so he aroused confidence in their souls. He also supported them to persist in the siege of the city. Finally, he opened their eyes and sent informers to disclose the king's plan, enabling them to capture him as he left through the diggings, as indeed happened.

This was all done by the hidden providence of God, and so we must diligently note these passages where God shows that whatever humans seem to accomplish is God's doing. The image of the net is compelling. We reckon we will always have some escape even in perplexity, and as often as we look around this way and that, some hope deludes us. But God proclaims that he has *"nets spread out"* surrounding us on all sides. When a way out appears, God has hidden snares to trap us.

As this passage compares God to a hunter, so we are the wild beasts. When a hunter pursues wild beasts, they look for space where the way is clear and rush thither, but hurl themselves into nets. So, too, when we try to escape God's hand, we are entrapped and held by him. When we want to evade God's providence, we deserve to be so blinded that we rush to our own destruction. Therefore: *"I will spread my net over him, and he will be caught in my snares. I will lead him away,"* he says, *"to Babylon."*

The prophet shows by degrees what formidable judgment awaited Zedekiah and the whole people. It was extremely miserable to be captured by the enemy and subjected to their passions and fury. If he had been slain, that would have been carried out easily in a moment. But God wanted him to drag out his life in exile. In addition, he says that although he would die in Babylon, he would still not see the city. Both things were fulfilled.

In a sense, Zedekiah rotted away in exile, for he lay in squalor and sordid conditions until he died. Although he was buried there, as we saw in Jeremiah, nevertheless it was a most pathetic situation to fear new wrath from the enemy during one's entire life. He was treated extremely barbarously and inhumanely. What is more, he was blinded on the journey itself, and for this reason it says that *"he will not see Babylon."* Nevertheless, he will reach there and *"there he will die."* After seeing his sons murdered in his presence, his eyes were torn out. That was a spectacle worse than death.

Now let us consider what life was like for this man in exile, in prison, and in chains — how he was bound in chains, as the sacred history relates. He grew weak through many slow deaths in a smelly prison that had no sight of the sun. This is what happened to Zedekiah. Hence we see why God thunders against the Israelites who thought they suffered miserably in exile, when they could have remained safe in Jerusalem. Next:

14 *"And all who are around him to help him, and all his wings* [that is, 'all his defenses'] *I will scatter to every* [or, 'to whatever'] *wind. And I will unsheathe the sword against them."*

He confirms the previous verse, and says that although Zedekiah had many soldiers in his garrison and also accustomed his people to bear arms, all this would be useless, because God would scatter all the troops in which he confided. Thus he says that *"he will scatter to all the winds whoever were around Zedekiah."* The unbelievers were deceived when they saw that the king was not destitute of external aids and that the people of the city were accustomed to warfare. Since Zedekiah was so prepared to defend the city, they thought it almost impossible that it would finally be captured by the Chaldaeans.

God teaches first that the war was waged under his auspices, and therefore no one should doubt that he fought against the city himself. He does not speak of the Chaldaeans; otherwise the unbelieving Israelites might make a judgment by comparison: "It is true that the Chaldaeans are besieging the city with a powerful and numerous army, but the city is impregnable. Besides, it is defended with great courage, and the king has adequate and solid forces to protect himself."

To prevent the unbelievers being deceived by this foolish analysis, God comes forward and turns their minds away from the Chaldaeans. This is why he ascribes to himself whatever was done by their foreign enemies. We gather from this that the profane nations are in God's hands, because he not only governs his own by the Spirit of regeneration but also compels the ungodly who desire to abolish his rule, to obey his commands. God did not unsheathe his sword from heaven, nor did angels publicly appear with unsheathed swords. This was done by the Chaldaeans. But as it says in Isaiah 10: "Will the axe boast against the one who wields it?"[4] Since there was no strength in the Chaldaeans of themselves, God armed them and then provided such success as he wanted. Next:

15 *"And they will know that I am Yahweh after I have expelled them among the nations* [or, 'dispersed,' or, 'scattered'; הפיצי (*hᵃpîṣî*) indicates a violent

---

4. Mg., Is. 10:15.

expulsion] *and scattered them throughout the land* [that is, 'through various regions']."

Here God reviles the Judeans and the Israelites who joined together. He says that he would make known his power such that they would be compelled to acknowledge him — but in their destruction. Experiential knowledge is sometimes attributed to the faithful; because we are exceedingly slow, God shows us his power by unambiguous proofs. But what is said here should be restricted to the reprobate and the lost. They do not acknowledge God except in death. But Zedekiah was not completely devoid of the fear of God; he respected Jeremiah, and the seed of piety in his soul was not completely extinct. As for the people, since they offered sacrifices daily, they certainly nurtured some notion of God's grace and also his power. But they despised the prophets and were so completely unruly that threats were jokes to them; they are therefore said not to acknowledge God.

This must be noted very carefully. The wicked do not consider themselves so stupid as to deprive God of the honor due him. Yet when God calls them to himself, they turn their backs. When he proclaims his Word, even for their own salvation, they not only become deaf and plug their ears but also cause a tumult or deride all threats as fairy tales. It is certain that no knowledge of God flourishes when such contempt of his teaching prevails.

For this reason he now says that *"in the end the Jews would know,"* because contempt prevented them from praising God for his power. They should have been terrified by no more than his nod. Jeremiah steadfastly drove home God's Word to them, but they so were so calloused that they esteemed that Word for nothing. This is the most serious threat, as if God said, "when I strike you with my hand, you will know that I am God."

So when God speaks, let us learn to acknowledge him promptly with the sense of faith, because that is the opportune time for the knowledge of salvation. Let us not abuse his patience when he rages against us with an armed hand and pursues us so horribly. Certainly he castigates his own now and then — for their salvation. But when the point is reached that no hope remains of repentance in the reprobate, he reduces them to nothing. Now follows:

16 *"And out of them I will make people of number* [that is, 'a few people'] *a remnant, by the sword, by famine, by pestilence, so that they might declare all their abominations among the nations to which they will come; and they will know that I am Yahweh."*

Some think that God is speaking about the faithful whom he had determined to save miraculously from that death. There is certainly some mitigation of the earlier vengeance. But it does not make sense to interpret this of the faithful.

297

He is speaking of the common crowd. But as we saw before, the destruction of the city will be such that God would scatter some remnant to the wind.

The prophet now confirms this. Hence we must affirm in the first place that this promise is not directed only to the elect or the church of God. God shows instead that the exile would not be the end of evil for the captives, even though they will not be immediately murdered. Their situation might seem better, but God proclaims that he would be unyielding toward them. Not all would perish by the sword or famine or pestilence, but some remnant would remain. "But that will happen," he says, "not because I will be reconciled to them, but so that I might expose their sins among the nations." Therefore, when he says *"that they might declare,"* he does not mean that they would testify of their sins, as the pious (as we will see elsewhere) are accustomed to extol the mercy of God and sincerely confess their sorrow before their fellows. He does not mean a declaration that would be a sign of repentance but speaks instead of a message told by events.

That exile heralded with a clear voice that it was sinful people with whom God had dealt in such a hostile manner. He had chosen that people; he was the guardian of the city. He would have been a steadfast savior, if their perversity had not been an obstacle. Hence because they were destitute of his aid, robbed of all their goods, with tyrannical enemies prevailing over them, it is sufficiently clear that they were worse than sinful. So *they declare* their sins among the nations not by word of mouth but by their entire condition.

Now we understand God's meaning. Although some survived and not all were murdered or destroyed by sword, famine, or pestilence, nevertheless they would be cursed. He had no other purpose in driving them far away than to make their disgrace obvious and themselves detested by everyone. Then even the profane nations will acknowledge that their sins deserved such vengeance. Therefore he says, *"they will declare all their abominations among the nations, and they will know that I am Yahweh."*

He repeats again the point that they will acknowledge too late what they have despised; that is, God offered himself to them as a father, but they did not accept that grace, and in the end they were compelled to recognize him as their judge — to their eternal destruction.

> *Almighty God, since you warn us with so many examples how formidable is your wrath, particularly against the stubborn and unyielding who reject the Word given so personally to them, grant, I pray, that in the humility and reverence proper to your children we might embrace what has been offered to us in your name, and so repent of our sins and secure their pardon until at last, having been freed of all the corruptions of our flesh, we might partake of the eternal and heavenly glory that your only-begotten Son has obtained for us by his blood. Amen.*

Lecture 33

17 *And the word of Yahweh was to me, saying:*
18 *"Son of man, eat your bread in trembling, and drink your waters in tumult and sadness* [or, 'torment,' or, 'anxiety'].
19 *And you will say to the people of the land, 'Thus says Sovereign Yahweh to the inhabitants of* [or, "those dwelling in"] *Jerusalem in the land of Israel, "They will eat their bread in anxiety* [or, 'torment,' or, 'sorrow'; he repeats the same word], *and they will drink their waters in desolation, so that the land will be stripped* [or, 'despoiled'] *of its abundance, because of the violence of all who dwell in it." ' "*

Now the prophet is ordered to depict the famine that awaited the Jews both in the siege and in exile. But this prophecy ought to be referred primarily to the time of siege. The Jews were in constant fear. Although they depended on their resources and thought their defenses would make them impregnable, nevertheless the Lord often — even repeatedly — shattered their confidence. There was misery, anxiety, and fear, so that they could not eat their bread except in fear or drink their water except in turmoil.

A city besieged is always afraid; the enemy also harasses them so that fatigue itself compels the besieged to surrender. It is probable that the Chaldaean army could often attempt to capture the city without great loss, so that the Jews were struck with fresh terrors every day. Therefore they could not eat bread or drink water without anxiety and turmoil. But because simple and plain teaching was not effective among the ten tribes and the Jews, an outward symbol is added. The prophet is an image of the besieged people, and therefore is ordered to *"eat his bread in fear"* so that the sight would do more to arouse the slow, even foolish, people.

299

The application follows immediately: *"You will say to the people of the land."* I am sure he means the ten tribes. Hence "the land" means Chaldaea and other regions through which the ones dragged into exile were scattered. But hearing this benefited them, as we saw before, because they thought that all had gone splendidly for the Jews who still were at peace at home, while they themselves were so wretched; hence not only their complaints but out-bursts against God and his servants, especially Jeremiah. This is the reason why the prophet had to preach to the captives.

But it says next: *" 'Thus says Sovereign Yahweh to the inhabitants of Jerusalem in the land of Israel' ";* that is, to those who remained in the land of Israel. So we see that the land of Israel is distinguished from the other land just mentioned. The inhabitants of Jerusalem remained at ease in their inheritance; their condition was held to be better because nothing is sadder than exile and captivity.

But God proclaims that those in Jerusalem would be more miserable than the captives who had already endured the principal part of their misery. *" ' "They will eat their bread," ' "* he says, *" ' "in sorrow, or torment, and drink their waters in desolation." ' "* He does not repeat the same words that he just used but briefly shows that the Jews boasted in vain of being still unharmed, because a little later the enemy presses them, preventing them eating even a mouthful of bread in peace.

He says *" ' "that their land might be reduced to devastation from its abundance" ' ";* some translate this "after its abundance," which is forced and very farfetched. The prophet means that the land would be deserted and empty because it will be plundered. "Abundance" is taken to mean plenty of every-thing, as is well known. Judea would then be reduced from abundance to devastation, since the enemy plundered whatever was at hand. Thus the region was emptied of its riches.

The explanation follows: *" ' "on account of the violence of all who inhabit it." ' "* Some incorrectly expound this of the Chaldaeans, because in their greed they destroyed the entire land. Instead the prophet warns them that it is the just vengeance of God, because all the Jews had devoted themselves to violence, cruelty, and greed. חמס [*ḥᵃmas*] indicates every kind of injury but in many cases means violence and greed.

Now we understand the prophet's meaning, that the Jews were de-servedly threatened with this destruction, because the just reward of their sins is being meted out to them. In this way Ezekiel restrains all the complaints in which they indulged with excessive license, as if God dealt with them too rigidly and harshly. Thus he teaches briefly that they in no way deserved to be spared any longer. Next:

20   " ' "And the inhabited cities will be reduced to desolation, and the land will be devastated [or, 'deserted'], and you will know that I am Yahweh." ' "

He pursues the same theme. He threatened the destruction of Jerusalem and its citizens; now he adds other cities of Judah that were still inhabited. Finally he speaks of the entire land, saying in effect there was no reason for a single corner to assume it would be immune from destruction, since God's vengeance and the enemy's cruelty would spread through every region. Jerusalem was the head of the entire nation, and Ezekiel predicts its overthrow. It would then be easy to overturn and plunder the other cities. Hence it happened that the whole region was subjected to the enemy's passions.

Next he adds what we saw before: " ' "you will know that I am Yahweh." ' " Indeed, they had heard the prophets; from earliest childhood they ought to have been imbued with this teaching; and also by many evidences God had testified that he was the true God. His power had been sufficiently recognized and understood through his frequent aid in rescuing that miserable people from imminent death. But impiety numbed them so that they confidently condemned not only prophetic teaching but also the very judgments of God when he openly chastised them. Therefore this knowing of theirs is mentioned for good reason.

When God extends his hand for the last time to castigate them, he says that then his power would be obvious to them. His power had not been entirely hidden from them, but it was so obscured by their depravity that they held God to be nothing. But we must always maintain the contrast between the knowledge bred from experience and the knowledge derived from teaching. Those who plug their ears when God invites them through his servants must experience in the end that he is God when he is silent as well as when he carries out his vengeance against them. Next:

21   And the word of Yahweh was to me, saying,

22   "Son of man, what is this proverb among you in the land of Israel, which says, 'The days are continued [or, "prolonged"], and all prophecy has vanished?'

23   Therefore, you will say to them, 'Thus says Sovereign Yahweh, "I will act to silence [or, 'put an end to'] this proverb, and they will no more use this proverb in Israel." ' Instead, tell them: 'The days have drawn near, and the word of every vision.' "

Here God inveighs against the crude mockery that everywhere reigned among the Judeans at the time. Although the prophets continually threatened them, their steadfastness fell so far short of moving them finally to repent that they became more hardened instead — as if they had become calloused. They plunged into such stubbornness that they boasted of their escape; and with

301

such confidence in their impunity they raged increasingly against God. The prophet is therefore ordered to restrain their audacity.

It was monstrous to have that people, who from childhood imbibed the teaching of the Law and the Prophets, erupt against God, as if he had lied through his prophets. This was the implication of their boasting: " 'O, the days are continued; therefore, every vision has passed away and vanished.' " They concluded from this delay that there was nothing to fear, because whatever Jeremiah and others like him predicted was obsolete.

We see how unbelievers turn God's patience into material for stubbornness or stupor. God spares them so that through a respite he might summon them to repent. What do they do? They count the days and years; when they see that God does not immediately carry out the judgment that he presented through his servants, they laugh and reckon everything the prophets said to be fairy tales.

This is the kind of impiety the prophet rebukes when he says, "What is this?" The question is a denunciation. God somehow marvels at the people's foolishness and furor, because they dare to vomit forth their blasphemies openly. What remains when God is reputed to be false in both his promises and his threats? All religion is destroyed. Therefore it is not surprising if God denounces such a monstrosity, while he questions how it could happen that the Israelites would be submerged in such madness: "What is," he says, "this proverb among you?"

He seems to include his servant among the others; but because he belonged to the body of the people, what was completely alien to him is nevertheless attributed to him in common with the others. Furthermore, this passage must be carefully noted, when the ungodly conclude that there is nothing for them to fear since the days are prolonged. As we said, this is certainly a sign of extreme madness. But since they do not honor his teaching, it is not surprising if they imagine God to be a liar and his threats to be empty when his hand is not immediately evident.

Unless they are terrified by God's power, unbelievers are never frightened and not moved one whit. It is not surprising, then, if they take it all as a joke when they see him hesitate while his words still resound in people's mouths. Let the apostle's statement come to mind: "By faith Noah built the ark,"[1] because he feared God's hidden judgment of which he had been warned, no less than if his eyes already beheld the flood in which the entire earth would be immersed. So although God withholds his hand for a time, let us learn to fear his Word alone lest delay leads us into such sluggishness.

Now he adds: "Therefore, you will say to them, 'Thus says Sovereign Yahweh, "I will make this proverb cease from the land of Israel." ' " Here God

1. Mg., Heb. 11:7.

shows that his anger was increasingly kindled by their contempt. When the wicked insult him with their lies, they succeed in making him hasten to execute his judgments, which otherwise he would still be prepared to suspend. In the end, the wicked goad God to execute his vengeance, by inferring from the delay that they have escaped and the vision was fleeting and illusory — as though they deliberately provoked him into a struggle.

The confirmation of his judgment immediately follows, " 'that is, because the days have drawn near.' " God is proclaiming that since time made the Jews confident of impunity, the end was already at hand for them to realize that they were exceedingly blind thus to abuse his great tolerance. Thus " 'the days draw near,' " and then " 'the word of every vision.' " Here "word" is taken for "fulfillment." We know that רבד [dābār] is often taken for "some object, transaction, result." But in this passage the prophet uses the phrase "the word of the vision" for the fulfillment of the vision, saying in effect, "Whatever the prophets have said will be steadfast and firm." Next:

24 " 'For there will no longer be every [that is, "any"] vision of lying [or, "emptiness"] and divination of the flatterer in the midst of the house of Israel.' "

Here God snatches away from the Jews another source of confidence. They freely flattered themselves, but they also had their agitators, false prophets, to inflate their flatteries even more. So when they heard sad prophecies, they scorned them, and then became hardened, as if the prophets groundlessly terrified them. Everyone was too prone to this drunken confidence; but, as I said, those flatterers added enticements to deceive them. The false prophets said that God would not be so severe, and that the prophecies about the destruction of the city and the temple contradicted God's many promises.

Hence we see how the prophets were despised by the willful stubbornness of the people, as well as the perverse designs of the false prophets. After that, God asserted that " 'the days drew near' "; now he adds that " 'a vision of emptiness will be no more.' " Not that the false prophets would be taken from their midst, but their mouths were shut while their depravity was exposed by the events themselves.

Since the people were shamed by the destruction, he says for this reason and in this sense that " 'the prophecy of emptiness must be removed,' " and next " 'the divination of the flatterer in the midst of the house of Israel.' " In their ease and shade they promised a prosperous outcome to those miserable people. But when the city was captured, people were dragged into exile, others were executed, and all were robbed of their fortunes and shamelessly harassed, then became clear the character of these prophets who nourished the people's perverse confidence with their empty flattery. Now we understand the prophet's genuine meaning. Next:

303

25 " 'For I, Yahweh, will speak; the word that I will speak, I will do [the copula is superfluous]. It will not be prolonged any further; because in your days, O provocative [or, "rebellious"] house, the word that I will speak, I will do, says Sovereign Yahweh.' "

He confirms the previous verse. There is some obscurity in the construction, but as far as his point is concerned, the prophet simply wishes to teach that whatever God has spoken will be soon fulfilled. God himself wishes to assert his trustworthiness by executing the vengeance that he threatened through his servants. The prophet is maintaining that it was not right to separate God's Word from its fulfillment, because when God speaks he is not divided against himself. When he opens his mouth, he puts his hand to the task at the same time. Now we understand the prophet's meaning.

It is easy to infer from this the value of this teaching. Because God's Word is lifeless among us and seems to be scattered to the winds, we must always consider his hand. Whenever the prophets speak, let God come before our eyes — and come not only in the naked Word but armed with his power and his hand itself enclosed, as it were, in his Word. The entire verse ought to be referred to this point: " 'I Yahweh will speak a word; and whatever I have spoken, that I will do. It will not be continued any further, but what I have said many times will return. Even in your days, O rebellious house, I will do what I have said through my servants.' "

Here he describes what might still seem doubtful. Because a thousand years are like one day with God,[2] the time could be said to be near, even if the city were not captured and destroyed along with the temple for thirty years. But now God specifies in a human way that the time is near, because those who then remained will see the fulfillment of the prophecies they had scorned. Next:

26 And the word of Yahweh was to me, saying,
27 "Son of man, behold, the house of Israel says ['saying'], 'This vision that he sees extends to many days, and he prophesies about times far off.'
28 Therefore you will say to them, 'Thus says Sovereign Yahweh, "It will not be continued any more; all the words that I speak, the word I will also do [or, 'I will fulfill'']," says Sovereign Yahweh.' "

Here it is not so much detestable blasphemy that is condemned, as we saw earlier, as subtle ridicule whose purpose was first to weaken confidence in prophecy and then to abolish completely all heavenly teaching. Those who are now condemned did not dare to revel and bluster against God. But since

2. Mg., Ps. 90:4; 2 Pet. 3:8.

304

others concluded as time dragged on that the prophecies had lapsed and were negligible, such people said: "It may be that God will fulfill what he now proclaims to us through his servant; but in the meantime, let us feast in confidence, because we will die before these things happen."

We see then that there were two classes. Some completely rejected the prophets of God and impudently ridiculed their threats. That crass impiety was exposed before. Others did not openly or explicitly affirm that God was a liar but relegated to the far distance the fulfillment of the prophet's words. We see that the first group were so lost that they all but openly ridiculed God; because God prolonged the time for them, they drove all fear out of their awareness.

For many years Jeremiah had spent his labor in vain, daily calling them before God's tribunal with a loud trumpet and summoning the Chaldaeans before their eyes. Because Jeremiah had no success, Ezekiel helped him; and after inveighing against the foul impudence of scorning God, he now attacks the hypocrites who had not yet abandoned themselves to the kind of reckless-ness that openly vilifies God.

But as I mentioned earlier, the fall from this confidence to crass contempt of God is easy. They thought they would be at ease and out of danger; and since God patiently deferred his judgments, they finally determined that he was content in his leisure not to bother with human matters. Let us accordingly protect ourselves from Satan's snares, and not only abhor that foul blasphemy of which the prophet spoke, but as soon as God threatens us, anticipate his judgment and not promise ourselves a long truce that in the end might numb us and leave us unafraid. *"The house of Israel were saying, 'He prophesies for many days.' "* They did not openly taunt Ezekiel with coming forward by chance and arrogating to himself the title of prophet. But they said that he *" 'prophesies for many days and long times.' "*

Now he adds: *"You will say to them, 'It will not be continued any more.' "* Some divide the phrase this way: "all my words will not be continued any more"; and they want to change the number to render it: "not one of my words will be continued." But a different construction seems to make better sense: *" ' "it will not be continued any more. The word that I have spoken I will do." ' "* He confirms again what we saw before, that God does not speak in vain, because he is not divided. A human being may lie or make an empty promise he cannot fulfill, or change his plans. It is not appropriate to imagine anything like that in God. God's hand and Word are always joined.

Almighty God, since in real measure you spare us, and meantime warn us with unmistakable signs of your wrath, grant us in good time to repent, lest negligence possess our minds and hearts and also dissipate our judgment. May we be attentive both to your Word and to every evidence that we are incurring your vengeance, and may we be so zealous to reconcile ourselves to you that for the future, having been reborn of your Spirit, we might ever glorify your name in Jesus Christ our Lord. Amen.

Index of Subjects

Index of Names

Aaron, 92
Abraham, 50, 112, 115, 177, 269, 279, 280, 292
Absalom, 136
Adam, 274, 275, 277
Adonis, 208
Ahab, 15
Ammon, 17, 126
Antioch, 165
Antonine Brothers, 218
Apelles, 5, 5n
Apollos, 5
Asia Minor, 130, 208
Augustine, 277, 278, 284
Azzur, 251

Babylon, 17, 18, 126, 174, 294, 295
Benaiah, 251, 262
Beza, Theodore, 3, 9
Blandrata, George, of Piedmont, 52
Budé, Jean, 5, 10
Bullinger, Heinrich, 4
Buzi, 20

Cain, 159
Calvin, John, 3, 4, 5, 9, 15n, 52n, 61n, 78n, 109n, 132n, 218n, 219n, 251n
Canaan, 5, 121, 265
Cephas, 5

Chaldaea, 16, 18, 19, 20, 32, 125, 142, 174, 221, 258, 259, 266, 283
Chebar, the river, 13, 18, 89, 103, 198, 230, 233, 242, 243
Christ, 37, 43, 50, 123, 242, 246, 294
Cicero, 286
Cilicia, 38, 240
Coligny, Gaspar de, 3
Colloquy of Poissy, 4, 7
Conde, Prince of, 3, 8

Daniel, 51, 64, 221, 267
Dauphine, Gaston de, 218n
David, 14, 36, 46, 112, 148, 151, 187, 236, 271, 294
Diblatha, 164, 165

Egypt, 125, 126, 130, 204, 210, 219, 221
England, 3
Erasmus, 61n, 65n
Esau, 213
Euphrates, 18
Ezekiel, passim

Farel, Guillaume, 4
France, 3

Germany, 3, 8

314

INDEX OF NAMES

Index of Biblical References

INDEX OF BIBLICAL REFERENCES

Index of Words

Hebrew Words and Phrases

INDEX OF WORDS